The Supreme Court

JUSTICE AND THE LAW

January 1974

CONGRESSIONAL QUARTERLY

1414 22ND STREET, N.W., WASHINGTON, D.C. 20037

Congressional Quarterly Inc.

Congressional Quarterly Inc., an editorial research service and publishing company, serves clients in the fields of news, education, business and government. It combines specific coverage of Congress, government and politics by Congressional Quarterly with the more general subject range of an affiliated service, Editorial Research Reports.

Congressional Quarterly was founded in 1945 by Henrietta and Nelson Poynter. Its basic periodical publication was and still is the CQ *Weekly Report*, mailed to clients every Saturday. A cumulative index is published quarterly.

The CQ *Almanac*, a compendium of legislation for one session of Congress, is published every spring. *Congress and the Nation* is published every four years as a record of government for one presidential term.

Congressional Quarterly also publishes paperback books on public affairs. These include the twice-yearly *Guide to Current American Government* and such recent titles as *Watergate: Chronology of a Crisis* and *Energy Crisis in America*.

CQ Direct Research is a consulting service which performs contract research and maintains a reference library and query desk for the convenience of clients.

Editorial Research Reports covers subjects beyond the specialized scope of Congressional Quarterly. It publishes reference material on foreign affairs, business, education, cultural affairs, national security, science and other topics of news interest. Service to clients includes a 6,000-word report four times a month bound and indexed semi-annually. Editorial Research Reports publishes paperback books in its fields of coverage. Founded in 1923, the service merged with Congressional Quarterly in 1956.

Book Service Editor: Robert A. Diamond
Major contributor: Associate Editor Elder Witt.
Other contributors: Mary Costello, Leo Adde, Janice L. Goldstein, Diantha Johnson, Suzanne de Lesseps, Andrea W. Loewenstein.
Cover: Howard Chapman, Art Director.
Photo by Dan De Vay.
Production Supervisor: Donald R. Buck.
Assistant Production Supervisor: Richard Butler.

Library of Congress Cataloging in Publication Data

Congressional Quarterly, Inc.
    Supreme Court, justice, and the law.

    1. United States.   Supreme Court.   2. Justice,
Administration of—United States.   I. Diamond,
Robert A., ed.   II. Title.
KF8742.C65   347'.73'26   73-20492
ISBN 0-87187-051-7

TABLE OF CONTENTS

I am not aware that any nation of the globe has hitherto organized a judicial power in the same manner as the Americans. The judicial organization of the United States is the institution which a stranger has the greatest difficulty in understanding. He hears the authority of a judge invoked in the political occurrences of every day, and he naturally concludes that in the United States the judges are important political functionaries....

Scarcely any political question arises in the United States that is not resolved, sooner or later, into a judicial question. Hence all parties are obliged to borrow, in their daily controversies, the ideas, and even the language, peculiar to judicial proceedings.

—Alexis de Tocqueville,
Democracy in America, 1835

INTRODUCTION

December 1973 is an appropriate time to publish a book on the American judicial system and the Supreme Court. The year just ending has been described by some observers as the year of Watergate and by others as the year of scandal, but it is equally fitting to call it "the year of the courts." Repeatedly, key news stories of 1973 have taken place in the courtroom.

The reader of the daily press or the viewer of the nightly news has been bombarded with a glossary of technical terms more familiar to practitioners of law. The layman whose vocabulary did not include a grasp of expressions such as *in camera, subpoena duces tecum* and *nolo contendere* found himself handicapped in keeping up with the fast-breaking events.

During the summer, for example, a nationwide television audience witnessed abstruse discussions of the rules of evidence and points of constitutional law during the Senate Watergate hearings. In the early fall, it was difficult to follow the litigation between the office of the special prosecutor and the President over court and grand jury access to presidential tapes and documents without some comprehension of the doctrine of executive privilege. *(Watergate and the courts, p. 96, 100; glossary of legal terms, p. 105)*

By the end of the year, it appeared that among the leading candidates for designation as "man of the year" were two men known for their legal experience—"country lawyer" Sen. Sam J. Ervin Jr., a former North Carolina state supreme court judge, and John J. Sirica, chief judge of the federal district court for the District of Columbia.

Watergate and the Courts. Watergate has, of course, been the major story keeping the courts in the news. As this book goes to press, the potentially explosive issue of President Nixon's credibility is being examined in Judge Sirica's court through an inquiry into the failure of the White House to produce two of nine subpoenaed presidential tapes and the President's lawyers' inability to account for an 18-minute erasure of a segment of one crucial recording.

The unraveling episode of the tapes was but the latest Watergate development to reach the courts. In January, the seven original Watergate conspirators were convicted in connection with the June 1972 break-in of the Democratic National Committee headquarters in the Watergate office building in Washington. In May, former Nixon administration cabinet officers John N. Mitchell and Maurice H. Stans were indicted in New York City on charges of obstructing justice and perjury in connection with an investigation into a $200,000 cash contribution to the Nixon 1972 re-election campaign.

In August, Jeb Stuart Magruder, former deputy director of the Committee for the Re-election of the President, pleaded guilty to one count of conspiracy in connection with his role in the Watergate coverup. In September, a Los Angeles grand jury indicted four men for their alleged roles in the 1971 burglary of the office of Dr. Lewis Fielding, the psychiatrist of Pentagon Papers defendant Daniel Ellsberg. The four indicted were John D. Ehrlichman, formerly Nixon's top adviser on domestic issues; Egil Krogh Jr., former deputy assistant to the President; David R. Young, a former White House aide; and G. Gordon Liddy, a former counsel to the President's re-election committee, who had been convicted in January for his part in the original Watergate break-in. The case against Ellsberg had been dismissed in May on grounds of government misconduct. In November, Krogh pleaded guilty to a charge of violating Fielding's civil rights.

In October, John W. Dean III, former White House counsel, pleaded guilty to one count of conspiracy in connection with the Watergate coverup. In November, Dwight L. Chapin, a long-time Nixon aide, was indicted for perjury in connection with his alleged knowledge of the 1972 "dirty tricks" activities of Donald H. Segretti, a presidential campaign employee. Segretti himself had pleaded guilty to three misdemeanors and had been sentenced to six months in prison for his activities during the 1972 Democratic presidential primary in Florida.

By early December, the running count of former Nixon administration officials and campaign aides who had been indicted for Watergate-related offenses stood at 18, of whom 13 had been convicted. Other indictments and convictions appeared likely, and no one could guess where it all would end. But it was clear that much of the responsibility for resolution of the affair would be left to the courts—or possibly to Congress itself sitting in the extraordinary judicial proceedings of an impeachment and trial of impeachment.

Agnew's Plea Bargaining. The downfall of Vice President Spiro T. Agnew was yet another 1973 front page news story that took place in court. Agnew was linked by federal investigators to bribery and extortion dating to his days as a county executive and governor of Maryland. Following three weeks of plea bargaining with the Baltimore U.S. attorney and the Justice Department, Agnew resigned from office Oct. 10 and pleaded *nolo contendre* to the charge of income tax evasion. He was fined $10,000, placed on three years' probation and faced disbarment proceedings in Maryland.

Watergate and the Supreme Court. The Supreme Court was denied an opportunity to rule on a Watergate-related issue. That was when President Nixon chose not to appeal the decision of Judge Sirica, affirmed by the District of Columbia Circuit Court of Appeals, ordering him to turn over presidential tapes and documents for Sirica's inspection preliminary to release of the material to the Watergate grand jury. The President explained his decision not to seek Supreme Court review as follows:

> If it had gone to the Supreme Court—and I know many of my friends argued, "Why not carry it to the Supreme Court and let them decide it?"—that would, first, have had a confrontation with the Supreme Court, between the Supreme Court and the President. And second, it would have established very possibly a precedent, a precedent breaking down constitutionality that would plague future presidencies, not just this President.

Two aspects of the President's statement are noteworthy—first, his suggestion that a "precedent" was avoided by his refusal to take the case to the Supreme Court; second, his implicit tribute to the authority of a Supreme Court decision.

The President's suggestion that a "precedent" was avoided is true insofar as it asserts that the precedential value of a Supreme Court decision on a point of law is of more weight than a lower court ruling on the same point. But where the Supreme Court has not ruled on a point of law, the precedential weight of a lower court ruling is enhanced. Indeed, the key precedent cited by Judge Sirica and the court of appeals in ruling against the President's assertion of an unlimited scope for executive privilege was not an earlier Supreme Court case; it was an 1807 decision, *United States v. Burr*, decided by a lower federal court in Virginia.[1] *(p. 100, 102)*

The President's tribute to the authority of the Supreme Court was implicit in his very decision not to appeal to that tribunal. His decision suggests that he did not want to incur the political costs of defeat before the highest court in the land, the institution which in the public's mind is clothed with greater moral authority than the two other more clearly political and partisan branches of government. In short, the influence and presence of the Supreme Court can be keenly felt even in those cases in which parties choose not to litigate before it.

Judicial Review

Part II, "Supreme Court History," examines the origins and evolution of what Tocqueville astutely identified as America's unique contribution to legal theory, the doctrine of judicial review. Simply stated, judicial review is the power of a court to declare a state or federal statute unconstitutional. The power is as significant in the many instances when it is not exercised as it is on the infrequent occasions when it is. For example, since 1789, the Supreme Court has declared only 97 acts of Congress unconstitutional; during the same period of time, Congress has enacted almost 39,000 public laws. *(Appendix for list of acts ruled unconstitutional, p. 113)*

If one were to conclude from these statistics that the Supreme Court's power to declare acts of Congress unconstitutional is relatively unimportant because it is rarely used, he would miss the point. What matters more than what the Court has done is what the Court is capable of doing. Hence, drafters of legislation—at all levels of government—must repeatedly consider whether their proposals will withstand a constitutional challenge in court.

Part III, "Federal Judiciary, 1969-73," focuses on the Supreme Court, the federal judiciary and legislation on the courts since 1969. It details the transition from the Supreme Court of Earl Warren to the Court of Warren Burger. It presents an extensive discussion of major Supreme Court decisions from 1969 through 1972, organized into major subject areas for ease of reference. The chapter on the most recently completed Supreme Court term (1972-73) focuses on the judicial profiles of the nine incumbent justices and illustrates that Nixon's four appointees to the Court have not transformed the institution into an extension of the Nixon administration. The chapter on federal judgeships examines the somewhat anomolous fact that there are 497 important posts in the federal judiciary but presidential nominees for these posts are almost invariably confirmed by the Senate with perfunctory dispatch; the chapter also notes that President Nixon has named more federal judges than any other President in history. *(List of Nixon appointees, p. 107)*

Part IV, "Legal Institutions," discusses four institutions which are undergoing increasing pressures for modernization and change—the courts, the legal profession, the jury system and grand juries. Each of these chapters appeared earlier in *Editorial Research Reports* or the Congressional Quarterly *Weekly Report*. They retain the original date of publication on the first page of the chapter.

Credits. *Supreme Court, Justice and the Law* highlights an aspect of Congressional Quarterly's coverage that is perhaps overlooked by many of our readers. The *Weekly Report*, well known for its comprehensive coverage of Congress, politics, lobbying and the presidency, is equally thorough and systematic in its reporting on the Supreme Court. Associate Editor Elder Witt's excellent coverage of the Court over the past four years has provided much of the raw material for this volume. A word of appreciation is also due our sister publication, Editorial Research Reports, whose fine articles on the legal profession, juries and the grand juries are republished in this volume.

---

1 Supreme Court Chief Justice John Marshall wrote the *Burr* decision; at the time he was presiding over the federal circuit court in Richmond.

ROBERT A. DIAMOND
Book Service Editor
December 1973

SUPREME COURT HISTORY

Power To Rule Legislation

Unconstitutional Exerts Deterrent Effect

The Supreme Court, great interpreter of the law and guardian of the people against unconstitutional legislative or executive action, exerts a strong restraining influence upon Congress. Although the Constitution did not expressly authorize the Court to strike down acts it deemed unconstitutional, the Court assumed that important authority through its own broad interpretation of its vested powers. Without the process known as judicial review, there would be no assurance (not even the President's veto) against domination of the entire Government by runaway Congressional majorities.

Surprisingly, the incidence of Court rulings overturning acts of Congress is not high; only 97 statutes have been declared unconstitutional in the 184 years of the Republic. Among the measures invalidated, many were unimportant and others, such as the measures prohibiting the spread of slavery and those carrying out parts of Franklin D. Roosevelt's New Deal program, were replaced by legislation so revised as to pass muster with the Supreme Court. Most constitutional scholars agree that the significance of judicial review is not in the number or even in the types of statutes the Court has struck down, but in the deterrent effect on Congress of a possible Supreme Court veto.

With few exceptions, the Court has interpreted the right of Congress to enact specific legislation as broadly as it has its own authority to sit in review of the statutes. The Court's approach to its duties was defined in 1827, when Justice Bushrod Washington observed that "it is but a decent respect due to the wisdom, the integrity and the patriotism of the legislative body by which any law is passed to presume in favor of its validity until its violation of the Constitution is proved beyond all reasonable doubt." Justices, on almost every Court since Justice Washington's day have reaffirmed that attitude.

Changes in Court's Philosophy

Because Supreme Court Justices are appointed for life terms, the Court's philosophy is much slower to change than is that of the other two branches of the Federal Government. For a century and a half, the Court served primarily as a bulwark against encroachment on property rights, much to the chagrin of Populist-oriented Congresses. This concept was maintained even in the 1930s, when the need was evident for precedent-shattering legislation to grapple with the country's economic crisis. In 1935 and 1936, the Court struck down 11 New Deal statutes—the heart of the recovery program. But after President Roosevelt's overwhelming victory in the 1936 election and his threat to "pack" the Court with additional justices who presumably would favor his program, the Court relented and the remainder of the New Deal legislation was upheld. From that point on, the Court's philosophy leaned more toward a flexible reading of the Constitution to permit achievement of national social goals than it did toward the traditional practice of giving priority to protection of property. This shift of doctrine was completed during the term of Chief Justice Earl Warren (1954-1969), when the Court promulgated a series of decisions in support of individual rights. *(Burger court developments, p. 16, 33, 56)*

Whatever the Court's philosophy, it has always had its share of Congressional critics quick to accuse if of usurping undue powers. The early Anti-Federalists (later known as Democratic Republicans and finally as Democrats) thought the Court nullified the Constitution by a series of rulings strengthening Federal power at the expense of individuals and the states. New Deal Democrats thought the Court was attempting to seize the pre-eminent role in Government by voiding much of their legislative program. And in recent years, Republicans and southern Democrats were driven virtually to despair by the Court's decisions on school desegregation, civil rights, criminal law, internal security and voter representation.

Such criticism of the Court has led to a number of proposals to curb the tribunals' powers. Among the proposals have been a requirement of more than a majority vote to render a statute unconstitutional, removal of justices upon concurrence of the President and both houses of Congress, and restriction of the Court's appellate jurisdiction to exclude certain types of cases in which the Court has made decisions not to the liking of some Members of Congress. Although certain of these proposals have attracted wide support, none has ever been enacted into law. The only effective sanction available to Congress has been the Senate's refusal to confirm Court nominees. The Court's critics have been moderately successful in use of that sanction, blocking 27 of 136 Court nominations submitted by successive Presidents. Eleven of the 27 nominations were rejected outright, and the others were withdrawn or allowed to lapse in the face of Senate opposition.

Reference
See Appendix for list of Acts of Congress declared unconstitutional by the Supreme Court.

Sources of Power

Unlike the rebels who framed the Declaration of Independence, the men who met at Philadelphia in 1787 to shape the U.S. Constitution represented conservative financial interests. These interests had suffered heavily during the period of national confederation following the Revolution, when state legislatures, controlled mostly by agrarian interests, made repeated assaults on vested rights.

While the framers of the Constitution deprecated the excesses of the legislatures, they held a high respect for the courts, which gave judgments in favor of creditors and sent delinquent debtors to jail. As political scientist Charles A. Beard, a leading constitutional scholar, once put it, "The conservative interests, made desperate by the imbecilities of the Confederation and harried by the state legislatures, roused themselves from their lethargy, drew together in a mighty effort to establish a government that would be strong enough to pay the national debt, regulate interstate and foreign commerce, provide for national defense, prevent fluctuations in the currency created by paper emissions, and control the propensities of legislative majorities to attack private rights."

At the time the Framers met, judicial review had not yet been instituted in any country in the world. And despite considerable discussion of some means to check the excesses of Congress, the matter of a judicial veto never came up for a direct vote. The closest the Convention got to considering such a scheme was when it rejected the Virginia Plan of government. That plan contained a section establishing a Council of Revision, consisting of Supreme Court justices and the President, to consider the constitutionality of proposed acts prior to final Congressional passage. As submitted to the state conventions for ratification, the Constitution was not clear on the final arbiter of constitutional disputes. Wilfred E. Binkley and Malcom C. Moos have pointed out that there were matters the delegates "dared not badly assert in the Constitution without imperiling its ratification, but they doubtless hoped that implications would eventually be interpreted to supply the thing desired." Judicial review appeared to be one of those things. Most other constitutional scholars have supported this view.

In *The Federalist,* a series of essays written to promote adoption of the Constitution, Alexander Hamilton made clear that the Framers expected the Judiciary to rule on constitutional issues. In Number 78 of *The Federalist,* Hamilton wrote: "The complete independence of the courts of justice is pecularily essential in a limited constitution. By a limited constitution, I understand one which contained certain specified exceptions to the legislative authority, such for instance, as that it shall pass no bills of attainder, no ex-post facto laws, and the like. Limitations of this kind can be preserved in practice no other way than through the courts of justice, whose duty it must be to declare all acts contrary to the manifest tenor of the Constitution void. Without this, all the reservations of particular rights or privileges would amount to nothing."

In a 1912 study of the history of judicial review, Beard found that of the 25 members of the Convention who appeared to be most influential in shaping the Constitution, 17 (including Hamilton) were on record as favoring "the proposition that the Judiciary would, in the normal course of things, pass upon the constitutionality of acts of Congress." Of the less prominent members, Beard said, eight went on record as understanding and approving the doctrine. Opponents of the concept have placed five members of the Convention against judicial review, but only one of these, Pierce Butler of South Carolina, was in the influential group. Beard observed that "The accepted canons of historical criticism warrant the assumption that, when a legal proposition is before a lawmaking body (the Constitutional Convention) and a considerable number of the supporters of that proposition definitely assert that it involves certain important and fundamental implications, and it is nevertheless approved by that body without any protests worthy of mention, these implications must be deemed part of that legal proposition when it becomes law...." Binkley and Moos asserted: "Whether or not the Supreme Court 'usurped' the practice of judicial review is now purely an academic question. So completely has the practice been woven into the warp and woof of our constitutional fabric that the garment could now scarcely endure its elimination."

Acts Declared Unconstitutional

No major constitutional clashes occurred during the Republic's first decade. Congress and the Executive Branch were firmly in the hands of the Federalist party, which was united in its determination to stifle the political opposition—the states'-rights-minded Anti-Federalists. When Congress passed the far-reaching Sedition Act of 1798, which led to the imprisonment of several Anti-Federalist editors for criticizing the Government, the Court refused to strike down the Act despite Anti-Federalist assertions of its probable unconstitutionality.

Only once in that decade did the courts question an act of Congress, and that was on a minor matter. In the *Hayburn Case* of 1792, two Supreme Court Justices sitting on a circuit court (as they then had to do in addition to performing their Supreme Court duties) declined to implement an act requiring the circuit courts to pass upon certain claims of invalid pensioners, subject to later revision by the Secretary of War and Congress. The Justices ruled the act unconstitutional because Congress was not empowered by the Constitution to add to the original jurisdiction of the Court. Article III of the Constitution gave the Supreme Court original jurisdiction over "cases affecting ambassadors, other public ministers and consuls, and those in which a state shall be party." In other cases the Supreme Court was given appellate jurisdiction "both as to law and fact, with such exceptions and under such regulations as the Congress shall make."

MARBURY v. MADISON

The doctrine of judicial review was first enunciated by the Supreme Court in the famous case of *Marbury v. Madison* (1 Cranch 137) in 1803.

After Republican Presidential candidate Thomas Jefferson had defeated Federalist John Adams in the latter's bid for re-election in 1800—but before the Republicans took office—Adams nominated a number of Federalists to judicial posts created by court-reform legislation passed by the lame-duck Federalist Congress. The nominations of 16 judges and some other officials were confirmed by the Senate and the commissions signed by Adams in the waning days and hours of his Administration. When Adams' term expired at midnight on March 3, 1801, several of the commissions had not been delivered. Jefferson, who entered office at the stroke of midnight, ordered that these commissions be withheld.

One of the appointees whose commission had not been delivered was William Marbury, who had been named to the post of justice of the peace for the District of Columbia. Marbury sought to test Jefferson's executive power by filing suit in the Supreme Court requiring Jefferson's Secretary of State, James Madison, to deliver the commission. Marbury filed the suit under terms of the Judiciary Act of 1789, which empowered the Court to issue writs of mandamus compelling Federal officials to perform their duties.

The Chief Justice at the time of the case was John Marshall, a staunch Federalist who had been Secretary of State in the Adams Administration and had been responsible in that capacity for delivering the commissions to Marbury and the other appointees. Notwithstanding his personal interest, Marshall refused to disqualify himself from participation in the Court's action in the case. On the contrary, he delivered the opinion of the Court.

Marshall first held that Marbury was entitled to his commission and that he should be granted the writ of mandamus if the Court had proper jurisdiction. Although the Judiciary Act of 1789 purported to grant the Supreme Court the jurisdiction necessary in this case, Marshall asserted that that part of the Act was unconstitutional because Congress had no power to enlarge the Court's original jurisdiction.

Under the guise of handing his Jeffersonian foes a political victory, Marshall had laid the cornerstone of Federal judicial power. Charles Warren, a leading constitutional authority, has commented: "Marshall naturally felt that in view of the recent attacks on judicial power, it was important to have the great principle firmly established, and undoubtedly he welcomed the opportunity of fixing the precedent in a case in which his action would necessitate a decision in favor of his political opponents.... In comprehensive and forceful terms, which for over 100 years have never been successfully controverted, he proceeded to lay down the great principles of the supremacy of the Constitution over statute law, and of the duty and power of the Judiciary to act as the arbiter in case of any conflict between the two."

Ironically, the doctrine of Supreme Court authority to strike down unconstitutional legislation, which Marshall established in the Marbury case, attracted little comment at the time. Republicans were critical instead of Marshall's comment that the mandamus should have been granted if the Court held proper jurisdiction. According to Charles Warren, Jefferson felt that Marshall and the other Federalists on the Court had "intentionally gone out of their way to rule on points unnecessary for the decision, and he regarded it as a deliberate assumption of a right to interfere with his executive functions." Jefferson remained indignant about that aspect of the decision until his death in 1826. As late as 1823, he wrote that "the practice of Judge Marshall in travelling out of his case to prescribe what the law would be in a moot case not before the Court" was "very irregular and very censurable" and amounted to an unwarranted lecture to the President from a political opponent on the bench.

DRED SCOTT DECISION

It was not until the eve of the Civil War that the Supreme Court again held an act of Congress unconstitutional. It did so in the case of *Scott v. Sanford* (60 U.S. 393) in 1857, probably the Court's most controversial decision of all time and the one most criticized by students of the Constitution.

Dred Scott, a slave, had been taken by his former master from the slave state of Missouri into territory made free by the act of Congress known as the Missouri Compromise. After returning to Missouri, Scott sued to establish his freedom on the ground that his sojourn in free territory had made him a free man. The Missouri Supreme Court held that he had indeed gained his freedom through being on free soil, but that he had lost it when he returned to the slave state of Missouri.

Since Scott's present master (Sanford) was a citizen of New York, the case could now be considered by a Federal court as a controversy between citizens of different states, provided that Scott was a citizen of Missouri. When the case reached the U.S. Supreme Court, a majority of the Justices decided initially that the case should have been dismissed in lower Federal court for lack of jurisdiction, because no Negro could be a citizen under terms of the Constitution. But the Court did not stop there despite the finding of no jurisdiction. Chief Justice Roger Brooke Taney, who wrote what is considered the majority decision in the case (although nine separate opinions were filed by the Justices), asserted that Scott was a slave because the Missouri Compromise—which had been repealed three years earlier by the Kansas-Nebraska Act—was unconstitutional. Congress, Taney declared, had no authority to limit the extension of slavery. (The decision was voided by the 13th Amendment outlawing slavery.)

The Dred Scott decision aroused tremendous resentment in the North, especially among members of the newly organized Republican party whose cardinal tenet was that Congress should abolish slavery in all of the territories. The *New York Tribune* asserted that the decision was entitled to "just so much moral weight as would be the judgment of a majority of those congregated in any Washington barroom.... Until that remote period when different judges sitting in this same court shall reverse this wicked and false judgment, the Constitution of the United States is nothing better than the bulwark of inhumanity and repression."

GREENBACK AND TAX CASES

Greenback Cases. The Dred Scott decision was a prime example of what a later Supreme Court Chief Justice, Charles Evans Hughes, called the Court's "self-inflicted wounds." As he noted, "It was many years before the Court, even under new judges, was able to retrieve its reputation." Before it had been able to do so, another decision on a constitutional issue brought the Court into further disrepute. In the case of *Hepburn v. Griswold* (8 Wallace 603), the Court by a 4-3 decision in 1870 ruled unconstitutional the provision of a Civil War statute making United States notes, popularly known as "greenbacks," legal tender in payment of debts contracted before passage of the Act.

On the day the opinion was rendered, President Grant, a proponent of the greenback clause, nominated

(Continued on p. 8)

The Federal Judicial System....

Under the United States system of checks and balances, the Supreme Court stands at the pinnacle of the Federal judicial structure as the final reviewing authority of Congressional legislation and executive action. However, as is implicit in a check and balance system of government, the High Court, and also the lower Federal judiciary, does not function with complete independence. On the one hand, the Judicial Branch is beholden to the Legislative Branch for its size, pay and, most importantly, for its scope of jurisdiction. On the other hand, the Judicial Branch is beholden to the Executive Branch for its membership.

Federal and State Courts. Two types of judicial systems, state and Federal, have provided forums for the resolution of litigated disputes. The state judicial systems are comprised of the state supreme court, or state court of appeals, and a group of lower courts, such as municipal, police and justice-of-the-peace courts. The Federal system forms a tri-level pyramid, comprised of district courts at the bottom, circuit courts of appeals in the middle, and the Supreme Court at the top.

Provision for a Federal judiciary was made by Article III, Section 1, of the Constitution, which stated: "The judicial power of the United States shall be vested in one supreme court, and in such inferior courts as the Congress may from time to time ordain and establish." Thus, aside from the required "supreme court," the structure of the lower Federal judicial system was left entirely to the discretion of Congress.

Congress and Federal Courts

The Judiciary Act of 1789 established the Supreme Court, 13 district courts, each with a single judge, and, above the district courts, three circuit courts, each presided over by one district and two Supreme Court judges. Thereafter, as the nation grew and the Federal judiciary's workload increased, Congress established additional circuit and district courts. There are now 11 **circuit courts of appeals, 97 district courts, and four** territorial courts (Canal Zone, Guam, Puerto Rico and Virgin Islands).

The influence of Congress over the Federal judiciary went beyond the creation of courts. Although the power to appoint Federal judges resided with the President, by and with the Senate's advice and consent, the power to create judgeships to which appointments could be made resided with Congress. It was in this area that politics historically played its most important role. For example, in 1801, the Federalist Congress created additional circuit court judgeships to be filled by a Federalist President. However, in 1802, when the Jefferson Republicans came into power, the new posts were abolished.

As Federal judges were appointed to serve during good behavior, the power of Congress to abolish judgeships was limited to providing in the creation of a judgeship that, when it became vacant, it could not be filled. The history of the Supreme Court's size provides the best illustration of the earlier habit of creating and abolishing judgeships. Originally, the Supreme Court was comprised of six justices. Subsequently, however, its membership varied: five justices, 1801-07; seven justices, 1807-37; nine justices, 1837-63; 10 justices, 1863-66; seven justices, 1866-69; and nine justices since 1869.

Jurisdiction of Federal Courts. Article III, Section 2, of the Constitution vested in the Supreme Court original jurisdiction over only a few kinds of cases. The most important of these were suits between two states, which might concern such issues as water rights, offshore lands, etc. Article III, Section 2, also extended to the Court "judicial power" over all cases arising under the Constitution, Federal laws and treaties. This jurisdiction, however, was appellate (i.e., limited to review of decisions from lower courts) and was subject to "such exceptions and...regulations as Congress shall make." Most of the High Court's present jurisdiction is defined by the Judiciary Act of 1925, largely drafted by the Court itself under Chief Justice Taft.

At that time, the Court was falling far behind in its docket—by as much as two years. It was felt that obligatory appellate jurisdiction was bringing before the Court far too many cases of relatively minor significance. In the Judiciary Act of 1925, the exercise of the Court's appellate jurisdiction was made largely discretionary.

Except for certain limited types of cases in which the Court was still "obligated" to take appeals, the Court was allowed to decide whether the decisions from the inferior tribunals presented questions or conflicts important enough or of such a constitutional nature as to warrant the Court's consideration on review.

In the relationship between Federal and state judicial systems, Federal courts had jurisdiction—usually where $10,000 or more was involved—over cases relating to Federal rights or actions in which the parties were citizens of different states. The state courts, on the other hand, were concerned with cases generally involving citizens of the specific states and their own state laws.

There was some overlap of jurisdiction. The state courts were empowered to hear litigation concerning some Federal rights, and Federal constitutional rights often formed the basis of decision in state court cases.

In the Federal courts, where jurisdiction is based on a "diversity of citizenship" (i.e., the litigants are from different states), the court is obliged to find and apply the pertinent law of the state in which the court is sitting. In state court cases, similarly, in those few instances where a "Federal question" might be resolved, the court is obliged to disregard its own precedents and apply appropriate Federal law.

....in the United States

Judicial Appointments

The power to name members of the Federal judiciary is perhaps the strongest and most controversial patronage lever possessed by an incumbent President. As a result, Federal judgeships, which are filled by the President with Senate confirmation, traditionally go to those having the same political affiliation as the President. Throughout the nation's history, however, Presidents generally have indicated their intention to make judicial appointments nonpartisan. Nevertheless, since a judge is appointed for life at a substantial salary, making the position a plum, appointees to the Federal bench, with few exceptions, have been of the same political party as the President appointing them.

Stages of Appointment Process. Two sections of the Constitution govern judicial appointments. Article II, Section 2, Clause 2, provided: The President "...shall nominate, and by and with the advice and consent of the Senate, shall appoint...judges of the Supreme Court, and all other officers of the United States...." Article II, Section 3, provided: The President "...shall commission all officers of the United States...."

From these two sections evolved three stages in the appointment process: (1) the nomination, (2) the appointment, and (3) the commission. The "nomination" was the independent act of the President, and was completely voluntary. In the selection, or nomination, of a prospective district or circuit court judge, however, the President usually took into consideration a number of things—for example, political views and party affiliation, the opinions of Congressional advisers who aided the President on other partisan matters, the recommendations of national, state and local political organizations and the qualification ratings given prospective nominees by national, state and local bar associations. In the selection of Supreme Court nominees, on the other hand, the President usually acted with more independence and gave more weight to political philosophy.

The "appointment" was also the sole act of the President, and was also a voluntary act, but could be performed only with the advice and consent of the Senate. In effect, the appointment was made automatically upon Senate confirmation, unless the President, for some previously unforeseen reason, decided to retract the nomination. Confirmation followed Senate Judiciary Committee approval and an affirmative floor vote in the Senate. Prior to confirmation, a Senator could object to a nominee for patronage or other reasons—for example, when a nomination to a district or circuit judgeship was made without consulting the Senators of the district or circuit concerned. Then a Senator could use the stock, but rare, objection that the nominee was "personally obnoxious" to him. In this case, other Senators usually —but not always—joined in blocking confirmation out of courtesy to their colleague.

The "commission" was also the sole act of the President, although merely a technicality provided for by the Constitution. It simply meant that the appointee was given by the President the authority to carry out the duties of his office.

Under the original agreement between the American Bar Association and the Senate, the ABA worked exclusively with the Senate Judiciary Committee, submitting its evaluation of the prospective nominee when informed by the Committee that hearings were going to be held. In 1952, the Justice Department as well asked for the ABA's evaluation of the candidate. In 1953, at the request of the Justice Department, the ABA stopped submitting the names of lawyers it considered qualified whenever a Federal judicial vacancy occurred. Thereafter it confined its reports to persons under active consideration by the Department.

Types of Appointments. There are two types of judicial appointments, including the regular appointment route outlined above. The other is the "recess" appointment prescribed by the Constitution's Article II, Section 2, Clause 3, which stated: "The President shall have power to fill up all vacancies that may happen during the recess of the Senate, by granting commissions which shall expire at the end of their (the Congress') next session."

The recess appointment is a frequently used and often criticized means of making appointments by temporarily bypassing Senate confirmation. Under this procedure, the President, when a judgeship becomes vacant and when Congress is not in session, can extend a "commission" for a judgeship, and the new judge can then take office without Senate confirmation. However, when Congress reconvenes, the President has to submit the name of his recess nominee for confirmation within 40 days. If he does not do so, the judge's pay is terminated. On the other hand, if the name is submitted in the required time and Congress fails to confirm or reject the nomination during the session, the appointment is good until Congress adjourns. When this happens, the President customarily gives the incumbent judge another recess appointment.

To prevent a President from leaving a vacancy which occurred in mid-session unfilled until Congress adjourns, so that he can make a recess appointment, law requires that the President nominate a person to fill a vacancy within 30 days. If the President fails to do this, he can still wait until Congress adjourns and then make the recess appointment, but the appointee would not be eligible to draw a salary.

William Strong and Joseph P. Bradley to fill two vacant seats on the Court. Soon after their confirmation, the Court ordered reargument of the case and reversed itself. In a 5-4 decision, with Bradley and Strong voting with the majority, the greenback statute was held constitutional. Even Chief Justice Salmon P. Chase joined critics in contending that the President had packed the court in order to win the reversal. The decision worked to the advantage of the railroads, whose long-term bonds were becoming due. The notes could now be paid in depreciated currency instead of gold, as would have been required under the first greenback decision.

In the opinion of Justice Hughes, "The reopening of the case was a serious mistake and the overruling in such a short time, and by one vote, of the previous decision, shook popular confidence in the Court." Hughes concluded: "The argument for reopening was strongly presented in view of the great importance of the question but the effect of such a sudden reversal of judgment might easily have been foreseen. Stability in judicial opinions is of no little importance in maintaining respect for the Court's work."

Income Tax Case. The next controversial overturning of a Congressional statute came in the income tax case of 1895, *Pollock v. Farmer's Loan and Trust Co.* (157 U.S. 429, 158 U.S. 601). Under assault in the case were the income tax provisions of the Tariff Act of 1894, which imposed a tax of 2 percent on incomes of more than $4,000. The Court at first held the statute constitutional by a 4-4 vote but later ruled it void by a vote of 5-4. The Court's reasoning was that the levy was a "direct tax," and the Constitution required that direct taxes be apportioned among the states according to population. The decision was widely interpreted as a predisposition by the Court to the doctrines of rugged individualism and Social Darwinism (survival of the fittest). This theme seemed to run through the concurring opinion of Justice Stephen J. Field, who said: "If the provisions of the Constitution can be set aside by an act of Congress, where is the course of usurpation to end? The present assault upon capital is but the beginning. It will be but the stepping stone to others, larger and more sweeping, till our political contests will become a war of the poor against the rich; a war constantly growing in intensity and bitterness." The decision was bitterly assailed by Democrats in Congress who contended that such protection of wealth was unconscionable in view of the severe depression then afflicting the country. The decision was nullified by the ratification in 1913 of the 16th Amendment empowering Congress to levy taxes on income without apportionment among the states.

INVALIDATIONS IN TAFT COURT

Solicitude for property rights reached its high-water mark on the Supreme Court during the Chief Justiceship of William Howard Taft, who served from 1921 to 1930. "In the last analysis," the former President once commented, "personal liberty includes the right of property, as it includes the right of contract and the right of labor. Our primary conception of a free man is one who can enjoy what he earns, who can spend it for his comfort or pleasure if he would.... This is the right of property.... Personal liberty and the right of property are indispensable to any possible useful progress to society."

To ward off what it regarded as unwarranted governmental intrusion on property rights, the Taft Court struck down an unusually large number of state and Federal statutes. While the Court had invalidated only two acts of Congress in the period from 1789 to 1865 (in the Marbury and Dred Scott cases), it struck down 22 in the period from 1920 to 1932. Among the Congressional statutes invalidated were curbs on the use of child labor (*Bailey v. Drexel Furniture Co.*, 259 U.S. 20) and a minimum wage for women and children in the District of Columbia (*Adkins v. Children's Hospital,* 261 U.S. 525). In the D.C. minimum wage case, decided in 1923, Justice George Sutherland wrote that the freedom of an individual to make his own labor arrangements was "the general rule and restraint the exception." Taft himself voted with the minority, but he wrote in dissent that "It is a disputable question in the field of political economy how far a statutory requirement of maximum hours or minimum wages may be a useful remedy" for the sweatshop system.

NEW DEAL LEGISLATION

The appointment in 1930 of Charles Evans Hughes to succeed Taft as Chief Justice seemed at the time to herald a new, less conservative era on the Supreme Court. In his six years on the Court as an Associate Justice (1910-1916), Hughes had become known for his liberal attitude in the field of civil liberties. As it developed, however, the Hughes Court became involved in an unprecedented clash with the Legislative and Executive Branches over the New Deal's intrusion on property rights.

One after another, the depression-born statutes passed by Congress at President Roosevelt's urging were struck down by the Hughes Court. During the 1935 and 1936 terms, laws invalidated by the Court included such key New Deal measures as the Railroad Retirement Act, the National Industrial Recovery Act (NIRA), the Agricultural Adjustment Act (AAA), the Bituminous Coal Conservation (Guffey) Act, a part of the Home Owners' Loan Act, an act providing for readjustment of municipal indebtedness, and the Frazier-Lemke Act designed to delay foreclosures of farm mortgages.

The only major New Deal statute to survive Supreme Court scrutiny (the important Reciprocal Trade Agreements Act did not come up for judicial review) was the Tennessee Valley Authority Act, which created a public regional development authority. In the NIRA and certain other cases, the Court ruled that Congress had made unconstitutional delegations of legislative power to the Executive Branch—unconstitutional because they set no standards to be followed in carrying out the acts or prescribed no findings of fact to be made before invoking the delegated powers. In most of the other cases, the Court narrowly interpreted the authority of Congress to regulate commerce or ruled that Congress was encroaching upon powers reserved to the states. Fear rose that the Court might strike down two 1935 New Deal enactments, the National Labor Relations (Wagner) Act and the Social Security Act, if given the opportunity.

President Roosevelt, stung by the Supreme Court's piecemeal destruction of his legislative program, resolved after the 1936 elections to do something about it. In a surprise message to Congress, Feb. 5, 1937, he asked for legislation that would authorize the President, when any Federal judge who had been in service for 10 years did not retire within six months after becoming 70 years old, to appoint an additional judge to the court in question.

Such a law would have made it possible for the President to add six Justices to the Supreme Court and thus presumably ensure a majority sympathetic to the New Deal. Speaking to the country on radio a month later, Roosevelt declared that he wanted "a Supreme Court that will enforce the Constitution as written—that will refuse to amend the Constitution by the arbitrary exercise of judicial power—amendment by judicial say-so."

Although the Court had come under heavy fire for its anti-New Deal decisions, the Court packing plan ran into strong opposition within and outside of Congress. Hughes presented an able defense of the Court before the Senate Judiciary Committee, which, on June 14, 1937, submitted an adverse report on the Administration bill. A measure finally approved in August provided only for procedural reforms in the lower courts.

Nonetheless, the President's campaign succeeded in bringing about a change of heart on the part of the Supreme Court. In *West Coast Hotel v. Parrish* (300 U.S. 379), decided soon after the court-packing plan was submitted to Congress, a minimum wage law, similar to one ruled unconstitutional a year before, was held to be valid. Revised versions of several of the other acts struck down by the Hughes Court were passed by Congress and sustained by the Court. On April 12, 1937, the Court in *NLRB v. Jones and Laughlin Steel Corp.* (301 U.S. 1) upheld the constitutionality of the Wagner Act. In that decision, Chief Justice Hughes put forward a broad and encompassing definition of interstate commerce, contending that Congress had power to protect the lifelines of the national economy from private industrial warfare. Arguments that had proved effective in the NIRA and coal cases were unavailing. "These cases," Hughes asserted, "are not controlling here." Of the Court's change of direction, it was said that "A switch in time saved nine."

CIVIL RIGHTS AND WARREN COURT

The Supreme Court under Chief Justice Earl Warren (1954-1969) clashed repeatedly with Congress over a series of Court rulings protecting individual rights. Although most of the controversy had to do with alleged Court usurpation of states' rights, several of the Court's decisions, including three important ones in the field of internal security, involved reversal of acts of Congress.

The first of the controversial rulings in the security field came in 1956, when the Court curbed dismissal of Government employees who were considered security risks. By a 6-3 decision in *Cole v. Young*, the Court ruled that the term "national security" in PL 81-733, the statute establishing the Government's industrial security program, was not used "in an all-inclusive sense, but was intended to refer only to the protection of 'sensitive' activities. It followed that an employee could be dismissed 'in the interests of the national security' under the Act only if he occupied a 'sensitive' position."

Another controversial decision was handed down the following year in the case of *Yates v. United States*. In that case the Warren Court ruled that the Smith Act of 1940 did not outlaw advocacy of forcible overthrow of the Government as an abstract doctrine but only as an incitement to action. The Court ruled also that the term "organize," as used in the Smith Act's prohibition against organizing a group advocating forcible overthrow, re-

ferred only to the initial act of bringing the group into being and not to continued organizing activities such as the recruitment of members. For the American Communist Party, the Court held, the act of organization had taken place in 1945, when the Communist Political Association was dissolved and the party brought into being. In 1962, Congress finally succeeded in enacting legislation to broaden the term "organize" to include continuing organizational activities.

A third major internal security case in which the Warren Court struck down Federal legislation was the 1964 case of *Aptheker v. Secretary of State*, in which the Court held unconstitutional a section of the Subversive Activities Control Act of 1950 depriving all U.S. Communist Party members of passport privileges. The Court, in a 6-3 decision, ruled that the clause was in violation of the due process clause of the Fifth Amendment. Other acts or parts of acts of Congress overturned by the Warren Court included provisions of the Uniform Code of Military Justice; a law depriving of citizenship (1) citizens leaving the country or remaining abroad during wartime in order to escape military service, (2) citizens voting in foreign elections, and (3) naturalized citizens having extended residence in the country of their birth or prior citizenship; a law prohibiting Communists from serving as officers or employees of labor unions; a provision for compulsory registration of Communist Party members; and several other minor statutes.

Congressional Investigations

Alleged abuse of Congressional investigatory powers has produced a number of Supreme Court decisions through the years. After some inconclusive disputes over the power of Congress to penalize contempt, the Supreme Court in 1821 (*Anderson v. Dunn*) upheld the authority of a house of Congress to punish "contempts committed against themselves." The power was limited to "the least possible power adequate to the end proposed," and imprisonment could not extend beyond the adjournment of Congress. Considering the limitation of imprisonment to the legislative session inadequate, Congress in 1857 enacted a law making it a criminal offense to refuse information demanded by either house. This statute is the original version of the law generally used by Congress today to enforce observance of its investigative authority.

In 1881 (*Kilbourn v. Thompson*), the Supreme Court asserted the right of the courts to review the investigative activities of Congress. The decision was an extension of the principle of judicial review established by Chief Justice Marshall in the 1803 Marbury decision. The 1881 decision concerned a House investigation of a private real estate pool, with one of whose bankrupt members the Federal Government had deposited funds. The Court held that "the investigation which the Committee was directed to make was judicial...and could only be properly and successfully made by a court of justice." The House, it said, was pursuing "a fruitless investigation into the personal affairs of individuals," which "could result in no valid legislation on the subject" of the inquiry.

Congress delegated its investigative powers to the Interstate Commerce Commission, established in 1887, and subsequently to other regulatory agencies. The Supreme Court in 1894 (*Interstate Commerce Commission v. Brimson*) sustained the ICC's investigative authority, but in 1906 *(Harriman v. Interstate Commerce Commission)* held that the power was limited to obtaining information connected with possible violations of law.

A series of Supreme Court decisions evolved a balance between the powers of investigating committees and the rights of witnesses. The most important of these decisions was made in 1927 *(McGrain v. Daugherty)*, when the Court ruled that the Senate could require information from Mally S. Daugherty, brother of former Attorney General Harry M. Daugherty. Justice Willis Van Devanter, speaking for the Court, stated that "the only legitimate object the Senate could have in ordering the investigation was to aid it in legislating; and we think the subject matter was such that the presumption should be indulged that this was the real object." Van Devanter sought to balance two general principles which he summarized as follows:

"One, that the two houses of Congress...possess not only such powers as are expressly granted to them by the Constitution, but such auxiliary powers as are necessary and appropriate to make the express powers effective; and the other, that neither house is invested with 'general' power to inquire into private affairs and compel disclosures, but only with such limited power of inquiry as is shown to exist when the rule...just stated is rightly applied."

In 1929 *(Sinclair v. United States)* the Supreme Court held that a witness who refused to answer questions asked by a Congressional committee could be punished if he were mistaken as to the ground on which he based his refusal, even if he acted in good faith on the advice of counsel. This precedent made any challenge of committee powers risky; a jail sentence might be in store for a witness seeking to test his rights in court.

Following World War II, the Supreme Court was far more protective of the rights of witnesses than of the rights of Congressional committees. In the 1953 case of *United States v. Rumely*, the Supreme Court upheld a Court of Appeals decision reversing the conviction for contempt of Congress of Edward A. Rumely. Rumely had refused to tell the House Select Committee on Lobbying Activities the names of individuals making bulk purchases of books distributed by the Committee for Constitutional Government, an arch-conservative organization. He had asserted to the Committee that "under the Bill of Rights, that is beyond the power of your Committee to investigate."

A majority of the Court avoided the constitutional questions by narrowly construing the authority granted by the resolution establishing the Committee. It held that the mandate to investigate "lobbying activities" was limited to "representations made directly to the Congress, its Members, or its committees," and excluded attempts to influence Congress indirectly through public dissemination of literature. Otherwise, the Court said, it would be confronted by "grave constitutional questions." Interpreting the authorizing resolution to include attempts to influence Congress indirectly, Justices William O. Douglas and Hugo L. Black contended that the requirement that a publisher disclose the identity of purchasers would violate the First Amendment guarantees of freedom of speech and the press.

The Court again placed strictures on the investigative powers of Congress in 1957, when it ruled in *Watkins v. United States* that John T. Watkins was not guilty of contempt of Congress for refusing to answer certain questions before the House Un-American Activities Committee. The Court based its decision on a finding that the Committee's legislative mandate was "loosely worded" and "excessively broad" and that the Committee had failed to show that its questions were pertinent to the subject of the inquiry.

The Court backtracked somewhat from this position in its decision in a 1959 case, *Barenblatt v. United States*. By a 5-4 vote, it ruled that First Amendment rights may be limited where the public interest outweighs the private interest. While the Court in that case criticized the "vagueness" of that section of House Rule XI defining the powers and duties of the Un-American Activities Committee (in the language of the resolution establishing the Committee), it concluded that "we may not read it in isolation from its long history in the House." *(See box.)* Shifting gears again, the Court in 1963, by another 5-4 decision, reversed the conviction of Edward Yellin for contempt of Congress on the ground that the Un-American Activities Committee violated its own rules by failing to consider his request for an executive session before he was questioned.

Court-Curbing Proposals

Intermittently throughout American history, Congressional critics of judicial power have sought to impose restrictions on the Supreme Court. The methods have ranged from proposed curbs on the Court's authority to the Senate's rejection of Court nominees.

Early Proposals. The first move against the Court was made in 1802, when the newly elected Congress dominated by Jeffersonian Republicans abolished additional Federal circuit courts set up the year before by the old Congress and staffed with 16 Federalist judges (the "midnight judges") appointed by President Adams on the eve of his departure from office. To delay a decision in the Marbury and controversial cases, Congress also enacted legislation postponing the Supreme Court's term for 14 months, until February 1803. In 1805, Rep. John Randolph, a Virginia Republican, proposed a constitutional amendment providing for removal of Supreme Court Justices by the President upon the approval of both houses of Congress. However, Randolph's proposal attracted little support and was dropped.

Alarmed by a series of Supreme Court decisions strengthening Federal power at the expense of the states, states' rights advocates in Congress introduced a variety of other Court-curbing proposals over the next several decades. In 1807, Republicans proposed a constitutional amendment providing for a limited tenure of office for Federal judges and for their removal by the President upon a two-thirds vote of each house. In 1831, Congressional Democrats (the old Jeffersonian Republican party) launched a determined effort to repeal Section 25 of the Judiciary Act of 1789, which authorized writs of error to the Supreme Court on state court judgements. (A writ of error is a process under which an appellate court may bring up a case from a lower court to examine the trial record as to questions of law but not of act.) On Jan. 29, 1831, the House rejected this proposal by a 51-158 roll-call vote, with all but six of the minority votes coming from southern and western states. Later that year, Democrats introduced another proposal directing the House

Judiciary Committee to study the feasibility of amending the Constitution to limit the tenure of Federal judges. That proposal was rejected by a 61-115 roll-call vote.

Another series of attacks on the Court was launched in the early 1900s, by critics of the Court's decisions protecting property rights. In 1923, Sen. William E. Borah (R Idaho) introduced a bill to require concurrence by seven of the nine justices to invalidate an act of Congress. The following year Sen. Robert M. LaFollette (Prog. Wis.) proposed a constitutional amendment providing that a statute once struck down by the Supreme Court could be declared constitutional and immune from further Court consideration by a two-thirds majority of both houses of Congress. Neither the Borah nor the LaFollette proposal received serious consideration.

After Congress rejected the Roosevelt court-packing plan in 1937, the Supreme Court experienced a period of relatively placid relations with Congress until the Warren Court launched on its course of judicial activism in the mid-1950s. The only proposed curb on the Court that attracted much support from the mid-1930s to the early 1950s was a 1953 proposal to amend the Constitution to make retirement mandatory for all Federal judges at age 75. The resolution proposing the amendment, suggested by the American Bar Association, was adopted by the Senate in 1954 but was shelved by the House.

Attacks on the Court

Congressional attacks on the Warren Court began in 1954, the year of the Court's famous school desegregation decision. On May 17, 1954, the Court had declared in the case of *Brown v. Board of Education of Topeka, Kansas* that racial segregation in public schools was inherently discriminatory and therefore in contravention of the equal protection clause of the 14th Amendment. The period of the next four years was a time of unusual anti-Court activity in Congress, spurred at first by southern Members. Some 19 Senators and 74 Representatives from the South signed a "Declaration of Constitutional Principles"—the so-called Southern Manifesto—on March 12, 1956, protesting the "decision of the Supreme Court in the school cases as a clear abuse of judicial power." The southerners were joined in time by colleagues from other sections who were dismayed by the Court's decisions in such matters as Federal-state relations, Communist activities, and contempt of Congress.

From 1955 through 1962, Congress considered legislation to curb the Supreme Court's power to strike down state laws under the doctrine of Federal legislative preemption. Under Article VI, Section 2, of the Constitution, making Federal law the "supreme law of the land," the courts had invalidated state laws in cases where: (1) Congress had stated an intention to take over ("preempt") a given field of legislation; (2) there was a direct conflict between a Federal law and a state law; or (3) Congressional intention to preempt a field of legislation could be inferred, even though it had not been specified by Congress (the doctrine of "preemption by implication"). In 1958, a broad anti-preemption bill was passed overwhelmingly by the House and was defeated in the Senate by only one vote.

Jenner-Butler Bill. Still to come in 1958 was another major court-curbing bill. The measure, known as the Jenner-Butler bill (for Republican Senators William E.

Jenner of Indiana and John Marshall Butler of Maryland), would have deprived the Supreme Court of authority to review several types of cases, including those concerning contempt of Congress, the Federal loyalty-security program, state anti-subversive statutes, and admission to the practice of law in any state. After lengthy committee hearings and bitter floor debate, the Senate tabled the bill by a vote of 49 to 41 on Aug. 20, 1958.

Attacks on the Supreme Court came not only from Congress but also from the Judiciary itself. Three days after the Jenner-Butler bill was shelved by the Senate, the Conference of State Chief Justices approved a statement asserting that the Court "too often has tended to adopt the rule of policy-maker without proper judicial restraint." The statement added: "We are not alone in our view that the Court, in many cases...has assumed what seem to us primarily legislative powers."

Dirksen Amendments. Congressional attacks on the Court intensified in the early 1960s. The Court in 1962 ruled unconstitutional the use of a 22-word prayer in New York State public schools. Justice Black, speaking for the Court in the case of *Engel v. Vitale* (370 U.S. 421), said the prayer requirement violated the First Amendment's clause forbidding laws "respecting the establishment of religion." Soon afterward, Senate Republican Leader Everett Dirksen (Ill.) championed a proposed constitutional amendment to legalize voluntary student participation in prayers in public schools. Four years later, the proposal came to a vote in the Senate and fell nine votes short of receiving the necessary two-thirds majority.

Dirksen was also leader of Congressional efforts to modify the Supreme Court's "one man, one vote" doctrine on legislative apportionment. The House passed a bill to deny Federal courts jurisdiction over apportionment of state legislatures, but it was blocked in the Senate. At this juncture, Court foes proposed a constitutional amendment to permit states to apportion one house of their legislatures on some basis other than population. The proposal came to a vote in the Senate in 1965 and again in 1966—each time failing by seven votes to achieve a two-thirds majority.

Court Pay Raises. Anti-Court sentiment triumphed in Congress in 1964 when pay raises of $7,500 were voted for Federal judges—except Supreme Court Justices, whose salaries were raised by only $4,500. The following year, an attempt to restore the pay differential was beaten down. For the next five years, the salary of the Chief Justice remained at $40,000 and that of Associate Justices at $39,500. In 1969, the Chief Justices' salary was raised to $62,500 and the salaries of Associate Justices to $60,000.

1968 Crime Act

A recent instance of anti-Court sentiment found expression in the Omnibus Crime and Safe Streets Act of 1968. Much of the publicity that attended final passage of the Act centered on three decisions of the Supreme Court—*Miranda*, *Mallory* and *Wade*. In *Mallory v.*

(Continued on p. 14)

Supreme Court 'Balances' Rights of Witnesses...

The leading Supreme Court decisions regarding the question of the First Amendment rights of witnesses and the investigating powers of Congress were Watkins v. United States (1957) *and* Barenblatt v. United States (1959). *A central issue in both cases was that section of House Rule XI defining the powers and duties of the House Un-American Activities Committee. Following are excerpts from Supreme Court opinions in these two cases:*

Watkins Case

(Majority opinion by Chief Justice Earl Warren)

"The controversy thus rests upon fundamental principles of the power of the Congress and the limitations upon that power. We approach the questions presented with conscious awareness of the far-reaching ramifications that can follow from a decision of this nature....

"We start with several basic premises on which there is general agreement. The power of the Congress to conduct investigations is inherent in the legislative process. That power is broad. It encompasses inquiries concerning the administration of existing laws as well as proposed or possibly needed statutes. It includes surveys of defects in our social, economic or political system for the purpose of enabling the Congress to remedy them. It comprehends probes into departments of the Federal Government to expose corruption, inefficiency or waste. But, broad as is this power of inquiry, it is not unlimited. There is no general authority to expose the private affairs of individuals without justification in terms of the functions of the Congress. This was freely conceded by the Solicitor General in his argument of this case. Nor is the Congress a law enforcement or trial agency. These are functions of the Executive and Judicial departments of government. No inquiry is an end in itself; it must be related to, and in furtherance of, a legitimate task of the Congress. Investigations conducted solely for the personal aggrandizement of the investigators or to punish those investigated are indefensible....

"Clearly, an investigation is subject to the command that the Congress shall make no law abridging freedom of speech or press or assembly. While it is true that there is no statute to be reviewed, and that an investigation is not a law, nevertheless an investigation is part of law-making. It is justified solely as an adjunct to the legislative process. The First Amendment may be invoked against infringement of the protected freedoms by law or by law-making.

"Abuses of the investigative process may imperceptibly lead to abridgment of protected freedoms. The mere summoning of a witness and compelling him to testify, against his will, about his beliefs, expressions or associations is a measure of governmental interference. And when those forced revelations concern matters that are unorthodox, unpopular, or even hateful to the general public, the reaction in the life of the witness may be disastrous. This effect is even more harsh when it is past beliefs, expressions or associations that are disclosed and judged by current standards rather than those contemporary with the matters exposed. Nor does the witness alone suffer the consequences. Those who are identified by witnesses and thereby placed in the same glare of publicity are equally subject to public stigma, scorn and obloquy. Beyond that, there is the more subtle and immeasurable effect upon those who tend to adhere to the most orthodox and uncontroversial views and associations in order to avoid a similar fate at some future time. That this impact is partly the result of nongovernmental activity by private persons cannot relieve the investigators of their responsibility for initiating the reaction....

"Accommodation of the Congressional need for particular information with the individual and personal interest in privacy is an arduous and delicate task for any court.... The critical element is the existence of, and the weight to be ascribed to, the interest of the Congress in demanding disclosures from an unwilling witness. We cannot simply assume, however, that every Congressional investigation is justified by a public need that overbalances any private rights to be affected. To do so would be to abdicate the responsibility placed by the Constitution upon the Judiciary to insure that the Congress does not unjustifiably encroach upon an individual's right to privacy nor abridge his liberty of speech, press, religion, or assembly....

"We have no doubt that there is no Congressional power to expose for the sake of exposure. The public is, of course, entitled to be informed concerning the workings of its government. That cannot be inflated into a general power to expose where the predominant result can only be an invasion of the private rights of individuals. But a solution to our problem is not to be found in testing the motives of committee members for this purpose. Such is not our function. Their motives alone would not vitiate an investigation which had been instituted by a house of Congress if that assembly's legislative purpose is being served....

(The Court took note of House Rule XI, which incorporated the resolution establishing the Un-American Activities Committee and authorizing it to investigate: "(1) the extent, character, and objects of un-American propaganda activities in the United States, (2) the diffusion within the United States of subversive and un-American propaganda that is insti-

...and Congressional Investigating Power

gated from foreign countries or of a domestic origin and attacks the principle of the form of government as guaranteed by our Constitution, and (3) all other questions in relation thereto that would aid Congress in any necessary remedial legislation.")

"It would be difficult to imagine a less explicit authorizing resolution. Who can define the meaning of 'un-American?' What is that single, solitary 'principle of the form of government as guaranteed by our Constitution?'....

"An excessively broad charter, like that of the House Un-American Activities Committee, places the courts in an untenable position if they are to strike a balance between the public need for a particular interrogation and the right of citizens to carry on their affairs free from unnecessary governmental interference. It is impossible in such a situation to ascertain whether any legislative purpose justifies the disclosure sought and, if so, the importance of that information to the Congress in furtherance of its legislative function. The reason no court can make this critical judgment is that the House of Representatives itself has never made it."

Barenblatt Case

(Majority opinion by Justice John Marshall Harlan)

"...Granting the vagueness of the Rule (House Rule XI), we may not read it in isolation from its long history in the House of Representatives. Just as legislation is often given meaning by the gloss of legislative reports, administrative interpretation, and long usage, so the proper meaning of an authorization to a Congressional committee is not to be derived alone from its abstract terms unrelated to the definite content furnished them by the course of Congressional actions. The rule comes to us with a 'persuasive gloss of legislative history,'...which shows beyond doubt that in pursuance of its legislative concerns in the domain of 'national security' the House has clothed the Un-American Activities Committee with pervasive authority to investigate Communist activities in this country....

"The precise constitutional issue confronting us is whether the Subcommittee's inquiry into petitioner's past or present membership in the Communist Party transgressed the provisions of the First Amendment, which of course reach and limit congressional investigations.

"The Court's past cases establish sure guides to decision. Undeniably, the First Amendment in some circumstances protects an individual from being compelled to disclose his associational relationships. However, the protections of the First Amendment, unlike a

proper claim of the privilege against self-incrimination under the Fifth Amendment, do not afford a witness the right to resist inquiry in all circumstances. Where First Amendment rights are asserted to bar governmental interrogation, resolution of the issue always involves a balancing by the courts of the competing private and public interests at stake in the particular circumstances shown. These principles were recognized in the Watkins case, where, in speaking of the First Amendment in relation to Congressional inquiries, we said: 'It is manifest that despite the adverse effects which follow upon compelled disclosure of private matters, not all such inquiries are barred.... The critical element is the existence of, and the weight to be ascribed to, the interest of the Congress in demanding disclosures from an unwilling witness....'

"That Congress has wide power to legislate in the field of Communist activity in this country, and to conduct appropriate investigations in aid thereof, is hardly debatable. The existence of such power has never been questioned by this Court, and it is sufficient to say, without particularization, that Congress has enacted or considered in this field a wide range of legislative measures, not a few of which have stemmed from recommendations of the very Committee whose actions have been drawn in question here. In the last analysis this power rests on the right of self-preservation, 'the ultimate value of any society.' Justification for its exercise in turn rests on the long and widely accepted view that the tenets of the Communist party include the ultimate overthrow of the Government of the United States by force and violence, a view which has been given formal expression by the Congress. On these premises, this Court in its constitutional adjudications has consistently refused to view the Communist party as an ordinary political party, and has upheld Federal legislation aimed at the Communist problem which in a different context would certainly have raised constitutional issues of the gravest character....

"To suggest that because the Communist party may also sponsor peaceable political reforms the constitutional issues before us should now be judged as if that party were just an ordinary political party from the standpoint of national security, is to ask this Court to blind itself to world affairs which have determined the whole course of our national policy since the close of World War II, and to the vast burdens which these conditions have entailed for the entire Nation....

"We conclude that the balance between the individual and governmental interests here at stake must be struck in favor of the latter, and that therefore the provisions of the First Amendment have not been offended."

United States (354 U.S. 449), the Court in 1957 ruled that if there was unnecessary delay in bringing a suspect before a judge for arraignment, any confession he made during that period could not be admitted in court as evidence against him. Although the Mallory decision affected only Federal police practices, it worried both Federal and state law enforcement officers. They said it would hamper police investigations. Sen. Strom Thurmond (R S.C.), a leading critic of the Court, denounced the Mallory decision when it was handed down and again, more than a decade later, during hearings before the Senate Judiciary Committee on the nomination of Associate Justice Abe Fortas to be Chief Justice of the Supreme Court.

"Mallory! Mallory! I want those words to ring in your ears," Thurmond told Fortas on July 18, 1968. "He raped a woman and confessed it in court and the Supreme Court turned him loose on a technicality." The Court had held that District of Columbia police violated Rule 5(a) of the Federal Rules of Criminal Procedure—that an arrested person should be arraigned "without unnecessary delay"—when they arrested Andrew Mallory, a 19-year-old Negro, and questioned him seven and one-half hours prior to arraignment. During that time, Mallory submitted to a lie detector test, made a confession and repeated it.

In *Miranda v. Arizona* (384 U.S. 436), the Court in 1966 set rules for stationhouse questioning of suspects. Before the police could conduct an interrogation or obtain a confession, the Court ruled, they must advise the suspect that anything he says may become evidence against him; that he has a right to remain silent, and that he is entitled to have a lawyer present during questioning. The following year, in the case of *United States v. Wade* (354 U.S. 449), the Court held that a pre-trial lineup in which a defendant is exhibited to identifying witnesses constitutes a critical step in a criminal prosecution and that the defendant is entitled to assistance of counsel at the lineup.

Title II of the 1968 Act contains language governing admissibility of evidence and eyewitness testimony which the magazine *Judicature* considered inconsistent with the three Court decisions. "These Supreme Court decisions are based on constitutional principles," the magazine commented in its June-July 1968 issue. "If the law enforcement practices to which *Miranda, Mallory* and *Wade* objected were unconstitutional, it is hard to see how an act of Congress alone can make them constitutional."

Rejection of Court Nominees

Congress exerts influence over the Judiciary in another major way—through the Senate's prerogative to "advise and consent" in the President's selection of candidates for judicial offices, including not only Supreme Court justices but also other Federal court judges.

Starting with George Washington, 15 Presidents have seen 27 of their nominees for the Supreme Court fail to win Senate confirmation—among a total of 136 appointments. In contrast, only eight Cabinet nominees have been rejected by the Senate. The last time a Cabinet nomination was rejected was in 1959, when Senate Democrats refused to approve President Eisenhower's selection of Lewis B. Strauss as Secretary of Commerce.

Although Congress also has authority to remove Federal judges by impeachment, this has been attempted with respect to a Supreme Court justice only once and that attempt failed. In 1804, the House impeached Justice Samuel Chase, a staunch Federalist who had rankled Republicans with his partisan political statements and his vigorous prosecution of the Sedition Act (which had finally been repealed in 1802). But Chase was not convicted by the Senate even though his opponents obtained a majority on three of the eight articles of impeachment. (A total of 23 Senators—two-thirds of the Senate—was necessary for conviction. The greatest number of votes for conviction on any of the articles was 19.) After the trial, President Jefferson, a strong foe of the Federalist-dominated Court, criticized impeachment as "a bungling way of removing judges" and "a farce which will not be tried again."

Senate rejection of Court nominations was common in the 19th century, when political ideology often colored the confirmation process. But from 1900 to 1968, the Senate refused a seat on the Supreme Court to only one man, John J. Parker in 1930. Then, in a 19-month period from late 1968 to early 1970, the Senate rejected four Supreme Court nominees—Abe Fortas and Homer Thornberry, nominated by President Johnson, and Clement F. Haynsworth Jr. and G. Harrold Carswell, nominated by President Nixon. (Fortas, already an Associate Justice, had been nominated for Chief Justice. Thornberry was to take his place as an Associate Justice. Both nominations were withdrawn when Senate supporters of the nominees were unable to break a Republican-southern Democratic filibuster on the Fortas nomination.)

Despite the low incidence of rejection for most of the 20th century, at least four other Court nominations faced stiff opposition—those of Louis D. Brandeis in 1916, Harlan F. Stone in 1925, Charles Evans Hughes in 1930, and Hugo L. Black in 1937. To this list might be added Thurgood Marshall, the only Negro ever named to the Court. The Senate Judiciary Committee, under the chairmanship of Sen. James O. Eastland (D Miss.), was able to induce President Johnson to hold back his intended nomination of Marshall for a year. When the nomination did come, in 1965, Marshall was confirmed, 54 to 16.

Action on the Brandeis nomination a half-century earlier was delayed for months by the same committee while it pondered the nominee's "radical views." When the nomination of Hughes as Chief Justice was made in 1930, the country was entering the Great Depression and the nominee's views were attacked as too conservative.

Despite the opposition to Hughes, voiced before his confirmation on Feb. 13, 1930, President Hoover thought Parker would be a non-controversial nominee. He was a Federal judge and a Republican from North Carolina. Hoover later wrote in his memoirs that "No member of the Court at that time was from the southern states, and the regional distribution of justices had always been regarded as of some importance." But Hoover misjudged the temper of the times. Social and economic issues were more important than was geography. A bipartisan group in Congress charged that Parker had made anti-Negro statements as a political candidate and an anti-Negro ruling from the bench. His nomination was rejected, 39 to 41, on May 7, 1930.

Hugo L. Black encountered difficulty getting confirmed because he had once been a member of the Ku

Supreme Court Nominations Not Confirmed by the Senate

From 1789 through 1973, 27 Supreme Court nominations have failed to receive Senate confirmation. Of these, 11 have been rejected outright and the remainder withdrawn or allowed to lapse when Senate rejection appeared imminent. Following is the complete list of nominees failing to receive confirmation:

Nominee	President	Date of Nomination	Senate Action	Date of Senate Action
William Paterson	Washington	Feb. 27, 1793	Withdrawn	(Later renominated and confirmed)
John Rutledge (for Chief Justice)	Washington	July 1, 1795	Rejected (10-14)	Dec. 15, 1795
Alexander Wolcott	Madison	Feb. 4, 1811	Rejected (9-24)	Feb. 13, 1811
John J. Crittenden	John Quincy Adams	Dec. 17, 1828	Postponed	Feb. 12, 1829
Roger Brooke Taney	Jackson	Jan. 15, 1835	Postponed	March 3, 1825 (Later nominated for Chief Justice and confirmed)
John C. Spencer	Tyler	Jan. 9, 1844	Rejected (21-26)	Jan. 31, 1844
Reuben H. Walworth	Tyler	March 13, 1844	Withdrawn	
Edward King	Tyler	June 5, 1844	Postponed	June 15, 1844
Edward King	Tyler	Dec. 4, 1844	Withdrawn	
John M. Read	Tyler	Feb. 7, 1845	Not Acted Upon	
George W. Woodward	Polk	Dec. 23, 1845	Rejected (20-29)	Jan. 22, 1846
Edward A. Bradford	Fillmore	Aug. 16, 1852	Not Acted Upon	
George E. Badger	Fillmore	Jan. 10, 1853	Postponed	Feb. 11, 1853
William C. Micou	Fillmore	Feb. 24, 1853	Not Acted Upon	
Jeremiah S. Black	Buchanan	Feb. 5, 1861	Rejected (25-26)	Feb. 21, 1861
Henry Stanbery	Andrew Johnson	April 16, 1866	Not Acted Upon	
Ebenezer R. Hoar	Grant	Dec. 15, 1869	Rejected (24-33)	Feb. 3, 1870
George H. Williams (for Chief Justice)	Grant	Dec. 1, 1873	Withdrawn	
Caleb Cushing (for Chief Justice)	Grant	Jan. 9, 1874	Withdrawn	
Stanley Matthews	Hayes	Jan. 26, 1881	Not Acted Upon	(Later renominated and confirmed)
William B. Hornblower	Cleveland	Sept. 19, 1893	Rejected (24-30)	Jan. 15, 1894
Wheeler H. Peckham	Cleveland	Jan. 22, 1894	Rejected (32-41)	Feb. 16, 1894
John J. Parker	Hoover	March 21, 1930	Rejected (39-41)	May 7, 1930
Abe Fortas (for Chief Justice)	Lyndon Johnson	June 26, 1968	Withdrawn	
Homer Thornberry	Lyndon Johnson	June 26, 1968	Not Acted Upon	
Clement F. Haynsworth Jr.	Nixon	Aug. 18, 1969	Rejected (45-55)	Nov. 21, 1969
G. Harrold Carswell	Nixon	Jan. 19, 1970	Rejected (45-51)	April 8, 1970

SOURCE: Library of Congress, Congressional Research Service.

Klux Klan in his native Alabama. Stone, at the time of his nomination, was U.S. Attorney General and was in the midst of prosecuting Burton K. Wheeler, a recently elected Democratic Senator from Montana. Wheeler was accused, but later acquitted, of charges of participating in an oil-land fraud. Wheeler's home state Democratic colleague, Sen. Thomas J. Walsh, used the committee hearings on Stone's nomination to criticize the Justice Department's handling of the Wheeler case.

The Senate's refusal to take up the Fortas and Thornberry nominations resulted largely from Fortas' affirmative votes in some of the most controversial decisions of the Warren Court and from the desire of Senate Republicans to have a Republican President name the new Chief Justice. The GOP strategy paid off when Republican Presidential candidate Richard M. Nixon won the 1968 election. But after Nixon's nominee for Chief Justice, Warren E. Burger, had been confirmed, Senate Democrats retaliated for the Fortas affair by successfully opposing confirmation of the President's next two Court nominees—Haynsworth and Carswell. *(Stories on Haynsworth and Carswell, p. 19, 22)* Critics of the nominations based their opposition primarily on allegations that both nominees had failed to observe high standards of professional ethics while serving on lower Federal courts. Republicans contended, however, that the avowedly conservative views of both men were responsible for their rejection.

FEDERAL JUDICIARY, 1969-73

Nixon's First Term Brings

New Personnel, Legislation and Key Court Decisions

The Supreme Court in 1973 looked quite different from the Supreme Court of early 1969. Gone was Chief Justice Earl Warren, the towering figure who had led the court longer than any other man in the century, whose name had become a synonym for the rulings affirming the rights of black citizens, the right of each citizen to an equal vote, and the rights of suspected criminals. In that center seat on the bench sat a new white-maned chief justice, Warren Earl Burger, a conservative appeals court judge selected by President Nixon to lead the court back to "interpreting...not making law."

Departed also from the bench as it was in 1969 were the articulate Abe Fortas, and two veteran justices—Hugo L. Black, fierce champion of First Amendment rights, and John M. Harlan, the court's conservative conscience. Now closer to the center of the redesigned bench as senior justices sat William O. Douglas, placed there by Roosevelt; Eisenhower nominees William J. Brennan Jr. and Potter Stewart; Kennedy choice Byron R. White, and Johnson nominee Thurgood Marshall.

Toward the ends of the now-curving bench (remodeled in the summer of 1972) sat the bespectacled Harry A. Blackmun, the quiet appeals court judge finally approved by the Senate to fill the Fortas seat; Virginia lawyer and former American Bar Association president Lewis F. Powell Jr. filling the "southern" seat held for 34 years by Black; and, in the Harlan seat, William H. Rehnquist, youngest and most conservative of the justices.

In June 1968 Warren had informed Johnson of his desire to retire as soon as a successor could be confirmed. But his departure was delayed for a year when the Senate, reacting to charges of "cronyism" and questionable extrajudicial activities, some of which involved the generally unpopular outgoing administration, refused to confirm Fortas, whom Johnson had chosen to promote to chief justice.

By a wry twist of fate Fortas left the court before Warren, the first justice in history to resign under charges of misconduct. *Life* magazine early in May 1969 published reports that Fortas, during his first year on the court, had received the first of what were to be annual fees of $20,000 from the family foundation of a wealthy industrialist convicted of violating federal securities laws. Demands for Fortas' resignation followed immediately, coming most loudly from the conservative wing of Congress.

Denying any wrongdoing and stating that the fee in question had been returned and the arrangement terminated, Fortas resigned on May 14, hoping to quiet the controversy and enable the court to "proceed with its work without the harassment of debate concerning one of its members." But his seat remained vacant for more

than a year: the legacy of bitterness remaining created a difficult atmosphere for the nomination of any possible successor.

As the court labored through Burger's first term—October 1969 to June 1970—with only eight members, its image was further dimmed during two painful and unsuccessful confirmation fights.

Soft-spoken Clement F. Haynsworth, a wealthy South Carolinian serving as chief judge of the court of appeals, 4th circuit, was named as Nixon's nominee for the Fortas seat in mid-August 1969. Still stinging from the criticism which had forced Fortas to resign, liberal members of the Senate attacked Haynsworth as "lacking in ethical sensitivity," questioning his participation in certain decisions involving parties in which he had some indirect financial interest. In November the Senate denied him confirmation, the first time in nearly 40 years that a Supreme Court nominee had been rejected by the Senate.

In January 1970 the second nominee for the Fortas seat was named, G. Harrold Carswell, a Floridian sitting as a judge on the court of appeals, 5th circuit. Criticism of his views as segregationist and of his ability as "mediocre," led to a Senate vote in April refusing him confirmation. Not since 1894 had a President had two Supreme Court nominees rejected outright.

A few days after the rejection of Carswell, Nixon named Blackmun to the empty seat. A respected member of the court of appeals, 8th circuit, a long-time friend of Burger, a fellow Minnesotan, and a specialist in medical law, Blackmun won quick approval from the Senate.

But a cycle of reaction appeared to be in motion: conservatives in Congress retaliated to the rejection of Carswell by calling for the impeachment of Douglas, who had apparently offended as many people by his liberal lifestyle as by his liberal views. But like an earlier removal effort, the 1970 impeachment move died young.

Just before the opening of its 1971-1972 term, predictions that age and illness would bring further changes in the court came true: Black, 85, resigned in mid-September and died within days; Harlan, 72, resigned a few days after Black and died at the end of the year.

To fill the gaping holes left by the departure of these two—whose total service on the court amounted to more than half a century—Nixon in October nominated Powell and Rehnquist. Never in doubt, Powell's confirmation was delayed by being linked to the more controversial Rehnquist nomination. But despite criticism of Rehnquist's personal views and those he had expressed as the administration's advocate to Congress during his years as assistant attorney general, both men were confirmed in December 1971.

Supreme Court Personnel

Following is a summary of changes in Supreme Court membership during the years 1969-72, with details on resignations, nominations and controversies over Senate confirmation.

Burger: A New Chief Justice

A judicial epoch of unprecedented impact upon the life of the average American ended on the morning of June 23, 1969. Behind the high Supreme Court bench, with President Richard Nixon watching, retiring Chief Justice Earl Warren administered the oath of his office to Warren Earl Burger, who became the nation's fifteenth chief justice. Warren had just adjourned the court's 1968 term, the sixteenth over which he had presided.

With the retirement of Warren, the California governor-turned-jurist who led the court longer than any other man in the century, an era ended. Led by Warren, the court had issued a series of landmark rulings beginning with its 1954 decision that it was unconstitutional for states to require that black and white children attend separate schools.

"Impeach Earl Warren" became a conservative by-word, emblazoned on billboards and bumpers, signaling a citizen's resentment of the decisions which outlawed school segregation or barred official school prayers or spelled out the rights of persons accused of crimes or laid down the rules of "one man, one vote" for drawing legislative district lines. *(Box on decisions, p. 18)*

Among the critics of the court's rulings was Richard Nixon, who made an unprecedented presidential visit to the Supreme Court on June 23 for the inauguration of his nominee as chief justice. During his 1968 campaign he had accused the Warren court of hamstringing law enforcement officials by its decisions safeguarding the rights of accused persons. He had promised to change the court's direction by any appointments he might make to fill its vacancies.

Yet on Warren's retirement Nixon praised Warren the man as an "example of humanity," symbolizing in his person the integrity, fairness and dignity of the nation's highest court. "His example," said Nixon, "as the chief law official of this country, has helped to keep America on the path of continuity and change, which is so essential for our progress."

Burger Record. In accord with his campaign statements describing the qualifications of the men he would appoint to the Supreme Court, Nixon named as the new chief justice a man known in legal circles for his conservative views on questions of criminal law. Burger, 61, and since 1956 a judge on the court of appeals for the District of Columbia circuit, had also criticized Warren court rulings: "This seeming anxiety of judges to protect every accused person from every consequence of his voluntary utterances is giving rise to myriad rules, subrules, variations, and exceptions which even the most alert and sophisticated lawyers and judges are taxed to follow. Each time judges add nuances to these 'rules' we make it less likely that any police officer will be able to follow the guidelines we lay down."

A native of Minnesota, Burger had worked his way through school and then practiced law for 22 years. First involved in national politics as a supporter of Minnesota Gov. Harold E. Stassen's 1948 bid for the Republican presidential nomination, Burger came to Washington to serve as assistant attorney general, civil division, in 1953. President Eisenhower appointed him from that post to the court of appeals in 1956.

More than a year before the Burger swearing-in, Chief Justice Warren had informed President Johnson that he would retire whenever his successor was confirmed. Johnson had quickly nominated his longtime friend and adviser, Associate Justice Abe Fortas, as Warren's successor. But the Senate, led by Republicans and conservative Democrats, filibustered the nomination, taking the opportunity to attack the decisions of the Warren court and to launch charges of 'cronyism' at the nomination. The Senate failed to invoke cloture to end debate on the nomination; Fortas asked the President to withdraw the nomination to avoid further attack on the court, and the President did so early in October 1968. In May of 1969 Fortas resigned from the court amid controversy over his off-the-bench activities. *(Story p. 19)*

A week after the Fortas resignation, President Nixon announced his nomination of Burger, then little-known outside of judicial and legal circles, on May 21. During the controversy surrounding the Fortas resignation various senators pledged that all future court nominations would be carefully scrutinized. But the Senate Judiciary Committee unanimously reported the Burger nomination on June 3 and the full Senate confirmed the nomination on June 9. The confirmation vote was 74-3; the three dissenters were Eugene McCarthy (D Minn.), Stephen Young (D Ohio) and Gaylord Nelson (D Wis.).

Burger Views. Excerpts from Burger's opinions written before his move to the Supreme Court added another dimension to the description of "strict constructionist"—the label selected by Nixon to depict his choice for what he termed "the most important nomination that a President...makes."

Burger was at times blunt, reserving some of his most severe criticism for members of the legal profession. Solidly committed to the constitutional concept of three coequal branches of government, he was anxious to guard against what he deemed judicial excess in any forum, including lower courts.

His statements included the following:

Court Conduct. "The government may prosecute vigorously, zealously with hard blows if the facts warrant, for a criminal trial is not a minuet. Nevertheless, there are standards which a government counsel should meet to uphold the dignity of the government. The language of the prosecutor here was hardly in keeping with what the courts and the public expect of its representatives." *(Taylor v. U.S., 1969)*

Rights of Accused Persons. "Each time judges add nuances to these 'rules' we make it less likely that any police officer will be able to follow the guidelines we lay down. We are approaching the predicament of the centipede on the fly paper—each time one leg is placed to give support for relief of a leg already 'stuck,' another becomes captive and soon all are securely immobilized. Like the hapless centipede on the flypaper, our efforts to extricate ourselves from this self-imposed dilemma will, if we keep it up, soon have all of us immobilized." *(Frazier v. U.S., 1969)*

The Warren Court Record: Activism and Controversy

Under the leadership of Earl Warren, the Supreme Court was more activist and more controversial than at any other time in the nation's history.

Liberalism and a willingness to deal with questions previously untouched by the high court and traditionally the domain only of Congress or the presidency made the Warren Court a target of unrelenting criticism.

The court ventured into the touchy areas of racial discrimination, religion, rights of accused persons and political redistricting. As such, it became a catalyst for social and political change.

The first year Earl Warren was chief justice of the United States, the court handed down its unanimous landmark decision (*Brown v. Board of Education of Topeka, 1954*) reversing the long-held "separate but equal" doctrine and declaring that racially segregated schools were unconstitutional and "inherently unequal." This was followed in 1955 by the second *Brown* decision which advised local school officials to proceed "with all deliberate speed" to end segregated school systems.

School segregation was only the first of a series of civil rights controversies with which the court dealt.

In several voting rights cases, the court declared unconstitutional the drawing of political districts along racial lines (*Gomillion v. Lightfoot, 1960*), the requirement that a candidate's race be noted on a ballot (*Anderson v. Martin, 1964*) and the collection of poll taxes in state elections (*Harper v. Virginia State Board of Elections, 1966*).

The court in 1967 struck down state antimiscegenation laws (*Loving v. Virginia*) and in 1968 held that a century-old Civil Rights Act (1866) banned all racial discrimination, public or private, in the sale or rental of property (*Jones v. Mayer*).

Criminal Due Process. The Warren Court spelled out in a series of rulings the rights of persons accused or suspected of crimes, restricting law enforcement officers to what it determined to be constitutional methods of obtaining evidence against an accused.

The court declared that states must supply indigent defendants with counsel (*Gideon v. Wainwright, 1963*), that juvenile offenders had the same basic constitutional rights as adult defendants (*In Re Gault, 1967*) and that the right of jury trial extended to trials in state courts (*Duncan v. Louisiana, 1968*).

The court reversed the rule allowing evidence obtained by state officers in an illegal search to be admitted in federal court, holding that no evidence obtained by illegal search was admissible (*Elkins v. U.S., 1960*).

The court in 1967 overturned a rule which had stood since 1928 and held that electronic eavesdropping or wiretapping, even that involving no physical trespass, constituted "search and seizure" and was unconstitutional and thereby inadmissible as evidence unless authorized by a warrant (*Katz v. U.S.*).

In 1969 the court held that, if illegal surveillance had occurred, defendants with standing to object must be allowed to examine the entire record of such surveillance without any preliminary screening of that record (*Alderman and Alderisio v. U.S.; Butenko v. U.S.; Ivanov v. U.S., 1969*).

Perhaps the court's most widely controversial criminal law decisions were those (*Escobedo v. Illinois, 1964* and *Miranda v. Arizona, 1966*) holding that police must—before interrogating a suspect—advise him that any statement he made might be used against him, that he had a right to have legal counsel and that he had the right to remain silent.

President Nixon criticized these decisions as "seriously hamstringing the peace forces in our society and strengthening the criminal forces." These controversial decisions were made by a closely divided court.

Prayers and Votes. The sensitive areas of political districting and religion also came under the purview of the Warren Court, in both instances engendering strong reaction from Congress and the public.

The court (*Baker v. Carr*) in 1962 reversed a statement by the court two decades earlier—that legislative apportionment was of "a peculiarly political nature and therefore not meet for judicial determination"—and ruled that federal courts could review that question.

A number of important decisions followed *Baker v. Carr*: the rule of "one man, one vote" was set forth (*Gray v. Sanders*, 1963) and applied to congressional (*Wesberry v. Sanders*, 1964; *Kirkpatrick v. Preisler* and *Wells v. Rockefeller*, 1969) and state legislative (*Reynolds v. Sims*, 1964) districts.

In the case of *Engel v. Vitale* (1962) the court declared that state officials could not require that an official prayer be recited in public schools.

This ruling was amplified the following year by the court's decision (*Abington Township School District v. Schempp*, 1963) that the state could not order recitation of the Lord's Prayer or Bible reading in public schools without violating the "establishment of religion" clause of the First Amendment, which was extended to the states by the Fourteenth Amendment.

Police and Arrests. "We need not blindfold the police, nor ask them to abandon their experience when they encounter situations which call for...effective intervention.... The test of probable cause (for arrest) is not what reaction victims—or judges—might have but what the totality of the circumstances means to police officers." (*Davis v. U.S., Sams v. U.S., 1969*)

Rule-making by the Supreme Court. Over these past dozen years...the Supreme Court has been revising the code of criminal procedure and evidence 'piecemeal' on a case-by-case basis, on inadequate records and incomplete factual data rather than by the orderly process of statutory rule-making.... I suggest to you that a large measure of responsibility for some of the bitterness in

American life today over the administration of criminal justice can fairly be laid to the method which the Supreme Court elected to use for this comprehensive—this enormous—task.... To put this in simple terms, the Supreme Court helped make the problems we have because it did not 'go by the book' and use the tested... process of rule-making through use of the advisory committee mechanism provided by Congress.... I question... not the court or the last decade's holdings...but its methodology and the loose ends, confusion and bitterness that methodology has left in its wake." (Address to the Ohio Judicial Conference at Columbus, Ohio, Sept. 4, 1968)

Fortas' Resignation

Abe Fortas became the first Supreme Court justice to step down under threat of impeachment when he resigned on May 14, 1969.

The resignation followed by less than eight months a successful Senate filibuster against President Johnson's nomination of Fortas to be chief justice. His departure from the court climaxed a furor brought on by the disclosure early in May that Fortas had received and held for 11 months a $20,000 fee from the family foundation of a man later imprisoned for illegal stock manipulation. The resignation was accepted May 15 by President Nixon. Fortas, a prominent Washington attorney, had been named an associate justice in 1965 by President Johnson.

According to an article in *Life* magazine, Fortas in January 1966 accepted a $20,000 check from a foundation established by multimillionaire industrialist, Louis E. Wolfson. In September 1966, Wolfson was indicted for selling unregistered securities. In December 1966, according to the article, Fortas returned the $20,000.

Wolfson was convicted in September 1967 and sentenced to one year in prison and fined $100,000. His appeal for review of the conviction was denied on April 1, 1969, by the Supreme Court, with Fortas taking no part in consideration of the case. His former law firm had on occasion represented Wolfson.

Fortas May 4 issued a statement saying that he did not feel that the fee in question implied any inducement for him to try to influence Wolfson's case. But that statement did nothing to quiet the rising furor.

Critics noted that the canons of judicial ethics state that "A judge should avoid giving ground for any reasonable suspicion that he is utilizing the power or prestige of his office to persuade or coerce others to patronize or contribute, either to the success of private business or to charitable enterprises." After Fortas resigned, the American Bar Association released an informal opinion from its committee on professional ethics which found Fortas' conduct "clearly contrary" to the canons.

Attorney General John N. Mitchell met May 7 with Chief Justice Warren; on May 8 it was reported that the Justice Department was investigating the Fortas-Wolfson relationship to determine possible violations of federal law.

A flurry of bills were introduced in Congress requiring financial disclosure by federal judges and Supreme Court justices. Rep. H. R. Gross (R Iowa) announced May 11 that he would present to the House articles of impeachment against Fortas if Fortas did not resign within a reasonable time. The articles accused Fortas of malfeasance, misconduct and impropriety, Gross said. That

same day Sen. Walter F. Mondale (D Minn.) became the first Democratic senator to call for Fortas' resignation.

On May 14 the resignation came. In a letter of that date to Warren, Fortas said that he was guilty of no wrongdoing, but that he was resigning in order that the court not continue to be "subjected to extraneous stress" which might adversely affect its performance.

Fortas detailed his acquaintance with Wolfson and his relationship to the Wolfson Family Foundation. When that relationship began late in 1965, he said, he saw no conflict between the nature of that work and his judicial duties and he thought his court duties would leave him time for such nonjudicial activities. He explained that the foundation paid him a $20,000 annual fee for his continuing services, and that the agreement provided for this fee to be paid to his wife, in the event of his death.

Fortas explained that in June 1966 he decided to terminate his role with the foundation due to the heavy demand on his time by the court's workload and to the fact that he learned that the Justice Department was considering prosecution of Wolfson for securities law violations. He terminated his role late in June via letter, he said, and returned the $20,000 fee in December.

Fortas concluded his letter: "There has been no wrongdoing on my part. There has been no default in the performance of my judicial duties in accordance with the high standards of the office I hold. So far as I am concerned the welfare and maximum effectiveness of the court to perform its critical role in our system of government are factors that are paramount to all others. It is this consideration that prompts my resignation which, I hope, by terminating the public controversy, will permit the court to proceed with its work without the harassment of debate concerning one of its members."

Haynsworth Rejected

In his effort to replace Abe Fortas with a southern conservative, Richard Nixon suffered his first major congressional defeat when the Senate in November 1969 rejected his nomination of Clement F. Haynsworth Jr. to the Supreme Court.

Haynsworth, a wealthy South Carolinian and chief judge of the court of appeals, 4th circuit, was named by Nixon Aug. 18 to fill the seat left vacant by the resignation of Fortas in May. A graduate of Harvard Law School, Haynsworth, 56 at the time of his nomination, had headed a Greenville, S.C., law firm which his father and grandfather had also led. In 1952 and 1956 a Democrat for Eisenhower, he became a Republican in 1964. Eisenhower appointed him to the appeals court in 1957. His record there became the target of his critics.

Opponents of the nomination, led by Birch Bayh (D Ind.), said repeatedly that they did not question Haynsworth's honesty or integrity. They did question his sensitivity to the appearance of ethical impropriety and his judgment regarding participation in cases where his financial interests could be said to be involved, even indirectly. Haynsworth was also opposed by labor and civil rights leaders.

Demands for President Nixon to withdraw the nomination merely stiffened the President's determination to stand behind his nominee and to reassert his confidence in him. Considerable political pressure preceded the final vote, brought to bear on individual senators by both opponents and advocates of the nomination.

The key to Haynsworth's defeat was the defection of liberal Republicans who voted with northern Democrats to deny confirmation Nov. 21, on a roll-call vote of 45-55. All three top Republican leaders in the Senate voted against confirmation.

Haynsworth was the 23rd man denied confirmation to the Supreme Court, the first to be formally rejected since 1930 when John J. Parker of North Carolina lost confirmation by one vote, 39-41.

Controversies. Overshadowing complaints about Haynsworth's record on labor and civil rights issues was the argument—reinforced by the recent Fortas charges—that Haynsworth was not sensitive enough to the need to avoid even the appearance of impropriety. His critics charged that he had participated in decisions indirectly affecting the welfare of companies in which he had a monetary interest.

The primary cases scrutinized during Senate Judiciary Committee hearings on the nomination in September were those growing out of a lengthy dispute between a textile mill—which was a subsidiary of Deering Milliken Inc.—and the Textile Workers Union. *(Deering Milliken Inc. v. Johnston, Darlington Manufacturing Co. and Deering Milliken v. NLRB)*

Critics of the nomination argued that Haynsworth should not have taken part in the decisions involving Deering Milliken, because he owned a one-seventh interest in a company, Carolina Vend-A-Matic Company, which held a contract to supply vending services to some Deering Milliken plants. The value of Haynsworth's share, at the time the company was sold to a larger operation, was about $450,000.

William Pollock, president of the union, said that Haynsworth should have disqualified himself from the case. But William H. Rehnquist, assistant attorney general in charge of the office of legal counsel, concluded that Haynsworth "was under a duty to take part in that decision." Rehnquist said that the question raised was "whether a judge, who owns stock in one corporation, which in turn does business with a second corporation, should disqualify himself when the second corporation is a party litigant in his court." For Rehnquist and the Justice Department, the answer was no.

Joseph L. Rauh Jr., vice chairman of Americans for Democratic Action, said that Haynsworth's action was "far worse than that of Justice Fortas; he decided an important case for a litigant with which a company partially owned by him did substantial business and sought more. Whereas Justice Fortas had a potential conflict of interest in his outside activities, Judge Haynsworth had an actual conflict of interest in a case before him at the bench."

Haynsworth said that at the time of his participation in the controversial decision, he had no conscious awareness of the business relationship between the vending company and affiliates of Deering Milliken. He said that had he known of the relationship, he would not have viewed it as a conflict of interest for him to take part in the decision. He said that the vending company was in no way affected by the outcome of the labor case. Haynsworth said he had disqualified himself from participation "in all cases in which (his) former law firm or any of its

Resigning Justices

Abe Fortas was the 41st Supreme Court justice to resign or retire from the court; he was the first to quit under charges of extra-judicial misconduct.

Justices quit for several reasons. Most resigning justices retired in advanced age and after lengthy service. Some 47 died while still serving. Some resigned for reasons of conscience, some to do other work, some because they were too ill to carry on. Three who quit died before their resignations became effective.

Benjamin R. Curtis resigned in 1857 after disagreements with Chief Justice Roger B. Taney over the Dred Scott decision. Curtis, whose brother had argued the case for Dred Scott, advocated freedom for slaves once they were on free territory.

John Campbell from Georgia resigned in April 1861 to return to the South, although he opposed secession and had freed all of his own slaves.

Tom Clark resigned in 1967 to avoid conflict of interest when his son, Ramsey Clark, was appointed U.S. attorney general.

John Jay left the court in 1795 to serve as governor of New York. He was reappointed to the court as chief justice in 1800, but declined. Jay felt the Supreme Court then lacked "the energy, weight and dignity which are essential to its affording due support to the national government."

Charles Evans Hughes resigned in 1916 to run for President.

Arthur Goldberg resigned in 1965 to serve as U.S. ambassador to the United Nations.

The only Supreme Court justice to be impeached was Samuel Chase. In 1804 the House charged him with "misconduct in trials impairing the confidence and respect for the courts," but he was acquitted by the Senate.

members were counsel, cases in which certain relatives were counsel, and all cases in which I had a stock interest in a party or in one which would be directly affected by the outcome of the litigation."

During the hearings, Haynsworth told the committee that the gross amount of business done by the vending company in 1963, the year of the decision, with plants controlled by Deering Milliken was $100,000—three per cent of the vending company's total gross for that year. The total after-tax profit which the company realized in 1963 from its business with the Deering Milliken subsidiaries was $2,730, of which his share was $390.

But, Haynsworth said, the Senate should decide the case for his nomination on the merits of the facts presented: "If there is substantial doubt about the propriety of what I did, I hope the Senate will resolve the doubts against me.... While I am concerned about my reputation, I am much more concerned about my country and the Supreme Court as an institution."

Among those speaking in behalf of Haynsworth, particularly in regard to the charges that he had ignored a conflict of interest in the Deering Milliken case, were John P. Frank of Phoenix, Ariz., an expert on the subject of judicial disqualification; Lawrence E. Walsh, chairman of the American Bar Association committee on the federal judiciary; and Judge Harrison L. Winter, a colleague from the court of appeals.

Among those leading the opposition testimony were George Meany, president of the AFL-CIO; Clarence Mitchell, director of the Washington bureau of the National Association for the Advancement of Colored People; Rauh, also representing the Leadership Conference on Civil Rights; and Pollock.

Committee Action. The Senate Judiciary Committee Oct. 9 voted 10-7 to report the nomination of Haynsworth favorably to the full Senate; the report was filed Nov. 12.

The majority set forth, in a 22-page report, its conclusion that Haynsworth was "extraordinarily well qualified" to fill the seat of an associate justice of the Supreme Court. It supported that conclusion with a point-by-point analysis and rebuttal of the ethical and philosophical charges against him.

Noting the high recommendation given Haynsworth by the American Bar Association and by his colleagues on the 4th circuit court of appeals, the majority described the nominee as a man of "outstanding judicial temperament" who approached controversial and complex legal matters in a balanced manner. The majority concluded that attacks on his ethical sensitivity were not substantiated and that "nothing in his judicial conduct...would in any way justify recommending against his confirmation."

The majority refuted the position which some opponents of the nomination had adopted—that even if ethical attacks could not be substantiated, the very fact that they were made constituted reason to deny confirmation. Such a position, the majority said, was contrary both to "traditional notions of fair play and to the lessons of history."

"To accede to such a view," the report stated, "would be to place a nominee's fate, not in the hands of those charged with advising and consenting to his nomination, but in the hands of his accusers. The most basic concept of fairness demands vindication where a charge is found to be unsubstantiated, just as surely as it demands condemnation where the objection is found to have merit."

The committee majority said that for Haynsworth to disqualify himself in the Deering Milliken case would have been contrary to all precedents for judicial disqualification. It said that judges had never been required to disqualify themselves simply because they owned stock in a parent corporation which controlled a litigant.

Those committee members voting against reporting the Haynsworth nomination favorably were Birch Bayh (D Ind.), who had spearheaded the Senate opposition, Philip A. Hart (D Mich.), Edward M. Kennedy (D Mass.), Quentin N. Burdick (D N.D.), Joseph D. Tydings (D Md.), Robert P. Griffin (R Mich.) and Charles McC. Mathias Jr. (R Md.).

Stating his views again, Bayh emphasized that the Senate must look at its action in confirming a Supreme Court nominee as one which should "shore up public confidence" in the judiciary. Bayh agreed that Haynsworth was an honest man, but he said that his record was nevertheless "blemished by a pattern of insensitivity to the appearance of impropriety."

Republican Defections. The loss of the votes of more than a third of the Republicans in the Senate was the key factor in the defeat of Haynsworth's nomination. The first indication of a crack in the Republican bloc came Oct. 1 —more than six weeks before the final vote—when Edward W. Brooke (R Mass.) wrote Nixon to request that the nomination be withdrawn. On the day before the vote in the Judiciary Committee, Assistant Senate Minority Leader Griffin and Margaret Chase Smith (R Maine), chairman of the Republican Conference, announced that they would oppose the nomination. Griffin, leader of the earlier fight against the Fortas nomination as chief justice, said that "legitimate and substantial doubt" had been raised about Haynsworth's ethical sensitivity. And Smith said that after opposing Fortas, she could not apply a double standard and support Haynsworth.

Ernest F. Hollings (D S.C.), Haynsworth's primary sponsor in the Senate, criticized the White House Oct. 9 for failing to rally Republican leadership behind the nomination. He said that Nixon had just sent the name to the Senate and left it there "hanging on the clothesline."

Floor Action. White House pressure mounted steadily during the weeks between the vote of the committee and that of the full Senate, alienating perhaps as many senators as it persuaded. Few issues had generated more pressure on his office, said Len B. Jordan (R Idaho), who voted against the nomination: "Support of the President is urged as if it were a personal matter rather than an issue of grave constitutional importance."

When the tense ten-minute roll call began Nov. 21 on the motion to confirm the nomination, there were only a dozen senators who had not made their positions known. When the vote ended—short by five of the 50 needed for confirmation (Vice President Agnew would have cast the deciding vote in favor of the nominee if the Senate had tied)—11 of the 12 had voted against the nomination. Of the 45 votes for Clement F. Haynsworth Jr., 26 were Republican and 19 Democrat—all but three from the South. Of the 55 votes against him 17 were Republican and 38 Democrats—only five of whom were from the South.

Republican opponents ranged from conservatives such as John J. Williams (Del.) and Jordan to liberals such as Charles H. Percy (Ill.) and Mark O. Hatfield (Ore.). The top Republican leaders in the Senate—Hugh Scott (Pa.), the minority leader; Griffin, the party whip; Smith, chairman of the Senate Republican Conference; and John J. William (Del.), chairman of the GOP Committee on Committees—all voted against Haynsworth.

Hollings told reporters after the vote, "We weren't in the ball park the last six weeks. You can't win if you can't get your leadership." Hollings said he told White House officials as long as two weeks before the vote that Haynsworth could not be confirmed.

Hatfield told Congressional Quarterly that lack of active support by the Senate's Republican leaders was one of the main factors leading to the Haynsworth defeat.

In a statement after the Senate vote, Nixon expressed regret that the Senate had failed to confirm "this distinguished man" and he deplored the attacks on Haynsworth, whose integrity he described as unimpeachable and whose ability, he said, was unquestioned. Referring to his campaign promises, he pledged to nominate another man selected by the same criteria as Hayns-

Supreme Court Membership, 1968-1973

Name	State	Date of Birth	Nominated By	To Replace	Date of Appointment	Date Confirmed	Date Resigned
Hugo L. Black	Ala.	2/27/1886	Roosevelt	Van Devanter	8/12/37	8/17/37	9/17/71
William O. Douglas	Conn.	10/16/1898	Roosevelt	Brandeis	3/20/39	4/4/39	
Earl Warren*	Calif.	3/19/1891	Eisenhower	Vinson	9/30/53	3/1/54	6/23/69
John M. Harlan	N.Y.	5/20/1899	Eisenhower	Jackson	1/10/55	3/16/55	9/23/71
William J. Brennan Jr.	N.J.	4/25/1906	Eisenhower	Minton	10/16/56	3/19/57	
Potter Stewart	Ohio	1/23/1915	Eisenhower	Burton	1/17/59	5/5/59	
Byron R. White	Colo.	6/8/1917	Kennedy	Whittaker	4/3/62	4/11/62	
Abe Fortas	Tenn.	6/19/1910	Johnson	Goldberg	7/28/65	8/11/65	5/14/69
Thurgood Marshall	N.Y.	6/2/1908	Johnson	Clark	6/13/67	8/30/67	
Warren E. Burger*	D.C.	9/17/1907	Nixon	Warren	5/21/69	6/9/69	
Harry A. Blackmun	Minn.	11/12/1908	Nixon	Fortas	4/14/70	5/12/70	
Lewis F. Powell Jr.	Va.	9/19/1907	Nixon	Black	10/21/71	12/6/71	
William H. Rehnquist	Ariz.	10/1/1924	Nixon	Harlan	10/21/71	12/10/71	

Chief Justice

Supreme Court appointments, 1789-1964, *Congress and the Nation Vol. I*, p. 1452
Supreme Court membership, 1965-1968, *Congress and the Nation Vol. II*, p. 340

worth had been: "The Supreme Court needs men of his legal philosophy to restore the proper balance to that great institution."

Carswell Rejected

The Senate dealt President Nixon a second stinging defeat in April 1970 when it rejected his second nominee to the Fortas seat on the Supreme Court, G. Harrold Carswell of Florida.

The rejection came two and a half months after Nixon had announced his selection Jan. 19 of Carswell, 50, a judge on the court of appeals, 5th circuit, as an associate justice. The Senate's action, on a roll-call vote of 45-51, took place on April 8, less than five months after its rejection of Clement F. Haynsworth Jr., whom Nixon had first chosen to fill the court vacancy.

Not since 1894, during the second Cleveland administration, had a President had two Supreme Court nominees rejected outright by the Senate. Carswell was the 24th man denied confirmation to a seat on the court.

Thirty-eight Democrats and 13 Republicans voted against Carswell, compared to 38 Democrats and 17 Republicans who voted against Haynsworth. Despite statements by administration spokesmen that the defeats of both Haynsworth and Carswell were partisan attempts to embarrass the President, only 23 of the 43 Republican senators voted for or announced their support of both nominees.

Whereas all four Republican leaders voted against Haynsworth—Minority Leader Hugh Scott (Pa.), Assistant Minority Leader Robert P. Griffin (Mich.), Margaret Chase Smith (Maine), chairman of the Republican Conference, and John J. Williams, chairman of the GOP committee on committees—only Smith voted against Carswell.

Background. Carswell, a native of Georgia, graduated from Duke University, served in the Navy during World War II and graduated from a small Georgia law school in 1948. He ran unsuccessfully for the Georgia legislature soon after his graduation from law school.

Moving to Tallahassee, Fla., in 1949, Carswell practiced law first with a firm in which LeRoy Collins, later governor of Florida, was a partner, and then with his own firm. Initially a Democrat, Carswell supported Eisenhower for President in 1952 and 1956, and changed his registration to Republican. In 1953 Eisenhower named Carswell federal attorney for northern Florida; five years later he nominated him as federal district judge for the same area—at 38, Carswell was the nation's youngest federal judge. In May 1969, less than a year before the Senate rejection of his Supreme Court nomination, Nixon elevated Carswell to the court of appeals. Within a month the Senate confirmed that nomination by voice vote and without opposition.

Early Opposition. Although the White House stated that Carswell had been thoroughly cleared, in advance of his nomination, of any of the financial conflict-of-interest and ethical impropriety charges that brought on the Haynsworth defeat, the news media disclosed Jan. 21 that during an unsuccessful campaign for a seat in the Georgia legislature in 1948 Carswell had made a speech supporting white supremacy. Carswell immediately repudiated any continuing belief in white supremacy, but civil rights groups charged that he was still a segregationist and that his record as a judge since 1948 had not reflected any change in his views or philosophy. Labor joined the opposition Jan. 26 when AFL-CIO President George Meany announced AFL-CIO opposition to the nomination and called it "a slap in the face to the nation's Negro citizens." Thus early opponents of the nomination included many of the same civil rights organizations and labor unions that had fought the Haynsworth nomination—the latter despite the fact that, unlike Haynsworth, Carswell was not accused of being anti-labor. In addition, the anti-Carswell forces later were joined by a substantial number of law school deans and professors from across the nation and by lawyers who objected to Carswell as mediocre, undistinguished and hostile to civil rights causes.

Opposition in the Senate to the nomination was slow to arise, largely because of a disposition by senators to avoid another bitter confirmation struggle. It was only with the persistent opposition of Edward W. Brooke (R Mass.) and the conviction, only belatedly held, of other senators that Carswell's record was such that he had to be opposed, that a concerted effort was mounted against him. As with Haynsworth, the Democratic opposition to Carswell was led by Birch Bayh (Ind.).

Controversies. Civil rights criticism of Carswell was much more strident than that of Haynsworth. The various points on which Carswell was attacked included the 1948 speech, his 1956 participation in the conversion of a municipal golf course to private ownership to avoid desegregation, his 1966 sale of a lot with a restrictive covenant, and his reported hostility to civil rights workers and lawyers appearing in his courtroom.

During Senate Judiciary Committee hearings on the nomination, which continued for five days in late January and early February, Carswell rejected charges that he was a racist. After the disclosure of the 1948 speech, Nixon said that he was not concerned by its contents, although he had not known of it previously. He instead pointed to Carswell's record of federal service since 1953, a record he described as "impeccable...without a taint of racism: a record of strict constructionism as far as interpretation of the Constitution and the role of the court, which I think the court needs."

But groups including the National Association for the Advancement of Colored People, the AFL-CIO, civil rights attorneys who had appeared before Carswell, and the National Organization of Women disagreed with this assessment. In the words of Joseph L. Rauh Jr., chairman of the Leadership Conference on Civil Rights, they felt that "Judge Carswell is Judge Haynsworth with a cutting edge, with a bitterness and a meanness that Judge Haynsworth never had."

The most telling element in the opposition which rose against the Carswell nomination was the criticism leveled at him from within the ranks of his own profession. Although the American Bar Association committee on the federal judiciary found him qualified for appointment to the court, many practicing lawyers and judges and legal scholars publicly challenged this assessment. By voicing their concern about his ability and competence as a jurist, they aroused concern in the minds of men undisturbed by the charges from civil rights and labor groups.

The liberal Republican Ripon Society characterized the nomination as "exceptionally inadequate." Derek Bok, dean of Harvard Law School, and 24 other faculty members said that Carswell lacked "minimum qualifications" for the court seat. More than 200 men who had served as law clerks to Supreme Court justices agreed that Carswell was only of "mediocre ability. His performance on the lower courts...reflects the absence of the qualities which, we believe, all Supreme Court nominees should possess." Faculty members from more than 35 other law schools across the country expressed their concern about Carswell's lack of qualifications for the legal profession's highest post.

Roman L. Hruska (R Neb.), ranking minority member of the Senate Judiciary Committee and leader of the fight for the Carswell nomination, attempted to respond to such charges in March when he said that "even if he was mediocre, there are a lot of mediocre judges and people and lawyers. They are entitled to a little representation, aren't they, and a little chance? We can't have all Brandeises, and Cardozos and Frankfurters and stuff like that there." Hruska aides later said that the remarks were made in jest, but they were repeated many times by Carswell critics.

Committee Action. After committee members twice delayed a vote on the Carswell nomination, the committee Feb. 16 approved it by a vote of 13-4. Voting against the nomination were Bayh, Philip A. Hart (D Mich.), Edward M. Kennedy (D Mass.) and Joseph D. Tydings (D Md.). The report was filed Feb. 27.

The majority of the committee found Carswell "thoroughly qualified" to serve on the court, noting that they felt he no longer held the "notions...expressed in his 1948 speech." The other charges of bias, they said, were insubstantial and unproved.

Bayh, Hart, Kennedy and Tydings found Carswell presenting "credentials too meager to justify confirmation."

Floor Action. A civil rights measure to amend the 1965 Voting Rights Act had long been set for consideration by the full Senate beginning March 1. Senate Majority Leader Mike Mansfield (D Mont.) said Feb. 17 that the Senate would complete action on that bill before considering the Carswell nomination. Those who opposed the Carswell nomination saw this delay, extended by southern opposition to the passage of the civil rights bill, as working to the advantage of the forces seeking to reject the nomination.

Debate on the nomination finally began March 13, but it was not until three weeks later that the Senate took its first vote on the matter. On April 6 the Senate rejected, 44-52, a motion to send the nomination back to the Judiciary Committee.

First conceived as a way of killing the nomination by burying it in committee, the motion had, by the time of the vote, become instead a diversionary tactic, a preliminary skirmish won by the administration. The vote was defective as a clear test of the strength of the opposition to Carswell because some senators oppose any recommittal motion in principle, and because others voted against the motion in order to bring the nomination to an up-or-down vote on the Senate floor. Seven senators who had voted against recommittal then voted against the nomination as well.

After rejecting recommittal, the Senate April 8 refused, 45-51, to confirm the nomination of Carswell to the Supreme Court. Of the 13 Republicans voting "nay," 10 had also voted against the Haynsworth nomination. One of the most surprising negative votes was cast by Marlow W. Cook (R Ky.), leader of the pro-Haynsworth forces. His vote, which brought a gasp from the packed Senate galleries, came early in the roll call and signaled the nomination's probable defeat.

Cook described his "nay" vote as the most politically dangerous of his career. He said he would like to see a southern conservative sit on the Supreme Court, but that he should be an outstanding southerner: "Haynsworth satisfied my standard of excellence. Carswell did not."

Also voting against the nomination were four southern Democrats—J. W. Fulbright (Ark.), William B. Spong Jr. (Va.), Albert Gore (Tenn.) and Ralph W. Yarborough (Texas). This vote by Gore and Yarborough was considered a significant factor in the primary defeats both suffered later in 1970.

In a speech before the final vote, Carswell supporter Robert Dole (R Kan.) virtually admitted defeat, and suggested that Nixon wait until after the November 1970 election to send up another nomination for the vacant court seat. "It may be easier," said Dole, "to change the Senate than the Supreme Court."

Expressing agreement with this sentiment, Nixon April 9 said that he felt the Senate "as presently constituted" would not confirm a southern court nominee "who believes as I do in the strict construction of the Constitution."

"As long as the Senate is constituted the way it is today, I will not nominate another southerner and let him be subjected to the kind of malicious character assassination accorded both Judges Haynsworth and Carswell," Nixon promised. He said, however, that "the day will come when men like Judges Carswell and Haynsworth can and will sit on the High Court."

(Haynsworth continued his work as chief judge of the court of appeals, 4th circuit. Carswell, only a few months after his Senate rejection, resigned his seat on the court of appeals, 5th circuit, to run unsuccessfully in 1970 for one of the Florida seats in the Senate.)

Blackmun Approved

Ending one of the longest court vacancies in history, the Senate May 12, 1970, confirmed Harry A. Blackmun of Minnesota as an associate justice of the Supreme Court. Blackmun filled the seat left vacant on May 14, 1969, by the resignation of Abe Fortas. The Senate vote on confirmation was 94-0 and came only a month after the nomination was announced. Blackmun formally took his seat on the court June 9, 1970.

Only six times had a Supreme Court seat remained vacant for as long as a year; the last such vacancy had occurred during the Civil War.

Background. Within a week after the Senate's rejection of the Carswell nomination, Nixon named Blackmun, a judge on the court of appeals, 8th circuit, to fill the empty seat. Like Haynsworth and Carswell, Blackmun suited the President's image of a strict constructionist, and came to the court from experience on one of the federal appeals courts.

Blackmun, a Phi Beta Kappa graduate of Harvard College and an honors graduate of Harvard Law School, was considered an expert in taxation matters, estate management and medical law. From 1950 to 1959, he was resident legal counsel for the Mayo Clinic in Rochester, Minn.

Blackmun was a member of the Interim Advisory Committee on Judicial Activities, established by Chief Justice Burger late in 1969 to render opinions concerning the extrajudicial activities of federal judges until a new set of guidelines for such activities was formulated and adopted.

Describing himself as a "nominal Republican," Blackmun said April 14 that he had never taken an active political role. His nomination, even before the White

---

Executive Prerogative

President Nixon April 1 declared that rejection of the Carswell nomination would impair the constitutional relationship of the President to Congress.

"What is centrally at issue in this nomination," Nixon said, "is the constitutional responsibility of the President to appoint members of the court—and whether this responsibility can be frustrated by those who wish to substitute their own philosophy or their own subjective judgment for that of the one person entrusted by the Constitution with the power of appointment. The question arises whether I, as President of the United States, shall be accorded the same right of choice in naming Supreme Court Justices which has been freely accorded to my predecessors of both parties."

President Nixon said he respected the right of any senator to differ with his selection. But, he continued, "the fact remains under the Constitution, it is the duty of the President to appoint and of the Senate to advise and consent. But if the Senate attempts to substitute its judgment as to who should be appointed the traditional constitutional balance is in jeopardy and the duty of the President under the Constitution impaired."

Senate Majority Leader Mike Mansfield (D Mont.) April 2 rejected Mr. Nixon's contentions concerning impairment of constitutional duty and relationships and said that the Senate, in advising and consenting, shared the appointive power with the President.

House announcement, was endorsed by former Vice President (and former Minnesota senator, 1948-1964) Hubert H. Humphrey. Humphrey said that Blackmun was "the kind of man I'd like to see on the court...completely devoid of any racial bias...(a man) of a moderate political persuasion."

Deputy Attorney General Richard G. Kleindienst April 15 sent to Judiciary Committee Chairman James O. Eastland (D Miss.) a letter detailing Blackmun's background, qualifications, major rulings and three cases in which he had ruled although he owned stock in one of the litigants.

According to the letter, Blackmun held approximately $75,000 in stocks, bonds and bank accounts and approximately $50,000 in equity in his house in Minnesota.

The letter, at Blackmun's request—in light of the controversy concerning Haynsworth's participation in cases involving litigants in which he had an interest—explained three instances in which Blackmun had participated in a case involving a company in which he held stock:

• *Hanson v. Ford Motor Co.* (1960)—Judge Blackmun in October 1957 bought 50 shares of stock in Ford Motor Co. for slightly more than $2,500. He later participated in this case, after discussing whether or not he should do so with the chief judge and deciding that his interest was too small to require disqualification. He wrote the opinion, reinstating a verdict against the Ford Motor Co.

• In 1964 Judge Blackmun was part of a court of appeals panel which decided the case of *Kotula v. Ford*

(Continued p. 26)

Douglas: House Committee Finds No Basis for Impeachment

The controversies over Fortas, Haynsworth and Carswell kindled many enmities and a renewed concern for the off-bench activities of federal judges and Supreme Court justices. One product of this concern was a second serious attempt, in 1970, to impeach Supreme Court Justice William O. Douglas.

Appointed to the court in 1939 by Franklin D. Roosevelt, Douglas quickly became one of the most controversial justices in history. His staunchly liberal views, his outspoken opinions, and his several marriages, two to women in their twenties, made him the target of continuing criticism. The first attempt to impeach him came in 1953 after he had stayed the execution of convicted spies Julius and Ethel Rosenberg.

The second was sparked in great part by frustration among supporters of the nomination of G. Harrold Carswell to the court. Even before the vote rejecting Carswell's nomination, Sen. Robert C. Byrd (D W.Va.) said that the House should begin impeachment proceedings against Douglas if Carswell were rejected.

The Charges

In an April 15 speech on the House floor a week after the rejection of the Carswell nomination, Republican Leader Gerald R. Ford (Mich.) began such a move. Ford made five major charges against Douglas:

• In 1966, Douglas dissented in a 5 to 4 decision that upheld the obscenity conviction of Ralph Ginzburg, publisher of *Eros.*

Sen. Barry Goldwater (R Ariz.) won a libel suit against *Fact,* another Ginzburg publication. On Jan. 26, 1970, the Supreme Court, with Justices Douglas and Black dissenting, affirmed the award of punitive damages against Ginzburg and *Fact.* In March 1969, *Avant Garde,* also published by Ginzburg, paid Douglas $350 for an article entitled "Appeal of Folk Singing: A Landmark Opinion." Douglas' failure to disqualify himself in the Ginzburg cases, according to Ford, amounted to a "gross impropriety."

• *Points of Rebellion,* a book written by Douglas and published by Random House Inc., presented the thesis that violence could be justified and perhaps only revolutionary overthrow of "the establishment" could save the country, Ford said. He charged the book violated the standard of good behavior.

• "Redress in Revolution," an article by Douglas in *Evergreen Review,* April 1970, appeared in the same issue with nude photographs.

• Associations by Douglas with Albert Parvin and the Albert Parvin Foundation resulted in his practicing law in violation of federal law.

Ford said Douglas assisted in the organization of the Albert Parvin Foundation, established in November 1960, and gave legal advice to the foundation in dealing with an investigation by the Internal Revenue Service. Douglas voluntarily ended his association with the foundation in May 1969.

• The Center for the Study of Democratic Institutions in Santa Barbara, Calif., Ford said, was a "left-

ish" organization. He said Douglas was a consultant at the same time the center was recipient of Parvin Foundation funds.

In his speech, Ford urged creation of a special House committee to investigate the behavior of Douglas. But instead, the impeachment resolution was referred, as is usual, to the House Judiciary Committee.

The Report

A special House Judiciary subcommittee created to investigate these charges voted 3-1 Dec. 3 that it had found no grounds for impeachment. The report containing its conclusions and findings was released Dec. 16. It was endorsed by the five-member subcommittee's Democratic majority—Reps. Emanuel Celler (N.Y.), Byron G. Rogers (Colo.) and Jack Brooks (Texas). Rep. Edward Hutchinson (R Mich.) filed a two-page dissent and Rep. William M. McCulloch (R Ohio) abstained.

In his dissent, Hutchinson said the subcommittee could not consider its work complete without testimony and cross-examination of Douglas and other principals.

The subcommittee reported that:

• Douglas did not violate the Canons of Judicial Ethics in submitting and receiving payment for the article on folk singing which appeared in *Avant Garde.* The Ginzburg case was not before the Supreme Court at the time Douglas submitted the article.

• Douglas did not violate federal law in failing to disqualify himself from participation in the Supreme Court decision on a petition by Ginzburg to overturn the libel verdict. The law requires disqualification only if there is a substantial interest in a case.

• Douglas was not guilty of practicing law on behalf of the Parvin Foundation. Another attorney assumed responsibility for authorship of the articles incorporating the foundation. The foundation retained outside tax counsel.

The subcommittee considered charges made against Douglas on the basis of his relationship to Parvin and the Parvin Foundation, but found them "difficult to analyze because of the extreme tenuousness of the circumstantial evidence."

• It was neither illegal nor unethical for Douglas to accept an annual salary of $12,000 plus traveling expenses from the Parvin Foundation.

• Douglas' participation in a program sponsored by the Center for the Study of Democratic Institutions did not constitute a violation of the Logan Act which makes it unlawful for private citizens, without the authority of the U.S. government, to communicate with foreign governments with the intent to influence government relations.

• Charges that Douglas published statements encouraging violence in his book, *Points of Rebellion,* were based on a misinterpretation of the book.

• Douglas had no control over publication by *Evergreen Review* of excerpts from his book. Douglas' publisher, Random House, made the arrangements with the magazine without informing Douglas.

(Continued from p. 24)

Motor Co. The court of appeals upheld a lower court's action setting aside a verdict against Ford.

- *Mahoney v. Northwestern Bell Telephone Co.* (1967) —Judge Blackmun in 1963-1964 acquired 22 shares of American Telephone and Telegraph Co. stock at a total cost of about $1,350. He later participated in this decision which dismissed Mahoney's complaint for lack of the required jurisdiction.

The American Bar Association's committee on the federal judiciary April 28 endorsed Blackmun as a man with "high standards of professional competence, temperament and integrity." Blackmun's fellow judges notified the Judiciary Committee April 26 that they enthusiastically supported his nomination.

Committee Action. The Senate Judiciary Committee held one day of hearings April 29 on Blackmun's nomination. On May 5 it unanimously voted to report the nomination favorably, recommending confirmation. The committee report, filed May 9, described Blackmun as "thoroughly qualified" for the post of associate justice.

Noting that Blackmun had "answered every inquiry intelligently, cooperatively and frankly," the committee report said that the judge had impressed the committee as a "man of learning and humility."

Birch Bayh (D Ind.), Robert P. Griffin (R Mich.), Philip A. Hart (D Mich.), Edward M. Kennedy (D Mass.) and Joseph D. Tydings (D Md.) included a more detailed description of Blackmun's procedures in regard to cases involving companies in which he held stock. The five senators also added a statement describing Blackmun as "fully devoted to the statutory and constitutional precepts which control in federal courts," and as "sensitive to the problems and challenges facing not only the courts, but the entire nation today."

Bayh, leader of the opposition to Haynsworth and Carswell, joined the committee views, stating that his study of Blackmun's conduct on ethical matters led him to conclude that Blackmun's record showed a high standard of integrity, "fully consistent with service on the High Court."

Robert C. Byrd (D W.Va.) stated that he supported Blackmun's nomination because of the judicial restraint evident in the nominee's "deference for the legislative branch of the government in legislative matters," and "his recognition of the nice delineation of powers between the legislative and judicial branches."

Floor Action. The Senate approved the Blackmun nomination May 12 by a 94-0 roll-call vote.

After several hours of uneventful debate May 11 and 12, the Senate unanimously approved the nomination. The six senators not voting were Bayh, Barry Goldwater (R Ariz.), Albert Gore (D Tenn.), Karl E. Mundt (R S.D.), Richard B. Russell (D Ga.) and John G. Tower (R Texas).

John L. McClellan (D Ark.), during debate May 11, expressed the hope that confirmation of Blackmun would close the unpleasant chapter in the court's history which began with the Fortas resignation and begin "restoring the Supreme Court to its rightful place of respect and reverence."

Black, Harlan Depart

The Supreme Court suffered a sudden and significant loss in September 1971, with the resignations of Hugo L. Black and John Marshall Harlan.

Black, 85, resigned Sept. 17, 1971; Harlan, 72, resigned Sept. 23. Both gave failing health as the reason. Black died Sept. 25; Harlan, Dec. 29.

BLACK: KINDLY COLOSSUS

The resignation of Hugo Lafayette Black from his seat as associate justice of the Supreme Court removed from that bench one of the most influential men ever to sit there.

The White House, announcing the resignation of the man who had served more than 34 years—longer than all but two other men in history, said that the President had accepted it with deep regret. Chief Justice Warren E. Burger called Black's retirement "a great loss to the court." Burger said that "no disagreement on legal issues has ever affected the warm friendship that he and I developed."

Hugo L. Black was born in rural Alabama in 1886, less than 20 years after the end of the Civil War. He graduated with honors from the University of Alabama law school in 1906, despite the fact that he had never gone to college.

For a time a country lawyer, Birmingham police court judge, county prosecutor and, by 1925, respected attorney specializing in labor union and personal injury cases, Black decided to go into politics.

In early 1927, Sen. Hugo L. Black (D Ala.), 41, arrived in Washington. Soon linked with the liberal forces in the Senate, Black was later one of the staunchest backers of the New Deal legislation.

On August 12, 1937, the President nominated Black to the Supreme Court to succeed Willis Van Devanter, who had resigned. The Senate confirmed the nomination, Roosevelt's first, Aug. 17, 1937, by a 53-16 vote.

Before he took his seat, a newspaper series pointed out that Black had been a member of the Ku Klux Klan early in the 1920s. The storm of criticism subsided when Black stated that he no longer had any ties with the KKK. Black took his seat on the bench Oct. 4, 1937.

Black left an indelible imprint upon constitutional law and the history of the Supreme Court. He sat on that bench with one-fourth of all the justices in history—and with one-third of all the chief justices. He participated in more than one of every four decisions ever announced by the court.

His fierce independence and absolute belief in the letter, as well as the spirit, of the Constitution were expressed in concise and vivid language. His most enduring legacy may well be the series of rulings by the court during the 1950s and 1960s which held that the 14th Amendment made the Bill of Rights binding upon the states, not just the federal government.

Among his other outstanding opinions are those which invalidated the seizure of the steel mills by President Truman during the Korean War, which barred the use of any officially prescribed prayer in public schools, which declared the right of an indigent defendant in a state court to have counsel and which upheld the action of Congress in granting the vote to 18-year-old citizens.

HARLAN: CONSERVATIVE CONSCIENCE

John Marshall Harlan, namesake of the fourth chief justice and of a grandfather who served on the Supreme Court for 34 years (1877-1911), had served almost 17 years. Chief Justice Burger expressed regret at his resignation and said that "the quality of his penetrating, incisive mind and the grace of his spirit have made him a unique figure and he will rank with the great justices of this court."

John Marshall Harlan was born in Chicago in 1899; his grandfather was at that time sitting on the Supreme Court bench.

Harlan graduated from Princeton in 1920 and spent three years at Oxford as a Rhodes Scholar. Beginning his study of law at Oxford, he completed those studies at New York Law School in 1924 and began his practice on Wall Street. Most of Harlan's life for the next 30 years centered on his New York practice. He became one of the city's leading trial lawyers.

After serving for two years as chief counsel for the New York State Crime Commission during its investigation of the ties between organized crime and the state government, Harlan was named to the court of appeals, 2nd circuit, in early 1954. He had served there only a matter of months when President Eisenhower on Nov. 8 nominated him to succeed Robert H. Jackson on the Supreme Court. He took his seat March 28, 1955.

A conservative member of the Supreme Court during one of its most innovative periods, Harlan often served, one biographer noted, as the "conservative conscience" of the court. Often in dissent and frequently in a separate or concurring opinion, Harlan's scholarly writings provided a balance for the majority position, expressing his devotion to the concept of judicial restraint.

In 1965, he wrote a dissenting opinion when the majority of the court ruled that a federal court could intervene to halt proceedings in a criminal trial in a state court *(Dombrowski v. Pfister)*. Six years later, the court issued a series of opinions agreeing with Harlan's view and severely limiting the circumstances under which such intervention could occur.

Harlan registered dissents to two of the Warren court's most controversial decisions. In 1964, the court held in *Reynolds v. Sims* that the standard for the reapportionment of legislative districts was "one man, one vote." Harlan disagreed: the court should not have ventured into this political thicket, he said.

Two years later, in the case of *Miranda v. Arizona*, the court held that police could not constitutionally interrogate a prisoner suspect unless he had been advised of his constitutional rights. Harlan dissented vigorously, saying that the decision created unnecessary problems for the police.

Powell, Rehnquist Confirmed

The Senate in December 1971 confirmed the nominations of Lewis F. Powell Jr. and William H. Rehnquist as associate justices of the Supreme Court, the third and fourth men placed on that bench by Richard Nixon. Not since Warren G. Harding had one President in his first term had the opportunity to appoint so many members of the Supreme Court.

Powell, 64, of Virginia, succeeded to the southern seat left vacant by the resignation of the late Hugo L. Black, and Rehnquist, 47, took the seat vacated by the resignation of ailing John Marshall Harlan.

President Nixon named Powell and Rehnquist to the court Oct. 21. Powell was confirmed by the Senate Dec.

6; Rehnquist—whose nomination aroused more controversy—was confirmed Dec. 10.

Powell, a former president of the American Bar Association (ABA), was nationally recognized as a leader in the legal profession. Rehnquist, since 1969 serving as the President's lawyer's lawyer in his role as assistant attorney general, office of legal counsel, was less well-known.

In a nationally televised announcement of the nominations, Mr. Nixon said Oct. 21 his two criteria for nominees were professional excellence and a judicial philosophy that judges should "interpret...not twist or bend the Constitution in order to perpetuate (their) personal political or social views."

Rehnquist had testified frequently before Congress in behalf of administration programs. He had offered legal opinions on presidential authority to conduct the war in Vietnam, government use of mass-arrest techniques against demonstrators, equal rights for women and other topics that could come before the court.

Powell, of Richmond, Va., was a senior partner in the law firm of Hunton, Williams, Gay, Powell & Gibson. He was a past president of the American Bar Association and was a member of President Johnson's Commission on Law Enforcement and the Administration of Justice.

Neither nominee had served before as a judge. Both had highly regarded academic backgrounds. Both were elected to Phi Beta Kappa in college, finished first in their law school classes and went on to earn masters' degrees from Harvard University. Rehnquist served as a law clerk to the late Supreme Court Justice Robert H. Jackson in 1952-53.

Congressional reaction the night of the announcement and the next day was almost uniformly favorable or guarded—with no immediate expressions of opposition.

Sen. Birch Bayh (D Ind.), who led opposition in the Senate to Nixon's previous Haynsworth and Carswell nominations, said Rehnquist and Powell "appear to be significantly better qualified than some of the other names leaked to the public." Senate Minority Leader Hugh Scott (R Pa.) said the two men "appear to be well qualified."

Judiciary Committee Chairman James O. Eastland (D Miss.) told reporters he did not know Powell but that Rehnquist was a "lawyer's lawyer" and would make an "outstanding justice."

Criticism of the two nominees was voiced Oct. 22 by George Meany, president of the AFL-CIO: "These appointments seem to be part and parcel of the administration's effort to pack the court with ultraconservatives who subscribe to the President's narrow views on human rights and civil rights."

During the week of Oct. 25, some opposition to Rehnquist's nomination was announced by groups that disagreed with his civil rights and civil liberties views. In an effort to defuse such opposition, the Justice Department Oct. 29 released three documents in which Rehnquist had taken positions in opposition to many civil rights advocates.

Two of the documents, written in 1964, expressed his opposition to a public accommodations law proposed —and enacted—for his home town of Phoenix, Ariz. Rehnquist argued that the ordinance would destroy "a measure of our traditional freedom."

Three years later, Rehnquist argued for the neighborhood school concept. "We are no more dedicated to an 'integrated' society, than we are to a 'segregated' society" he said. "We are instead dedicated to a free society in which each man is accorded the maximum amount of freedom of choice in his individual activities."

The only possible hitch in confirmation of Powell appeared to be the question of the manner in which he would deal with his investments while he sat on the court. Data provided to the Senate Judiciary Committee showed that Powell, his wife and son held stocks and other investments worth about $1.5-million. (A similar listing for Rehnquist and his immediate family placed their holdings' worth at about $77,000.) Powell had said earlier that he would make any arrangement necessary to insulate himself from holdings which might create conflicts of interest.

Hearings. The Senate Judiciary Committee held hearings on the nominations Nov. 3-4, and 8-10.

Opening the hearings, Eastland reported that the FBI investigations of the nominees had uncovered no flaw in either man's background or character. The American Bar Association committee on the federal judiciary had also found both men qualified for the nominations, Eastland said.

The ABA committee unanimously recommended Powell as meeting, to an exceptional degree, high standards of professional competence, judicial temperament and integrity. "He is one of the best qualified lawyers available," the report concluded. Rehnquist received a similar highly favorable endorsement from nine members of the ABA committee, but three members—while not opposing his nomination—did not give him such a high rating.

Appearing Nov. 3-4 before the committee, Rehnquist was questioned closely as committee members attempted with relatively little success to uncover his personal philosophy. He did agree with conservative members that the Constitution should not be interpreted in order to achieve socially desirable ends, and that previous Supreme Court decisions should be given great weight in present and future rulings.

He promised to dissociate his personal philosophy "to the greatest extent possible" from his role on the court, but said too that he would not hesitate, as a justice, to adopt a position different from one he had advocated during his days in the Nixon administration. He said that those positions were not necessarily in accord with his personal feelings, but that he would have resigned his post, had those views been obnoxious to him.

Rehnquist disclaimed his 1964 writings on the public accommodations issue, saying that he no longer opposed such laws and that he had "come to realize the strong concern of minorities for the recognition of these rights." But he said he still opposed the use of busing for racial balance in school systems which had not formerly been dual segregated systems.

Declining to expound his personal views on various controversial matters on which the administration had taken a position, Rehnquist said that "it is a generally applicable principle in a lawyer-client relationship that the lawyer does not express personal views as to the merits of the client's case.... It would be disadvantageous to the government's position if I did disagree with it

after having acted as an advocate for it)." His clients, he said, were the attorney general and the President.

Bayh, interested in probing Rehnquist's views further, wrote Nixon and Attorney General John N. Mitchell asking them to waive this lawyer-client privilege. Mitchell responded that this would be inappropriate because it would expose to the public confidential policy discussions within the executive branch.

"There is a limit beyond which no nominee can go in expressing an opinion at this particular juncture," said Roman L. Hruska (R Neb.). "Since Franklin Roosevelt, philosophy has played a part in the selection of court nominees. And...they have, since that time, all been of liberal views. It's about time for some balance."

Appearing before the committee Nov. 8, Powell told them that he would disqualify himself from any case involving a party in which he had any interest. He said that he would move promptly to limit his holdings .but that he would retain certain investments in which sale of the stock would not remove his interest, such as those in companies which were clients of his firm.

The device of a "blind trust"—used to insulate a public official from knowledge of the holdings he has—accomplished little, Powell said. A judge needed to know what he owned in order to avoid inadvertent participation in cases in which he did have an interest, he said.

Powell said his concept of the role of the Supreme Court was based upon these tenets:

"I believe in the doctrine of the separation of powers...and that the court should not encroach upon the responsibility of the executive or the legislature; I believe in the federal system...; I believe in the importance of judicial restraint...that the court should avoid making a decision on constitutional grounds when other grounds are present; I believe in the power of precedent and a strong presumption in favor of upholding precedent; I believe that cases should be decided on the basis of the Constitution, the law and the facts before the court, putting aside one's own political and economic views and, to the extent possible, what one brings with him from his own background and experience. The court is the final authority and has great responsibility to uphold the rule of law...and to protect and safeguard the rights and liberties...of all our people."

Rehnquist Opposition. A number of witnesses appeared Nov. 9-10 to express opposition to the Rehnquist nomination. Among them were:

• Joseph L. Rauh, vice chairman, Americans for Democratic Action (ADA), who criticized Rehnquist for lacking respect for the rights of minorities and for the Bill of Rights. "This nominee," said Rauh, "is probably further to the right than any Supreme Court justice of this century."

• Clarence Mitchell, director, Washington bureau, National Association for the Advancement of Colored People (NAACP), and legislative chairman, Leadership Conference on Civil Rights, warned against this "self-proclaimed segregationist." "The Rehnquist nomination," he said, "raises a grim warning. Through that nomination the foot of racism is placed in the door of the temple of Justice. The Rehnquist record tells us that the hand of the oppressor will be given a chance to write opinions that will seek to turn back the clock of progress."

• Andrew J. Biemiller, AFL-CIO, described Rehnquist as a "right wing zealot" nominated to the court because he had demonstrated his "complete fealty to the administration's programs." "It is precisely because he is the administration's man," said Biemiller, "rather than his own that he should not sit on the high court."

Committee Action. After a delay of almost two weeks, the committee Nov. 23 voted unanimously to report favorably the Powell nomination and voted 12-4 to report favorably the Rehnquist nomination. The reports were filed Nov. 30.

Powell. The committee found Powell "thoroughly qualified" for the post of associate justice. It noted that supporting statements had come from black and white Virginians of different views, all "attesting to their respect for Mr. Powell's competence and fairness."

The committee said that in examining Powell's role in public education after the Supreme Court's 1954 school desegregation decision, it found that his predominant interest was in preserving and obtaining quality education for all Virginians, white and black. "He is remembered by those involved in the controversies of those years," wrote the committee, "as a moderating influence, seeking always to avoid hasty or extreme solutions and at the same time striving to obey the law of the land." The committee said it was entirely satisfied that Powell was dedicated to the concept of equal justice under law for all Americans.

Bayh, Philip A. Hart (D Mich.), Edward M. Kennedy (D Mass.) and John V. Tunney (D Calif.) supported the nomination, explaining their decision in light of some of the questions raised during the hearings about Powell's stand on questions of civil liberties and civil rights.

Questions about Powell's civil rights views—raised primarily in regard to his role in Virginia education—were resolved, the four senators said, by the record of his courageous efforts to keep the public schools open in the face of the massive resistance efforts to close, rather than desegregate, the schools.

"What his critics all too often have failed to realize," wrote the four senators, "is that it would be unfair to judge his individual specific actions without reference to the political context. We are convinced that...Powell was bucking the tide of opposition to change, pushing slowly but steadily toward the time when all the schools could be integrated."

Rehnquist. The committee found Rehnquist "thoroughly qualified" for the post of associate justice.

The committee felt that Rehnquist was "as responsive as he could be (in testimony before the committee) in view of his position in the government (as adviser to the President and the attorney general) and in view of the possibility that some of the questions he was asked might ultimately come before the Supreme Court."

The committee found the charges of Rehnquist's insensitivity on questions of civil rights to be "totally unfounded."

In a general observation, the committee majority pointed out that a judge and an advocate have essentially different roles: "The former must carefully weigh the strengths of competing arguments and public policy considerations while the latter owes a duty to his client to argue vigorously in support of his client's case.... Thus to draw sweeping generalizations from the positions an advocate has taken as a means of determining his fitness to be a judge is...mistaken."

The committee found that Rehnquist fully understood and believed in the guarantees of individual freedom embodied in the Bill of Rights: "He sees both sides of the difficult questions in this area, which require working out the delicate balance established by the Constitution between the rights of individuals and the duty of government to enforce the laws." His views, the committee concluded, "reflect a deep and unwavering commitment to the Constitution and represent advocacy in the best tradition of our legal system."

Bayh, Hart, Kennedy and Tunney included a lengthy memorandum outlining their reasons for opposing the Rehnquist nomination.

The Senate's role in confirmation of Supreme Court nominees, they said, went beyond rejecting those who were "obviously flawed by impropriety or incompetence." The Senate should weigh "the nominee's attitude toward the fundamental values of our constitutional system: limits on government power, individual liberty, human equality. A man takes what he is and believes to the bench," they said.

Rehnquist's record presented no problems of integrity or excellence, they said, but it raised serious questions about his commitment to those fundamental values.

Rather than reflecting a strict constructionist's point of view, said the committee minority, Rehnquist's statements mirrored a "strangely elastic approach to constitutional interpretation: The Bill of Rights and decisions upholding them...are read as narrowly as possible.... But provisions and precedents conferring executive power and declaring the general purposes of government are read loosely and expansively to justify the most intrusive kinds of official interference with those rights."

Furthermore, the four Democrats said, Rehnquist's record was "one of persistent indifference to the evils of discrimination and an almost hostile unwillingness to accept the use of law to overcome racial injustice in America."

Floor Action. The Senate Dec. 6, after three days of discussion, confirmed Powell by a vote of 89-1. The dissenting vote was cast by Fred R. Harris (D Okla.), who found Powell an elitist lacking compassion for "the little people."

Not a single critical word was directed at the nomination during debate. Paul J. Fannin (R Ariz.) pointed out that "debate is not very exciting when—as in this case—there is nothing to debate. After the first round of wonderful praise for Mr. Powell, all else is repetition."

William B. Spong Jr. (D Va.) remembered that "in the bitter aftermath of the Senate's rejection of the nomination of Judge Harrold Carswell, it was believed by many that a southerner could never be confirmed to a seat on the Supreme Court. I contested that view. I have always believed that a qualified southerner should be nominated, and, if nominated, could be confirmed, and if confirmed would serve the court and the nation with great distinction...Lewis F. Powell Jr...is such a man."

After the vote to confirm Powell, debate began on the more controversial Rehnquist nomination. Supporters complained that opponents of the nomination were filibustering, but the Senate, after four days of debate, refused Dec. 10 to limit debate. That day a cloture motion was rejected 52-42; a two-thirds majority—63 in this case—was needed for approval.

Bayh, leader of the opposition, then moved that the Senate put off the Rehnquist vote until Jan. 18, 1972. The Senate soundly rejected this motion, 22-70, and then voted, on a key roll-call vote of 68-26, to confirm Rehnquist. Opposing the nomination on the final vote were three Republicans—Edward W. Brooke (Mass.), Clifford P. Case (N.J.) and Jacob K. Javits (N.Y.)—and 23 Democrats.

Chronology

Of Legislation

On the Courts,

1969-1972

FEDERAL JUDGESHIPS. During his first term Nixon named almost as many federal judges and Supreme Court justices as had any President. Franklin D. Roosevelt held the existing record at 194 during his more than 12 years as President, but Nixon's 177 showed him certain to break that record during his second term. Nixon's achievement in this area was given substantial help by the Democratic Congress, which in 1970 approved legislation creating 58 additional permanent federal judgeships and three temporary ones.

1969. The Senate June 23 by voice vote and without debate passed and sent to the House a bill (S 952) creating 67 new permanent district judgeships and three temporary judgeships, most of which had been recommended by the U.S. Judicial Conference in 1968. The House Judiciary Committee held one day of hearings in October but took no further action.

The Senate Oct. 29, by a vote of 61-25, passed and sent to the House another bill (S 1508) which would allow federal judges to retire after 20 years on the federal bench, regardless of their age. The House failed to pass the bill. Under existing law, a federal judge could retire at age 65 after 15 years of service or at 70 after 10 years.

1970. Congress May 20 cleared S 952 for the White House. As finally approved, the bill created 58 new permanent federal district judgeships and three temporary posts. As signed by the President, the bill (PL 91-272):

- Authorized new permanent district judgeships for Alabama (2), Arizona (1), California (8), Colorado (1), Florida (3), Georgia (4), Illinois (2), Kentucky (2), Louisiana (3), Maryland (2), Michigan (2), Missouri (1), Nebraska (1), New Jersey (1), New Mexico (1), New York (4), Ohio (2), Pennsylvania (8), Puerto Rico (1), South Carolina (1), Tennessee (1), Texas (4), Virginia (1), Virgin Islands (1), West Virginia (1).
- Made permanent temporary judgeships in Kansas, Pennsylvania and Wisconsin.
- Authorized temporary judgeships in New Jersey, Pennsylvania and North Carolina.

The House Judiciary Committee had cut the number of judgeships in the bill by 13; the House had approved the amended bill March 18, 366-18. Conferees had com-

promised by adding to the House bill four more judgeships, one each in Maryland, Florida, Nebraska and West Virginia. The House adopted the conference report, 333-20, May 19; the Senate by voice vote the following day. The last judgeships bill cleared by Congress before 1970 was in 1966.

1971. The House Judiciary Committee Nov. 18 reported a bill (HR 11394) creating a new judicial district in Louisiana, and providing additional federal judgeships for Indiana, Florida, Texas and Missouri.

1972. The House Feb. 2 approved by voice vote HR 11394, providing five new federal district judgeships, one each in Indiana, Florida, Texas, Missouri and Wisconsin. The Senate took no action on the bill.

During floor consideration, the provisions creating a new judicial district for Louisiana were deleted without opposition; the same provisions had been attached to a private bill (HR 3749—PL 92-208) signed into law Dec. 18, 1971.

Congress July 31 cleared a bill (HR 6745—PL 92-376) altering the boundaries of the judicial district for the state of South Dakota. The state is one district made up of four divisions served by two district judges. The House passed the bill Feb. 7; the Senate July 31.

JUDICIAL SALARIES. A pay raise for Supreme Court justices and federal appeals and district judges went into effect Feb. 14, 1969, after Congress failed to veto the proposed increases. The pay raises increased the salary of the chief justice to $62,500 from $40,000, of associate justices to $60,000 from $39,500, of appeals court judges to $42,500 from $33,000, and of district judges to $40,000 from $30,000. The last judicial pay raise had been in 1964.

1972. Congress Aug. 9 cleared a bill (S 2854—PL 92-397) increasing the annuities paid to widows of Supreme Court justices to $10,000 each year from $5,000, and creating a contributory annuity system for retired and active justices. The Senate approved the bill June 30; the House approved a revised version Aug. 7; the Senate accepted the House version Aug. 9.

COURT PERSONNEL. Responding to the interest of Chief Justice Warren E. Burger in more efficient administration of the federal courts, Congress in 1970 cleared a bill (HR 17901—PL 91-647) providing for an executive to handle administrative duties for each of the 11 federal court circuits.

As signed into law, PL 91-647:

- Authorized the judicial council of each circuit to appoint a court executive and to delegate to him whatever administrative duties it considered advisable to delegate, subject to the general supervision of the circuit's chief judge.
- Established a five-member board of certification to set standards for and to certify qualified court executives.
- Authorized the Judicial Conference of the United States to set each executive's salary.

The court executive would, it was hoped, free the circuit's chief judge from many day-to-day administrative tasks; the concept was backed by the Justice Department, the Administrative Office of the U.S. Courts, and the American Bar Association (ABA). With ABA backing, an institute was established to train these executives.

The House approved the bill by voice vote under suspension of rules Oct. 5. The Senate approved the bill without change Dec. 22.

National Court of Appeals

Creation of a new high federal court to decide what cases the Supreme Court should consider was formally proposed Dec. 19, 1972, by a study group appointed by Chief Justice Warren E. Burger.

Headed by Harvard law professor Paul A. Freund, the study group was assembled under the aegis of the Federal Judicial Center. After a year's study, the group recommended:

• Creation, by law, of a National Court of Appeals to screen all requests for review of cases that now go to the Supreme Court and to decide certain cases in which courts within two judicial circuits have issued conflicting rulings.

• Elimination, by statute, of three-judge federal district courts (most often convened to hear constitutional questions) and elimination of the provision for direct review by the Supreme Court of three-judge court decisions, and of decisions in Interstate Commerce Commission (ICC) and antitrust cases.

• Establishment, by law, of a nonjudicial body to investigate and report on the complaints of prisoners.

• Increased staff support for the justices.

The new court was not to have a permanent set of its own judges, but would instead be composed of seven judges, drawn from the judges sitting on federal courts of appeals, to sit for staggered three-year terms.

All cases (except, it is assumed, those which go to the court under its own special original jurisdiction) which are now filed in the Supreme Court would go to this National Court of Appeals. There, they would be screened and denied or referred to the Supreme Court.

The study group's recommendations were expected to go to Congress and to the newly established federal Commission on Revision of the Federal Court Appellate System.

1971. The House approved a bill (HR 8699) on July 13, by a 263-139 vote, providing the Chief Justice with an administrative assistant similar to that provided by PL 91-647 for the chief judges of the federal circuits. The Senate took no action.

1972. Congress Feb. 18 cleared HR 8699 (PL 92-238) authorizing the Chief Justice to appoint himself an administrative aide, to assign certain duties to him and to pay him a salary of up to $40,000. Final action came with Senate passage, by voice vote, of the bill as approved by the House.

JUDICIAL REFORM. Two Senate Judiciary subcommittees held hearings in 1969 on legislation dealing with judicial reform in the aftermath of the resignation of Associate Justice Abe Fortas, but Congress left the matter of setting limits on the extrajudicial activities of federal judges to the federal judiciary.

1969. The Senate Dec. 9 approved by voice vote a bill (S 2624) to modernize the customs courts.

1970. Congress May 19 cleared S 2624 (PL 91-271) which:

• Provided a single, continuous procedure for deciding all issues in any entry of merchandise.

• Increased the length of time for importers to file requests for administrative and judicial review.

• Eliminated automatic referrals to the Customs Court by the bureau of denials of appeals, and set a two-year limit on the period the bureau had to dispose of an appeal.

• Provided that normally all customs cases before the Customs Court should be tried by a single judge (instead of by a three-judge panel as previously required).

The House approved an amended bill May 18 by a 310-0 roll-call vote; the Senate concurred May 19.

1972. Congress Oct. 4 cleared HR 7378 (PL 92-489) establishing a Commission on Revision of the Federal Court Appellate System of the United States to study and recommend changes in the geographic boundaries of the circuit courts and the structure and procedure of all federal appeals courts.

The House approved one version of the bill May 15, by a 317-25 roll-call vote, only authorizing the study of the geographic boundaries of the appeals courts circuits. The Senate approved an amended bill by voice vote June 30, expanding the time and scope of the mandate, and authorizing the commission to look into all facets of the problems of the appellate courts.

Conferees, reporting Sept. 28, gave the 16-member commission six months to study and recommend changes in the boundaries of the circuits, and 15 months to study and recommend more structural and procedural changes. The 16 members were to be appointed, four each by the chief justice, Senate, House and President. The Senate adopted the conference report by voice vote Sept. 29, the House Oct. 4.

MAGISTRATES. Congress in 1972 cleared two bills concerning U.S. magistrates, the judicial officers of federal district courts. Their functions include issuing search and arrest warrants, fixing bail, holding preliminary hearings and conducting trials for minor offenses.

On Feb. 18 the Senate by voice vote approved and cleared HR 9180 (PL 92-239), which authorized temporary assignment of magistrates outside their regular jurisdictions during emergencies. The bill, backed by the Justice Department, was an amendment to the Federal Magistrates Act of 1968. The House had approved HR 9180 by a 344-10 roll-call vote Nov. 1, 1971.

Congress Sept. 12 cleared a bill (HR 7375—PL 92-428) increasing the statutory ceiling for magistrates' salaries to $30,000 annually from $22,500. The ceiling for part-time magistrates was increased to $15,000 from $11,000. The House approved the bill by voice vote May 16; the Senate approved an amended version by voice vote Aug. 18. The House agreed to the Senate changes Sept. 12.

CLAIMS AND JURIES. Congress in 1972 cleared a bill (HR 12979—PL 92-375) providing for the temporary recall of retired senior commissioners of the U.S. Court of Claims when the court needed them. The commissioners hold hearings to determine facts and make recommendations and determinations which are reviewed by the court. The House approved the bill by voice vote April 17; the Senate by voice vote July 31.

Congress in 1972 also cleared a bill (S 1975—PL 92-269) lowering the required age for federal jury service to 18 from 21. The Senate had approved the bill Dec. 1, 1971, by voice vote; the House approved an amended bill March 6 by voice vote; the Senate cleared the bill by accepting the House changes March 24.

1973 Legislation

RULES OF EVIDENCE. In an unpublicized but significant assertion of authority, Congress in 1973 took an active role in developing the technical rules by which evidence—the crucial factor in any case—is admitted into federal courtrooms.

Led by Rep. William L. Hungate (D Mo.), a subcommittee of the House Judiciary Committee worked for most of the year on the proposed rules, sent to Congress by Chief Justice Burger early in February. Since 1792 the Supreme Court has been empowered by Congress to prescribe the procedures to be followed in certain federal cases. Since 1934, Congress had required, in most cases, that the rules be reported to Congress and that a certain period of time elapse before they became effective.

A dozen years of study and work by judges and attorneys under the aegis of the Judicial Conference of the United States produced the proposed rules of evidence which the Supreme Court formally made public in November 1972. Even at that time, Justice William O. Douglas expressed his concern that the court might have exceeded the scope of its delegated authority, moving from matters of procedure to matters of substance in approving rules of evidence.

As sent to Congress Feb. 5, the rules were to go into effect July 1, unless Congress blocked them within 90 days of Feb. 5. Concerned about the warning from Douglas, and about the contents of these rules, Sen. Sam J. Ervin Jr. (D N.C.), chairman of the Senate Judiciary subcommittee on separation of powers, quickly introduced a bill (S 583) delaying the effective date until the end of the current congressional session. The Senate approved the bill two days after the rules reached the Hill.

The House Judiciary Committee, feeling "that there is enough controversy wrapped up in the 168 pages of rules...that the rules should not be permitted to become effective without...an affirmative act of Congress," approved an amended bill to delay the effective date until such time as Congress had approved the rules of evidence. In her maiden speech in the House, freshman Elizabeth Holtzman (D N.Y.), a member of the judiciary subcommittee, pointed out that: "The proposed rules of evidence do not deal with abstruse legal technicalities .... They seek to resolve social issues over which there is now vast national debate: executive secrecy, the newsman's privilege, and individual privacy." The House approved the amended bill March 14; the Senate agreed to the House version five days later.

Then the careful, time-consuming, technical work of the judiciary subcommittee began in earnest as each rule was examined—and approved, deleted, or amended. Between late March and late June, the subcommittee held 17 meetings to work on the rules; the result was a new draft of the rules which was circulated for comment from the legal profession for 30 days. All comments were considered and a revised draft, drawn up in five additional mark-up sessions, was reported to the full Judiciary Committee on Oct. 10. After three meetings dealing with the rules, the full committee ordered the rules (HR 5463) reported to the House (H Rept 93-650) on Nov. 6.

Rules Reported. As approved by the House Judiciary Committee, the bill (HR 5463) contained the first uniform set of rules of evidence for the federal courts. There had been, as the committee report noted, controversy over the actual need for a uniform set of such rules. Those who advocated such a code said it would assist federal judges assigned to districts or circuits other than their own in order to help out their over-burdened colleagues, and would also help younger members of the bar, who would only have one set of rules to learn. Opponents of such a code of evidence said there was no real need for the proposed rules, that evidence was a subject which should be left to case-by-case development and not codified. The subcommittee concluded that there should be a uniform set of rules of evidence.

More than half of the rules in HR 5463 as reported were not amended at all by the committee or were amended only in nonsubstantive ways, the report noted. Five proposed rules were deleted and significant changes were made in 24 others. Those deleted by the committee were proposed rules which would have:

- Set forth guidelines for judges to use in summing up evidence and commenting to the jury upon its weight and the credibility of the witnesses. The section of the rule dealing with the comments was highly controversial.
- Dealt with the use of presumptions in criminal cases, and the weight they should be given. This subject, commented the report, was under consideration by the Judiciary Committee in its work on the proposed new federal criminal code.
- Provided for a certain method of proof that some practice was a habit or routine. This, said the report, was a matter to be dealt with by courts on a case-by-case basis.
- Allowed new exceptions to the general rule that hearsay testimony is not admissible as evidence. The proposed exceptions would have injected "too much uncertainty into the law of evidence," said the report.

Among the rules substantially amended by the committee were those which:

- Defined specific non-constitutional privileges (lawyer-client, husband-wife, state secrets etc.) which federal courts must recognize, and provided that only those privileges or others granted by Congress would be recognized in the federal courts. These were the most controversial of all the proposed rules, and were seen as limiting most privileges while expanding the protection granted through privilege to state secrets and government information.

The committee eliminated all of the rules setting forth specific privileges, leaving the law on that point in its present state and providing that privileges "shall continue to be developed by the courts of the United States under a uniform standard applicable both in civil and criminal cases."

- Allowed character witnesses to give opinion, as well as reputation, testimony. References to opinion testimony were deleted by the committee which feared that such an allowance "might tend to turn a trial into a swearing contest between conflicting character witnesses."
- Allowed the credibility of a witness to be attacked by the introduction of evidence that he had been convicted of a felony or of a crime which involved dishonesty or false statement. The committee amended the rule to allow such evidence to be so used only if the witnesses' crime involved dishonesty or false statement.

The bill also authorized the court to propose amendments to the rules, and provided that either house of Congress could prevent a rule from going into effect by passing a resolution within 180 days of receiving the rules.

Supreme Court Decisions, 1969-1972

"We need a court which looks upon its function as being that of interpretation rather than of breaking through into new areas," declared candidate Richard Nixon in 1968. He promised to rebalance the court with men who realized that some Warren court decisions had "tended to weaken the peace forces as against the criminal forces."

Between 1969 and 1972 Nixon placed a new chief justice and three new associate justices on the court, more in a four-year period than any president since Harding. But by 1972 it was apparent that Nixon's reshaping of the court had not had quite the result he envisioned: over administration protest the court had outlawed the death penalty, refused to halt publication of the Pentagon Papers articles in *The New York Times* and *The Washington Post,* approved the use of busing to desegregate public schools, and rejected the administration's claim that it did not have to get court approval of wiretaps on domestic groups suspected of subversion.

No Warren court ruling had been overturned: the very decisions decried by Nixon had hardened quickly into precedent requiring respect from the new conservative justices. The court chipped away at the scope of some of these rulings, such as the *Miranda* decision, announced in 1966 by a 5-4 court. In that ruling the court had barred use as evidence of any statements made by a defendant whom police had not properly informed of his constitutional rights. Joined by Blackmun and Burger, the three *Miranda* dissenters who remained—Harlan, Stewart and White—formed a new majority by 1971 in ruling that such statements, if voluntary, could be used under certain circumstances to impeach a defendant's credibility.

Another way in which the force of some earlier rulings was limited was by holdings condoning certain violations of rights as merely harmless error, given other facts in a particular case. Rehnquist, in the first majority opinion he wrote, applied this approach to violation of the right to face one's accusers.

Criminal Law. Because of Supreme Court rulings in criminal law during this post-Warren period, by 1972 *(Criminal law decisions, p. 34):*

● The death penalty as it had been imposed in the United States was outlawed.

● If a defendant had been overheard on an illegal wiretap, the government had to chose between disclosing to him all material obtained from the wiretap and dropping the case against him.

● The government had to go to court to get approval for electronic surveillance of domestic groups suspected to be subversive.

● State juries of fewer than 12 persons could try persons charged with non-capital offenses; but states had to provide jury trials for all persons charged with offenses entailing possible sentences of more than six months.

● State juries could find a person guilty by a less than unanimous vote.

● Judges could order disruptive defendants bound, gagged and removed from the courtroom if necessary to proceed with the trial; but if the judge charged a defendant with contempt for behavior during the trial, another judge would preside over the contempt trial.

● Juveniles had the right to be found guilty or delinquent—beyond a reasonable doubt, but did not have a constitutional right to trial by jury.

● The right to legal counsel applied to all persons charged with any offense involving possible imprisonment, and to persons at certain preliminary stages of the criminal proceedings, but not to persons in pre-indictment line-ups.

● States could not make the private possession of obscene material or the distribution of contraceptives to unmarried persons a crime.

● Judges could no longer sentence a guilty man to "$30 or 30 days"; nor could poor prisoners be held in jail beyond their maximum sentence to "work off" fines they could not pay.

Civil Rights. All court-ordered efforts to erase the effects of legal school segregation continued to win Supreme Court backing. In other civil rights cases, the court held that community swim clubs could not exclude black residents from membership when all white residents were accepted, but that federal civil rights law did not reach a private club with a state liquor license and a discriminatory guest policy.

A city, held the court, could close all its municipal swimming pools rather than desegregate them; states could condition all construction of low-income housing projects on approval by local referendum. But employers could not impose job requirements on applicants if those criteria were unrelated to job performance and disqualified more black job applicants than whites.

Congress could, by law—not just by constitutional amendment—lower the voting age to 18 for federal elections, held the court, at the same time disapproving congressional enactment of the lower voting age for state and local elections. State residency requirements of more than 30 days for voters were invalidated. And the court insisted on strict mathematical equality of population between congressional districts within a state.

First Amendment Rights. Watching over the separation of church and state, the court in 1970 backed property tax exemptions for church-owned lands used for religious purposes; but the next year it invalidated state laws allowing state reimbursement of private schools for certain educational costs. In 1972 it approved the exemption of Amish children from compulsory public school attendance laws.

The fairness doctrine for broadcasters was upheld and libel protection for newspapers was reinforced. In a historic confrontation, the court sided with the press in denying the government's plea to halt publication of newspaper articles based on the once-classified Pentagon Papers. A year later, the court held that the First Amendment did not protect newsmen from grand jury efforts to obtain information, even confidential information. And it narrowed congressional immunity by holding that a senator could be prosecuted for accepting a bribe to cast a certain vote.

New Horizons. Despite Nixon's desire that the Supreme Court stick to interpreting the law and not break through into new areas, the court by 1972 was dealing with the problems of sex discrimination, the rights of consumers, of tenants and of welfare recipients, and the growing concern over man's effect on his environment. The court's docket reflected the new concern of the nation it served, and the court in 1972 evidenced its traditional caution but no reluctance in grasping those issues and blazing—carefully—new legal trails.

Crime and Constitutional Rights

Spinelli v. U.S., decided by a 5-3 vote, Jan. 27, 1969. Harlan wrote the opinion; Marshall did not participate; Black, Fortas and Stewart dissented.

Just a report of a reliable informer's tip containing some specific details is not sufficient cause for issuing search warrant, even though tip was corroborated by other sworn charges resulting from independent investigation and by reputation of suspect.

Davis v. Mississippi, decided by a 6-2 vote, April 22, 1969. Brennan wrote the opinion; Fortas did not participate; Black and Stewart dissented.

John Davis, a young black Mississippian, was convicted of rape after his fingerprints, obtained by the police during his warrantless detention as part of a police dragnet, matched those found at the scene of the crime. The court reversed his conviction, finding that this taking of his fingerprints violated the Fourth Amendment guarantee against unreasonable search and seizure. The fingerprints so obtained could thus not be used as evidence against him, held the court, directing that henceforth, such "investigatory arrests" must be authorized by warrants if the evidence obtained during them was to be used in court.

"Nothing is more clear," stated the majority, "than that the Fourth Amendment was meant to prevent wholesale intrusions upon the personal security of our citizenry, whether these intrusions be termed 'arrests' or 'investigatory detentions'." In dissent, Justice Black lamented the decision as "one more in an ever-expanding list of cases in which this court has been so widely blowing up the Fourth Amendment's scope that its original authors would be hard put to recognize their creation."

Chimel v. California, decided by a 6-2 vote, June 23, 1969, Stewart wrote the opinion; Black and White dissented.

Over complaints from Justices Black and White that the court was imposing unreasonable restrictions upon police action, the court overruled a 20-year-old decision *(U.S. v. Rabinowitz, 1950)* to narrow the area which could be searched, without a warrant, incident to an lawful arrest. If police wished to search further than the immediate area from which the arrested person could reach to obtain a weapon or destroy evidence, they must obtain a search warrant, held the court. A person's entire dwelling could not be subjected to a warrantless search simply because he was arrested there.

Colonnade Catering Corp. v. U.S. decided by a 5-3 vote, Feb. 25, 1970. Opinion by Douglas; Burger, Black and Stewart dissented.

Congress has not authorized federal tax agents, forcibly and without a warrant, to enter the premises owned or operated by a liquor dealer. Congress has instead made it an offense for a dealer to refuse to admit the inspecting agent.

Vale v. Louisiana, decided by a 6-2 vote, June 22, 1970. Stewart wrote the opinion; Blackmun did not participate; Burger and Black dissented.

Police without a warrant cannot constitutionally search a suspect's house incident to his arrest just outside. Burger and Black criticized the majority for failing to appreciate the problem faced by a police officer who had now to leave the premises—and possible evidence— to obtain a search warrant. The ruling, they said, made "unnecessarily difficult the conviction of those who prey upon society."

Whiteley v. Warden, decided by a 6-3 vote, March 29, 1971. Harlan wrote the opinion; Black, Burger and Blackmun dissented.

Police cannot constitutionally arrest someone on the basis of information broadcast over police radio when that information had been considered insufficient for issuing an arrest warrant. Black complained that this decision was "a gross and wholly indefensible miscarriage of justice," a decision "calculated to make many good people believe our court actually enjoys frustrating justice by unnecessarily turning professional criminals loose to prey upon society with impunity."

Williams v. U.S., Hill v. California, decided by a 6-2 vote, April 5, 1971. White wrote the opinions; Douglas did not participate; Harlan and Marshall dissented in part.

The court refused to make its *Chimel* decision retroactive, applying it only to searches occurring after that ruling. The court in *Hill* refused to invalidate the warrantless, pre-*Chimel* search of the entire apartment of a defendant incident to the mistaken warrantless arrest there of a person resembling the defendant.

Coolidge v. New Hampshire, decided by a 5-4 vote, June 21, 1971. Stewart wrote the opinion; Burger, Black, Blackmun and White dissented in part.

Evidence cannot be used at trial if it was seized, held the court, by officers acting with a search warrant issued by an official actively involved in prosecuting the particular case: warrants must be authorized by "neutral and detached magistrates" in order to be constitutionally valid. Evidence obtained by police from a defendant's home without a warrant but with his wife's permission is admissible at trial, but not evidence obtained from his car by a warrantless search.

Search and Seizure

The right of the people to be secure in their persons, houses, papers and effects, against unreasonable searches and seizures, shall not be violated, and no warrants shall issue, but upon probable cause, supported by oath or affirmation and particularly describing the place to be searched, and the persons or things to be seized.

Fourth Amendment, U.S. Constitution

Bivens v. Six Unknown Federal Agents, decided by a 6-3 vote, June 21, 1971. Brennan wrote the opinion; Burger, Black and Blackmun dissented.

A person whose dwelling was searched illegally by federal agents who arrested him may sue those agents for damages for violation of his constitutional right against unreasonable search and seizure. Chief Justice Burger dissented, arguing that Congress alone could create this remedy—of a damage suit—against the federal government.

U.S. v. Harris, decided by a 5-4 vote, June 28, 1971. Burger wrote the opinion; Harlan, Douglas, Brennan and Marshall dissented.

The court upheld as probable cause for a search of a suspected moonshiner's premises an affidavit based on an informer's tip and the suspect's reputation.

U.S. v. Biswell, decided by an 8-1 vote, May 15, 1972. White wrote the opinion; Douglas dissented.

A warrantless inspection of a gun dealer's storeroom during business hours was not an unreasonable search if necessary for effective enforcement of federal firearms law.

Adams v. Williams, decided by a 6-3 vote, June 12, 1972. Rehnquist wrote the opinion; dissenting were Douglas, Brennan and Marshall.

Police, with informer's tip but without search warrant, can properly and reasonably stop a person and search him for an illegally possessed weapon.

WIRETAPPING

Alderman v. U.S., Butenko v. U.S., Ivanov v. U.S., decided by a 5-3 vote, March 10, 1969. White wrote the opinion; Marshall did not participate; Black, Harlan and Fortas dissented.

The court, to the dismay of the Justice Department, ruled that the federal government must turn over for examination all material obtained by illegal electronic surveillance to a defendant whose rights were violated by the surveillance and against whom they might be used, even if the surveillance involved the national security. The court also held that such material, although unusable as evidence against anyone whose constitutional rights against unreasonable search and seizure had been violated in the surveillance, might be usable as evidence against another defendant whose rights had not been so violated.

Justice White, in his opinion, made clear the "search and seizure" aspect of electronic surveillance; "the right to be secure in one's house against unauthorized intrusion is not limited to protection against a policeman viewing or seizing tangible property." This right is "as clearly invaded when the police enter and install a listening device in his house as they are when the entry is made to undertake a warrantless search for tangible property.... Like physical evidence which might be seized overheard conversations are fruits of an illegal entry and are inadmissible in evidence," against the owner, whether or not he was present or participating in the conversations.

The court rejected the government's argument that a judge should first determine, through inspection in his chambers the "arguably relevant" information in the illegally obtained material and then turn over to the defendant only such relevant matter:

"The task is too complex, and the margin for error too great, to rely wholly on the...judgment of the trial court to identify those records which might have contributed to the government's case."

Desist v. U.S., decided by a 5-3 vote, March 24, 1969. Stewart wrote the opinion; Marshall did not participate; dissenting were Harlan, Fortas and Douglas.

The court refused to apply its landmark 1968 decision on wiretapping in the case of *Katz v. U.S.* retroactively. In *Katz* the court had reversed a 40-year-old decision *(Olmstead v. U.S. 1928)* to hold that whether or not actual physical trespass occurs (as in the installation of an electronic device), any electronic surveillance which is not approved ahead of time by a court is unconstitutional as an unreasonable search and seizure. Stewart said that the court felt the decision should only apply to cases occurring after it because it was a "clear break" with the 1928 holding.

U.S. v. White, decided by a 6-3 vote, April 5, 1971. White wrote the opinion; Douglas, Harlan and Marshall dissented.

Opening a loophole in its wall of disapproval of warrantless electronic surveillance, the court held that it was not unconstitutional for an electronic device to be voluntarily carried by an informer, without a warrant, to overhear conversations between the informer and another person. In his dissent, Douglas argued that such monitoring of conversations stifled free speech: "Free discourse...may be frivolous or serious, humble or defiant, reactionary or revolutionary, profane or in good taste; but it is not free if there is surveillance.... Must everyone live in fear that every word he speaks may be transmitted or recorded and later repeated to the entire world? I can imagine nothing that has a more chilling effect on people speaking their minds and expressing their views on important matters."

U.S. v. U.S. District Court, Eastern Michigan, decided by a 6-2 vote, June 19, 1972. Powell wrote the opinion; Rehnquist did not participate; Burger and White dissented.

The court rejected the Justice Department's claim that it did not have to get court approval for the use of electronic surveillance of persons or domestic groups suspected to be subversive. Powell wrote: "The price of lawful public dissent must not be a dread of subjection to an unchecked surveillance power. Nor must the fear of unauthorized official eavesdropping deter vigorous citizen dissent and discussion of government action in private conversation. For private dissent, no less than open public discourse, is essential to our free society."

"Unreviewed executive discretion," warned Powell, "may yield too readily to pressures to obtain incriminating evidence and overlook potential invasions of privacy and protected speech.... We cannot accept the government's argument that internal security matters are too subtle and complex for judicial evaluation.... If the threat is too subtle or complex for our senior law enforcement officers to convey its significance to a court, one may question whether there is probable cause for surveillance."

Gelbard v. U.S., U.S. v. Egan, decided by a 5-4 vote, June 26, 1972. Brennan wrote the opinion; Burger, Blackmun, Powell and Rehnquist dissented.

A grand jury witness may refuse to testify—without risking contempt charges—until the government proves that the evidence on which he was called to appear was not obtained by illegal electronic surveillance. The Nixon nominees, in dissent, complained that the majority had "stood on its head both the language and the legislative history" of the law to reach this result; neither the 1968 Omnibus Crime Control and Safe Streets Act nor the 1970 Organized Crime Control Act supported such "expansive and novel claims" as those upheld by the majority. *(Story p. 265; Congress and the Nation Vol. II p. 323)*

DOUBLE JEOPARDY

Benton v. Maryland, decided by a 6-2 vote, June 23, 1969. Marshall wrote the opinion; Harlan and Stewart dissented.

In the last announced decision of the Warren Court, the court overruled its 32-year-old holding in *Palko v. Connecticut (1937)* to apply the constitutional guarantee against double jeopardy to the states. The double jeopardy clause was thus the last of the provisions of the Bill of Rights to be found to apply to the states through the Fourteenth Amendment guarantee of due process. In an earlier decision the majority had held that if a right guaranteed by the Bill of Rights is "fundamental to the American scheme of justice," it must also apply to the states. The double jeopardy clause was certainly fundamental, ruled the court.

North Carolina v. Pearce, Simpson v. Rice, decided by a 6-2 vote, June 23, 1969. Stewart wrote the opinion; Black and Harlan dissented in part.

The double jeopardy clause requires that a judge credit punishment already exacted when resentencing a defendant who has been retried for an offense for which he has already once been convicted and sentenced. If a more severe sentence is imposed after the retrial, the judge must place in the record affirmative reasons for the heavier penalty, based objectively on the conduct of the defendant since his original sentencing.

Ashe v. Swenson, decided by a 7-1 vote, April 6, 1970. Stewart wrote the opinion; Burger dissented.

After a jury has acquitted a man on charges of robbing one victim of a multi-victim single robbery, that same man cannot be retried on charges of robbing another of the victims. The majority held that the doctrine of collateral estoppel was part of the double jeopardy guarantee: "when an issue of ultimate fact once has been determined by a valid and final judgment, that issue cannot again be litigated between the same parties in any future lawsuit."

Waller v. Florida, decided by a 8-0 vote, April 6, 1970. Burger wrote the opinion.

State cannot try person on charge arising from same action for which he has already been tried and convicted by municipal court.

Price v. Georgia, decided by an 8-0 vote, June 15, 1970. Burger wrote the opinion; Blackmun did not participate.

Once a man has been tried on murder charges, convicted only of manslaughter, and had that conviction overturned, he cannot be retried by the state on any more serious charge than manslaughter. A guilty verdict on a lesser included offense, such as manslaughter, is an "implicit acquittal" on a greater charge, such as murder.

SELF-INCRIMINATION

Orozco v. Texas, decided by a 6-2 vote, March 25, 1969. Black wrote the opinion; Fortas did not participate; White and Stewart dissented.

The court's landmark ruling in *Miranda v. Arizona* —that a suspect, before interrogation by police, must be advised of his constitutional right to remain silent and to have legal counsel—applied to questioning of a suspect in custody outside as well as inside a police station, even in bed in his own home. White complained that the court was tightening the constitutional straitjacket into which *Miranda* had laced law enforcement officials. *(Congress and the Nation Vol. II p. 323)*

Leary v. U.S., decided by an 8-0 vote, May 19, 1969. Harlan wrote the opinion.

Reversing the conviction of former Harvard psychologist Timothy F. Leary for failing to pay a federal tax on marijuana transfers, the court found the law imposing the tax unconstitutional as a violation of the right not to incriminate oneself. Anyone complying with the federal law would provide evidence which would incriminate him under state laws forbidding the possession of marijuana.

Minor v. U.S., Buie v. U.S., decided by a 6-2 vote, Dec. 8, 1969. White wrote the opinion; Douglas and Black dissented.

Refusing to reverse convictions of men for selling heroin and marijuana without the federal order forms required by law, the court held that the law requiring use of those forms did not violate the privilege against self-incrimination. Drug dealers were not forced to incriminate themselves by selling without the required forms; they did have the alternative of not selling the drugs at all.

Turner v. U.S., decided by a 6-2 vote, Jan. 20, 1970. White wrote the opinion; Black and Douglas dissented.

The court upheld a federal law presuming that a person possessing heroin—not stamped with federal tax stamps—knows that it is illegally produced, purchased, possessed and distributed—because heroin is not produced in the United States or legally imported. But the court invalidated a similar law concerning possession of unstamped cocaine, because some cocaine is produced in the United States, and some is legally imported.

Brady v. U.S., decided by an 8-0 vote, ***Parker v. North Carolina,*** decided by a 5-3 vote, May 4, 1970. White wrote the opinions; Douglas, Brennan and Marshall dissented in the second case.

A guilty plea entered in a capital case to avoid a possible death sentence is not an involuntary guilty plea in violation of the right against self-incrimination.

McMann v. Richardson, decided by a 5-3 vote, May 4, 1970. White wrote the opinion; Douglas, Brennan and Marshall dissented.

Prisoner's claim that his guilty plea, entered with advice of counsel, was induced by an earlier coerced confession does not win him a federal *habeas corpus* hearing on the voluntariness of the plea.

North Carolina v. Alford, decided by a 6-3 vote, Nov. 23, 1970. White wrote the opinion; Douglas, Brennan and Marshall dissented.

A murder defendant's claim to innocence did not foreclose court acceptance of his plea of guilty to second-degree murder when the plea was made with the advice of counsel, supported by substantial evidence and motivated by the desire to avoid the death penalty.

Harris v. New York, decided by a 5-4 vote, Feb. 24, 1971. Burger wrote the opinion; Black, Douglas, Brennan and Marshall dissented.

Modifying its ban imposed in *Miranda v. Arizona (1966)* on any in-court use of statements made by defendants not properly advised of their rights, the court held that these statements, so long as they were voluntary, could be used to impeach a defendant's credibility if he contradicted them in testifying in his own behalf. Burger wrote that "every criminal defendant is privileged to testify in his own defense or to refuse to do so. But that privilege cannot be construed to include the right to commit perjury.... The shield provided by *Miranda* cannot be perverted into a license to use perjury by way of a defense, free from the risk of confrontation with prior inconsistent utterances." In dissent, Brennan warned that the court was undoing much of the progress made by the Warren court in requiring police methods to remain within constitutional bounds.

U.S. v. Freed, decided by a 9-0 vote, April 5, 1971. Douglas wrote the opinion.

As revised in 1968, the existing federal gun control law, requiring registration of firearms only by transferor and forbidding use of information provided by registration for prosecution, does not violate the privilege against self-incrimination.

California v. Byers, decided by a 5-4 vote, May 17, 1971. Burger wrote the opinion; Black, Douglas, Brennan and Marshall dissented.

The five-man majority declined to overthrow, as a violation of the Fifth Amendment right not to incriminate oneself, state laws requiring motorists involved in acci-

---

Fair Trial

In all criminal prosecutions, the accused shall enjoy the right to a speedy and public trial, by an impartial jury of the state and district wherein the crime shall have been committed,...and to be informed of the nature and cause of the accusation; to be confronted with the witnesses against him; to have compulsory process for obtaining witnesses in his favor, and to have the assistance of counsel for his defense.

—Sixth Amendment, U.S. Constitution

---

dents to stop and identify themselves even though no restriction is imposed on prosecutorial use of that information.

Lego v. Twomey, decided by a 4-3 vote, Jan. 12, 1972. White wrote the opinion; Douglas, Brennan and Marshall dissented.

A confession could be used as evidence, held a bare majority, if it was proved voluntary by a preponderance of the evidence (not beyond a reasonable doubt). Brennan, writing for the dissenters, argued that "it is...critical to our system of criminal justice that when a person's words are used against him, no reasonable doubt remains that he spoke of his own free will."

Kastigar v. U.S., decided by a 5-2 vote, May 22, 1972. Powell wrote the opinion; Rehnquist and Brennan did not participate; Douglas and Marshall dissented.

The court upheld the narrowed witness immunity provisions of the 1970 Organized Crime Control Act, approving—as no infringement of the Fifth Amendment—a limited grant of immunity from prosecution to a witness compelled to testify. The court did specify however that in any subsequent prosecution of the witness, the prosecution must show that the evidence against the witness was derived from sources independent of his own testimony.

Brooks v. Tennessee, decided by a 6-3 vote, June 7, 1972. Brennan wrote the opinion; Burger, Blackmun and Rehnquist dissented.

A defendant's Fifth Amendment right against self-incrimination is violated by a state law which requires him to testify first in his defense presentation or not at all.

FAIR TRIAL

Illinois v. Allen, decided by an 8-0 vote, March 31, 1970. Black wrote the opinion.

The right to be present at one's own trial is not absolute, ruled the court. A defendant can lose his right to be present if, after being warned that he will be removed from the courtroom if he continues to disrupt the trial, he continues to act in such a way that the trial cannot continue while he is present. Black noted that it would also be constitutionally permissible, if necessary, for a judge to have an obstreperous defendant bound and gagged.

Dickey v. Florida, decided by an 8-0 vote, May 25, 1970. Burger wrote the opinion.

The right to a speedy trial is denied by a seven-year-delay between arrest and trial, even if the defendant is, for that period, in federal prison in another state.

Williams v. Florida, decided by a 7-1 vote, June 22, 1970. White wrote the opinion; Blackmun did not participate; Marshall dissented.

In non-capital cases a six-member jury can try a defendant just as constitutionally as a 12-member panel. The number 12 as applied to jury composition was merely an "historical accident"; the number had significance only to mystics; the jury could perform its role just as well with six as with 12 members.

On a secondary question, the court ruled, 6-2, that a defendant's rights are not violated by a state requirement that he inform the prosecution of his alibi defense and the related witnesses ahead of time. Black and Douglas dissented.

Baldwin v. New York, decided by a 5-3 vote, June 22, 1970. White wrote the opinion; Blackmun did not participate; Burger, Harlan and Stewart dissented.

States must provide trial by jury for all persons charged with offenses punishable by more than six months imprisonment.

Coleman v. Alabama, decided by a 6-2 vote, June 22, 1970. Brennan wrote the opinion; Blackmun did not participate; Burger and Stewart dissented.

The right to counsel applies at a preliminary hearing which is a critical stage in a state's criminal proceedings.

California v. Green, decided by a 7-1 vote, June 22, 1970. White wrote the opinion; Blackmun did not participate; Brennan dissented.

A sworn pre-trial statement made by a witness may be used as evidence at trial if the witness at the trial contradicts the earlier statement; it may also be used as evidence even if the witness is not present at the trial so long as the defense had opportunity to cross-examine at pretrial hearing.

Dutton v. Evans, decided by a 5-4 vote, Dec. 14, 1970. Stewart wrote the opinion; Black, Douglas, Brennan and Marshall dissented.

The right to confront witnesses testifying against oneself is not violated by Georgia's law allowing, as an exception to the rule against hearsay evidence, the use, as evidence, of a statement made by a non-testifying co-conspirator, during a conspiracy's "concealment" phase.

Mayberry v. Pennsylvania, decided by a 9-0 vote, Jan. 20, 1971. Douglas wrote the opinion.

Criminal defendant charged with contempt for insulting the trial judge while disrupting trial proceedings is entitled to a public trial by another judge on the contempt charges.

Groppi v. Wisconsin, decided by an 8-1 vote, Jan. 25, 1971. Stewart wrote the opinion; Black dissented.

State law barring change of place of trial for any misdemeanor case deprives defendant—who could be sentenced to one year in prison—of his right to trial by an impartial jury.

Nelson v. O'Neil, decided by a 6-3 vote, June 1, 1971. Stewart wrote the opinion; Douglas, Brennan and Marshall dissented.

The right to confront witnesses testifying against oneself was not denied the defendant whose jointly-tried co-defendant came to the witness stand after his statement implicating the defendant was admitted into evidence, denied making the statement and testified favorably to the defendant.

McKeiver v. Pennsylvania, decided by a 6-3 vote, and *In Re Burrus,* decided by a 5-4 vote, June 21, 1971. Blackmun wrote the opinion; Douglas, Black and Marshall dissented in both, joined by Brennan in the second case.

The Sixth Amendment does not establish a right to trial by jury for a juvenile delinquent.

U.S. v. Marion, decided by a 7-0 vote, Dec. 20, 1971. White wrote the opinion.

The right to a speedy trial does not require dismissal of an indictment returned three years after the alleged crime became known to the government; that right concerns the interval between arrest or charges and the trial. The right to due process may bar excessive and unjustified delay in seeking the indictment, but harm from the delay must be shown before the indictment can be dismissed on that basis.

Adams v. Illinois, decided by a 5-2 vote, March 6, 1972. Brennan wrote the decision; Powell and Rehnquist did not participate; Douglas and Marshall dissented.

The court held that its 1970 decision in *Coleman v. Alabama*—requiring that counsel be provided at preliminary hearings—was not retroactive and applied only to hearings held after the date of its announcement.

Schneble v. Florida, decided by a 6-3 vote, March 21, 1972. Rehnquist wrote the opinion; Douglas, Marshall and Brennan dissented.

The right to confront witnesses against oneself was not violated by use, as evidence against murder defendant, of out-of-court statement by non-testifying jointly-tried co-defendant which contradicted an initial out-of-court statement of innocence by defendant and corroborated a later confession. If this use of evidence violated the court's 1968 decision *(Bruton v. U.S.)* guaranteeing this right of confrontation, it was only a harmless error. The dissenters said that the court had emasculated the 1968 decision.

Johnson v. Louisiana, Apodaca v. Oregon, decided by a 5-4 vote, May 22, 1972. White wrote the opinion; Douglas, Brennan, Stewart, and Marshall dissented.

The constitutional guarantee of a jury trial, as applied to states, does not require the jury to be unanimous in its verdict; lack of unanimity on the question of guilt does not itself indicate reasonable doubt of guilt. Douglas found the decision "a radical departure from American tradition." He and the other dissenters warned that this would allow nine jurors to ignore the views of their fellow jurors who were of a different race or class. And Marshall viewed this as cutting the heart out of the right to a jury trial and the right to be found guilty beyond a reasonable doubt.

Kirby v. Illinois, decided by a 5-4 vote, June 7, 1972. Stewart wrote the opinion; Douglas, Brennan, Marshall and White dissented.

Before indictment, the right to counsel does not apply at post-arrest investigatory confrontations, like line-ups.

Argersinger v. Hamlin, decided by a 9-0 vote, June 12, 1972. Douglas wrote the opinion.

The right to counsel applies to all offenses, state or federal, which involve any potential incarceration.

Barker v. Wingo, decided by a 9-0 vote, June 22, 1972. Powell wrote the opinion.

When defining the precise meaning of the constitutional right to a speedy trial, the court "cannot definitely say how long is too long in a system where justice is supposed to be swift but deliberate." No inflexible rule can be set, but a balancing test must be applied in which the conduct of both the prosecution and the defense are considered. Among the factors which should be considered also are: length of delay, reason for delay, defendant's assertion of his right to a speedy trial and the harm to the defendant resulting from the delay.

CAPITAL PUNISHMENT

Furman v. Georgia, Jackson v. Georgia, Branch v. Texas, decided by a 5-4 vote, June 29, 1972. Unsigned opinion with separate opinions filed by Douglas, Brennan, Stewart, White and Marshall in the majority; Burger, Blackmun, Powell and Rehnquist each in dissent.

"The court holds that the imposition and carrying out of the death penalty in these cases constitutes cruel and unusual punishment in violation of the Eighth and Fourteenth Amendments." And so the death penalty, as it was at that time imposed in each of the 50 states, was declared unconstitutional.

Brennan and Marshall held executions *per se* "cruel and unusual punishment." "The calculated killing of a human being by the state," wrote Brennan, "involves, by its very nature, a denial of the executed person's humanity."

Continuing, Brennan wrote: "The punishment of death is inconsistent with...four principles: Death is an unusually severe and degrading punishment; there is a strong probability that it is inflicted arbitrarily; its rejection by contemporary society is virtually total, and there is no reason to believe it serves any penal purpose more effectively than the less severe punishment of imprisonment. The function of these principles is to enable a court to determine whether a punishment comports with human dignity: Death, quite simply, does not."

Douglas found that the laws allowing imposition of the death penalty at the discretion of judge or jury provided the opportunity, which was often taken, he said,

---

Due Process, Equal Protection

"...Nor shall any state deprive any person of life, liberty, or property, without due process of law; nor deny to any person within its jurisdiction the equal protection of the laws."
Fourteenth Amendment, U.S. Constitution

for discrimination, for imposing that sentence on the "poor and despised...lacking political clout...a member of a suspect or unpopular minority."

Stewart and White found that the present system of imposing the death penalty under which "this unique penalty...(is) so wantonly and freakishly imposed" was clearly unconstitutional.

Stewart wrote that these death sentences were "cruel and unusual in the same way, that being struck by lightning is cruel and unusual. For of all the people convicted of rapes and murders in 1967 and 1968...the petitioners are among a capriciously selected random handful upon whom the sentence of death has been imposed."

In dissent, Chief Justice Burger was quick to point out that the opinions of White and Stewart implied that states might enact a constitutional capital punishment law: "Since the two pivotal concurring opinions turn on the assumption that the punishment of death is now meted out in a random and unpredictable manner, legislative bodies may seek to bring their laws into compliance with the court's ruling by providing standards for juries and judges to follow in determining the sentences in capital cases or by more narrowly defining the crimes for which the penalty is to be imposed."

DUE PROCESS

Foster v. California, decided by an 8-1 vote, April 1, 1969. Fortas wrote the opinion; Black dissented.

Use at trial of victim's identification of suspect without legal counsel after a suggestive line-up, an individual confrontation, and a second line-up (in which no other participants in the first were present) violates due process. Judged by the "totality of the circumstances," the identification procedures were conducted in such a suggestive way that they constituted a denial of due process, held the court.

In Re Winship, decided by a 5-3 vote, March 31, 1970. Brennan wrote the opinion; Burger, Black and Stewart dissented.

Due process requires that the guilt of juveniles like that of adults be found "beyond a reasonable doubt," not just "by a preponderance of the evidence." This decision, complained Burger and Stewart, further strait-jacketed "an already overly restricted (juvenile court) system.... I cannot regard it as...progress to transform juvenile courts into criminal courts."

McGautha v. California, Crampton v. Ohio, decided by a 6-3 vote, May 3, 1971. Harlan wrote the opinion; Douglas, Brennan and Marshall dissented.

States do not violate due process by giving juries complete discretion in deciding in what capital cases to impose a death sentence; states do not violate the privilege against self-incrimination by allowing one jury simultaneously to determine guilt and punishment.

Loper v. Beto, decided by a 5-4 vote, March 22, 1972. Stewart wrote the opinion; Burger, Powell, Blackmun and Rehnquist dissented.

Prior invalid convictions cannot be used to impeach the credibility of a defendant—if their use influences the outcome of his case.

McNeil v. Director, Patuxent Institution, decided by a 9-0 vote, June 19, 1972. Marshall wrote the opinion.

Defendant convicted, sentenced to five years' imprisonment, and referred as possible defective delinquent to institution for psychiatric examination, cannot be held in that institution longer than five years, without violation of his constitutional rights.

Morrissey v. Brewer, decided by an 8-1 vote, June 29, 1972. Burger wrote the opinion; Douglas dissented in part.

Parole revocation proceedings must adhere to certain standards and procedural safeguards to protect the liberty of the paroled person and to ensure that revocation is based on verified facts.

EQUAL PROTECTION

Williams v. Illinois, decided by an 8-0 vote, June 29, 1970. Burger wrote the opinion; Blackmun did not take part.

Equal protection of the laws requires that the maximum imprisonment for any offense be the same for all defendants, rich and poor. Therefore, states cannot hold poor people in prison beyond the maximum sentence merely to work off a fine they cannot pay. (Forty-seven of the 50 states allowed such further imprisonment.)

Tate v. Short, decided by a 9-0 vote, March 2, 1971. Brennan wrote the opinion.

The "$30 or 30 days" sentence was an unconstitutional denial of equal protection; that guarantee barred any state or municipality from limiting punishment for an offense to a fine for those who could pay, but expanding punishment for the same offense to imprisonment for those who could not pay the fine.

Younger v. Gilmore, decided by a 7-0 vote, Nov. 8, 1971. Unsigned opinion.

States must provide poor prisoners with sufficient legal research materials to ensure that they have equal access to advice and courts as do wealthier prisoners.

Mayer v. Chicago, decided by a 7-0 vote, Dec. 13, 1971. Brennan wrote the opinion.

States must supply a free trial transcript to every poor person appealing a misdemeanor conviction.

Schilb v. Kuebel, decided by a 4-3 vote, Dec. 20, 1971. Blackmun wrote the opinion; Douglas, Brennan and Stewart dissented.

States do not violate equal protection or due process when they impose a bail administration fee on persons released on bail when they have deposited only ten per cent of the bail amount, but impose no fee on those who deposit the full amount of bail.

Eisenstadt v. Baird, decided by a 6-1 vote, March 22, 1972. Brennan wrote the opinion; Powell and Rehnquist did not participate; Burger dissented.

States cannot, without violating the equal protection guarantee, ban distribution of contraceptives to unmarried individuals.

Alexander v. Louisiana, decided by a 7-0 vote, April 3, 1972. White wrote the opinion; Powell and Rehnquist did not participate.

A black man indicted for rape by all-white state grand jury selected from class which was partially black by an all-white jury commission was denied equal protection of the laws by obvious racial discrimination in jury selection.

Jackson v. Indiana, decided by a 7-0 vote, June 7, 1972. Blackmun wrote the opinion; Powell and Rehnquist did not participate.

Equal protection and due process guarantees require state, after a reasonable period, to release or civilly commit defendant who was found incompetent to stand trial and confined as criminally insane, since law makes release more difficult in criminal than in civil cases.

Peters v. Kiff, decided by a 6-3 vote, June 22, 1972. Marshall wrote the opinion; dissenting were Burger, Rehnquist and Blackmun.

White defendant indicted and convicted by juries from which blacks had been systematically excluded was by that discrimination denied his rights to equal protection and due process.

Civil Rights

SCHOOL DESEGREGATION

U.S. v. Montgomery County Board of Education, decided by an 8-0 vote, June 2, 1969. Black wrote the opinion.

Federal district judge may order Alabama school board to desegregate faculty and staff of schools according to specific mathematical ratio.

Alexander v. Holmes County Board of Education, decided by an 8-0 vote, Oct. 29, 1969. Unsigned opinion.

In the first decision of Chief Justice Warren E. Burger's first term, the court rebuffed the Nixon administration's request for further delay in desegregation of 33 Mississippi school systems. The court held that continued segregation of public schools was no longer constitutionally permissible and that the schools must desegregate immediately.

Northcross v. Memphis Board of Education, decided by a 7-0 vote, March 9, 1970. Unsigned opinion; Marshall did not participate.

Memphis school system must eliminate dual schools during current school year. In a concurring opinion, Burger said that the full court should consider some of the basic problems of school desegregation, such as whether a particular racial balance must be achieved and whether busing must be or may be used. The court, he said, had defined a unitary school system as one "from which no person is to be effectively excluded from any school because of race or color."

Swann v. Charlotte-Mecklenburg County Board of Education, decided by a 9-0 vote, April 20, 1971. Burger wrote the opinion.

Busing, racial balance ratios, and gerrymandered school districts are all permissible interim methods of eliminating the vestiges of state-imposed segregation from southern schools.

The court said remedies which might be authorized under this decision and previous decisions might be "administratively awkward, inconvenient and even bizarre in some situations and may impose burdens on some; but all awkwardness and inconvenience cannot be avoided in the interim period when the remedial adjustments are being made to eliminate the dual school systems."

There were limits to the remedies which might be used to eliminate the vestiges of segregation, the court said, but no fixed guidelines setting such limits could be established.

The court pointed out that federal courts entered the desegregation process only when local school authorities did not fulfill their obligation to eliminate the dual school system. If school authorities do default—as the lower federal court found that the school board of Charlotte, North Carolina, had in the case before the court—then the federal judge has wide discretion in selecting the means of desegregating the school system.

The court did not deal with *de facto* segregation resulting from factors other than state law. It specifically said that it did not reach the question of the action which would be taken concerning schools which are segregated as a result of "other types of state action, without any discriminatory action by the school authorities."

Limited use of mathematical racial ratios—as a starting point for the remedial process—is within the discretion of the federal court. But "if we were to read the holding of the district court to require, as a matter of substantive constitutional right, any particular degree of racial balance or mixing, that approach would be disapproved and we would be obliged to reverse. The constitutional command to desegregate schools does not mean that every school in every community must always reflect the racial composition of the school system as a whole."

The existence of a few schools within a system, which are attended almost completely by children of one race, is not in itself a mark of a still-segregated system, but school authorities will have to prove to courts that such schools are not the result of present or past discriminatory action on their part.

As "an interim corrective measure" courts may order drastically gerrymandered school districts and attendance zones, and pairing, grouping or clustering of schools. Without a constitutional violation there would be no basis for court orders directing the assignment of pupils on a racial basis.

Bus transportation of students has been an "integral part of the public education system for years" and is a permissible remedial technique when ordered by a court to implement desegregation. "Desegregation plans cannot be limited to the walk-in school."

There may be some valid objections to busing when so much time or distance is involved as to risk the children's health or to impinge significantly on the educational process. "Limits on time of travel will vary with many factors but probably with none more than the age of the students."

The court concluded its opinion with the statement—in apparent reference to the resegregation which might follow the achievement of a unitary school system: "Neither school authorities nor district courts are constitutionally required to make year-by-year adjustments of the racial composition of student bodies once the affirmative duty to desegregate has been accomplished and racial discrimination through official action is eliminated from the system.

"This does not mean that federal courts are without power to deal with future problems; but in the absence of a showing that either the school authorities or some other agency of the state has deliberately attempted to fix or alter demographic patterns to affect the racial composition of the schools, further intervention by a district court should not be necessary."

U.S. v. Scotland Neck Board of Education, decided by a 9-0 vote, *Wright v. Emporia City Council,* decided by a 5-4 vote, June 22, 1972. Stewart wrote the opinions; Burger, Blackmun, Powell and Rehnquist dissented in the second case.

Federal court can halt state or local action creating new school district with the effect of impeding school desegregation.

HOUSING, JOBS, JURIES, PARKS, CLUBS

Hunter v. Erickson, decided by an 8-1 decision, Jan. 20, 1969. White wrote the opinion; Black dissented.

A city cannot constitutionally require that any local fair housing ordinance be subject to approval by referendum; such a requirement is a real, substantial and invidious denial of equal protection. Official action cannot any more disadvantage any particular group by making it difficult to enact legislation in its behalf than it can dilute any person's vote.

Daniel v. Paul, decided by a 7-1 vote, June 2, 1969. Brennan wrote the opinion; Black dissented.

Civil Rights Act of 1964 prohibits privately owned recreational club, which serves some interstate travelers and qualifies as place of public accommodation, from excluding persons on the basis of race.

Sullivan v. Little Hunting Park Inc., decided by a 5-3 vote, Dec. 15, 1969. Douglas wrote the opinion; Burger, Harlan and White dissented.

Civil Rights Act of 1866—which expressly protects the right to lease property—prohibits a community recreational club from refusing membership to a black man who received a club share as part of his lease of a home in the neighborhood.

Carter v. Jury Commission of Greene County, decided by a 7-1 vote, Jan. 19, 1970. Stewart wrote the opinion; Douglas dissented.

State law providing for jury selection is not unconstitutional, despite abuse of discretion under law to exclude blacks systematically from jury service.

Turner v. Fouche, decided by an 8-0 vote, Jan. 19, 1970. Stewart wrote the opinion.

State law governing selection of jurors and school board members is not unconstitutional, despite systematic exclusion of blacks from juries and school boards; exclusion must cease; property requirement for membership on school board is unconstitutional violation of equal protection.

Evans v. Abney, decided by a 5-2 vote, Jan. 26, 1970. Black wrote the opinion; Marshall did not participate; Brennan and Douglas dissented.

Termination of a trust, and reversion of property to heirs, is not unconstitutional when purpose of trust —to create a park for use by white people only—has failed. Individual action was the cause for termination of the trust; state law had only allowed inclusion of such racial restrictions in bequests. Termination of the trust followed a neutral application of state law; ·both races shared the loss of the park.

Adickes v. Kress and Co., decided by a 5-2 vote, June 1, 1970. Harlan wrote the opinion; Marshall did not participate; Brennan and Douglas dissented.

Civil Rights Act of 1871 allows person to recover damages from restaurant owners for refusing service on the basis of race only if discrimination was based on state-enforced custom of segregation.

Griggs v. Duke Power Co., decided by an 8-0 vote; March 8, 1971. Burger wrote the opinion; Brennan did not participate.

Civil Rights Act of 1964 bars employer requirement of high school diploma or score on general intelligence test—as condition for employment or promotion—so long as neither is related to job skills and so long as both tend to disqualify more black than white applicants.

James v. Valtierra, decided by a 5-3 vote, April 26, 1971. Black wrote the opinion; Douglas did not participate; Brennan, Blackmun and Marshall dissented.

Equal protection guarantee not violated by language in state constitution forbidding construction of any low-income housing projects not expressly approved by a referendum in affected area.

Griffin v. Breckenridge, decided by a 9-0 vote, June 7, 1971. Stewart wrote the opinion.

Federal civil rights law barring conspiracy to deprive persons of equal protection reaches private conspiracies.

Palmer v. Thompson, decided by a 5-4 vote June 14, 1971. Black wrote the opinion; White, Douglas, Brennan and Marshall dissented.

Constitution does not bar city from closing public swimming pools which had been directed by a court to cease segregated operation, but which could not be operated safely and economically in integrated fashion.

Moose Lodge 107 v. Irvis, decided by a 6-3 vote, June 12, 1972. Rehnquist wrote the opinion; Douglas, Brennan and Marshall dissented.

Private club's possession of state liquor license does not render club's discriminatory guest policy state action within the reach of the equal protection guarantee.

SEX DISCRIMINATION

Phillips v. Martin Marietta Corp., decided by a 9-0 vote, Jan. 25, 1971. Unsigned opinion.

1964 Civil Rights Act bars job discrimination on basis of sex against mother of pre-school children and, in absence of *bona fide* occupational qualification, requires one hiring policy for men and women. "The existence of such conflicting family obligations, if demonstrably more relevant to job performance for a woman than for a man could arguably be a basis for distinction."

Reed v. Reed, decided by a 7-0 vote, Nov. 22, 1971. Burger wrote the opinion.

Guarantee of equal protection invalidates state law which automatically prefers father over mother as executor of son's estate: "To give a mandatory preference to members of either sex over members of the other...is to make the very kind of arbitrary legislative choice forbidden by the equal protection clause."

Stanley v. Illinois, decided by a 5-2 vote, April 2, 1972. White wrote the opinion; Powell and Rehnquist did not participate; Burger and Blackmun dissented.

Guarantee of equal protection invalidates state law which presumes that unwed father is unfit custodian of child while allowing all other parents, whose custody of child is challenged, including the unwed mother, a hearing to determine their fitness as a parent.

Election Laws

Oregon v. Mitchell, Texas v. Mitchell, U.S. v. Idaho, U.S. v. Arizona, decided by a 5-4 vote on the lower voting age, by an 8-1 vote on residency requirements, and by a 9-0 vote on literacy test ban, Dec. 21, 1970. Black wrote the opinion; Stewart, Burger, Harlan and Blackmun dissented on the question of age; Harlan dissented alone on the residency issue.

Congress has the power to lower the voting age to 18 for federal elections, but not for state and local elections; Congress has the power to restrict state residency requirements to 30 days for persons wishing to vote in presidential elections; Congress has the power to ban the use of literacy tests as voter qualification devices in any national, state or local election.

Black wrote the majority opinion and cast the pivotal vote: his position—that Congress had the power to lower the voting age in federal, but not state or local, elections—prevailed, although the was the only justice holding that view in its entirety.

Four justices—Brennan, Douglas, Marshall and White—considered the 18-year-old vote provision fully constitutional for federal and state elections. Four others—Burger, Blackmun, Harlan and Stewart—believed it was unconstitutional as to both state and federal elections. None agreed completely with Black's position.

"I believe that Congress has the final authority over federal elections," Black said but added, "I would hold that Congress has exceeded its powers in attempting to lower the voting age in state and local elections."

In a concurring opinion, Douglas wrote: "It is said, why draw the line at 18? Why not 17? Congress can draw lines and I see no reason why it cannot conclude that 18-year-olds have that degree of maturity which entitles them to the franchise.... It is a reasoned judgment that those who have such a large 'stake' in modern elections as 18-year-olds, whether in times of war or peace, should have political equality."

Stewart in dissent emphasized that the Supreme Court was not attempting to determine the value of lowering the voting age. "Our single duty as judges is to determine whether the legislation before us was within the constitutional power of Congress to enact.... A casual reader could easily get the impression that what we are being asked in these cases is whether or not we think allowing people 18 years old to vote is a good idea. Nothing could be wider of the mark."

Stewart, joined by Burger and Blackmun, argued that state laws that deny the vote to persons under 21 "do not invidiously discriminate against any discrete and insular minority." They concluded that the laws do not violate the Fourteenth Amendment's antidiscrimination ban and thus Congress was in error when it passed the law to combat the "discrimination" against youths.

Dun v. Blumstein, decided by a 6-1 vote, March 21, 1972. Marshall wrote the opinion; Powell and Rehnquist did not participate; Burger dissented.

State cannot constitutionally restrict franchise to persons who have lived in state at least one year and in county at least three months.

Allen v. State Board of Elections, decided by an 8-1 vote; **Bunton v. Patterson** and **Whitley v. Williams,** decided by an 8-1 vote; **Fairley v. Patterson,** decided by a 7-2 vote, March 3, 1969. Warren wrote the opinions; Black dissented in each case, joined by Harlan in *Fairley.*

Enactments by certain states which are covered by the Voting Rights Act of 1965—changing from district to at-large election of county officials, changing from elective to appointive selection of a county official, imposing stricter requirements for the inclusion of independent candidates upon a ballot, and changing write-in procedures—are "standard(s), practice(s) or procedure(s) with respect to voting" within the meaning of Section 5 of the Act and must, therefore, be submitted to the Attorney General before they can be enforced. *(Congress and the Nation Vol. II, p. 356)*

Hadnott v. Amos decided by a 6-2 vote, March 25, 1969. Douglas wrote the opinion; White and Stewart dissented; Black did not take part.

Unequal application of state laws which had the effect of disqualifying candidates, usually Negroes, from place on the ballot violated Fifteenth Amendment; new election law requiring independent candidates to file declaration of intent at same time as primary candidates is "standard practice or procedure with respect to voting" which, without approval required by the Voting Rights Act of 1965, cannot be enforced.

Gaston County v. U.S. decided by a 7-1 vote, June 2, 1969. Harlan wrote the opinion; Black dissented.

Previous maintenance of segregated land and unequal school systems in county required denial of county's request under the Voting Rights Act of 1965 for judicial reinstatement of literacy test because such test, in conjunction with previous deprivation of equal educational

opportunity for black residents now of voting age, had the effect of abridging the right to vote on account of race. Because of such past discrimination, the court held that " 'impartial' administration of the literacy test today would serve only to perpetuate these (past) inequities in a different form."

Perkins v. Matthews, decided by a 7-2 vote, Jan. 14, 1971. Brennan wrote the opinion; Harlan and Black dissented.

Towns and cities covered by the 1965 Voting Rights Act cannot annex territory or relocate polling places without federal approval.

NEW DISTRICTS

Kirkpatrick v. Preisler, decided by a 6-3 vote, April 7, 1969. Brennan wrote the opinion; Harlan, Stewart and White dissented.

Missouri redistricting statute producing congressional districts with a maximum population variance of 3.1 per cent from perfect mathematical equality was unconstitutional without justification or proof that such variation was unavoidable.

Brennan held that states must strive to create congressional districts of precisely equal population. Any variance in population, "no matter how small," must be justified by the state or shown to result despite a "good-faith effort." There is no fixed population variance small enough to be considered negligible. "Equal representation for equal numbers of people is a principle designed to prevent debasement of voting power and diminution of access to elected representatives. Toleration of even small deviations detracts from these purposes."

Fortas, concurring in the rejection of the Missouri plan, disagreed with the standard of mathematical precision announced in the court's opinion. Fortas said he would accept districts with "small disparities" in population: "The majority's pursuit of precision is a search for a will-o'-the-wisp." Legislatures implementing the standard "might have to ignore the boundaries of common sense, running the...district line down the middle of the corridor of an apartment house or even dividing the residents of a single-family house between two districts."

Harlan complained that the court had transformed "a political slogan into a constitutional absolute." He said: "Strait indeed is the path of the righteous legislator. Slide rule in hand, he must avoid all thought of county lines, local traditions, politics, history and economics, so as to achieve the magic formula: one man, one vote."

Wells v. Rockefeller, decided by a 6-3 vote, April 7, 1969. Brennan wrote the opinion; White, Harlan and Stewart dissented.

New York redistricting statute not producing congressional districts of equal population is unconstitutional, although the statute did produce districts of nearly equal population within the regions in the state.

Population must be equal in all the districts of a state, not just in "defined substates." The court noted that "New York...does not claim that the legislature made a good-faith effort to achieve precise mathematical equality among its 41 congressional districts."

Whitcomb v. Chavis, decided by a 5-4 vote, June 7, 1971. White wrote the opinion; Douglas, Stewart, Brennan and Marshall dissented.

Without actual proof that black residents' votes are diluted by the creation of multi-member legislative districts, the court cannot find multi-member districts in themselves unconstitutional.

ELECTIONS

Williams v. Rhodes, decided by a 6-3 vote; ***Socialist Labor Party v. Rhodes***, decided by an 8-1 vote, Oct. 15, 1968. Opinion by Black.

State's imposition of substantially greater burden upon small or newly organized political parties than upon the Democratic or Republican party for obtaining a place on the ballot violated the equal protection of the law guaranteed by the Fourteenth Amendment. (The *Williams* case was initiated by presidential candidate George C. Wallace's American Independent party in Ohio and resulted in Wallace's name appearing on the ballot in Ohio in the Nov. 5, 1968, elections.)

Moore v. Ogilvie, decided by a 7-2 vote, May 5, 1969. Douglas wrote the opinion; Stewart and Harlan dissented.

State requirement that nominating petitions for independent presidential electors must include at least 200 signatures from each of 50 counties among the required 25,000 signatures violates the "one-man, one vote" principle guaranteed under the equal protection clause of the Fourteenth Amendment by discriminating against voters residing in populous counties.

In 1948 the Supreme Court upheld this particular requirement as constitutional and not denying equal protection (*MacDougall v. Green*). (*Congress and the Nation Vol. I, p. 116a*)

The court in 1969 overruled *MacDougall v. Green* as out of line with the court's more recent decisions on apportionment.

Kramer v. Union Free School District No. 15, decided by a 5-3 vote, June 16, 1969. Opinion by Warren; Stewart, Black and Harlan dissented.

State cannot bar from voting in school district elections persons who are neither owners or lessees of real estate within the district nor parents or guardians of children attending the public schools without violating the constitutional guarantee of equal protection.

Cipriano v. City of Houma, decided by an 8-0 vote, June 16, 1969. Unsigned opinion.

Louisiana law providing that only "property taxpayers" might vote in elections to approve the issuance of municipal utility revenue bonds violates the guarantee of equal protection.

Hadley v. Junior College District of Metropolitan Kansas City, Mo., decided by a 5-3 vote, Feb. 25, 1970. Black wrote the opinion; Harlan, Burger and Stewart dissented.

The "one-man, one-vote" rule must be applied to any election—state or local—of persons to perform governmental functions.

There was no valid reason, the court held, for courts to try to apply the "one-man, one-vote" rule selectively, distinguishing between types of elections or between types of elected officials: "If one person's vote is given less weight through unequal apportionment, his right to equal voting participation is impaired just as much when he votes for a school board member as when he votes for a state legislator.... The crucial consideration is the right of each qualified voter to participate on an equal footing in the election process.

"We therefore hold today that as a general rule, whenever a state or local government decides to select persons by popular election to perform governmental functions, the equal protection clause of the Fourteenth Amendment requires that each qualified voter must be given an equal opportunity to participate in that election, and when members of an elected body are chosen from separate districts, each district must be established on a basis which will insure, as far as is practicable, that equal numbers of voters can vote for proportionally equal numbers of officials."

Phoenix v. Kolodziejski, decided by a 5-3 vote, June 23, 1970. White wrote the opinion; Blackmun did not participate; Burger, Stewart and Harlan dissented.

Equal protection guarantee bars states from excluding nonproperty owners from voting in elections to approve the issuance of general obligation bonds.

Evans v. Cornman, decided by an 8-0 vote, June 15, 1970. Marshall wrote the opinion; Blackmun did not participate.

State may not deny the right to vote to persons living within federal enclave in state and otherwise treated as state residents.

Gordon v. Lance, decided by a 7-2 vote, June 7, 1971. Burger wrote the opinion; dissenting were Brennan and Marshall.

Equal protection guarantee is not violated by requirement that a political subdivision cannot exceed constitutionally set limits of bonded indebtedness or tax rates without an affirmative vote of 60 per cent in a referendum.

Roudebush v. Hartke, decided by a 5-2 vote, Feb. 22, 1972. Stewart wrote the opinion; Powell and Rehnquist did not participate; Douglas and Brennan dissented.

State vote recount procedures are part of its electoral process and do not usurp the Senate's power to act as exclusive judge of its members' qualifications.

Bullock v. Carter, decided by a 7-0 vote, Feb. 24, 1972. Burger wrote the opinion.

State filing fee, the amount of which is based on the estimated total cost of the election, is an unconstitutional discrimination against the political candidate who cannot pay such a large fee.

Church and State

Epperson v. Arkansas, decided by a 9-0 vote, Nov. 12, 1968. Fortas wrote the opinion.

State "monkey law" forbidding public school teaching of the Darwinian theory of evolution violates First Amendment ban on establishment of religion and its guarantee of freedom of religion: "The First Amendment mandates governmental neutrality between religion and religion and between religion and nonreligion."

Walz v. Tax Commission of the City of New York, decided by a 7-1 vote, May 4, 1970. Burger wrote the opinion; Douglas dissented.

Property tax exemption for church-owned land used solely for religious purposes does not violate First Amendment guarantee against establishment of religion as applied to the states by the Fourteenth Amendment. Such exemptions were only evidence of the state's "benevolent neutrality" toward religion, held the court:

"There is no genuine nexus between tax exemption and establishment of religion... The exemption creates only a minimal and remote involvement between church and state and far less than taxation of churches. It restricts the fiscal relationship between church and state, and tends to complement and reinforce the desired separation insulating each from the other."

Tilton v. Richardson, decided by a 5-4 vote, June 28, 1971. Burger wrote the opinion; Douglas, Black, Marshall and Brennan dissented.

Higher Education Facilities Act of 1963—under which federal grants are provided for construction of buildings by colleges and universities, regardless of religious affiliation, so long as buildings are used exclusively for secular educational purposes—does not violate First Amendment; First Amendment does invalidate provision of law limiting to 20 years the restriction of use of facility to secular educational purposes.

Lemon v. Kurtzman, decided by an 8-0 vote, June 28, 1971. Burger wrote the opinion; Marshall did not participate.

First Amendment invalidates state law authorizing state reimbursement of nonpublic school for costs of teachers' salaries, textbooks and instructional materials in secular subjects; First Amendment invalidates state law authorizing supplementary salary grants to nonpublic school teachers of secular subjects while barring such grants to teachers in schools that spend more per pupil on secular education than do public schools; such laws foster excessive entanglement between government and religion.

Religion, Speech, and Press

Congress shall make no law respecting an establishment of religion, or prohibiting the free exercise thereof; or abridging the freedom of speech, or of the press; or the right of the people peaceably to assembly, and to petition the Government for a redress of grievances.

—First Amendment, U.S. Constitution

Wisconsin v. Yoder, decided by a 6-1 vote, May 15, 1972. Burger wrote the opinion; Powell and Rehnquist did not participate; Douglas dissented.

First Amendment guarantee of freedom of religion prohibits the application of state's compulsory education law requiring school attendance until a child is 16 to members of the Amish sect, "whose long-established, self-sufficient agrarian lifestyle is essential to their religious faith" and is threatened by the exposure of their children to modern educational influences.

Free Speech

Tinker v. Des Moines Independent Community School District, decided by a 7-2 vote, Feb. 24, 1969. Fortas wrote the opinion; Harlan and Black dissented.

Students have the right to engage in peaceful nondisruptive protest. The wearing of black armbands to protest the Vietnam war was "closely akin" to the "pure speech" protected by the First Amendment, and therefore a public school ban on this form of protest, which did not disrupt the school's work or offend the rights of others, violated these students' rights. "In the absence of a specific showing of constitutionally valid reasons to regulate their speech, students are entitled to freedom of expression of their views."

Street v. New York, decided by a 5-4 vote, April 21, 1969. Harlan wrote the opinion; Warren, Fortas, White and Black dissented.

State law making it a crime to "cast contempt" upon American flag by words or acts is unconstitutional in allowing persons to be punished merely for speaking derogatory words about the flag.

Harlan concluded that "disrespect for our flag is to be deplored no less in these vexed times than in calmer periods of our history.... Nevertheless, we are unable to sustain a conviction that may have rested on a form of expression, however distasteful, which the Constitution tolerates and protects."

Brandenburg v. Ohio, decided by an 8-0 vote, June 9, 1969. Unsigned opinion.

State law making a crime of advocating violence or terrorism as a mode of reform and of meeting with any group formed to advocate such ideas is unconstitutional violation of the freedoms of speech and association.

Any law, the court held, which did not make the distinction between "mere abstract teaching" of the need for the use of force and violence and the actual preparation of a group for such violent action, impermissibly intruded upon individual freedom and condemned constitutionally protected speech.

Bachellar v. Maryland, decided by an 8-0 vote, April 20, 1970. Opinion by Brennan.

Disorderly conduct conviction of antiwar protesters must be overturned because it may have rested upon the unconstitutional grounds—suggested by the judge—that their views were offensive to bystanders.

Schacht v. U.S., decided by an 8-0 vote, May 25, 1970. Black wrote the opinion.

Actors, as well as other citizens, have the right openly to criticize the government, ruled the court, invalidating a law which made it a crime for an actor to wear an official military uniform in a production which was unfavorable to the armed forces.

Organization for a Better Austin v. Keefe, decided by an 8-1 vote, May 17, 1971. Burger wrote the opinion; Harlan dissented.

State court cannot constitutionally order community group to cease peacefully distributing leaflets charging real estate broker with "blockbusting" or to cease picketing in the broker's community.

Coates v. Cincinnati, decided by a 6-3 vote, June 1, 1971. Stewart wrote the opinion; White, Burger and Blackmun dissented.

City ordinance is unconstitutionally broad and vague in barring any assembly of three or more persons on sidewalk to annoy passers-by.

Lloyd Corporation v. Tanner, decided by a 5-4 vote, June 22, 1972. Powell wrote the opinion; Douglas, Brennan, Marshall and Stewart dissented.

First Amendment is not violated by ban imposed by privately owned and operated shopping mall on distribution of handbills by peaceful group without any grievance against the merchants in the mall.

Laird v. Tatum, decided by a 5-4 vote, June 26, 1972. Burger wrote the opinion; Douglas, Brennan, Stewart and Marshall dissented.

Persons who cannot claim that their own activities have been affected by military surveillance of legal civilian political activity cannot bring a court challenge to the constitutionality of that surveillance.

Kleindienst v. Mandel, decided by a 6-3 vote, June 29, 1972. Blackmun wrote the opinion; Douglas, Brennan and Marshall dissented.

Congress has properly delegated to the executive branch the power to exclude aliens or prescribe the conditions for their entry into the United States; when the Attorney General decides for a good reason not to waive the statutory exclusion of an alien, that decision will not be scrutinized by the courts or weighed against the free speech rights of persons wishing to speak with the excluded alien.

Obscenity

Stanley v. Georgia, decided by a 9-0 vote, April 7, 1969. Marshall wrote the opinion.

The First Amendment guarantee of freedom of expression bars states from making it a crime to privately possess obscene material: "The Constitution protects the right to receive information and ideas.... Also fundamental is the right to be free, except in very limited circumstances, from unwanted governmental intrusions into one's privacy.... Whatever may be the justifications for other statutes regulating obscenity, we do not think they reach into the privacy of one's own home.... If the First Amendment means anything, it means that the

Shift to Restraint

A signal of the Supreme Court's return to a less activist position was sounded on Feb. 23, 1971. In a series of decisions, the court sharply curtailed the application of a 1965 decision which allowed federal courts to halt state criminal proceedings, when the law involved was challenged as unconstitutional by the defendant.

Before the 1965 decision, federal courts observed the doctrine of judicial abstention, refraining from intervention in any ongoing state court proceedings. In 1965, the Supreme Court ruled, 5-2, that this doctrine did not apply in cases involving laws which defendants challenged as unconstitutional infringements of their freedom of expression *(Dombrowski v. Pfister).*

Defendants prosecuted under state laws subject to such challenge did not hesitate to take full advantage of this ruling. A wave of petitions in federal courts produced an increasing number of injunctions halting state trials.

In the 1971 decisions, Justice Black—with only Justice Douglas dissenting—wrote that "the normal thing to do when federal courts are asked to enjoin pending proceedings in state courts is not to issue such injunctions."

However, as Justices Stewart and Harlan pointed out in a concurring opinion, there were certain limited circumstances in which a federal court could intervene in pending state proceedings. Such circumstances existed when there was a great and immediate threat of irreparable injury, when a state law was flagrantly unconstitutional on its face, or when there had been official lawlessness.

The principle of federal restraint, wrote Black, was based on "a proper respect for state functions ...and a continuance of the belief that the national government will fare best if the states and their institutions are left free to perform their separate functions in their separate ways." With this pronouncement, the court, by varying votes, disapproved the actions of federal courts:

• Halting prosecution of a movie exhibitor for showing the allegedly obscene movie "I Am Curious (Yellow)" *(Byrne v. Karalexis).*

• Suppressing allegedly obscene materials during an obscenity trial *(Perez v. Ledesma).*

• Halting prosecution under the California criminal syndicalism law *(Younger v. Harris).*

• Considering the constitutionality of the New York criminal anarchy law *(Samuels v. Mackell, Fernandez v. Mackell).*

• Declaring a Texas obscenity law unconstitutional and halting the prosecution of a newspaper publisher under that law *(Dyson v. Stein).*

But a year later, in a decision announced by a unanimous seven-man court on June 19, 1972, the court held that federal courts could halt state court proceedings when citizens whose constitutional rights were threatened by actions under authority of state law requested federal courts to halt that threat *(Mitchum v. Foster).*

state has no business telling a man, sitting alone in his own house, what books he may read or what films he may watch."

Rowan v. U.S. Post Office Dept., decided by 8-0 vote, May 4, 1970. Burger wrote the opinion.

Neither freedom of the press nor freedom of speech is violated by the 1967 law authorizing individuals to request the Postmaster General to order a company to cease sending that individual obscene material. The right of privacy was paramount in this case, held the court: "To hold less would tend to license a form of trespass and would make hardly more sense than to say that a radio or television viewer may not twist the dial to cut off an offensive or boring communication." *(1967 Almanac p. 593)*

Blount v. Rizzi, U.S. v. The Book Bin, decided by a 9-0 vote, Jan. 14, 1971. Brennan wrote the opinion.

The court invalidated two laws—one enacted in 1950 and the other in 1960—which allowed the Post Office to stop mail to businesses under investigation for or found to sell pornographic material. The laws did not contain sufficient safeguards against unconstitutional curtailment of free speech, according to the court. *(Congress and the Nation Vol. I, p. 1671, 1672)*

U.S. v. Reidel, decided by a 7-2 vote, May 3, 1971. White wrote the opinion; Black and Douglas dissented.

The court upheld a law which forbade use of the mails to deliver obscene material, even if the material was being distributed to willing adult recipients.

U.S. v. 37 Photographs, decided by a 6-3 vote, May 3, 1971. White wrote the opinion; Black, Douglas and Marshall dissented.

Federal laws authorizing customs officials to seize imported obscene material do not violate First Amendment, nor does seizure of obscene matter privately possessed at port of entry by person who intends it for commercial distribution.

Cohen v. California, decided by a 5-4 vote, June 7, 1971. Harlan wrote the opinion; Burger, Black, White and Blackmun dissented.

The court invalidated the conviction—under a state disturbing-the-peace law which forbade offensive conduct—of a demonstrator who wore a jacket inscribed "Fuck the Draft" into a courthouse.

Free Press

Red Lion Broadcasting Co. v. Federal Communications Commission and ***U.S. v. Radio Television News Directors Assn.,*** decided by a 7-0 vote, June 9, 1969. White wrote the opinion; Douglas did not take part.

The court held that the general public's right to fair treatment of all aspects of important issues by news media required broadcasters to comply with the fairness doctrine set forth by the Federal Communications Commission. Therefore, the court ruled, broadcasters must continue to provide free time for persons to reply to broadcasts of political editorials or endorsements.

The right of broadcasters to free speech must be balanced with the right of the people as a whole to free speech and their "collective right to have the medium function consistently with the ends and purposes of the First Amendment." This right—of viewers and listeners—the Court held paramount.

"It is the purpose of the First Amendment to preserve an uninhibited marketplace of ideas in which truth will ultimately prevail, rather than to countenance monopolization of that market, whether it be by the government itself, or a private licensee."

Greenbelt Cooperative Publishing Assn. v. Bresler, decided by an 8-0 vote, May 18, 1970. Stewart wrote the opinion.

First Amendment guarantee of free press protects newspaper against libel suit for accurate reporting of charges made against a public figure. The fundamental meaning of a free press would be subverted if newspapers could be punished for publishing accurate, truthful reports of matters of public importance.

Monitor Patriot Co. v. Roy, Ocala Star-Banner Co. v. Damron, decided by 7-2 votes, Feb. 24, 1971. Stewart wrote the opinions; Black and Douglas dissented in part.

Any allegation of criminal activity, no matter how remote, is relevant to the fitness of a candidate for office; therefore—unless such allegation is printed with knowledge that it is false or with actual malice, no libel judgment can be entered against the publication printing the charge.

Time Inc. v. Pape, decided by a 8-1 vote, Feb. 24, 1971. Stewart wrote the opinion; Harlan dissented.

Mere omission of the word 'alleged' from an article reporting a charge of police brutality does not show malice nor provide grounds for a libel judgment against the publisher of the article.

Rosenbloom v. Metromedia Inc., decided by a 5-3 vote, June 7, 1971. Brennan wrote the opinion; Douglas did not participate; Harlan, Stewart and Marshall dissented.

Rule of *New York Times v. Sullivan* (1964)—that defamatory falsehood concerning public official is libel only if it is proven to have been uttered with knowledge of its falsity or in reckless disregard of its truth or falsity—applies to libel action brought by private individual for falsehood used by radio news program about individual's arrest.

New York Times Co. v. U.S., U.S. v. The Washington Post, decided by a 6-3 vote, June 30, 1971. Unsigned opinion; each justice wrote a separate opinion expressing his views. Dissenting were Burger, Blackmun and Harlan.

The government failed to show sufficient justification for its request for court orders barring publication—by *The New York Times* and *The Washington Post*—of articles based on classified documents, a multi-volume history of U.S. involvement in Indochina, popularly known as the Pentagon Papers.

Black, joined by Douglas, wrote: "I believe that every moment's continuance of the injunctions against these newspapers amounts to a flagrant, indefensible, and continuing violation of the First Amendment.... In my view, it is unfortunate that some of my brethren are apparently willing to hold that the publication of news may sometimes be enjoined. Such a holding would make a shambles of the First Amendment."

"The press was to serve the governed, not the governors. The government's power to censor the press was abolished so that the press would remain forever free to censure the government."

Marshall wrote: "The issue is whether this court or the Congress has the power to make law.... It would...be utterly inconsistent with the concept of separation of power for this court to use its power of contempt to prevent behavior that Congress has specifically declined to prohibit.... The Constitution provides that Congress shall make laws, the President execute laws and courts interpret law.... It did not provide for government by injunction in which the courts and the executive can 'make law' without regard to the action of Congress."

White, joined by Stewart, wrote: "I concur...but only because of the concededly extraordinary protection against prior restraints enjoyed by the press under our constitutional system. I do not say that in no circumstances would the First Amendment permit an injunction against publishing information about government plans or operations.... But...the United States has not satisfied the very heavy burden which it must meet to warrant an injunction against publication in these cases."

And Stewart, joined by White, said: "The only effective restraint upon executive policy and power in the areas of national defense and international affairs may lie in an enlightened citizenry.... Without an informed and free press there cannot be an enlightened people."

Brennan wrote: "The error which has pervaded these cases from the outset was the granting of any injunctive relief whatsoever, interim or otherwise.... The First Amendment tolerates absolutely no prior judicial restraints of the press predicated upon surmise or conjecture that untoward consequences may result."

Douglas, joined by Black, wrote: "The dominant purpose of the First Amendment was to prohibit the widespread practice of government suppression of embarrassing information.... The First Amendment was adopted against the widespread use of the common law of seditious libel to punish the dissemination of material that is embarrassing to the powers-that-be.... The present cases will, I think, go down in history as the most dramatic example of that principle.... Secrecy in government is fundamentally anti-democratic, perpetuating bureaucratic errors."

In dissent, Harlan, joined by Burger and Blackmun, declared: "The Court has been almost irresponsibly feverish in dealing with these cases.... The scope of the judicial function in passing upon the activities of the executive branch of the government in the field of foreign affairs is very narrowly restricted."

Blackmun dissented: "The First Amendment, after all, is only one part of an entire Constitution. Article II... vests in the executive branch primary power over the conduct of foreign affairs....

"Each provision...is important and I cannot subscribe to a doctrine of unlimited absolutism for the First Amendment at the cost of downgrading other provisions."

Burger dissented: "To me it is hardly believable that a newspaper long regarded as a great institution in American life would fail to perform one of the basic and simple duties of every citizen with respect to the discovery or possession of stolen property or secret government documents. That duty, I had thought—perhaps naively—was to report forthwith, to responsible public officers. This duty rests on taxi drivers, justices and *The New York Times.*"

Branzburg v. Hayes, In re Pappas, U.S. v. Caldwell, decided by a 5-4 vote, June 29, 1972. White wrote the opinion; dissenting were Douglas, Brennan, Stewart and Marshall.

The constitutional freedom of the press does not privilege newsmen to refuse—without risking contempt charges—to provide information to grand juries concerning a crime or the sources of evidence concerning a crime. White wrote that the majority saw no basis "for holding that the public interest in law enforcement and in ensuring effective grand jury proceedings is insufficient to override the consequential but uncertain burden on newsgathering which is said to result from insisting that reporters, like other citizens, respond to relevant questions put to them in the course of a valid grand jury investigation or criminal trial." Stewart in dissent complained about the court's "crabbed view of the First Amendment." He saw the right to gather news as a corollary of the right to publish.

Freedom of Association

In Re Stolar, Baird v. State Bar of Arizona, decided by 5-4 votes, Feb. 23, 1971. Black wrote the opinion; Burger, Blackmun, Harlan and White dissented.

First Amendment bars state from excluding applicant for admission to bar solely because he or she refused to state whether he had belonged to any organization advocating violent overthrow of the government.

Law Students Civil Rights Research Council v. Wadmond, decided by a 5-4 vote, Feb. 23, 1971. Stewart wrote the opinion; Black, Douglas, Marshall and Brennan dissented.

Constitutional rights are not infringed by state requirements that applicants for state bar be of good moral character and loyal to the Constitution (even if latter is interpreted to require sworn support for state and federal constitution and statement concerning any membership in organization advocating violent overthrow of government).

Connell v. Higginbotham, decided by an 8-1 vote, June 7, 1971. Unsigned opinion; Stewart dissented in part.

State requirement that teachers swear to support state and federal constitutions is constitutional, but due process bars dismissal of teacher—without hearing—for failure to swear that he or she does not believe in the overthrow of the government by force.

Cole v. Richardson, decided by a 4-3 vote, April 18, 1972. Burger wrote the opinion; Douglas, Brennan and Marshall dissented.

First Amendment is not violated by a state requirement that all employees take oath to "oppose the overthrow of the government by force, violence or by any illegal or unconstitutional method."

Healy v. James, decided by a 9-0 vote, June 26, 1972. Powell wrote the opinion.

University's denial of recognition to student group—in this case a local chapter of Students for a Democratic Society—is an unconstitutional infringement of the freedom of association; nonrecognition could be justified by showing that group's activities would be disruptive influence on campus.

Rights of Individuals

Sniadach v. Family Finance Corp., decided by a 7-1 vote, June 9, 1969. Douglas wrote the opinion; Black dissented.

State cannot constitutionally allow garnishment of wages to pay debts before allowing notice and hearings for debtor.

Perez v. U.S., decided by an 8-1 vote, April 26, 1971. Opinion by Douglas; Stewart dissented.

Consumer Protection Act of 1968 is proper exercise of Congressional authority under the commerce power to bar loansharking; no explicit connection need be provided between loan shark and interstate commerce to convict loan shark of illicit activities.

Lynch v. Household Finance Corp., decided by a 4-3 vote, March 23, 1972. Stewart wrote the opinion; Burger, Blackmun and White dissented.

Federal courts have power to halt state court proceedings in cases involving impairment of property rights as well as in cases involving impairment of personal liberties: "The dichotomy between personal liberties and property rights is a false one. Property does not have rights. People have rights. The right to enjoy property without unlawful deprivation, no less than the right to speak or the right to travel, is in truth a 'personal' right, whether the 'property' in question be a welfare check, a home or a savings account. In fact, a fundamental interdependence exists between the personal right to liberty and the personal right in property. Neither could have meaning without the other. That rights in property are basic civil rights has long been recognized." *(p. 46)*

Fuentes v. Shevin, decided by a 4-3 vote, June 12, 1972. Stewart wrote the opinion; Burger, Blackmun and White dissented.

Due process invalidates state laws which allow summary seizure of goods from installment purchasers without prior notice or hearing, upon application of creditor.

Thorpe v. Durham Housing Authority, decided by a 9-0 vote, Jan. 13, 1969. Warren wrote the opinion.

Tenants of public housing projects cannot be evicted without being given reasons for any notice to vacate and an opportunity to reply to those reasons, as directed in 1967 regulations by the Department of Housing and Urban Development.

Lindsey v. Normet, decided by a 5-2 vote, Feb. 22, 1972. White wrote the opinion; Rehnquist and Powell did not participate; Douglas and Brennan dissented.

Equal protection does not invalidate state law which requires trial for nonpayment of rent within six days of service of a formal complaint of nonpayment and which bars a tenant from using, as a defense to the complaint, the fact that the landlord had failed to maintain or repair the rented premises.

Labine v. Vincent, decided by a 5-4 vote, March 29, 1971. Black wrote the opinion; Douglas, Brennan, White and Marshall dissented.

Neither due process nor equal protection bars state from denying illegitimate children an equal right of inheritance from father with legitimate children.

Weber v. Aetna Casualty and Surety Co., decided by an 8-1 vote, April 24, 1972. Powell wrote the opinion; Rehnquist dissented.

Equal protection invalidates workmen's compensation laws which prefer acknowledged illegitimate children to unacknowledged illegitimate children in allocating benefits of deceased father. "Imposing disabilities on the illegitimate child is contrary to the basic concept of our system that legal burdens should bear some relationship to individual responsibility or wrongdoing.... Courts are powerless to prevent the social opprobrium suffered by these hapless children, but the equal protection clause does enable us to strike down discriminatory laws relating to status of birth where—as in this case—the classification is justified by no legitimate state interest."

Shapiro v. Thompson, Washington v. Legrant, Reynolds v. Smith, decided by a 6-3 vote, April 21, 1969. Brennan wrote the opinion; dissenting were Warren, Black, Harlan.

State or federal requirement that person must reside within a certain jurisdiction for one year before becoming eligible for welfare assistance violates individual rights to due process and equal protection of the laws; no compelling government interest has been presented to justify this infringement of the right to travel.

Wheeler v. Montgomery, Goldberg v. Kelly, decided by 5-3 votes, March 23, 1970. Brennan wrote the opinion; Burger, Black and Stewart dissented.

Due process requires state to give welfare recipient opportunity for full hearing before terminating his or her welfare payments. The crucial factor in the situation, noted the court, was that "termination of aid pending resolution of a controversy over eligibility may deprive an eligible recipient of the very means by which to live."

Dandridge v. Williams, decided by a 5-3 vote, April 6, 1970. Stewart wrote the opinion; Douglas, Brennan and Marshall dissented.

States do not violate federal law or the equal protection guarantee by limiting the amount of welfare aid which one family may receive.

Rosado v. Wyman, decided by a 6-2 vote, April 6, 1970. Harlan wrote the opinion; Burger and Black dissented.

New York revision of welfare program to reduce benefits does not comply with requirements of 1967 Social Security Amendments that states readjust the standard of need in welfare programs in order to reflect the increased cost-of-living.

Lewis v. Martin, decided by a 6-2 vote, April 20, 1970. Douglas wrote the opinion; Burger and Black dissented.

State cannot reduce welfare aid to children because there is a man living in the same house unless he actually contributes to the support of the children. (This followed up a 1968 ruling in the case of *King v. Smith* in which the court had invalidated a state regulation which terminated all welfare aid to children if a man was living in the same house.)

Wyman v. James. decided by an 8-1 vote, Jan. 12, 1971. Blackmun wrote the opinion; Douglas dissented.

Constitutional protection against unreasonable searches does not invalidate state law conditioning receipt of aid to dependent children on periodic, warrantless visits to home by caseworker.

California Department of Human Resources v. Java, decided by a 9-0 vote, April 26, 1971. Burger wrote the opinion.

Federal law forbids state withholding unemployment compensation payments pending outcome of employer's appeal of initial valid determination of recipient's eligibility.

Graham v. Richardson, decided by a 9-0 vote, June 14, 1971. Blackmun wrote the opinion.

Equal protection guarantee violated by state laws denying welfare benefits to aliens who have lived in the United States less than 15 years or denying benefits to all resident aliens.

Richardson v. Belcher, decided by a 4-3 vote, Nov. 22, 1971. Stewart wrote the opinion; Douglas, Brennan and Marshall dissented.

Federal law allowing reduction in disability payments to reflect workman's compensation payments, but not other payments, is not in violation of due process.

Jefferson v. Hackney, decided by a 5-4 decision, May 30, 1972. Rehnquist wrote the opinion; Douglas, Brennan, Stewart and Marshall dissented.

Neither federal law nor equal protection guarantees are violated by state reducing its aid to dependent children by a larger percentage than it reduced its aid to aged and disabled persons.

Carleson v. Remillard, decided by a 9-0 vote June 7, 1972. Douglas wrote the opinion.

State cannot deny aid to dependent children of servicemen absent without leave from duty.

Boddie v. Connecticut, decided by an 8-1 vote, March 2, 1971. Harlan wrote the opinion; Black dissented.

Due process bars states from denying persons divorces simply because the applicants are too poor to pay the court fees.

Wisconsin v. Constantineau, decided by a 6-3 vote, Jan. 19, 1971. Douglas wrote the opinion; Burger, Black and Blackmun dissented.

Due process bars states from posting the names of excessive drinkers in liquor stores without giving individuals named notice and opportunity for hearing on listing.

Rogers v. Bellei, decided by a 5-4 vote, April 5, 1971. Blackmun wrote the opinion; Douglas, Black, Brennan and Marshall dissented.

Foreign-born child of alien and American parents is not citizen within Fourteenth Amendment protection of due process and loses citizenship if he or she fails to live in United States for a period of five years between the ages of 14 and 28. Black complained that the court was overruling a 1967 decision that Congress had no power to strip anyone of citizenship not voluntarily renounced *(Afroyim v. Rusk).*

U.S. v. Vuitch, decided by a 5-4 vote, April 21, 1971. Black wrote the opinion; Douglas, Brennan, Marshall and Stewart dissented.

Law barring all abortions except those performed to save the life or health of the mother is not void as over-vague, since "health" has been interpreted to include mental well-being; law can be constitutionally applied because it requires prosecution to prove that abortion was unnecessary in order to convict physician.

Bell v. Burson, decided by a 9-0 vote, May 24, 1971. Brennan wrote the opinion.

State cannot constitutionally suspend, without hearing, car registration and driver's license of uninsured motorist after accident unless he posts security for damages, while exempting from this suspension motorists who are released by victim from liability or who are found non-liable by court.

Military Law

Oestereich v. Selective Service System Board, decided by a 6-3 vote, Dec. 16, 1968. Douglas wrote the opinion; Stewart, Brennan and White dissented.

Draft board did not have authority to withdraw divinity student's draft exemption because of his participation in anti-war protest.

McKart v. U.S., decided by an 8-0 vote, May 26, 1969. Marshall wrote the opinion.

Draft exemption of sole surviving son continues even after the death of all family members except son.

Gutknecht v. U.S., decided by an 8-0 vote, Jan. 19, 1970. Douglas wrote the opinion.

Selective service system is not authorized to accelerate induction of man found delinquent for turning in his draft card in anti-war protest. The court held that the law allowed the system to prosecute such delinquents, but not to punish them through accelerated induction.

Breen v. Selective Service System Local Board, decided by a 6-2 vote, Jan. 26, 1970. Black wrote the opinion; Stewart and Burger dissented.

Selective Service System is not authorized to reclassify person holding valid student deferment as punishment for turning in his draft card as protest against war; person so reclassified may challenge legality of his induction prior to actual induction.

Toussie v. U.S., decided by a 5-3 vote, March 2, 1970. Black wrote the opinion; Burger, Harlan and White dissented.

A man who failed to register for the draft at the time of his 18th birthday cannot—under the statute of limitations—be prosecuted after his 23rd birthday.

Welsh v. U.S., decided by a 5-3 vote, June 15, 1970. Black wrote the opinion; Blackmun did not take part; White, Burger and Stewart dissented.

Persons objecting to war because of deeply held moral or ethical beliefs are entitled to conscientious objector exemption even if any religious basis for their belief is expressly disavowed.

"What is necessary," Black said, "for a registrant's conscientious objection to all war to be 'religious'...is that this opposition to war stem from...(his) moral, ethical or religious beliefs about what is right and wrong and that these beliefs be held with the strength of traditional religious convictions."

All persons "whose consciences, spurred by deeply held moral, ethical, or religious beliefs, would give them no rest or peace if they allowed themselves to become part of an instrument of war" are entitled to exemption as conscientious objectors.

Mulloy v. U.S., decided by an 8-0 vote, June 15, 1970. Stewart wrote the opinion; Blackmun did not participate.

A draft board must—when presented with a registrant's nonfrivolous request for reclassification—reopen his case, and decide again on his classification, so that he may have the right to appeal an adverse decision.

Gillette v. U.S., Negre v. Larsen, decided by an 8-1 vote, March 8, 1971. Marshall wrote the opinion; Douglas dissented.

Neither First Amendment nor federal law are violated by selective service system's denial of conscientious objector exemption and discharge to persons objecting only to participation in a particular war.

Ehlert v. U.S., decided by a 6-3 vote, April 21, 1971. Stewart wrote the opinion; Douglas, Brennan and Marshall dissented.

Individual's right not to be involuntarily subject to combatant training or service is not violated by policy that conscientious objector applicant—whose antiwar beliefs crystallized after receipt of his induction notice—will receive hearing and, until decision, be employed in duties involving minimum conflict with beliefs.

Clay v. U.S., decided by an 8-0 vote, June 28, 1971. Unsigned opinion; Marshall did not participate.

Conviction of Cassius Clay for refusing induction must be reversed because appeals board, in refusing his conscientious objector claim, failed to specify the reasons for its disapproval, two of which—as suggested by the Justice Department—were incorrect.

Parisi v. Davidson, decided by a 7-0 vote, Feb. 23, 1972. Stewart wrote the opinion; Powell and Rehnquist did not participate.

Federal district court can move on *habeas corpus* petition alleging wrongful denial by army of conscientious objector discharge, even though military man filing petition is presently being court-martialed for refusal to board plane for Vietnam.

O'Callahan v. Parker, decided by a 5-3 vote, June 2, 1969. Douglas wrote the opinion; Harlan, Stewart and White dissented.

A serviceman is entitled to trial by civilian court, not court-martial, for non-service-connected crimes committed during peacetime while off post, on leave and out of uniform.

Only service-connected crimes came under military jurisdiction. Otherwise, the court said, military jurisdiction might be expanded to deny all members of the armed services in all cases the benefits of an indictment by grand jury and a trial by jury.

Relford v. Commandant, decided by a 9-0 vote, Feb. 24, 1971. Blackmun wrote the opinion.

Court-martial had jurisdiction to try soldier charged with on-base kidnaping and rape, since on-post offenses are "service-connected."

Congressional Powers, Immunities

Powell v. McCormack, decided by a 7-1 vote, June 16, 1969. Warren wrote the opinion; Stewart dissented.

The House of Representatives does not have the authority to exclude from membership a duly elected Representative who meets the constitutional qualifications of age, residence and citizenship.

Background. Adam Clayton Powell Jr. (D N.Y.) was in 1966 elected for his 12th term as Representative from New York's 18th Congressional District (Harlem).

On the first day of the 90th Congress, Jan. 10, 1967, the House (H Res 1) decided that Powell's eligibility to be sworn in and seated as a Member should be determined by a select committee.

The committee, Feb. 23, 1967, concluded that Powell had claimed an unwarranted immunity from the New York courts, submitted false expense reports to the Committee on House Administration and misused House funds. The House March 1, 1967, voted 307-116 to exclude Powell from the 90th Congress.

Powell and a number of his constituents March 8 filed suit in federal district court for the District of Columbia against House Speaker John W. McCormack (D Mass.) and other House leaders and officials.

The suit requested a declaratory judgment that the exclusion of Powell by the House was unconstitutional, a permanent order forbidding McCormack to refuse to administer the oath to Powell, the Clerk to refuse to perform duties due a Representative, the Sergeant-at-Arms to refuse to pay Powell his salary, and the Doorkeeper to threaten not to admit him to the House Chamber.

The federal district court dismissed the suit because, it said, it did not have jurisdiction over its subject matter. The court of appeals, District of Columbia circuit, Feb. 28, 1968, affirmed the action of the lower court in dismissing the suit. The court of appeals held that the lower court did have jurisdiction over the subject matter but that the case involved a political question, which if decided, would constitute a violation of the separation of powers and produce an embarrassing confrontation between Congress and the courts. Judge Warren E. Burger wrote the court of appeals opinion.

While *Powell v. McCormack* was pending on the Court's docket, the 90th Congress ended. Powell was elected again to represent New York's 18th District in the House. He was seated in January 1969 by the 91st Congress and fined $25,000.

Opinion. Chief Justice Warren, for the court, ruled that the House had improperly excluded Powell, a duly elected Representative who met all constitutional qualifications.

Warren then proceeded to the question whether the speech or debate clause of the Constitution (Article I, Section 6) protected those named by Powell in his suit from judicial review of their actions.

Freedom of legislative activity, the objective of the constitutional clause, was protected, the court held, so long as legislators were not forced to defend themselves for their legislative actions. Therefore, the action against McCormack and the other members was dismissed. The court, however, allowed Powell to maintain the suit against the House employees.

The Constitution, the court ruled, in giving to the House the power to "be the Judge of the...Qualifications of its own Members," (Article I, Section 5, clause 1) left the House without the authority to exclude any duly elected Representative who met the requirements for membership expressly stated in the Constitution.

The court did not deny the unquestionable interest of the Congress in maintaining its own integrity. In most cases, however, the court felt that that interest could be properly safeguarded by the use of each House's power to punish or expel its Members. "The Constitution does not vest in the Congress a discretionary power, to deny membership by a majority vote."

The court dismissed the argument that the case presented a "political question" which, if decided by the court, could produce an explosive confrontation between the legislative and judicial branches. Determination of Powell's right to his seat in the 90th Congress, the court held, required only the interpretation of the Constitution, the traditional function of the court.

The Supreme Court sent the case back to the court of appeals with instructions to enter a declaratory judgment stating that the House action was unconstitutional and to conduct further proceedings on the unresolved issues of seniority, back pay and the $25,000 fine.

Stewart dissented, holding that the end of the 90th Congress and the seating of Powell in the 91st Congress rendered the case moot.

U.S. v. Brewster, decided by a 6-3 vote, June 29, 1972. Burger wrote the opinion; Brennan, Douglas and White dissented.

The constitutional immunity conferred on members of Congress does not protect them from prosecution for accepting a bribe in order to vote a certain way on a legislative matter.

Background. Former Sen. Daniel B. Brewster (D Md. 1963-1969) was indicted in 1969 on charges of accepting $24,000 in bribes between 1966 and 1968 from the mail order firm of Spiegel Inc. During that time, Brewster was a member of the Senate Post Office and Civil Service Committee, which was considering proposed

changes in postal rates. The indictment alleged that he was influenced in his action on these proposals by the bribes.

In November 1970, a federal district judge in the District of Columbia, George L. Hart, dismissed the charges against Brewster, stating that the immunity granted members of Congress by the Constitution shielded him from prosecution for bribery related to performance of a legislative act. The Justice Department immediately asked the Supreme Court to review this decision.

Opinion. Chief Justice Burger, for the court, reversed the lower court ruling and held that Brewster could indeed be prosecuted on the bribery charges. The constitutional protection granting members of Congress freedom from prosecution "in any other place" for "any speech or debate in either House" did not protect members' illegal actions in accepting bribes, even if the bribe was directed at a legislative act, such as a committee vote. Taking a bribe is illegal, is no part of the legislative process, and is therefore subject to prosecution and punishment in the nation's courts, held the court.

In dissent, the justices argued that the majority was weakening the independence of Congress and should leave the disciplining of Brewster to Congress itself: "The speech or debate clause does not immunize corrupt congressmen. It reserves the power to discipline (them) in the houses of Congress."

Gravel v. U.S., U.S. v. Gravel, decided by a 5-4 vote, June 29, 1972. White wrote the opinion; Douglas, Stewart, Brennan and Marshall dissented.

The constitutional immunity of members of Congress extends also to their aides, if the conduct in question would be a protected legislative act if performed by the member himself; immunity does not shield an aide or member from testifying to a grand jury about acts unconnected with the legislative process.

Background. At the peak of the controversy over publication of the Pentagon Papers in 1971, Sen. Mike Gravel (D Alaska) called a nocturnal meeting of the public works subcommittee of which he was chairman. Before an audience composed of members of the press and general public, Gravel read, hour after hour, from the classified documents. Later he arranged for the Beacon Press to publish the record of these hearings, known as the Gravel version of the Pentagon Papers.

In August 1971 a grand jury investigating the release of the papers called Leonard S. Rodberg, an aide to Gravel, to appear before it. Rodberg moved to quash his subpoena on the basis that he was protected by congressional immunity from such questioning; Gravel backed that motion. The Justice Department opposed it.

A federal district court held that no witness including Rodberg could be questioned about Gravel's conduct at the subcommittee meeting or about preparations for the meeting. The court of appeals, 1st circuit, held that Gravel and Rodberg could be questioned about the later publication of the subcommittee record.

Opinion. White, for the court, made clear that neither Gravel nor Rodberg could be questioned about the events at the subcommittee meeting. However, the majority agreed that this protection did not extend to cover arrangements that were made for publication of the papers nor information about the source of the classified documents. Gravel, as well as Rodberg, could be required to testify about these non legislative matters, held the majority.

Stewart dissented from the ruling insofar as it held that a member of Congress could be forced to tell a grand jury about the sources of information used to prepare for legislative activity. Douglas, Brennan and Marshall would hold that the constitutional immunity protected Gravel and Rodberg and Beacon Press from questions concerning the publication of the papers.

Antitrust Law

Citizen Publishing Co. v. U.S., decided by a 7-1 vote, March 10, 1969. Douglas wrote the opinion; Fortas did not participate; Stewart dissented.

A joint operating agreement combining the advertising and circulation departments of two competing newspapers and involving price-fixing, market control and pooling of profits was clearly a restraint of trade in violation of the Sherman Antitrust Act. The "failing company" doctrine can serve as defense in antitrust suits only if acquiring company has been shown to be the only available purchaser; burden of proof that conditions of doctrine have been satisfied rested on those using doctrine as defense.

The court refused to hold that the First Amendment guarantee of freedom of the press bars application of antitrust laws to newspapers: "The First Amendment affords not the slightest support for the contention that a combination to restrain trade in news...has any constitutional immunity.

Utah Public Service Commission v. El Paso Natural Gas Co., decided by a 4-2 vote, June 16, 1969. Warren wrote the opinion; White and Marshall did not participate; Harlan and Stewart dissented.

Supreme Court's mandate that natural gas company divest itself of stock and assets of acquired pipeline company—and that district court reapportion gas reserves between two companies—was not effectively implemented by court order permitting gas company to acquire stock in pipeline company and not returning divested company to same competitive premerger position.

U.S. v. Interstate Commerce Commission (ICC), Brundage v. U.S.; Auburn v. U.S.; Livingston Anti-Merger Committee v. ICC, decided by a 7-0 vote, Feb. 2, 1970. Burger wrote the opinion; Douglas did not participate.

ICC approval of merger of the Great Northern Railway Company and the Northern Pacific Railway Company was proper, despite the fact that the competitive merging lines were in sound financial health.

U.S. v. Phillipsburg National Bank, decided by a 5-2 vote, June 29, 1970. Brennan wrote the opinion; Blackmun and Stewart did not participate; Burger and Harlan dissented.

Anticompetitive effects of merger between small competing banks in town must be measured in same geographic area as are benefits of the merger.

U.S. v. Armour and Co., decided by a 4-3 vote, June 1, 1971. Marshall wrote the opinion; Black and Blackmun did not participate; Douglas, Brennan and White dissented.

A company with retail food subsidiaries can acquire majority stock of meatpacking company without violating Meat Packers Consent Decree of 1920 which prohibits meatpacking company from engaging in retail food operations.

U.S. v. Greater Buffalo Press Inc., decided by a 9-0 vote, June 1, 1971. Douglas wrote the opinion.

Acquisition of profitable major printer which results in concentration of 75 per cent of independent color comic supplement printing business violates Clayton Act; passage of time in itself is not barrier to divestiture of stock acquired as result of unlawful merger.

Hawaii v. Standard Oil of California, decided by a 5-2 vote, March 1, 1972. Marshall wrote the opinion; Powell and Rehnquist did not participate; Douglas and Brennan dissented.

State is not authorized by Clayton Act to sue for damages for economic interests of its citizens even if the alleged damage is attributed to violation of the antitrust laws.

Federal Trade Commission v. Sperry and Hutchinson Company, decided by a 7-0 decision, March 1, 1972. White wrote the opinion; Powell and Rehnquist did not participate.

Federal Trade Commission is empowered to protect consumers as well as competitors and to judge challenged practices against standards of fair competition and fair practices as well as against the letter and spirit of the antitrust laws.

Ford Motor Co. v. U.S., decided by a 5-2 vote, March 29, 1972. Douglas wrote the opinion; Powell and Rehnquist did not participate; Burger and Blackmun dissented.

Antitrust laws are violated by practice of cooperative and assets of second largest domestic independent spark plug manufacturer by nation's second largest automobile producer.

U.S. v. Topco Associates, decided by a 6-1 vote, March 29, 1972. Marshall wrote the opinion; Powell and Rehnquist did not participate; Burger dissented.

Antitrust laws are violated by practice of cooperative association of small supermarket chains in allocating territory among members to minimize competition between member stores, even if this territorial arrangement is needed to enable the small chains to compete with national chains; association limitations on resale of private label products are also in violation of antitrust laws.

Flood v. Kuhn, decided by a 5-3 vote, June 19, 1972. Blackmun wrote the opinion; Powell did not participate; Douglas, Brennan and Marshall dissented.

Professional baseball remains exempt from federal antitrust laws, an exception in which Congress has acquiesced, and therefore the reserve clause, which allows a monopoly over the services of an individual player, is allowed to stand.

Business

Anderson's-Black Rock Inc. v. Pavement Salvage Co., decided by a 7-0 vote, Dec. 8, 1969. Douglas wrote the opinion; Burger did not participate.

A useful combination of already-patented elements which added nothing to the nature and quality of the elements did not qualify as patentable invention.

First National Bank v. Dickinson, Camp v. Dickinson, decided by a 6-2 vote, Dec. 9, 1969. Burger wrote the opinion; Douglas and Stewart dissented.

A national bank operating within a state was subject to the same limitations which state law imposed upon banks chartered within the state.

City of Chicago v. U.S., decided by an 8-0 vote, Dec. 9, 1969. Douglas wrote the opinion.

Individual persons can obtain judicial review of orders of the Interstate Commerce Commission continuing investigation of termination or changes in operation of interstate passenger trains.

Ross v. Bernhard, decided by a 5-3 vote, Feb. 2, 1970. White wrote the opinion; Burger, Harlan and Stewart dissented.

Stockholders bringing suit in federal court on behalf of a corporation are entitled to a jury trial so long as the issues, if contested by the corporation in its own behalf, merit a jury trial.

U.S. v. Kordel, decided by a 7-0 vote, Feb. 24, 1970. Stewart wrote the opinion; Black did not participate.

Federal regulatory agencies have the right to demand information from manufacturers in civil suits under threat of forfeiting their products, even if the information so gained might incriminate the manufacturer.

Association of Data Processing Service Organizations v. Camp, decided by an 8-0 vote, March 3, 1970. Douglas wrote the opinion.

Data processing companies have standing to bring court challenge to 1966 ruling by currency comptroller which allowed national banks to sell data processing services to other banks and to businesses which were bank customers.

U.S. v. Key, decided by an 8-0 vote, March 30, 1970. Marshall wrote the opinion.

Insolvent corporation reorganizing under federal bankruptcy law must pay federal tax claims before other debts.

Investment Company Institute v. Camp, decided by a 6-2 vote, April 5, 1971. Stewart wrote the opinion; Burger did not participate; Harlan and Blackmun dissented.

Banks are barred by the Banking Act of 1933 from operating mutual investment funds.

Labor

Detroit and Toledo Shore Line Railroad Co. v. United Transportation Union, decided by a 6-2 vote, Dec. 9, 1969. Black wrote the opinion; Burger and Harlan dissented.

The "status quo" preserved by the Railroad Labor Act of 1927 pending resolution of labor-carrier disputes included all actual working conditions regardless of their inclusion in or omission from an existing collective bargaining agreement.

National Labor Relations Board (NLRB) v. Rutter-Rex Manufacturing Co., decided by a 5-3 vote, Dec. 15, 1969. Marshall wrote the opinion; Burger, Harlan and Douglas dissented.

Back wages ordered by NLRB to be paid to wrongfully discharged employees may not be reduced because of NLRB delay in issuing order.

Czosek v. Mara, decided by a 7-1 vote, Feb. 24, 1970. White wrote the opinion; Burger dissented.

Discharged railroad employees can seek damages against union officers for failing adequately to press their claims. Such a complaint is adequate allegation of the union's breach of its duty of fair representation.

H. K. Porter Co. v. NLRB, decided by a 4-2 vote, March 2, 1970. Black wrote the opinion; White and Marshall did not participate; Douglas and Stewart dissented.

NLRB cannot compel a party to agree to any substantive contractual provision of a collective bargaining agreement.

The National Labor Relations Act pre-empts state jurisdiction to enjoin peaceful pickets protesting substandard wages paid by foreign-flag ships to American longshoremen in American ports.

NLRB v. Raytheon Co., decided by an 8-0 vote, May 18, 1970. Marshall wrote the opinion.

Company found guilty of unfair labor practice does not automatically escape judicial proceedings in enforcement of NLRB cease-and-desist order because a valid election has intervened.

Boys Markets Inc. v. Retail Clerk's Union, decided by a 5-2 vote, June 1, 1970. Brennan wrote the opinion; Marshall did not take part; Black and White dissented.

Federal judges are empowered to halt strikes which occur in violation of no-strike provisions in labor contract when contract also provides for binding arbitration. (Reversal of *Sinclair Refining Co. v. Atkinson,* 1962.

Atlantic Coast Line Railroad Co. v. Brotherhood of Locomotive Engineers, decided by a 5-2 vote, June 8, 1970. Black wrote the opinion; Marshall did not participate; Brennan and White dissented.

Federal judge may not issue order blocking state court action—even if state court's authority to act is unclear—unless the federal court is specifically authorized to act or is obligated to act to protect its own jurisdiction.

NLRB v. Operating Engineers, decided by a 7-2 vote, Jan. 12, 1971. Marshall wrote the opinion; Douglas and Stewart dissented.

Union pressure on neutral contractor to bind all subcontractors to particular form of job assignment or suffer strike is unfair labor practice.

Boilermakers v. Hardeman, decided by an 8-1 vote, Feb. 24, 1971. Brennan wrote the opinion; Douglas dissented.

Federal court has jurisdiction over expelled union member's claim for damages for union's violation of his rights by failure to give him full hearing at disciplinary proceedings.

Chicago and Northwest Railway Co. v. United Transportation Union, decided by a 5-4 vote, June 1, 1971. Harlan wrote the opinion; Black, Douglas, Brennan and White dissented.

Railway Labor Act imposes judicially-enforceable duty on carriers and employees to exert every reasonable effort to reach agreement and legally obligates parties to negotiate with desire to reach agreement; federal court not barred from issuing strike injunction if injunction is only practical and effective means of enforcing duty to negotiate to agreement.

Chemical Workers v. Pittsburgh Plate Glass Co., decided by a 6-1 vote, Dec. 8, 1971. Brennan wrote the opinion; Douglas dissented.

Retired employees' benefits are not, under the National Labor Relations Act, a mandatory subject of bargaining.

NLRB v. Scrivener, decided by a 7-0 vote, Feb. 23, 1972. Blackmun wrote the opinion; Powell and Rehnquist did not participate.

Employer cannot lawfully discharge employees for giving sworn written statements to NLRB field examiner investigating charges against employer.

NLRB v. Burns International Security Services, decided by a 5-4 vote, *Burns v. NLRB,* decided by a 9-0 vote, May 15, 1972. White wrote the opinion; Burger, Brennan, Rehnquist and Powell dissented.

Successor employers are not bound to substantive provisions of collective-bargaining agreement negotiated by predecessors, held the court unanimously. But successor employers, the court held, 5-4, are bound to bargain with the union recognized by the predecessor employer.

Central Hardware Co. v. NLRB, decided by a 6-3 vote, June 22, 1972. Powell wrote the opinion; Douglas, Brennan and Marshall dissented.

Union organizer not representing employees is not entitled by First Amendment to solicit store employees in store parking lot unless he shows that he cannot otherwise communicate with them.

Pipefitters Local Union v. U.S., decided by a 6-2 vote, June 22, 1972. Brennan wrote the opinion; Blackmun did not participate; Burger and Powell dissented.

Corrupt Practices Act, which bars contributions by any labor organization to any federal election, does not bar union contributions and expenditures to campaigns from political funds financed by voluntary contributions from members; solicitation of contributions is not banned if conducted without deception or threat of reprisal.

Environmental Rights

Growing concern for the quality of the environment was reflected in the quadrupling of environmental law cases on the Supreme Court's docket from 1969 to 1972. In the most significant of these, the court ruled that:

• Federal highways can only be built through public parks in the most unusual situations. The court, 8-0 on March 2, 1971, directed a lower court to determine whether or not the secretary of transportation had acted arbitrarily or capriciously in authorizing the construction of a highway through a city park. Marshall wrote the opinion; Douglas did not participate. *(Citizens to Preserve Overton Park v. Volpe).*

• State courts were better equipped than the Supreme Court to rule on the local legal issues and matters of complex technical fact involved in a suit by Ohio against several chemical companies for allegedly polluting Lake Erie with mercury deposits. The court agreed, 8-1 on March 23, 1971; Harlan wrote the opinion; Douglas dissented *(Ohio v. Wyandotte Chemicals Corp.).*

• Federal law regulating the discharge of radioactive waste from nuclear power plants could not be superseded by stricter state pollution laws. Over the dissents of Douglas and Stewart, the court, 7-2, April 2, 1972, refused to review—and thus upheld—this ruling by a lower court *(Minnesota v. Northern States Power Co.)*

• The Sierra Club and other conservation groups could not mount a court challenge to federal action allowing development of a commercial ski resort in a national forest unless the club or its members claimed to suffer actual injury from the development. By a 4-3 vote, April 19, 1972, the court ruled in this case. Stewart wrote the majority opinion; Powell and Rehnquist did not participate; Douglas, Brennan and Blackmun dissented *(Sierra Club v. Morton).*

• Federal district courts were the proper original forums for a case brought by 18 states against the nation's four largest car manufacturers, charging them with conspiring to delay development of effective antipollution devices for car engines. The court unanimously sent the case to the lower courts on April 24, 1972; Douglas wrote the opinion *(State of Washington et al v. General Motors Corp. et al).*

• Lower federal courts had sufficient power to resolve a dispute between Illinois and four Wisconsin cities for allegedly polluting Lake Michigan with raw sewage. The court agreed unanimously on this point April 24, 1972; Douglas wrote the opinion *(Illinois v. Milwaukee)*

• A three-judge federal court had correctly refrained from ruling on a challenge to a state law requiring all Great Lakes vessels—even those with federal licenses operating in interstate commerce—to equip themselves with sewage holding tanks. The court reached this conclusion by a 7-2 vote; Brennan wrote the opinion; Burger and Powell dissented; the decision was announced May 30, 1972 *(Lake Carriers Association v. MacMullan).*

THE SUPREME COURT IN 1973: STILL INDEPENDENT AND EQUAL

Defying efforts to label it and forecast its actions, the Supreme Court in its 1972-73 term made its continued independence perfectly clear. Four of its nine members had come to the bench by the personal choice of President Nixon, but the decisions of the first full term in which all four participated demonstrated forcefully that the court was not an extension of the Nixon administration.

As desired by Nixon, the court did rewrite the definition of obscenity to allow stricter state and local limits on its availability, and it did refuse to expand on various rights guaranteed to criminal defendants by earlier decisions.

But the same court rejected positions endorsed by Nixon when it voided laws making abortion a crime and invalidated state plans for aid to parents of nonpublic school children. Nixon nominee Harry A. Blackmun wrote the abortion decision; Nixon nominee Lewis F. Powell wrote the parochaid ruling. In a further rebuff to administration efforts, the court in April refused an administration request that it review and reverse a lower court's decision barring construction of the oil pipeline across Alaska. Had all four Nixon justices voted to hear the case, it would have been set for argument.

The balance on any given matter within the court was not static, but shifting. The closeness of the margin on many issues was illustrated when Powell did not participate in two major cases and the court deadlocked 4-4, thus upholding lower court rulings which:

• Reversed a court order directing merger of the Richmond, Va., city schools with those in two neighboring counties in order to create a better racial mix within the metropolitan area schools.

• Directed the Environmental Protection Agency to disapprove any state air quality control plan which allowed deterioration of existing air quality.

By June 1973, each of the nine justices had established his juridical personality, providing ample material in his majority and dissenting opinions for observers to begin to draw his judicial portrait.

The Conservative Chief...

Proudly announcing the court's new definition of obscenity, Chief Justice Warren E. Burger admonished his colleagues that "no amount of 'fatigue' should lead us to adopt...an absolutist view of the First Amendment... because it will lighten our burdens." The new guidelines upon which a five-man majority of the court agreed were premised upon a non-absolutist view of the freedom of speech. Basic to the new 'local option' system of controlling pornography was the assumption that the First Amendment ban on laws restricting freedom of expression did not foreclose laws affecting obscene material.

"It is neither realistic nor constitutionally sound to read the First Amendment as requiring that the people of Maine or Mississippi accept public depiction of conduct found tolerable in Las Vegas or New York City," wrote the Minnesota native, directing local communities to use

Warren E. Burger

their own standards by which to judge whether or not a particular book or movie was offensive enough to deserve censorship. Furthermore, "to equate the free and robust exchange of ideas and political debate with the commercial exploitation of obscene material demeans the grand conception of the First Amendment and its high purposes," Burger concluded. (*Miller v. California*)

This particular ruling fell neatly into line with the expressed unhappiness of President Nixon with the permissive attitude fostered by earlier court decisions and resulting in widespread distribution of debatable material, books and films. But Burger, chosen by Nixon for his conservative views, did not always vote on that side of an issue. During the term, he wrote the majority opinion when the court:

• Held, 5-4, that consumers were entitled under law to be informed fully of the terms and total cost of any item purchased through an installment plan. (*Mourning v. Family Publications Service Inc.*)

• Unanimously ordered charges dismissed against a defendant who had been denied his right to a speedy trial, holding that half-way measures, such as a reduced sentence, were not acceptable remedies. (*Strunk v. U.S.*)

• Refused, by a 7-2 vote, to find that the First Amendment required broadcasters to sell time to every group or individual wishing to air its or his views on a controversial matter. "It would be anomalous for us to hold...that the day-to-day editorial decisions of broadcast licensees are subject to the kind of restraints urged.... To do so in the name of the First Amendment would be a contradiction." (*CBS v. Democratic National Committee*)

And when the conservative chief justice disagreed with the majority, his position was not always easily categorized. He dissented when the court:

• Dismissed, by a 6-2 vote, a huge antitrust judgment against Hughes Tool Company in favor of Trans World Airlines. The majority said the challenged transactions were immune from antitrust complaints because they were under the supervision of the Civil Aeronautics Board. Burger objected to such "repeal" of federal antitrust laws. (*Hughes Tool Co. v. TWA*)

• Struck down state laws providing aid to parents who sent their children to nonpublic schools. Burger argued that "where state law is genuinely directed at enhancing the freedom of individuals to exercise a recognized right, even one involving both secular and religious consequences as is true of the right of parents to send their children to private schools...then the establishment clause no longer has a prohibitive effect." *(Committee for Public Education and Religious Liberty v. Nyquist)*

• Upheld, by a 5-4 vote, a city ordinance forbidding newspapers to carry sex-designated want ads. "Freedom of the press," wrote Burger," includes the right of a newspaper to arrange the content of its paper, whether it be news items, editorials or advertising, as it sees fit." *(Pittsburgh Press Co. v. Pittsburgh Commission on Human Relations)*

...A Flexible Follower

"Our law should not be that rigid," wrote Harry A. Blackmun, refuting a technical point raised against the legal challenge to state laws limiting abortions. And Blackmun himself in the 1972-73 term began to demonstrate a new flexibility, breaking out of his role as Burger's "Minnesota Twin" and displaying his own legal personality.

It was the soft-spoken, bespectacled Blackmun, whose speciality is medical law developed in years of work with the famous Mayo Clinic, who wrote the term's most controversial decision—that striking down all existing state laws which made abortion a crime under most circumstances. Carefully balancing medical, legal, and social considerations in the lengthy and comprehensible opinion, Blackmun held that "the right of privacy...is broad enough to encompass a woman's decision whether or not to terminate her pregnancy."

Harry A. Blackmun

Thus the second man placed on the court by Nixon came forth with one of that court's most far-reaching decisions, one which ran directly counter to Nixon's expressed opinion. During the first six months of pregnancy, wrote Blackmun for the seven-man majority, a woman with a doctor's agreement and under state-approved conditions had a right to an abortion. Only during the last three months of pregnancy could a state bar abortions. *(Roe v. Wade)*

In other majority opinions he authored during the term, Blackmun returned to the more conservative path in cases in which the court:

• Refused to extend the equal protection of the laws to cover the right to receive relief from one's debts through bankruptcy. For a five-man majority, Blackmun held that every applicant for this relief must pay the $50 filing fee, even if it was paid in installments. Blackmun suggested that the indigent debtor involved in the case might save the money for the fee by foregoing a weekly movie or two packs of cigarettes each week. *(U.S. v. Kras)*

• Refused to expand the right to a lawyer, holding 6-3 that a defendant did not have a right to have his lawyer present when a witness was shown photographs of persons including the defendant in an effort to win identification of the criminal at the trial. *(U.S. v. Ash)*

With the chief justice, Blackmun dissented when the court dismissed the Hughes-TWA antitrust judgment and when it upheld the city ordinance barring "Men Wanted" and "Women Wanted" classified ads. Alone he dissented when the majority held it unfair for a union to fine a member who resigned during a strike and went back to work, so long as there were no rules making clear that a member could not resign without a penalty under those circumstances. Blackmun defended the union, speaking of the need for solidarity: "The mutual reliance of his fellow members...outweighs, in the circumstances here presented, the admitted interest of the individual who resigns to return to work." *(NLRB v. Granite State Joint Board)*

Blackmun the conservative would prefer to avoid overturning congressional action whenever possible. This inclination was reflected in his dissent from the decision to throw out language added by Congress to the law setting up the food stamp program in order to prevent receipt of this aid by college students. The language was "not happily drafted," Blackmun agreed, but rather than voiding it, he would add procedural guarantees to ensure that it did not sweep more broadly than it should in its application. *(U.S. Department of Agriculture v. Murry)*

Common Sense and Caution

"The ultimate solutions must come from the lawmakers and from the democratic pressures of those who select them," wrote Lewis F. Powell Jr., giving his view of the judicial role in reform. And so, for the five-man majority, he wrote that it was not unconstitutional for states to finance public schools chiefly through local property tax revenues. This Supreme Court decision reversed a trend begun in 1971-72 by several lower courts which had held the system of school financing unconstitutional because it produced wide variation between the amount which districts in the same state could spend to educate each student.

Both the Constitution and common sense supported the majority's conservative holding, wrote Powell. Education was not one of the fundamental rights guaranteed by the Constitution; furthermore, the financing system under challenge did not deny any child an education—it only meant that one child's education would not be as well-financed as another's.

Lewis F. Powell Jr.

In addition, wrote Powell—reflecting his years of experience as a member of the Richmond and Virginia school boards—"the alternatives proposed are only recently conceived and nowhere yet tested." State legislatures were the appropriate bodies to deal with this matter, he concluded, and they should move to do so: "The need is apparent for reform in tax systems which may well have relied too long and too heavily on the local property tax." *(San Antonio Independent School District v. Rodriguez)*

The most articulate of the Nixon appointees, Powell wrote frequent majority opinions during the 1972-73 term. It was he who authored the opinions resoundingly rejecting Nixon-endorsed schemes of state aid to parents whose children attended nonpublic schools. Dealing a death blow to state reimbursement of tuition and tuition tax credits —and to administration plans to institute the same form of aid on a federal level—Powell made clear that this form of aid was unconstitutional because it aided religion, in direct conflict with the First Amendment ban on government action to establish religion. That ban was clearly worded, he wrote, and "with that judgment we are not free to tamper." *(Committee for Public Education and Religious Liberty v. Nyquist, Sloan v. Lemon)*

Taking on yet a third major issue concerning the future of the nation's public schools, Powell stated that "the evil of operating separate schools is no less in Denver than in Atlanta." Concurring in the court's 8-1 ruling warning nonsouthern schools on the subject of segregation, Powell urged the court to discard the worn-out distinction between *de jure* and *de facto* segregation. In any system with a substantial number of segregated schools, the school board should have to prove that the system was nevertheless genuinely integrated. Powell urged reasonableness, balance and flexibility in the use of any method, including busing, to encourage integration. *(Keyes v. Denver School District No. 1)*

In other majority opinions which he wrote during the term, Powell set forth the court's reasoning when it:

• Reversed, 8-1, the murder conviction of a black Mississippian who had been prevented, by a state hearsay rule, from showing at his trial that someone else had confessed to the murder for which he was being tried. *(Chambers v. Mississippi)*

• Unanimously directed a lower court to take a second look at the refusal of McDonnell Douglas Corporation to rehire a black mechanic who had led an illegal civil rights protest against the company's hiring policies. The court must make certain, wrote Powell, that the company was not using the protest as an excuse for job discrimination. *(McDonnell Douglas Corp. v. Green)*

• Declined, 5-4, to extend a 1969 decision which forbade a judge to give a harsher sentence on retrial to a defendant who had won a new trial. In a second trial of this type, Powell wrote, a jury could hand down a harsher sentence than the original one. *(Chaffin v. Stynchcombe)*

• Upheld, 5-4, the ordinance barring sex-designated want ads. Such ads are purely commercial speech which is not protected by the First Amendment, wrote Powell.

The Young Radical...

At 48 the youngest justice, William H. Rehnquist made clear, during his first full term on the court, that he was also its radical conservative. Speaking often for the conservative majority, it was Rehnquist who set forth the new double standard by which the "one person, one vote" rule was applied to state and congressional districts. State legislative districts were judged less strictly against this standard, Rehnquist wrote for a five-man majority in a case involving Virginia: "Application of the 'absolute equality' test...to state legislative redistricting may impair the normal functioning of state and local governments.... So long as the divergences...are based on legitimate considerations incident to the effectuation of a rational state policy, some deviations from the equal population principles are constitutionally permissible." *(Mahan v. Howell)*

Early in the term Rehnquist had issued a majority opinion foreshadowing the court's new stricter role in  regard to obscenity. The court held, 5-4, that the states' power to regulate the importation of liquor, a power granted by the 21st Amendment, included the power to license bars and nightclubs and other places to serve liquor. And that power to license encompassed the power to ban 'topless' and other allegedly obscene forms of entertainment in the places which received licenses. *(California v. LaRue)*

William H. Rehnquist

And following presidential intentions faithfully in the area of criminal law, Rehnquist wrote majority opinions in which the court:

• Refused, 5-4, to allow a man charged with illegal drug production to defend himself with the fact that an undercover federal agent had been closely involved in the production process. *(U.S. v. Russell)*

• Refused, 6-3, to allow a man who entered a guilty plea in his 1948 trial to attack his conviction because blacks were excluded from his jury. "A guilty plea," wrote Rehnquist, "represents a break in the chain of events which has preceded it in the criminal process. When a criminal defendant has solemnly admitted in open court that he is in fact guilty...he may not thereafter raise independent claims relating to the deprivation of constitutional rights that occurred prior to the entry of the plea. He may only attack the voluntary and intelligent character of the guilty plea." *(Tollett v. Henderson)*

Rehnquist was more frequently in the dissenting column than the other Nixon nominees; among the decisions with which he disagreed were those in which the court:

• Struck down state anti-abortion laws. Rehnquist criticized the majority for its "conscious weighing of competing factors...far more appropriate to a legislative judgment than to a judicial one."

• Voided as discriminatory armed forces rules which made it more difficult for a servicewoman to claim her husband as a dependent for purposes of benefits than for a serviceman to claim his wife as a dependent. *(Frontiero v. Richardson)*

• Warned nonsouthern school systems that they might be subject to desegregation requirements. Rehnquist complained that this was a "long leap" from such actions in areas where segregation had been once required by law.

• Voided state efforts to aid the parents of children attending nonpublic schools.

...the Old Absolutist

"The materials before us may be garbage. But so is much of what is said in political campaigns, in the daily press, on TV or over the radio," wrote William O. Douglas, dissenting from the court's obscenity rulings and explaining his absolutist view of the First Amendment.

All forms of speech and expression—be it obscenity, commercial speech, the political speech of civil servants, or broadcast speech—are protected by the First Amendment, Douglas insisted. It was "astounding" that five of the justices would find that that constitutional guarantee allowed persons to be punished for disseminating "offensive" material. Use of that standard, he wrote, "would make it possible to ban any paper or any journal or magazine in some benighted place."

And so Douglas found himself in the dissenting minority in most of the court's rulings concerning the First Amendment. When the court upheld federal laws barring the importation or carrying from state to state of obscene material, even that intended for the personal use of the possessor, Douglas noted that the court had earlier held it was not a crime for a person to have obscene material in his home for his use there. Now, he reasoned, the only way a person could enjoy this right was if he "wrote or designed a tract in his attic, printed or processed

William O. Douglas

it in his basement, so as to be able to read it in his study."

Succinctly stating his view of government's role under the First Amendment, Douglas joined the majority in the Burger opinion holding that broadcasters could not be required by the government to sell time to groups wishing to air controversial issues: "One hard and fast principle which it (the First Amendment) announces is that the government shall keep its hands off the press." Naturally this view led him to dissent—again with the chief justice —from the majority vote upholding the ordinance barring sex-designated want ads.

Douglas, the court's most frequent dissenter, also disagreed when the majority:

• Held, 5-3, that the courts did not have the authority to review decisions by the executive branch to classify information related to the national security. Even the time of day could thus be classified top secret, protested Douglas. (*Environmental Protection Agency v. Mink*)

• Refused, 5-4, to allow a man to defend himself on narcotics charges by claiming that he had been trapped into illegal production of drugs by a federal undercover agent who had supplied a crucial element for the process. "Federal agents play a debased role when they become the instigators of the crime, or partners in its commission, or the creative brain behind the illegal scheme.... May the federal agent supply the counterfeiter with the kind of

paper or ink that he needs in order to get a quick and easy arrest?"

But Douglas, 74, the court's most senior member, marking his 34th year on the court in April 1973, was not always in dissent. Two of his majority opinions came in cases of environmental law, one went for environmentalists and one against. He wrote the opinions when the court:

• Unanimously held that Florida's stricter clean-up standards for water polluters did not conflict with the Federal Water Quality Improvement Act of 1970. (*Askew v. American Waterways Operators*)

• By a 5-4 vote held that federal authority to control noise resulting from jet aircraft was supreme, barring local curfews on jet take-offs and landings designed to cut nighttime noise. (*Burbank v. Lockheed Air Terminal*)

• Held, 4-3, that privately owned electric utilities were subject to federal antitrust laws. (*Otter Tail Power Co. v. U.S.*)

• Reinforced by a series of 7-0 votes the power of the Food and Drug Administration to act quickly and comprehensively in taking ineffective drugs off the market. (*Weinberger v. Hynson, Westcott and Dunning*)

The Liberal Spokesman...

"A long and unfortunate history of sex discrimination ...(has) put women not on a pedestal, but in a cage," wrote William J. Brennan Jr. in the clearest judicial call yet heard for an end to such discrimination. Brennan,

William J. Brennan Jr.

joined by Douglas, Byron R. White and Thurgood Marshall, wrote in 1973 that sex-based classifications should be treated as equally suspect and potentially unconstitutional as racial classifications.

Although Brennan, the second most senior justice, found himself more and more often in dissent during the 1972-73 term, he did occasionally rally a majority as in opinions he authored for the court which:

• Discarded, by a 8-1 vote, Pentagon regulations making it more difficult for a servicewoman to claim her husband as a dependent than for a serviceman to claim his wife as a dependent. (*Frontiero v. Richardson*)

• Upheld, 6-3, an 1899 federal ban on dumping refuse into navigable waterways without a permit, despite the fact that no formal permit program had existed until 1970. (*U.S. v. Pennsylvania Industrial Chemical Corp.*)

• Warned, 8-1, nonsouthern cities that their school systems might also be judged against desegregation requirements and directed another judicial examination of the policies of the Denver, Colo., school board which resulted in some segregated schools within that system. (*Keyes v. Denver School District No. 1*)

Concluding that "we are manifestly unable to describe it (obscenity) in advance except by reference to concepts so elusive that they fail to distinguish clearly between protected and unprotected speech," Brennan literally threw up his hands in frustration with the effort to set standards for some control of obscene material. He dissented from the court's new definition, enunciated by Burger, but said he was also abandoning the earlier definition, which he had set forth in a 1966 ruling.

Dissenting also when the court allowed state legislative districts to depart from the strict "one person, one vote" standard of equal population which applied to congressional districts, Brennan wrote that "the Constitution does not permit a state to relegate considerations of equality to secondary status." Later, in a similar case, he explained: "The demand for precise mathematical equality rests neither on a scholastic obsession with abstract numbers nor a rigid insensitivity to the political realities of the reapportionment process. Our paramount concern has remained an individual and personal right—the right to an equal vote."

Among the rulings with which Brennan also disagreed were those in which the court:

• Refused to require broadcasters to sell time to groups wishing to air controversial views on public issues across the airwaves.

• Held, 6-3, that a person can waive his constitutional right of protection against warrantless searches—even if he does not know he has the right to refuse consent to the search. *(Schneckloth v. Bustamonte)*

• Held, 7-2, that it is not unconstitutional for police, without a warrant, to search and take fingernail scrapings from a murder suspect detained at the police station, even if the evidence was taken over his protest. *(Cupp v. Murphy)*

...and the Man in the Middle

Moving case-by-case along a middle road between liberal and conservative labels, Potter Stewart charted an independent course, which was illustrated by the majority opinions he authored on the issue of the Fourth Amendment protection against unreasonable searches. "It is well settled," he wrote in the first of these, "that a search conducted without a warrant...is '*per se* unreasonable...subject only to a few specifically established exceptions.'" Such exceptions were found by Stewart and the court majority:

• When a man, halted by police, consented to a warrantless search of his car—even though he did not realize he could refuse his consent. *(Schneckloth v. Bustamonte)*

• When a murder suspect, detained at the police station, was, over his protest, searched by police who without a search warrant took evidence from him. *(Cupp v. Murphy)*

But, later in the term, Stewart drew the line on government searches, holding that the government had exceeded constitutional limits in conducting warrantless searches of cars within a 100-mile zone of the U.S.-Mexico border. Writing for a five-man majority in which he was joined by Douglas, Brennan, Marshall and Powell, Stewart held that "it is not enough to argue, as does the govern-

Potter Stewart

ment, that the problem of deterring unlawful entry by aliens across...national boundaries is a serious one. The needs of law enforcement stand in constant tension with the Constitution's protections of the individual against certain exercises of official power. It is precisely the predictability of these pressures that counsels a resolute loyalty to constitutional safeguards." *(Almeida-Sanchez v. U.S.)*

Stewart appeared on the liberal side of the issue in other cases, such as that in which he wrote the majority opinion enlarging the right of citizens to challenge government actions affecting the environment. Rebuffing the administration's arguments, Stewart held that just because an action adversely affecting the environment could be said to harm a large number of persons, it did not follow that individuals in that group did not have the legal standing to bring a court challenge to that action. To deny standing to persons "who are in fact injured simply because many others are also injured would mean that the most injurious and widespread government actions could be questioned by nobody," Stewart wrote, finding that an unacceptable conclusion. *(U.S. v. SCRAP)*

Stewart also disagreed from the decisions in which the court by 5-4 votes:

• Revised the definition of obscenity to allow more local and state censorship of objectionable material.

• Refused to allow use of the entrapment defense when a federal agent had participated in the illegal drug production for which another man was convicted. "It is the government's duty to prevent crime, not to promote it," complained Stewart.

• Allowed a city to ban sex-designated want ads. This was "the first case," wrote Stewart, "that permits the government agency to enter the composing room of a newspaper and dictate...the layout and makeup."

Plaintive Protest

"It is disgraceful for an interpretation of the Constitution to be premised upon unfounded assumptions about how people live," Thurgood Marshall blasted at the conservative majority which refused to waive the $50 bankruptcy filing fee for an indigent debtor. The target of Marshall's criticism here was Blackmun's suggestion that the debtor might save up the $50 by foregoing a movie or two packs of cigarettes each week.

"It may be easy for some people to think that weekly savings of less than $2 are no burden," rebutted Marshall, "but no one who has had close contact with poor people can fail to understand how close to the margin of survival many of them are.... A pack or two of cigarettes may be, for them, not a routine purchase, but a luxury indulged in only rarely. The desperately poor almost never go to see a movie.... They have more important things to do with what little money they have."

Almost invariably voting with his liberal colleagues Douglas and Brennan, Marshall offered his most significant statements during the term in his dissenting opinions. A former solicitor general, who had made history earlier as the civil rights lawyer who argued the initial school desegregation cases in the early 1950s, Marshall joined the majority in the Denver desegregation ruling. But he dissented vigorously when the court refused to overturn the property tax system for financing public schools, a step which had been heralded as the second giant step forward in the battle for equal educational opportunity.

Thurgood Marshall

The court's ruling, wrote Marshall, "can only be seen as a retreat from our historic commitment to equality of educational opportunity and as unsupportable acquiescence in a system which deprives children...of the chance to reach their full potential.... I...am unsatisfied with the hope of an ultimate 'political' solution sometime in the indefinite future while, in the meantime, countless children unjustifiably receive inferior educations that 'may affect their hearts and minds in a way unlikely ever to be undone.'" The last is a quotation from the court's ruling in the initial desegregation case.

Several of the conservative rulings on matters of criminal law also evoked strong dissents from Marshall, among them the majority's holdings that:

• Juries could, on re-trial, hand down harsher sentences than those resulting from the initial trial. This holding, wrote Marshall, "unquestionably burdens a defendant's choice of a jury trial after a successful appeal" and award of a new trial.

• A man could waive a constitutional right to be protected against warrantless unreasonable searches without knowing he had the right. "When the court speaks of practicality," Marshall lamented, "what it really is talking of is the continued ability of the police to capitalize on the ignorance of citizens so as to accomplish by subterfuge what they could not achieve by relying only on the knowing relinquishment of constitutional rights."

No Nixon Nominee, But...

Because Congress chose to acquiesce in the executive's determination that certain papers were highly sensitive by virtue of their concern with national security and should therefore be classified, Congress placed these papers beyond public reach by exempting them from coverage of the Freedom of Information Act. The Supreme Court by a 5-3 vote early in 1973 followed that lead, refusing to allow a judge to second-guess the executive decision to classify such material. Byron R. White wrote this opinion, in line with administration arguments.

White, the second youngest justice at 56 and a Kennedy appointee, voted more like a Nixon choice during the 1972-73 term than did some of the Nixon justices. White provided the crucial fifth vote to make the ma-

jority in favor of the revised obscenity definition which was in line with the President's own ideas. When the court rebuffed administration positions on abortion, parochaid and the matter of citizen authority to challenge government actions affecting the environment, White dissented each time.

Byron R. White

Some observers described White as a "one man Supreme Court," in an effort to characterize his ability to make a majority of the four other Warren Court members if he voted with them or of the four Nixon justices if he joined them. But more accurately, White could be called a charter member of the conservative bloc, frequently joining it when Powell or Blackmun did not. The majority opinions written by White included those in which the court:

• Indicated some acceptance of the administration's argument that the effect of a merger on potential competition should be considered in antitrust challenges by directing, 5-2, a district court to look again at a merger. (*U.S. v. Falstaff Brewing Corp.*)

• Held, 5-4, with Powell, Brennan, Marshall and Douglas forming a majority with White, that there are limits to the immunity accorded to members of Congress by the Constitution. "The business of Congress is to legislate; congressmen and aides are...immune when they are legislating. But when they act outside the 'sphere of legitimate legislative activity'...they enjoy no special immunity." (*Doe v. McMillan*)

• Reiterated, 6-3, its double standard for state and congressional redistricting, but overturned as discriminatory in historical context certain multi-member state legislative districts.

• Upheld, 5-4 and 6-3, restrictions on the political activity of government employees. White refused to find them invalid as too broad and vague, holding that the need for a nonpolitical government bureaucracy overrode any possible constitutional problems in the ban. (*Civil Service Commission v. National Association of Letter Carriers, Broadrick v. Oklahoma*)

Again taking the conservative view, White dissented when the court:

• Struck down state laws against abortion. White complained that the court was imposing its values and its will on the states in "an improvident and extravagant exercise of the power of judicial review."

• Struck down state laws providing aid to parents sending children to nonpublic schools. The court "should not, absent a clear mandate in the Constitution, invalidate these...statutes and thereby not only scuttle state efforts to hold off serious financial problems in their public schools but also make it more difficult, if not impossible, for parents to follow the dictates of their conscience.

• Restricted the government's power to conduct warrantless 'border searches.'

• Granted standing to sue to citizens who alleged that they were injured by government action affecting the environment.

BIOGRAPHIES OF SUPREME COURT JUSTICES

WARREN EARL BURGER, 66, was appointed in 1969 by President Nixon to be the 15th Chief Justice of the United States. Burger, hardly known outside the legal profession, served as a judge on the U.S. Court of Appeals for the District of Columbia from 1956 until his nomination to the nation's highest court.

Born of Swiss-German stock in St. Paul, Minn., Judge Burger spent his early years on a farm outside the city. He attended public schools in St. Paul and worked his way through the University of Minnesota and the St. Paul College of Law, now Mitchell College of Law, attending school at night and working days in the office of the Mutual Life Insurance Company of New York. He was graduated magna cum laude from St. Paul in 1931. Following admission to the Minnesota Bar the same year, he combined a career in private practice with a career of teaching at his alma mater.

From 1931 on, he was an associate in Boyesen, Otis and Faricy, and partner in the successor firm of Faricy, Burger, Moore & Costello. During his 22 years in private practice, his range of cases ran the gamut of civil and criminal law. He argued about a score of cases before the United States Supreme Court and dozens more before state supreme courts and United States appellate courts. During the same period, he did postgraduate work at both the New York University School of Law and the Hague Academy of International Law in Holland.

Burger was part of a group of younger men who in 1938 brought about the election of Harold E. Stassen (R) as the youngest governor in the history of Minnesota and who in 1948 supported Stassen's candidacy for the Republican nomination for the presidency. Gov. Thomas E. Dewey (R N.Y.) defeated Stassen for the nomination, but in the contest Burger became acquainted with Dewey and Herbert Brownell, his campaign manager. It was Brownell who, after the election of Dwight D. Eisenhower, recommended Burger's appointment as Assistant Attorney General of the United States for civil affairs. He served in that position until shortly before his appointment to the U.S. Court of Appeals.

During his appellate court tenure, Judge Burger's decisions were marked with a tone of toughness against crime, calling for a balance between the rights of the accused and the rights of society. Burger also has been dedicated to strictly upholding the rights of the three branches of government and believes the judiciary should try to avoid making policy that would interfere with the prerogatives of the other branches. His philosophy calls for restraint by judges when making decisions which go beyond their areas of competence, such as how a school system should be operated. He is a strong believer in a code of judicial conduct.

Born Sept. 17, 1907, St. Paul, Minn., University of Minnesota, St. Paul College of Law, LLB. (1931); married, two children; lawyer, Assistant U.S. Attorney General, 1953-1955, Judge, U.S. Court of Appeals for the District of Columbia, 1956-1969; nominated as Chief Justice by President Nixon May 21, 1969.

WILLIAM H. REHNQUIST, 49, is the youngest member of the court and the fourth justice to be nomi-

nated by President Nixon and confirmed by the Senate. As assistant attorney general in the Justice Department's Office of Legal Counsel since 1969, Rehnquist was called "the President's lawyer's lawyer." He often appeared before congressional committees as a spokesman for Nixon administration policies, which usually matched his own generally conservative personal philosophy. Rehnquist has supported federal wiretapping, surveillance of citizens suspected of subversive activities, mass arrests of demonstrators, *de facto* school segregation and expanded presidential war powers. He has criticized the Supreme Court's *Miranda* decision guaranteeing the pretrial rights of suspects and once suggested it should be overruled. After serving as a law clerk to former Justice Robert H. Jackson in 1952-53, Rehnquist began practicing law in Phoenix, Ariz., where he was an official in a Republican party "ballot security" program to challenge voter qualifications during the 1960 and 1964 presidential elections. Rehnquist denied that he ever challenged anyone personally, however. In 1964 he wrote a letter to a Phoenix newspaper criticizing a new city ordinance on public accommodations and defending the rights of property owners to refuse service if they wished. During confirmation hearings he said he had since changed his opinion.

Born Oct. 1, 1924, in Milwaukee, Wis.; Stanford University, B.A., M.A. (1948), LL.B (1952); Harvard University, M.A. (1949); Phi Beta Kappa; World War II veteran; married, one son, two daughters; lawyer; member, American Bar Association, Maricopa County (Ariz.) Bar Association; with Phoenix law firms of Evans, Kitchel & Jenckes, 1953-55, Ragan & Rehnquist, 1956-57, Cunningham, Carson & Messenger, 1957-60, Powers & Rehnquist, 1960-69, nominated as associate justice by President Nixon on Oct. 21, 1971.

WILLIAM O. DOUGLAS, 75, is the outspoken and, in the eyes of his critics, the doctrinaire liberal of the court. In that regard, he has lived up to all the expectations of President Roosevelt, who named him to the court in 1939 to succeed Justice Brandeis. Justice Douglas is seldom content with the court's position, even its most liberal stands. His opinions insist that the essence of the Constitution is freedom—as much as possible—for the individual. He resists what he considers governmental invasions of that freedom, even though arguably supported by other constitutional provisions. Justice Douglas practiced law in New York and Washington, D.C., and taught it at Yale and Columbia Universities. He came to the capital in the New Deal days. (Douglas was a member of the Securities and Exchange Commission from 1936-39, serving as chairman from 1937-39.) He has gained a reputation as an enthusiastic outdoorsman and conservationist and has hiked through and written about many spectacular regions of the world.

Born Oct. 16, 1898, in Maine, Minn.; Whitman College, A.B. (1920) Phi Beta Kappa; Columbia University Law School, LL.B. (1925); World War I veteran; married fourth wife 1966, one daughter, one son; lawyer, law professor, government official; nominated as associate justice by President Roosevelt on March 20, 1939.

LEWIS F. POWELL JR., 66, was the third justice appointed by President Nixon to be confirmed to the Supreme Court. The only Democrat of the Nixon court nominees, Powell is the first justice from Virginia since 1841. He was the only southerner Nixon named successfully to the court. A prominent Richmond attorney, Powell was chairman of the Richmond school board during Virginia's period of massive resistance to integration movement in the 1950s. Powell led in the fight to keep Virginia's schools open. Powell leans toward the conservative side on such issues as the constitutional rights of demonstrators and the extent to which pre-trial publicity should be allowed. He believes demonstrations have reduced respect for laws. As president of the American Bar Association from 1964-65, he formulated a program to compile a set of "Standards of Official Conduct," which proposed, among other things, expanded rights for the accused. Out of this project grew the ABA guidelines against pre-trial publicity. In 1966, as a member of the Presidential Commission on Law Enforcement and Administration of Justice, he criticized the controversial Supreme Court *Miranda* decision, which provides that a suspect must be told his legal rights before pre-trial interrogation.

Born Sept. 19, 1907, in Suffolk, Va.; Washington and Lee University, B.S., 1929, Phi Beta Kappa, LL.B., 1931; Harvard, LL.M., 1932; LL.D. degrees from Hampden Sydney College, 1959; Washington and Lee University, 1960; College of William and Mary, 1965; and University of Florida, 1965. World War II veteran; married, three daughters, one son; vice president, National Legal Aid and Defender Association, 1964-65; president, American College of Trial Lawyers, 1969-70; partner in the firm of Hunton, Williams, Gay, Powell and Gibson since 1937; nominated as associate justice by President Nixon on Oct. 21, 1971.

WILLIAM J. BRENNAN JR., 67, is one of eight children of an Irish immigrant couple who came to the United States in 1890; his father was a coal-heaver in a brewery and later a union leader. Justice Brennan won a scholarship to Harvard Law School and entered private practice in New Jersey, specializing in labor-management relations. A Democrat, although not an active one, he was appointed to the New Jersey Superior Court in 1949 by Gov. Alfred E. Driscoll, a Republican. He soon attracted the attention of the judiciary by initiating pretrial conferences with litigants and disposing of many cases, thus keeping his docket relatively clear. In 1952, Governor Driscoll named him to the New Jersey Supreme Court where he developed a reputation as a generally liberal jurist. President Eisenhower in 1956 named him to the U.S. Supreme Court. Justice Brennan usually aligns himself with the "liberal-activist" element of the court, but he has the judge's strong sense of precedent. Thus in 1957 he joined Justice Harlan in dissenting from a case which held that professional football is a business within the meaning of the antitrust laws. The dissenters argued that only four years before, the court had held that professional baseball was a sport and not a business within the meaning of those laws. Any such differentiation, they said, should be made by Congress.

Born April 25, 1906, in Newark, N.J.; Wharton School of Finance and Commerce (University of Pennsylvania), B.S. (1928); Harvard University Law School LL.B. (1931); World War II veteran; married, one daughter, three sons;

lawyer, judge; received recess appointment as associate justice from President Eisenhower on Oct. 15, 1956; nominated as associate justice by President Eisenhower on Jan. 14, 1957.

POTTER STEWART, 58, was the fifth and last justice named by President Eisenhower. As did Justice Brennan (in 1957), he joined the court during its stormy years after the landmark school desegregation case in 1954. Justice Stewart soon became known for independence of mind and, when the court divides evenly, he often casts the deciding vote. He generally leans toward a liberal position. Justice Stewart practiced law in New York City and Cincinnati, serving on the City Council and as vice mayor of the latter city. He assisted the late Sen. Robert A. Taft in his efforts to gain the Republican presidential nomination in 1948, and in 1952 worked in the Eisenhower presidential campaign. President Eisenhower appointed him to the 6th Circuit Court of Appeals in 1954 and to the U.S. Supreme Court five years later.

Born Jan. 23, 1915, in Jackson, Mich.; Yale College, A.B. (1937); Phi Beta Kappa; Cambridge University Law School, LL.B. (1941); World War II veteran; married, one daughter, two sons; cub reporter, lawyer, city official, judge; received recess appointment as associate justice from President Eisenhower on Oct. 14, 1958; nominated as associate justice by President Eisenhower on Jan. 17, 1959.

BYRON R. WHITE, 56, is the first native of Colorado to become a justice. When he was first named to the court in 1962 by President Kennedy, a long-time friend, his accomplishments were considerable: Phi Beta Kappa, Rhodes Scholar, All-America football star, professional football player, member of the Football Hall of Fame, decorated naval officer, lawyer, major assistant in a presidential election campaign and deputy attorney general. On the court, he has aligned himself with the conservative element. The son of the mayor of Wellington, a small town in Colorado, Justice White achieved an outstanding academic and athletic record at the University of Colorado and was named an All-America halfback. To earn money for his law training, he played for the Pittsburgh Pirates (now Steelers) in 1938 and was the leading ground gainer in the National Football League. Then followed a period at Oxford University as a Rhodes Scholar, interrupted by the beginning of World War II. Justice White entered Yale Law School, and played in 1940 and 1941 for the Detroit Lions at the same time. He served in the Navy in the Pacific, where he renewed his acquaintance with John F. Kennedy, whom he had met in England. Completing law school after the war, he was law clerk to the late Chief Justice Vinson and then established a practice in Denver, Colo., eventually handling considerable corporation work. He took little part in politics until 1960, when he went to work with the Kennedy forces, and was credited with delivering 27 of Colorado's 42 convention votes for Kennedy. He then ran the Citizens for Kennedy organization during the 1960 campaign, and after the election was appointed deputy attorney general.

Born June 8, 1917, in Fort Collins, Colo.; University of Colorado, A.B. (1938); Phi Beta Kappa; Oxford University (1939) as Rhodes Scholar; Yale Law School, LL.B. (1946); World War II veteran; married, one daughter, one son; professional football player, lawyer, deputy attorney general; nominated as associate justice by President Kennedy on April 3, 1962.

THURGOOD MARSHALL, 65, in 1967 became the first Negro ever named to the court. The son of a Pullman car steward and great-grandson of a slave, Marshall has made a career out of causes but seldom has been a controversial man personally. He has the reputation of being the man who led the Negro civil rights revolution to its first and often its biggest victories in the courts. His most notable victory came in the Supreme Court's 1954 decision, *Brown v. Board of Education*, which outlawed racial segregation in the schools. Assessing his successes, one friend said Marshall's chief asset was "his ability to take very sticky situations and patch them over with his personality." A long-time white associate said perhaps Marshall's most "obvious characteristic" was his capacity "to put you at ease on the matter of race." He has been likened to former Chief Justice Warren in his views, reportedly sharing the conviction that difference of opinion can be negotiated and being more interested in the background of a case than in its purely technical side. In 25 years as counsel for the National Assn. for the Advancement of Colored People and the NAACP Legal Defense and Educational Fund, Marshall argued 32 cases before the court, emerging the winner 29 times. Born July 2, 1908, in Baltimore, Md., Lincoln University (1930); Howard University Law School (1933); recess appointment to Second Circuit Court of Appeals

by President Kennedy, October 1961; appointed solicitor general of the United States August 1965 by President Johnson; married twice (first wife deceased), two sons; lawyer, civil rights leader, nominated as associate justice by President Johnson on June 13, 1967.

HARRY ANDREW BLACKMUN, 65, appointed associate justice by President Nixon, is a lifelong friend of Chief Justice Burger. The two attended grade school together in Minnesota. A scholarly man, Justice Blackmun worked his way through Harvard University, where he was elected to Phi Beta Kappa, and through Harvard Law School, tutoring mathematics. From 1959 until his appointment to the Supreme Court in 1970, he was judge of the U.S. Court of Appeals for the 8th Circuit, succeeding the judge for whom he was once a law clerk. He is an expert on medical law, having been resident counsel at the Mayo Clinic in Rochester, Minn., 1950-1959. Prior to 1950, Justice Blackman was general partner in a Minneapolis law firm specializing in tax work. He also taught at the University of Minnesota Law School. A Republican, he has never been active in politics. He is considered a conservative, although as a judge his record has shown him to be liberal on civil rights and moderate to conservative on criminal issues.

Born Nov. 12, 1908, in Nashville, Ill.; Harvard University, B.A., summa cum laude, 1929; LLB, Harvard University, 1932; married, three daughters; lawyer, judge; nominated as associate justice by President Nixon on April 14, 1970.

Reference Guide to the Supreme Court

The United States Law Week—The most complete single source of current developments, opinions and rulings. Opinions are mailed the day they are delivered. Published by the Bureau of National Affairs Inc., Washington, D.C. $164.32 per year.

Supreme Court Bulletin—A weekly newsletter on actions of the Court with reviews of cases on the docket. Published by Commerce Clearing House, Chicago, Ill., $100 per year.

The Constitution: Analysis and Interpretation—One volume that discusses the Constitution phrase by phrase, citing relevant Court decisions. Available from GPO, $15.50.

The United States Reports—Official publication of the Court decisions is made in "slip opinions" ($15 a term), "Preliminary Prints" ($15 a term) and in volumes of Reports (now numbering 399). (All are available from GPO.)

Lawyers' Edition of the United States Supreme Court—(Published by Lawyers Co-operative Publishing Co., Rochester, N.Y.) and *Supreme Court Reporter*—(Published by West Publishing Co., St. Paul, Minn. $742.55 for 91 volumes). Court opinions are mailed rapidly by both of these services. These advance sheets are later bound in volumes as permanent reports. The Lawyer-Edition gives summaries of ar-

guments, while the Reporter series has the West "key number" breakdown for facilitating legal research. Both series publish digests of all Court decisions.

Fundamentals of Legal Research, by Ervin H. Pollack, published by Foundation Press. ($8.)

Effective Legal Research, by Miles O. Price and Harry Bitner, published by Little, Brown. ($9.)

How to Find the Law, Willam R. Roalfe, general editor, published by West Publishing Co., St. Paul Minn. ($8.)

The Justices of the United States Supreme Court 1789-1969. Edited by Leon Friedman and Fred L. Isreal. Four volumes on the lives and major opinions of the 97 Supreme Court justices. Published by Bowker. $110.

Black's Law Dictionary. Definitions of the terms and phrases of American and English jurisprudence, ancient and modern. By Henry C. Black. Published by West Publishing Co. $12.50.

The Supreme Court in United States History. By Charles Warren. Published by Little, Brown and Co. Two volumes. $20.

Reference guides in this book are adapted from "Understanding Government" charts by Clement E. Vose, Wesleyan University.

FEDERAL JUDGES: A RECORD NUMBER OF NIXON NOMINEES

Federal judgeships are the juiciest of patronage plums bestowed by the party of the President: Richard Nixon will, in his two terms as President, name more men to the federal bench than any other President. His first-term total of 177 federal district and appeals court judges, plus four Supreme Court members, moved him within easy striking distance of the existing record set by Franklin D. Roosevelt, who in his 12 years placed 194 men on the federal bench and nine men on the Supreme Court. (Appendix, p. 107)

Late in 1973, when the Senate confirmed his 17th and 18th nominees of that year, Nixon surpassed the Roosevelt record for nominees to the lower federal courts.

This Nixon legacy will exert an influence on American life continuing long after 1976. The persons who sit as federal judges rule on questions of far-reaching significance to the nation, among them desegregation, freedom of the press, environmental protection, consumer's rights.

But who are the people who sit in these seats? And how are they chosen? The public generally ignores the process of their selection, and the press rarely records any but the bare fact of their nomination and confirmation —in sharp contrast to the attention turned on Supreme Court nominations. Federal judges hold their posts for life "during good behavior" at a current annual salary of $40,000 for district judges and $42,500 for judges on courts of appeals.

In apparent contradiction of the American ideal of an independent judiciary free of partisan flavor, the process through which federal judges are selected is purely political. No constitutional guidelines exist: Only custom directs that the President nominate federal judges below the Supreme Court level with the Senate's advice and consent. Only tradition requires that judges be residents of their districts or that they be lawyers.

In conflict with the intent of the men who wrote the Constitution as spelled out by Alexander Hamilton in *The Federalist*—tradition has, since 1840, awarded to senators of the President's party the prerogative of naming persons for federal judgeships within their states. If the senators are not of the President's party, the White House looks to its party organization within that state for suggested nominees.

Loyalty to the Republican party, said Richard G. Kleindienst in 1969, would play a "very very minor part" in the selection of federal judges during the Nixon administration. Yet, of the 176 men and one woman named to the federal bench in the first Nixon term, 165 were Republicans, many with long records of service to the Grand Old Party. Kleindienst, as deputy attorney general from 1969 until 1971, had the major responsibility for processing those nominations. Of the 1973 judicial nominees, only one—who called himself an independent —was not a Republican.

As President Nixon began his second term, there were 400 federal district judgeships and 97 court of ap-

'Such Inferior Courts'

The Constitution makes no mention of federal district or appeals courts nor of the persons who would preside over them. It established one Supreme Court and left it to Congress to create "such inferior courts" as might be necessary. The first Congress did create a federal district court (with one judge) for each of the 13 original states plus three intermediate courts of appeals which were presided over each by one Supreme Court justice, who traveled to the site of the case, and the district judge from the area.

This initial judicial structure had its problems —not least of which was that justices and judges were obliged to review their own decisions. But judicial reform was immediately a question deeply embroiled in political considerations.

Late in the administration of John Adams, his party won passage of a bill revising the original judicial structure and creating additional judge-ships for Adams to fill just before leaving office. The incoming administration of Thomas Jefferson objected to this "midnight judges bill", repealed it and passed its own, creating judgeships for Jefferson to fill with men of his choice.

Similar patronage considerations motivated a Democratic-controlled Congress to refuse—in 1957, 1958, 1959, and 1960—to enact a bill creating 73 new federal judgeships, which would have been filled by Republican President Dwight D. Eisenhower. Not even Eisenhower's offer to name Democrats to half of the new seats moved Congress to act. But after John F. Kennedy was inaugurated in 1961, the bill glided through Congress, giving the new posts to Kennedy to fill.

peals seats—almost exactly double the number when Harry S Truman took office in 1945. An ever-increasing caseload has provided the rationale—and desire for additional patronage posts no hindrance—for Congress to enact six separate bills since 1945 to create additional judgeships.

Congress in 1970 created 70 new judgeships for Nixon to fill, but again in 1973 it was asked to consider further expansion of the judiciary. The Judicial Conference of the United States, the judiciary's policy arm headed by Chief Justice Warren E. Burger, a Nixon nominee, recommended late in 1972 that Congress create 40 new federal district judgeships and 11 more seats on the courts of appeals.

Although it takes a recommendation from this non-partisan body to start congressional consideration of a bill creating judicial posts, the final version of the act often reflects the politics of the legislative process. The 1970 act included three judgeships not requested by the Judicial Conference—one each in Maryland, Nebraska and West Virginia. A senator from each of those states sat on the subcommittee which originated the bill.

For Services Rendered

"The judiciary has long been treated as the place to put political warhorses out to pasture," writes Philip B. Kurland, professor of law at the University of Chicago. "The great majority of American judges have their posts because—and only because—of prior services rendered to the dominant political party."

When Attorney General Elliot Richardson was revamping Justice Department leadership in mid-1973, a seat on the court of appeals, 9th circuit, proved to be a convenient reward for Deputy Attorney General Joseph Sneed, who had held that post for only a few months, but whom Richardson wished to replace with William D. Ruckleshaus.

These well-paid positions are often consolation prizes for defeated politicians—or career-capping posts for those who have retired from active political life. Among Nixon nominees for federal district judgeships were unsuccessful Republican gubernatorial candidates C. Stanley Blair of Maryland and Raymond J. Broderick of Pennsylvania, former New Mexico Governor and Senator (R 1962-64) Edwin L. Mechem and former Representatives James F. Battin (R Mont. 1961-69) and Robert V. Denney (R Neb. 1967-71). Nixon also promoted former South Carolina Governor and Senator (D 1965-66) Donald Stuart Russell from the federal district bench to the court of appeals.

But only rarely does a President name a member of the opposition party to a federal judgeship. Only about one of every 30 judges appointed by Roosevelt was a Republican; only one of every 18 Eisenhower nominees was a Democrat. Of Nixon's first-term nominations, about one of 14 was a Democrat. *(Graph next page)*

Strong political motivation is usually behind any White House decision to deviate from choosing members of its own party for these posts. Such was the case in South Carolina when in 1971 there were two federal district judgeships to be filled. One went to former Republican State Chairman Robert F. Chapman. But the other —to the consternation of the state's Republicans but with the acquiescence of the Republican senator, Strom Thurmond—went to Solomon Blatt Jr., the son of the long-time Democratic speaker of the South Carolina House. Observers attributed this move to the fact that the Democratic Party still controlled the major sources of political power within the state—a fact of significance to Nixon and to Thurmond, both of whom faced re-election campaigns in 1972.

One of the few other Democrats named to a federal judgeship during the Nixon administration was Eldon B. Mahon, U.S. attorney for northern Texas—and nephew of the powerful chairman of the House Appropriations Committee, George Mahon (D Texas). Such a nomination appeared explicable in light of the Nixon effort to win Texas Democrats' votes in 1972, and in light of the administration campaign to reduce federal spending—and congressional appropriations.

Republican Rewards. But many of the federal judges selected by Nixon had records of service to some part of the Republican Party; many served as delegates or alternates to one or more Republican conventions in the 1950s and 1960s. Some of these judges include: Republican National Committee Vice Chairman Donald R. Ross of Nebraska—who left that post when chosen to fill a seat on the court of appeals in 1970; former state Republican officials Sam C. Pointer Jr. of Alabama—at 38 the youngest sitting federal judge, Charles A. Moye Jr. and William C. O'Kelley in Georgia, John Feikens of Michigan, William M. Steger of Texas and Chapman of South Carolina, all in 1972 serving as federal district judges.

This use of federal judgeships as rewards for Republican service was illustrated by the 1970 nominations of L. Clure Morton and Harry W. Wellford as federal district judges in Tennessee. Morton, a Knoxville attorney, was brother to one of the major figures in the successful 1966 senatorial campaign of Howard H. Baker Jr., the state's first Republican senator in almost a century. Wellford, from Memphis, was active in that campaign and in the 1970 Tennessee Republican gubernatorial campaign. Wellford's nomination came within a month of the November election in which his candidate, Winfield Dunn (R), was chosen the state's first Republican governor in 50 years.

Morton, however, chosen with an eye to his conservative credentials, in 1971 issued an order directing an increase in the busing of school children in Nashville, Tenn., in order to desegregate the schools. Baker, an avowed opponent of busing, was heard to wonder aloud what would have happened had he recommended someone with liberal credentials for that judgeship.

Former Vice President Agnew's influence was a factor in nominations such as those of Blair, a former Agnew adviser, for a federal judgeship after his unsucessful 1970 gubernatorial campaign; of James R. Miller Jr., who had served as liaison in 1968 between Nixon and Agnew campaign headquarters; of Joseph H. Young, who headed the 1968 Maryland Lawyers for Nixon-Agnew, and of Charles R. Richey, whom Agnew, during his term as governor, had named general counsel of the state's public service commission.

The extent of Agnew's influence was indicated in August 1973, when every federal judge in Maryland withdrew from involvement with the investigation of Agnew for bribery and extortion. Each of the nine judges disqualified himself "because of the unique position of the Vice President and his relationships to the state of Maryland." Chief judge Edward S. Northrup said that at least six of the judges had felt that they were too closely connected to Agnew's own political career.

Public Service Award. Among the men elevated to federal judgeships by Nixon are a number known for some form of generally nonpartisan public service:

• Frederick B. Lacey, the U.S. attorney who successfully prosecuted former Newark, N.J., mayor Hugh Addonizio for extortion.

• Thomas A. Flannery, chief federal prosecutor for the District of Columbia and strong advocate of the Nixon administration's war on crime and its omnibus D.C. crime bill enacted in 1970.

• Lawrence W. Pierce, former chairman of the New York State Narcotics Addiction Control Commission.

• Richard W. McLaren, assistant attorney general for antitrust (1969-71).

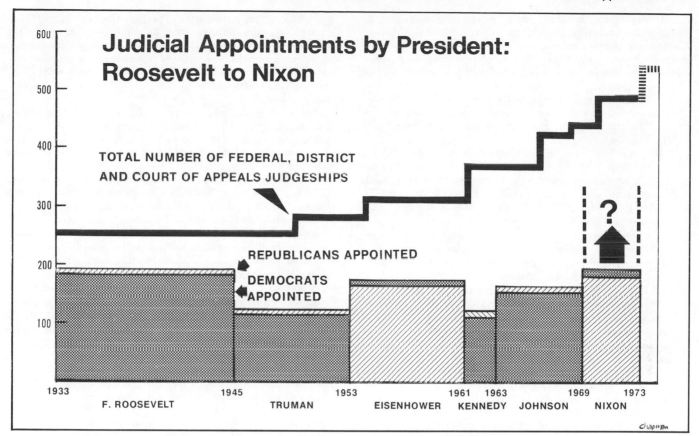

Judicial Appointments by President: Roosevelt to Nixon

TOTAL NUMBER OF FEDERAL, DISTRICT AND COURT OF APPEALS JUDGESHIPS

REPUBLICANS APPOINTED

DEMOCRATS APPOINTED

?

1933 F. ROOSEVELT 1945 TRUMAN 1953 EISENHOWER 1961 KENNEDY 1963 JOHNSON 1969 NIXON 1973

chapman

• Whitman Knapp, chairman of the commission which investigated police corruption in New York City in 1971.

• William M. Byrne Jr., former executive director of the President's Commission on Campus Unrest and a Democrat whose nomination in 1969 as a federal district judge by Lyndon Johnson had been withdrawn by the Nixon administration after it took office. Byrne was the judge who dismissed the government's case against daniel Ellsberg in May 1973.

Nomination: The Crucial Stage

When a judicial post becomes vacant or is created within a state, the senator or senators from the state who are of the President's party send to the office of the deputy attorney general a list of prospective nominees.

This first step is not always simple. No federal judge was named for New York State during 1969 or 1970—despite a mounting caseload and a number of vacancies rising to 10 in early 1971. Just before the November 1970 election, the state's two liberal Republican senators, Jacob K. Javits and Charles E. Goodell, submitted a list.

But Goodell was almost immediately defeated by conservative James L. Buckley, who thus moved into a position to block any or all of the Goodell-Javits nominees by invoking the tradition of 'senatorial courtesy.' This long-standing custom dictates that the Senate not confirm any nominee to whom a senator of the President's party from the homestate of the nominee objects.

Mindful of the potential impasse, the Justice Department took no action on the Javits-Goodell list. Early in 1971, Buckley submitted his own list which contained none of the names of the first list.

Negotiations then began between Javits, Buckley and the Justice Department, but it was mid-May before the Nixon administration named its first federal judges for New York State. Among those finally nominated was Murray Gurfein, a New York attorney. Only a few days after taking his seat, Gurfein found himself confronted with the administration's request that he halt publication of *The New York Times* articles based on the Pentagon Papers. Gurfein refused to issue such an order and was subsequently upheld by the Supreme Court.

Prospective nominees recommended by senators or party organizations undergo scrutiny by the White House, the FBI and the American Bar Association (ABA) committee on the federal judiciary. A number of prospective nominees during the Nixon administration have failed to survive this examination—for a variety of reasons.

Philosophy and Geography. An unsatisfactory judiciary philosophy, according to the Justice Department, was the reason that the administration blocked the nomination of Clarence Clyde Ferguson, a distinguished black attorney and ambassador to Uganda, to a seat on the Court of Appeals, 3rd Circuit. For three years the seat remained vacant while New Jersey's Republican senator, Clifford Case, worked to win it for Ferguson, former dean of Howard University Law School and general counsel for the Civil Rights Commission. But the administration was adamant in its opposition, which observers saw as founded on a view that Ferguson was "soft" on issues of law and order. Case regretfully withdrew his recommendation.

Senatorial recommendations carry less weight in the choice of persons for the prestigious seats on the courts of appeals, of which there are 11, each with jurisdiction over cases from a number of states.

White House relations with Hawaiian Sen. Hiram L. Fong, a high-ranking Republican on the Senate Judiciary Committee, were strained in 1969 after the White House ignored Fong's well-known feeling that a Hawaiian judge should be named to one of three empty seats on the Court of Appeals, 9th Circuit, with jurisdiction over cases from Hawaii. Of the 10 judges on the court of appeals at that time, not one was from Hawaii. Fong had selected a federal district judge then sitting in Hawaii for one of the three vacancies.

But instead the White House nominated Federal District Judge John F. Kilkenny of Oregon, named to his post by Eisenhower; Eugene A. Wright of Seattle, a bank vice-president and friend of White House aide John D. Ehrlichman, and Ozell M. Trask, Phoenix attorney and former law partner of Kleindienst.

To demonstrate his irritation, Fong delayed committee approval of the nominees for two months; eventually all three were confirmed. When the next vacancy on that appeals court occurred—in 1971—it was filled by Fong's law partner from Honolulu, Herbert Y.C. Choy.

Public Reaction. Adverse reaction to the rumors of a potential nominee can also block a particular choice as in the case of Joseph O. Rogers Jr., recommended by Thurmond to the Justice Department in 1970 to fill a new judgeship in South Carolina. Rogers was then a federal attorney, a post to which it was said he had been nominated with the understanding that he would move on to the judicial post once it was created.

Civil rights groups protested the idea of Rogers' possible nomination, pointing to his decade of service as one of the leaders of a state committee devoted to preserving segregation. The nomination was never made; Rogers subsequently returned to private practice.

ABA Veto. To ensure that his judicial nominations met a certain professional standard, Nixon in 1969 became the first President to pledge that he would not name to a judgeship—except to the Supreme Court—anyone found not qualified for the post by the ABA committee.

Just about one of every three names sent to the committee during 1969 and 1970 was of someone found not qualified—and therefore not nominated. A report from the committee in August 1972 showed that about half the Nixon administration nominees had been given minimal clearance as qualified, that slightly less than half had been found well qualified, and that only 11 had been awarded top marks as exceptionally well qualified.

Confirmation: Advise and Consent?

The Senate has virtually abdicated its function of advising and consenting to judicial nominations.

With the exception of Supreme Court nominations, the difficult part of the selection process is over by the time a judicial nomination is sent to the Senate. Very rarely does the Senate reject a judicial nomination.

The most controversial recent incident came in 1965 when Edward M. Kennedy (D Mass.) was forced to withdraw the nomination of family friend Francis X. Morrissey as a federal district judge. Strong opposition had developed to Morrissey's nomination for the stated reason that he was not qualified for the job. The Senate sent the nomination back to committee, which had approved it by a 6-3 vote earlier. Kennedy then withdrew the nomination.

When the nomination reaches the Judiciary Committee, a blue slip is sent to each senator from the nominee's homestate. To indicate approval, the senator signs and returns the slip. If a senator disapproves, he does not return the slip and he usually talks with Committee Chairman James O. Eastland (D Miss.) to explain his opposition.

Lawrence Walsh, chairman of the ABA committee, has noted that "it's virtually impossible to have a person confirmed for a federal judgeship if one of the senators (from his homestate) is openly or secretly opposed to the nomination."

The objection may not be personal but may instead reflect partisanship. Late in the Johnson administration, Case blocked certain nominations recommended by the Democratic senator from New Jersey, Harrison A. Williams Jr. In 1969, Williams returned the disfavor, blocking for four months confirmation of four Republicans recommended by Case to fill those vacant seats. Late in the year, Williams withdrew his objection.

But usually the blue slips are quickly returned to the committee. A special subcommittee, composed of Eastland, ranking committee minority member Roman L. Hruska (R Neb.) and John L. McClellan (D Ark.), sets a public hearing on the nomination. A week's advance notice is given publicly and to the ABA and others who have expressed a particular interest in a nomination.

Eastland alone sees the FBI report on the nominee. The ABA committee informs the committee of the results of its examination of the nominee's professional qualifications. The hearing is held with the nominee present, usually escorted by one or both his senators. The hearings are usually quite brief and routine.

The subcommittee then makes its recommendation to the full committee which usually acts within days to send the nomination to the floor with the recommendation that it be confirmed, and usually without any printed report. The nomination is routinely confirmed within a matter of seconds by the Senate once it is brought up for consideration.

The perfunctory nature of the Senate's advising and consenting to judicial nominations was pointed up when, in 1969 and 1970, the Senate rejected the nominations of two men, Clement F. Haynsworth Jr. and G. Harrold Carswell, to the Supreme Court who had earlier been confirmed as judges on federal courts of appeals.

Birch Bayh (D Ind.) a leader in opposing both the nominations, said afterwards that he hoped that the Senate would exercise more care in confirming nominees to federal judgeships in order to avoid such embarrassment. But, three years later, Bayh's concern had produced no specific proposal for strengthening this senatorial role.

No change appears likely in the process of judicial nomination and confirmation: Senators of the proper state and party will continue to play a major part in the selection of federal judges for their states while the Senate will continue to play only a perfunctory role. In his study of this process, *Lawyers and Judges*, Joel B. Grossman points out that actual investigation of each nominee by the Judiciary Committee would result in that committee's curbing the prerogatives of members of the Senate, who, he notes, frequently choose men for reasons of local politics or for other reasons which would not bear public scrutiny.

Legal Institutions

JUDICIAL REFORM: SOLID PROGRESS BUT A LONG ROAD AHEAD

"In the supermarket age, we are like a merchant trying to operate a cracker barrel corner grocery store with the methods and equipment of 1900."
> —Chief Justice Warren E. Burger soon after assuming the leadership of the federal judiciary in 1969.

In 1973 Burger was still calling for change in the system which, as he put it, was "suffering from long deferred maintenance and reliance on methods and procedures that are inefficient, outworn and inadequate to deliver prompt justice at reasonable cost to the consumers of justice."

Looking back over the innovations of the last few years, Burger conceded, in his 'state of the judiciary' address to the American Bar Association (ABA) in August: "We have made solid progress, but the reality is that we have a long way to go. Like caring for a garden or any growing thing, it is a task never finished."

Even before Burger moved to modernize the judiciary, the breezes of change had begun to blow. Since 1967, a variety of improvements in the federal judicial machinery had been proposed, approved and implemented. Among them were:

• Creation in 1967 of the Federal Judicial Center, a research arm for the judiciary which President Johnson envisioned would "enable the courts to begin the kind of self-analysis, research and planning necessary for a more effective judicial system—and for better justice." Retired Supreme Court Justice Tom C. Clark was the center's first director. He was succeeded in 1971 by retired Federal Appeals Court Judge Alfred P. Murrah.

• Abolition in 1968 of the out-moded system of U.S. commissioners, "overgrown justice-of-the-peace-type officers" in the federal courts; and creation in its place of the federal magistrates system. Magistrates are attorneys who serve as officers of the court, authorized to issue warrants, fix bail, hold preliminary hearings and conduct trials for petty offenses. The magistrate can also be authorized by the judge with whom he works to assume other functions, including screening the petitions which come to the court from prisoners seeking review of their sentences or convictions. In 1972, Congress upped the salary ceiling for magistrates to $30,000.

• Establishment by Congress in 1968 of a Judicial Panel on Multidistrict Litigation, authorized to consolidate in one court the pretrial proceedings in civil suits all of which involved one common fact situation, such as an airline crash, but many lawsuits in different federal districts.

• The addition of nine new federal appellate judgeships in 1968 and 58 new federal district judgeships in 1970.

The Price of Justice

In 1970, Chief Justice Warren E. Burger conceded that the long overdue improvements in the federal judicial system would cost money, but he noted that the increase in the budget of the judiciary would still "be a small fraction, for example, of the $200-million cost of a C-5A airplane.... Military aircraft are obviously essential in this uncertain world, but surely adequate support for the judicial branch is also important."

And the budget of the federal judiciary did double from fiscal 1969 to fiscal 1974, rising from $103-million to $205.5-million. But that total remained small in comparison to the chunks of the federal budget consumed by the other two branches. In fiscal 1973, the judiciary received $193.6-million. Congress appropriated almost three times as much for its own operations—$513.8-million—and just one of the executive departments, the Department of Justice, received more than $1.8-billion.

• Creation in 1970 of the post of circuit court executive, allowing each of the eleven judicial circuits to name an administrator to its staff to assume some of the administrative duties which burdened the chief judge of each appeals court. Each such executive had to be certified as qualified by a special board; his salary was set at $36,000.

• Authorization, two years later, for similar assistance for the chief justice, by creation of the post of administrative assistant to the chief justice. The salary for this post was not to exceed $40,000, the same as that of director of the Federal Judicial Center and the director of the Administrative Office of the U.S. Courts, the federal judiciary's 'staff' organization. Mark W. Cannon, expert in political economy and government, was the first person named to this post. He had previously held the post of director of the Institute of Public Administration in New York, the oldest center for public administration research and training in the country.

• Establishment in 1972 of a commission to study the structure and procedures of the federal appellate system and recommend changes in the geographical boundaries of the circuits—each of which contains a number of states—and changes in the procedures used by the appeals courts.

Crime and Congested Courts

Burger came to the post of chief justice already known for his concern about the way in which the machinery of justice operated. And he reached the peak of the federal judicial system at a time when expanding public concern over the rising incidence of crime had given new meaning and impetus to efforts to update the cumbersome and old-fashioned judicial machinery.

"Crime statistics started shooting up" during the 1960s, Sen. Quentin N. Burdick (D N.D.), head of the Senate subcommittee on improvements in judicial machinery, pointed out, "and we started paying great attention to crime—and hence to the courts."

More crime meant more arrests, more trials and more work for the courts. Conversely, as Burger pointed out, many persons felt that the crime rates would drop sharply if punishment for crime came swiftly, if the courts were equipped to try all criminal cases within 60 days of indictment.

"I prefer that we risk some false starts rather than make no starts at all."

—Chief Justice
Warren E. Burger

In 1960, there were approximately 89,000 cases—criminal and civil—filed in federal district courts; by 1970, the figure had increased 43 per cent to 127,000. Even more dramatic, appeals filed in federal appellate courts tripled from 1961 to 1971, rising from 4,204 to 12,788.

The traditional response to such burgeoning of judicial business was for the Judicial Conference, the "board of directors" of the federal judiciary, 24 federal judges led by the chief justice, to ask for—and Congress to grant—more federal judgeships. Four times in the decade of 1961-1971—in 1961, 1966, 1968 and 1970—Congress authorized an increase in federal judgeships. When President Nixon began his second term, there were twice as many federal judges as in 1945 when Harry S Truman became President.

But this traditional approach did not appear to solve the problems of the federal judiciary. "The mere addition of judges to the courts," noted President Johnson in 1967, "will not bring about the efficient administration of justice that simple justice demands."

That same year, in an address which caught the eye of Nixon, a federal appeals judge named Warren E. Burger spoke of the need for reform: "Is a society which frequently takes five to ten years to dispose of a single criminal case entitled to call itself an 'organized' society?"

Two years later, as Burger told it, he went to work on the problem "within 24 hours after I took office on June 23, 1969. The next morning, I had the first meeting on the problem of court administration." And, he has also noted, "Everything I've done since in the way of public utterance on the subject has been directed at this broad problem.... We cannot blindly cling to methods and forms designed for the 17th and 18th centuries."

To deal with the "colossal and immediate" challenge Burger gave priority attention "to methods and machin-

ery, to procedures and techniques, to management and administration of judicial resources even over the much needed re-examination of substantive legal institutions."

Moving first to create a corps of trained court executives, whom he described as similar in role to hospital administrators, Burger asked the ABA in August 1969 to set up a training program for such personnel. Less than six months later, Burger and ABA President Bernard C. Segal announced the creation of the foundation-funded Institute of Court Management, sponsored by the ABA, the American Judicature Society and the Institute of Judicial Administration. Burger predicted that the assistance provided by individuals trained in this program, headquartered at the University of Denver, would "improve the efficiency of each judge by more than 25 per cent."

Congress, which had been considering the circuit executives bill in 1969, had not completed action by late summer 1970. "We have at least 58 astronauts capable of flying to the moon," Burger lamented to the ABA then, "but not that many authentic court administrators.... The federal courts need immediately a court executive...for each of the eleven circuits and for every busy federal trial court." By Christmas 1970, Congress had completed work on the bill; two years later the chief justice was also granted such an assistant.

Efficiency, not "more money and more judges," was the best solvent for the administrative tangle of the judicial system in Burger's view. And he made clear the link he saw between efficiently operating courts and the quality of justice: "Efficiency must never be the controlling test of criminal justice, but the work of the courts can be efficient without jeopardizing basic safeguards. Indeed, the delays in trials are often one of the gravest threats to individual rights. Both the accused and the public are entitled to a prompt trial."

And in a statement in September 1973, Burger explained his concern: "A more productive judicial system is essential for justice by giving litigants their relief promptly.... By making the judicial system more productive, we are making the federal courts accessible to all Americans at less personal financial expense and less emotional expense—all in addition to saving citizens' taxes."

"Judges have been too timid and the bar has been too apathetic to make clear to the public and the Congress the needs of the courts," Burger told the ABA in 1970. "But I believe the days of apathy are past," he added.

A Change in Congress

"The traditional response to increased litigation has been for the judicial branch...to request, and for the legislative branch to create, additional judgeships," a report of the Senate Judiciary Subcommittee on Improvements in Judicial Machinery said. As a result, "in 23 years, the number of district court judges has almost doubled... (and) the Federal Judicial Center in...March 1971...predicted that by 1990 we would need three times the present number of district court judges."

Basing its request on such projections, the Judicial Conference late in 1972 asked Congress to authorize 51 new federal district judgeships and 10 new appellate posts. Similar past requests have been routinely rubber-stamped by Congress once strategic members added one or two new posts within their state, adding one more plum to their patronage pie.

But, in 1971, Sen. Quentin N. Burdick (D N.D.) became chairman of the Senate Judiciary Subcommittee on Improvements in Judicial Machinery. And a difference in that body's approach to federal judgeships became apparent in 1973 as the subcommittee went to work on the request for additional federal district judgeships.

"We don't need more judges," Burdick said, "just more efficient ones." Acting in line with his idea that Congress should take a more active role in judicial reform, Burdick saw to it that in 1973 the subcommittee worked to evolve objective principles to guide its decisions on the creation of new judgeships. The subcommittee heard testimony for 15 days, scrutinizing the present workload of the judge in each district where a new post was recommended by the Judicial Conference.

"Thorough inquiry was made concerning the workload of the judges...the number of days spent on the bench, the use made of U.S. magistrates, the use made of various court procedures and techniques leading to the settlement of...cases...and the amount of time spent by active judges of the particular district in holding court in other judicial districts," the report said. Applying its new criteria, the subcommittee cut the number of recommended judgeships almost in half.

Looking back, Burdick commented that in the 1960s "there were two ways to go to improve the situation: create more judgeships or develop new procedures to relieve the congestion. We moved on both fronts." The court administrators, he noted, have relieved the chief circuit appeals judges of much "bookwork," and the magistrates are functioning in many districts practically as "sub-judges." These two developments alone, he says, "have made efficient operations possible in the early stages of the judicial process."

Emphasizing his point, Burdick noted figures showing that in 1968 the average number of cases terminated by a federal district judge was 310; three years later, despite the creation of additional judgeships, the rate had risen only slightly—to 315. But in 1972, the first full year in which the magistrate system was in operation, the termination rate jumped to 358.

"We now see a turn-around," Burdick said. "The latest report from the Administrative Office of the U.S. Courts shows a clear downward trend in filings. For about three years they had been tapering downward; this year they definitely turned down."

The chief justice, in his continuing expression of concern for the overloaded system, "hasn't given due weight to the downward trend in filings," said Burdick.

Burger was clearly keeping his eye on the progress made within the system, however, although he perhaps interpreted the need for further improvement differently. On Sept. 20, 1973, Burger issued a statement taking pleased note of the fact that in fiscal 1973 federal judges had settled cases at a rate 30 per cent above that of fiscal 1968. "The adoption of modern techniques,...(and) judges working harder than ever before," were responsible for this improvement, he said. But he reiterated the need for the additional judge manpower requested in order that some dent might be made in the backlog mounting up to some 126,000 cases.

Cutting the Caseload

"The federal court system is for a limited purpose," Burger reminded the nation in his 1970 state of the judiciary speech, signaling the second thrust of his effort to deal with the administrative problems of the judiciary. "Lawyers, the Congress and the public must examine each demand they make on that system."

"We don't need more judges...just more efficient judges."

—Sen. Quentin N. Burdick

Directing attention to changes which could reduce the flood of cases into the federal judicial system, Burger suggested a number of measures:

• Requiring a 'court impact statement' to accompany any bill reported from a congressional committee which would bring more cases into the federal courts. Making this suggestion in 1972, Burger hastened to note that he was not suggesting "that Congress reject legislation simply because it would increase litigation, but only... that Congress consider the needs of the courts."

• Redrawing the jurisdiction of the federal courts to remove cases not involving a substantial federal question. High on the list of matters to be deleted are diversity cases—those involving citizens resident in different states. There is "no rational basis" for these cases being litigated in federal courts instead of state courts, he said. More than one-fourth of all federal civil cases are diversity cases, Burger said in a 1972 interview, giving a typical example: "Suppose a man from Kansas goes to San Francisco...and has an automobile accident there and is injured, with damages estimated to exceed $10,000. Then he can sue in federal district court...instead of the California courts."

• Revising the boundaries and procedure and, possibly the structure, of the federal appellate courts. The National Commission on Revision of the Federal Court Appellate System is expected to submit its report on the suggested boundary revisions in mid-December; its report on the questions of procedure and structure is due in September 1974. The December report was expected to recommend division into two circuits of the Deep South 5th circuit—which Burger in 1971 labeled "an unmanageable, administrative monstrosity"—and of the Northwest 9th circuit, which includes Alaska and Hawaii.

Again more judges are not the primary answer: the 15 members of the court of appeals, 5th circuit, the nation's largest, voted to ask that no more judges be added to their bench but that other methods be considered to ease the burden of their workload. As Burger noted, there is no courtroom in which all 15 judges could comfortably sit to hear a case together.

Change at the Top

"We recommend creation of a National Court of Appeals which would screen all petitions for review now filed in the Supreme Court and hear and decide... many cases of conflicts between the circuits.... Several hundred would be certified annually to the Supreme Court for...choice of cases to be heard."

This highly controversial suggestion of the study group headed by Harvard Law Professor Paul A. Freund was based upon the unit's findings that "the conditions essential for the performance of the conditions essential for the performance of the court's mission do not exist.... (T)he pressures of the docket are incompatible with the appropriate fulfillment of its historic and essential functions."

Chief Justice Warren E. Burger, who had appointed the study group, urged the legal profession and the nation to consider the proposal, and alternative suggestions, seriously. But vocal and highly placed opposition to the idea continued to develop throughout the year after the study group made its recommendation in December 1972. That very month, Justice William O. Douglas, in an opinion, asserted that "the case for our 'over-work' is a myth."

Charging that fundamental damage could be done under the guise of procedural reform, former Chief Justice Earl Warren in May described the proposed court as "a national court of glorified law clerks" which would result in "irreparable harm to the prestige, the power and the function of the Supreme Court." And later in the year, Justice William J. Brennan Jr., in a rare public statement, said that the study group had "regrettably misconceived both the nature and the importance of the screening process.... It is a task that should...be performed only by the members of the court."

Already, some internal changes had been made to provide increased assistance to the nine justices. A third law clerk had been provided and in 1973 the chief justice began experimenting with the idea of a career legal assistant, an experienced attorney who would become part of a justice's staff in place of one of the law clerks, at a higher salary and for a period of time longer than the year or two that law clerks traditionally remain. In addition, the court in 1972 hired its first legal officer, a special problems lawyer, to provide assistance in particularly complex or unusual legal matters.

"Realignment alone is not the answer" either, says Commission Director Leo Levin, a University of Pennsylvania law professor. And so the commission in 1974 will consider other ways to expedite the work of the appeals courts, very likely looking at proposals to create specialized courts of appeals, to merge all the circuits into a national appeals court and perhaps to require that a litigant secure permission from the appeals courts—as now is required from the Supreme Court for most cases—to file an appeal.

Other measures likely to come under scrutiny by the commission—which is composed of men named by the chief justice, the President, the House and the Senate—include measures which might increase the workload of the appeals courts by eliminating the present right of direct appeal—from the district to Supreme Court—for litigants in certain cases. These measures include:

• The elimination of the three-judge district panels now convened to hear cases challenging the constitutionality of state laws. These panels, composed of one appellate and two district judges, cause serious disruption of the work schedules of the courts on which all three men ordinarily sit, Levin noted. Burger, telling the ABA in 1972 that the original reasons for the convening of these courts no longer existed, explained that direct review of these cases has "seriously eroded the Supreme Court's power to control its workload, since appeals from three-judge district courts now account for one of five cases heard." Burger asked for the total elimination of such courts; a bill (S 271) approved in 1973 by the Senate eliminated all but those convened to consider challenges to reapportionment plans.

• Repeal of the Expediting Act which allowed direct appeal to the Supreme Court for litigants in civil antitrust cases. A section of another Senate-approved bill (S 782) would accomplish this.

Supreme Court Overload

The problems of the federal judiciary did not stop short of the Supreme Court, Burger quickly made clear after becoming chief justice. The court's greatest challenge in the 1970s, Burger said in 1971, was simply "to try to keep up with the volume of work that ought to come from this court."

Improvements in the efficiency of district and appellate courts did little to reduce the chief problem of the nation's highest court, a caseload that was growing rapidly, rising from 1,463 in 1953 to 4,640 in 1973. The improved judicial machinery at the lower levels of the system might in fact compound the Supreme Court's problem, by making it possible for the lower courts to handle more cases and thus increasing the number of possible appeals.

The Supreme Court has adopted various innovations within its own structure, chiefly in matters of personnel, but the most controversial of suggested remedies is the proposal that a new court be created to screen cases before they reach the Supreme Court. This was recommended late in 1972 by a study group, appointed by Burger under the aegis of the Federal Judicial Center. *(Box this page)*

Burger has not officially endorsed the concept of a new court, but in August 1973 he renewed his plea for some remedy for the overworked court: "No person who looks at the facts can rationally assume that nine justices today can process four or five times as many cases as the courts that included Taft, Holmes, Brandeis and Hughes ...and do the task as it should be done."

"I prefer that we risk some false starts rather than make no starts at all," Burger told the ABA in his 1973 address. He warned that "dispensing justice is not a matter in which we should provide the bare minimum required to keep judges' heads above water. Justice is not a commodity—and whether people experience the injustice of delay or injustice in some other form it is not as tolerable as denial of some other services we ask from government."

LEGAL PROFESSION SUBJECT TO CONFLICTING PRESSURES

The legal profession which once seemed securely anchored to traditional practices and conservative values is busy today trying to determine if the activism of young lawyers and law students has brought lasting changes. The profession may still be predominantly conservative and traditional, but nobody is quite sure at this time. One school of thought that is being voiced in numerous books, bar journal articles and other published studies is that all the ferment is only skin deep and, in time, will fade. Another school maintains that even if the commitment to public service is weaker among some of the young lawyers than they pretend, and less than sincere among established law firms with new *pro bono* departments,[1] it is still strong enough to have undermined past smugness. *(Footnotes p. 81)*

In this setting of uncertainty and hope, the American Bar Association conducted its 95th annual meeting Aug. 11-17, 1972, in San Francisco. Indicative of change that was taking place, there were sectional discussions of natural resources law, with its environmental implications, and of minority-group challenges to the present method of financing public school education. Still another topic which received attention, though not on the agenda, was the possibility that soon there may not be enough jobs in the legal profession for all the new and future law-school graduates.

Leon Jaworski of Houston, the ABA president, announced at the association's mid-year meeting at New Orleans in February 1972 that a nine-member Task Force on Professional Utilization had been formed to study the problem. Robert W. Meserve of Boston, who succeeded Jaworski at the conclusion of the San Francisco meeting, said: "If you think we've seen disruption before, think what it would be if we were pouring out 15,000 qualified lawyers each year who could find nothing to do but raise hell with the system."

Total enrollment in the nation's 147 accredited law schools has more than doubled during the past decade and for women it has increased sixfold, as is shown in the following table:

Year	Total law students	Women law students
1961	41,499	1,489
1971	94,469	8,914

Nationally, law schools report an average of about three applicants for every opening while at such prestige schools as Harvard, Yale, Michigan, Pennsylvania, Stanford and the University of California at Berkeley the ration runs as high as 10 to 1. It has been calculated that if the present rate of increase continues, the number of yearly law school graduates will double by 1974 and result, by 1985, in a doubling of the entire legal profession's membership, now about 350,000.[2]

Legal Career Attractions. Why are so many young men and women attracted to the law as a career? There seem to be many reasons, both idealistic and pragmatic. To some it is "where the action is"—where the reform-minded individual can make the law a tool "to turn the system around." Others may be impressed with the availability of jobs and the relatively high pay, especially in a time of job scarcity in many other professions.

Despite the current talk of too many lawyers in the years ahead, the picture is not entirely bleak. A Supreme Court ruling in June 1972 that every defendant in a criminal case was entitled to an attorney was described editorially in *The Washington Post* as "the 1972 employment act for lawyers." Moreover, a number of observers see American society becoming increasingly legalistic.[3] As for income, students may well be attracted by statistics showing that the earnings of lawyers more than quadrupled between 1950 and 1970, going up from $6,000 to $25,000 a year on the average, while the cost of living increased by just 61 per cent.

Still others may wish to follow a family tradition, or share in glory that covers such diverse heroes as Perry Mason and Justice Holmes. Many regard the law as a stepping stone to leadership in politics. Twenty-two of the 36 American Presidents have been lawyers.[4] About 60 per cent of the men and women serving in the national and state legislatures come from the legal profession. Lawyers are frequently named to high positions in government and as heads of universities, corporations and foundations. The presidents of Harvard, Yale and Chicago are all former law professors.

Theoretically, the law-school graduate has a wide variety of career choices—from the Wall Street law firm to the metropolitan legal-aid office, and from government service to private practice in a small town. The opportunities, in fact, depend to a great extent on the law school he attended and his performance there. It is estimated that 70 to 75 per cent of the large Wall Street firms are staffed by honor graduates of Harvard, Yale and Columbia law schools. The graduate can expect a starting salary of $16,000 or more at the better-known firms. Senior partners may earn $200,000 to $700,000 a year. Richard M. Nixon earned $300,000 a year at the Wall Street firm of Mudge, Rose, Guthrie, and Alexander— $100,000 above his presidential salary.

Between 200,000 and 250,000 lawyers, roughly two-thirds of the total, are in private practice. Of these, more than 100,000 are in practice alone. Most of them put in long hours for relatively low pay, an average of $15,000 a year, according to a study conducted in 1971 by *Forbes* magazine. However, they have control over the cases they accept, the hours they keep and the way they deal with their clients. The remaining private practitioners are in partnership. *Forbes* found that the larger firm, the more each partner tends to make. "An ordinary partner in a six-man firm gets $35,000; he gets $45,000 in a nine-man firm and roughly $50,000 to $125,000 in one of the 50 largest firms with 10 to 200 men."[5] Lawyers who are not in private practice, almost 100,000 altogether, work for the government and for corporations in about equal numbers. Government lawyers were reported to make as much as solo practitioners, and company counsels as much as lower-level partners in large firms.

Many young lawyers see the law as a vehicle for social change and are attracted to it for that reason. *Fortune* writer Peter Vanderwicken traces the origin of this activism to the summer of 1964 when some 400 law students and young lawyers went to Mississippi to defend civil-rights workers who were enrolling Negroes to vote. "They discovered there that the blacks' problems were compounded by their inability to get legal advice and protection."[6]

Activism of Young Lawyers. Since that time the activists have discovered other causes, including poverty, consumerism, the environment, and the Viet Nam war. "Poverty Lawyers," who are continuing what the civil rights lawyers started, aid the poor and blacks in cases arising from discrimination, consumer fraud and similar matters. A well known, and controversial, public legal program for the poor is the legal services program of the Office of Economic Opportunity (OEO). It was established as part of President Johnson's war on poverty in 1965 and has continued to stay alive—even grow—despite criticism from former Vice President Spiro T. Agnew, among others, for using government-paid attorneys to sue some other agency of government.

The program has been endorsed by the ABA and has had enough support in Congress to survive annual budget battles. The agency's 2,000 lawyers operate about 250 community programs and concentrate on services for the 25.5 million Americans who fall below the officially defined poverty line.

Still another type of public-service lawyer is personified by Ralph Nader. His work for the American consumer has attracted a host of young volunteers to his many investigative activities.[7] A lawyer who is considerably more controversial than either the poverty lawyer or those of the Nader stamp is the political radical who specializes in defending draft evaders, anti-war groups, drug defendants, Black Panthers, and other political and social rebels. William Kunstler, Michael Tigar, and Leonard Boudin are among the best known of the leftist attorneys who have aroused a storm of criticism.

The most prominent critic has been U.S. Chief Justice Warren E. Burger. In a speech before the American Law Institute on May 18, 1971, Burger asserted:

> All too often, overzealous advocates seem to think the zeal and effectiveness of a lawyer depend on how thoroughly he can disrupt the proceedings or how loud he can shout or how close he can come to insulting all those he encounters—including the judges.... At the drop of a hat—or less—we find adrenal-fueled lawyers cry out that theirs is a 'political trial.' This seems to mean in today's context-at least to some—that rules of evidence, canons of ethics and codes of professional conduct—the necessity for civility—all become irrelevant.... I submit that lawyers who know how to think but have not learned how to behave are a menace and a liability, not an asset, to the administration of justice.

Burger's philosophy of "judicial restraint" also clashes with the activism of many young lawyers who do not necessarily share the radicals' ideas and methods. In an interview with *The New York Times,* published July 4, 1971, Burger said: "Young people who decide to go into law primarily on the theory that they can change the world by litigation in the courts I think may be in for some disappointments.... That is not the route by which basic changes in the country should be made."

The National Lawyers Guild often is the institutional home of radical lawyers. The Guild was started in 1937 by leftist lawyers and Communist Party members. During the McCarthy era it lost much of its standing and most of its members. There were only a few hundred members in four chapters in the mid-1960s. But by 1971 the Guild claimed 3,000 members, 43 chapters and an annual budget of more than $200,000. Members are unabashedly political. A Guild pamphlet states: "Certainly one role of the radical lawyer is to use whatever legal procedures are available on behalf of those struggling against the system.... An organization which believes in basic social change can and must be revolutionary, particularly in the way it confronts institutions and defines itself."

Many Guild members also participate in law communes, accepting cases on the basis of whether they help radical causes. Salaries of commune members are based on need rather than on case load. The top salary is usually about $175 a week and few of these attorneys earn more than $10,000 a year. Some cases are handled free. Decisions on which cases to accept are made collectively. Mike Haroz, founder of the Cambridge (Mass.) Law Commune, told an interviewer: "We operate on the principle of picking and choosing political groups and political activities we want to be involved in...those that would generally advance the kind of left movement now going on in the country."[8]

Question of Commitment. A Gallup Poll taken for *Redbook* magazine in January 1971 found that of 137 graduating law students at 20 of the nation's leading law schools, Nader, the public-service lawyer, was the person they admired most. But at Columbia University Law School, a questionnaire in the spring of 1971 showed that only four of the 136 third-year students said they had accepted public-service jobs whereas 88 said they planned to work for private law firms. Mrs. Ruth Traynor, then the director of the school's placement office, told a reporter from *The Wall Street Journal:* "When the graduates have to choose between public service and a $16,000 a year salary. I'm cynical enough to believe that the dollar sign wins out."

Derek Bok, the president of Harvard University who was formerly dean of its law school, wrote in the *Harvard Alumni Bulletin* in the fall of 1971: "Critics such as Ralph Nader, Edgar (S.) Cahn and Mark (J.) Green have asserted that students from leading law schools seem much less inclined to go to established law firms.... One still looks in vain for reliable factual support for these claims. Despite the sincere interest of many students in social service and the advocacy of unpopular causes, the alternatives to the law firm are unlikely to attract them in the end."

In response, Green wrote that his first impulse was "to do verbal battle" with Bok on the issue but "Now I write...to admit error." He added: "The tide of change now seems only a trickle, and the longevity of law student activism has equaled that of the Nehru jacket. For while many law students are still speaking the rhetoric of the advocacy profession—perhaps even slaying some legal dragons during summers or in class—most still go to work for corporate law firms when the moment of decision arrives."[9]

Robert F. Buckhorn, in his book *Nader: The People's Lawyer* (1972), writes that Nader's vision of a public-interest bar is questioned by detractors who say he cannot realistically expect lawyers to be more self-sacrificing than persons in other professions or society as a whole. They say money must be provided, and over the long term. "Nader doesn't dispute this," Buckhorn adds. "He realizes that money from foundations is not long-term financing, and government financing is too controversial and too restrictive. His real hope is that the legal community itself will supply much of the funding needed to make public interest attractive." Nader has proposed that lawyers give 10 per cent of their earnings to public-service law.

Lawyers in America

Almost all blueprints for an ideal society—from Thomas More's *Utopia* to Karl Marx's *Communist Manifesto*—have dispensed with lawyers. Marx believed that the legal profession was part of the capitalist structure that kept the workers subjugated. Immediately following both the French and Russian revolutions, the legal profession was proscribed. But in a less-than-perfect world, it has been the lawyers and not the utopians who have thrived.

Colonial America, deeply suspicious of English common law and its harshness toward dissenters, visualized a new society without lawyers. To the Puritan emigre, the practice of law was a "dark and knavish business." In New England, the clergy dispensed justice according to the "word of God." The Quakers sought to establish a system of "amicable adjustment of relations by friendly neighbors." By the early 18th century, however, most colonists had come to realize the futility of law by biblical injunction and the wastefulness of allowing each man to be his own advocate. The need for lawyers was acknowledged but the profession itself continued to be held in low esteem. John Adams wrote in 1759: "Looking about me in the country I found the practice of law grasped into the hands of deputy sheriff's, pettifoggers and even constables who filled all the writs upon bonds, promissory notes, and accounts, received the fees established for lawyers, and stirred up many unnecessary suits."[10]

Around 1765, in reaction against these untrained and unethical practitioners, a number of lawyers, some trained at the Inns of Court in England, tried to correct the abuses. A number of reformers became political leaders. Twenty-five of the 56 signers of the Declaration of Independence and 31 of the 55 delegates to the Constitutional Convention of 1787 were lawyers.

Ambivalence Toward Lawyers. Still. There was a profound distrust of professionalism, which was looked on as undemocratic. John Dudley, a New Hampshire Supreme Court justice early in the 19th century, summed up this feeling: "Gentlemen, you have heard what has been said in this case by the lawyers, the rascals.... They talk of law. Why gentlemen, it is not law we want, but justice. They would govern us by the common law of England. Common sense is a much safer guide.... It is our duty to do justice between the parties, not by any quirks of the law out of Coke or Blackstone—books that I never read and never will."[11]

Public ambivalence toward the legal profession has continued to the present day. There is on the one hand the picture of the lawyer as a shyster, a fixer, and an ambulance chaser. Balancing this is the Louis Auchincloss figure of the dignified, attractive counselor and the Ralph Nader-type fighter for the rights of the underdog. A study of the public's attitude toward lawyers, undertaken by the Missouri Bar Association in 1960, recorded more negative than positive feelings about the legal profession. Of the 6,000 persons who responded to a questionnaire, the majority rated lawyers below bankers, clergymen, doctors, dentists and teachers. Those who had retained a lawyer thought less highly of the profession than those who had not. Only 37 per cent of the respondents said they thought lawyers were honest and truly dedicated to their work; almost 57 per cent of those who had dealt with lawyers thought that they created lawsuits unnecessarily.[12]

Organizations of lawyers go back to pre-Revolutionary times and the first state bar association originated in New Hampshire as early as 1788. However, by the second third of the 19th century these organizations had disbanded or become purely social clubs. Professions and particularly organized professional groups were deemed un-American and undemocratic. The revival of professional organizations for lawyers can be said to have begun in 1870. In February of that year, the first meeting of the Association of the Bar of the City of New York was held and a constitution adopted which pledged "to maintain the honor and dignity of the profession, to cultivate social intercourse among its members, and to increase its usefulness in promoting the due administration of justice." Between 1870 and 1878, eight city and eight state bar associations were established in 12 states.

Bar Associations in United States. The American Bar Association, the first national organization for lawyers, was formed at Saratoga Springs, N.Y., in 1878. For the first 25 years of its existence, the ABA was primarily a social organization composed of conservative, wealthy East Coast attorneys. Its aims were the improvement of legal education, the tightening of standards for admission to the bar, and the adoption of uniform state laws. In the early years of the 20th century, the activities and membership of the organization grew rapidly and its orientation changed. The ABA adopted a code of ethics in 1908 and took a stand on controversial issues, beginning in 1903 when it issued a report condemning business monopoly. In 1914 the ABA advocated the adoption of a uniform workmen's compensation act, and in 1917 its Conference of Bar Association Delegates recommended that all bar associations foster legal aid societies.

During the 1920s, the association continued to take a liberal stand on issues—for the regulation of business, the abolition of "lame duck" sessions of Congress, U.S. support of the Permanent Court of International Justice, and legislation to facilitate the peaceful adjustment of labor disputes. Since 1923 the association has carried on a program of law school inspection and approval. Membership has grown from 552 in 1880 to about 150,000 today.

During the past few years there have been widening divisions between conservative and liberal members on the legality of the war in Viet Nam and the conduct of some activist lawyers in the courtroom. Probably the most publicized of recent ABA actions has been its recommendations on the judicial qualifications of Supreme Court nominees. The association's Committee on the Federal Judiciary was widely criticized for having approved the fitness of Clement Haynsworth in 1969 and J. Harrold Carswell in 1970. Both were federal judges named to the Supreme Court by President Nixon but rejected by the Senate.

The committee, which had been evaluating the qualifications of Supreme Court nominees since 1950, gave a rating other than "qualified" for the first time in 1971. Given a list of six potential nominees, the committee found one of them, Herschel H. Friday of Little Rock, to be "unqualified"; it deadlocked in a 6 to 6 vote on a motion of being "not opposed" to another of the six, Judge Mildred L. Lillie of the California Court of Appeals at Los Angeles. In fact, none of the six was nominated,[13] and John N. Mitchell, then the Attorney General, said the Nixon administration would no longer ask the ABA to review nominations. He accused it of making "unauthorized disclosure" of the names under consideration.

Changes in Legal Training. Until well into the second half of the 19th century, most lawyers received their training by assisting an established attorney and by reading law in his office. "The lawyers of those days were reluctant to accept the idea of university training. They clung tenaciously to the notion that legal education was nothing more than the mastering of a craft, the skills for which had to be passed on from the practitioner to the novice."[14] A small number of lawyers did seek insitutional legal training. During the colonial period, the wealthier young men were sent to England to study at the Inns of Court. The College of William and Mary, upon the advice of Thomas Jefferson, began giving legal instruction in 1779. Five years later, the first independent law school was opened in Litchfield. Conn. In its 50 years of existence, the Litchfield Law School was attended by over 1,000 students, among whom were John C. Calhoun and Horace Mann. Its alumni included 129 members of Congress, 34 Supreme Court justices, and 14 governors. Profesor Joel Parker of Harvard Law School wrote later: "Perhaps no law school has had—perhaps I may add ever will have—so great a proportion of distinguished men on its catalogue."[15]

Harvard established the first university-connected law school in 1817, attracting a first-year class of six students. The number of law schools and students grew slowly at first. By 1870 there were 31 law schools and about 1,700 students. Almost any young man wishing to attend was accepted. Standards were low; the usual requirement for the LL.B—bachelor of laws—degree was completion of a four-to-six month session followed by passage of a brief oral examination. The situation at Harvard Law School, considered the best in the country, prompted Oliver Wendell Holmes Jr., the Supreme Court justice, to write in 1870: "The condition of the Harvard Law School has been almost a disgrace to the Commonwealth of Massachusetts."

The year 1870 marks the beginning of modern legal education in the United States. Law schools began to establish more stringent educational requirements for admission, some states started making specific training a prerequisite for the practice of law, and most important of all, a New York lawyer named Christopher Columbus Langdell was made dean of Harvard Law School. Langdell set high standards for faculty and students, and he introduced the "case method" to replace the lecture system. The method relied primarily on class discussion of actual court cases. The instructor became merely a discussion leader. Gradually, over considerable opposition, the case method was accepted by most of the country's law schools.

The ABA was also influential in pressing for quality legal education. Under the chairmanship of Elihu Root, the section on legal education issued a report in 1922 recommending minimum standards for law schools, inspection by the ABA, and a listing of schools that met its approval. Another factor leading to the improvement of the country's law schools was the establishment of the National Conference of Bar Examiners in 1931. This organization tended to make educational standards for admission to the bar more uniform and to ensure that the law schools prepared their students for the exam. By the mid-20th century, most ABA-approved law schools required four years of undergraduate study followed by three years of law study. Until recent times, most law schools were open only to men. The exceptions were Michigan, Yale and Cornell which admitted women in the latter part of the 19th century. Women were excluded at Columbia until 1929 and at Harvard until 1950.

Even more difficult was the women's fight for admission to bar associations and to status positions in the profession. In 1899 the National Association of Women Lawyers (NAWL) was formed because the ABA barred women members. It finally consented to admit women in 1943 but even in 1972 only two women are among the 315 members of the ruling House of Delegates.[16] After years of suffering job discrimination the woman law-school graduate may now be more sought after by law firms than her male counterpart, according to a Columbia University Law School report issued March 13, 1972. It said that the job market for graduating law students had changed dramatically within the past year, with more jobs going to women and fewer to blacks.

Large Law Firms. The history of the legal profession in the United States is closely linked to the economic philosophy of the particular era in which it existed. In the Jacksonian period, when a frontier-style democracy flourished, the profession was open to almost anyone able to meet a few minimum requirements. With the enormous growth of American industry toward the end of the 19th century, the more ambitious members of the bar left the courtroom for the executive suite. As such, they served big business as "adviser, counselor, administrator of affairs—in contrast to the image of the frock-coated Daniel Webster, which was the mid-19th century sterotype of the bar."[17] The "railroad lawyer" became the first symbol of this change in the generation after the Civil War.

Law firms were first established in cities—notably New York and Chicago—where financial and industrial power was concentrated. Their growth was slow until the early 20th century. In 1872 only one New York City firm had more than five partners and by 1900 only two had more than eight. By 1948 there were 284 law firms in the country with eight partners or more. Seventy-three of these firms were in New York and 25 in Chicago. The growth of large law firms brought on a degree of specializaton; a large corporate client could obtain a number of different services from the firm.

Legal specialization has long been an object of criticism. In a speech before the American Bar Association in 1910, Woodrow Wilson warned that specialization removed many of the nation's leading lawyers from any contact with important pulbic issues and causes. Supreme Court Justice Harlan F. Stone told the 1934 graduating class at the University of Michigan:

> Steadily the best skill and capacity of the profession has been drawn into the exacting and highly specialized service of business and finance. At its best the changed system has brought to the command of the business world loyalty and a superb proficiency and technical skill. At its worst it has made the learned profession of an earlier day the obsequious servant of business, and tainted it with the morals and manners of the market place in its most antisocial manifestations.

Adolf A. Berle Jr., a specialist in corporation law and finance, wrote at about the same time in a similar vein: "Many of the great American law firms of today, recognized as the leaders of the bar, owe their origin to the safe navigation of clients through some scandal of the latter part of the 19th century: the defense of the Tweed ring, the safeguarding of the interests of Jay Gould in Erie, the wreck of the Pere Marquette railroad.... The law firm became virtually an annex to some group of financial promoters, manipulators or industrialists; and such firms have dominated the organized profession although they have contributed little of thought, less of philosophy and nothing at all of responsibility or idealism. What they have contributed, however, is the creation of a legal framework for the new economic system, built largely around the modern corporation."[18]

Ever since the government began to take an active part in the direction of American business in the New Deal days, the Washington lawyer has been an object of widespread interest. In his book *The Superlawyers* (1972), Joseph C. Goulden writes: "The Washington Lawyer[19] is an important figure in contemporary America because he is often the interface that holds together the economic partnership of business and government. In the decades following the New Deal, at a pace that sharply accelerated during the 1960s, some Washington Lawyers directed a counter-revolution unique in world economic history. Their mission was not to destroy the New Deal, and its successor reform acts, but to conquer them, and to leave their structures intact so they could be transformed into instruments for the amassing of monopolistic corporate power."

Goulden maintains that the Washington Lawyer in recent decades has stepped beyond the attorney's tradidtional role as legal representative. "The Washington Lawyer affects public policy when it is being shaped in the Congress and the regulatory agencies and in the executive departments, either as a proponent of original ideas or in reaction to those from elsewhere. He is a markedly more sophisticated man than knee-jerk conservatives of the 1930s, for he recognizes the government as a source of subsidies, as a partner in legalized price fixing, as a deterrent to competition. The lawyer's historic role was

that of advising clients how to *comply* with the law. The Washington Lawyer's present role is that of advising clients how to *make* laws, and to make the most of them."

Access to the Law

A common theme underlies much of the criticism of the American legal system. It is that many people are denied access to the law because they cannot pay the prevailing legal fees.[20] Lawyers have outpriced themselves," Ralph Nader has said. "They have permitted the legal system to be congested, and justice delayed. Most Americans, in effect, have very little access to the legal system to resolve their complaints grievances."[21] Charges vary from lawyer to lawyer and from area to area. Some leading lawyers on Wall Street and in Washington charge $250 an hour for consultation while small-town practitioners may settle for $10 or less.

Lawyers charge by the hour, by the job or by a percentage of the amount they win for the client. The percentage or contingency fee is used extensively in cases involving personal injury, wills, property and taxes. It is outlawed in divorce matters, criminal proceedings, lobbying, and the negotiation of government contracts. The only advantage of the percentage system for the client is that the lawyer may receive nothing if he loses the case. Contingency fees are often criticized as excessive. The *Consumer Newsletter* reported: "Some lawyers ask for 25 per cent, others ask for 50 per cent—not including expenses. In Miami, a 10 year-old boy injured in an auto accident was awarded $2,578. The lawyer demanded $1,260 as his fee, and tacked on $657 for expenses. The kid was left with a little over a quarter of his award: $661."[22]

There are no limits on the amount a lawyer may ask for his services. However, minimum-fee schedules have been set in about two-thirds of the states. Because county bar associations usually draw up the schedules, there is often great variance from place to place. Minimum fees, it has been pointed out appeal to lawyers for several reasons:

> They are a helpful guide to beginners, and in difficult fee-setting situations can be helpful to experienced lawyers as well. They tend to reduce client dissatisfaction and apprehension that the lawyer is overcharging him.... But the major attraction...is that they help keep fees up and reduce competition based on the price of services. As most schedules are periodically revised upwards, they are a means of raising fees. Depending on who is talking about them, they can be considered as preventing cutthroat competition or as encouraging monopoly price fixing."[23]

If the client feels that the fee is too high he can appeal to the bar association which sets the fee scale or he can hire another lawyer to sue the first one—and pay another minimum fee for that case. Lawyers who charge less than the minimum fee are courting trouble. The ABA's Committee on Professional Ethics and Grievances stated in 1961 that while lawyers are not forced to charge the minimum, "the habitual charging of fees less than those established by a minimum fee schedule, or the charging of such fees without proper justification, may be evidence of unethical conduct."

Curricula Revision. The American Bar Foundation, with funding from the Ford Foundation, has sponsored a study of what the legal profession is doing to help more people gain access to the law. The study, headed by F. Raymond Marks,[24] shows that many law firms are engaged in *pro bono* work far more than they were only a few years ago. Law schools also have revised their curricula to meet the demands that they train their students for public service. Mark J. Green, in his writing, has called the traditional law school "a boot camp for corporate lawyering" where students were told "what was really worth studying" was "corporation law, accounting and taxation (otherwise known as making money, counting money and keeping it from the government)." Ralph Nader has found fault with law schools on many counts.

"Normative thinking—the 'shoulds' and the 'oughts' —was not part and parcel of rigorous analytic skills." he wrote in 1969. "The nation's law schools downplayed the normative inquiry as something of an intellectual pariah. Thus the great legal challenges of access to large governmental and corporate institutions, the control of environmental pollution, the requisites of international justice suffered from the inattention of mechanical minds."

> Courses on estate planning proliferated (he continued); there were none for environmental planning until a few years ago. Other courses dealt with collapsible corporations, but the cupboard was bare for any student interested in collapsing tenements. Creditors' rights were studied deeply; debtors' remedies were passed by shallowly. Coursees tracking the lucre and the prevailing ethos did not embrace any concept of professional sacrifice and service to the unrepresented poor or public interests being crushed by concern of legal charity, to be dispensed by starved legal aid societies.[25]

At the time Nader wrote his indictment of law schools, many of them were extensively revising their curricula. A survey conducted by the Association of American Law Schools showed that 126 courses in environmental law were offered by law schools in 1970. The Council on Legal Education for Professional Responsibility, a group sponsored by the Ford Foundation, found that 100 of the 107 law schools it contacted in 1970 allowed students to receive credit for work in community legal-aid offices, OEO Neighborhood Law Programs and public-interest law firms.

The emphasis is on "clinical"—in contrast to classroom—work. Public-interest law firms have been founded in several major cities, often with financial backing from foundations, and are largely staffed by students who receive academic credit from their law schools. Antioch College at Yellow Springs, Ohio, opened a law school in Washington, D.C., in September 1972 which is described as "a totally new institution, functioning both as a law firm with the Urban Law Institute as its nucleus and as a law school—similar to a medical school's affiliation with a hospital."[26] More than a thousand applications were received for the opening class of 125 students. Plans also include the training of about 15 persons in an 18-month course as "certified legal technicians." It is hoped that they may relieve lawyers of some duties and thus cut client costs.

The Urban Law Institute was founded in 1968 by a black civil rights lawyer, Jean Camper Cahn, as an OEO pilot project for reforming legal education. She and her husband, Edgar S. Cahn, who are credited with drawing up the OEO's legal services program, will be co-deans of the Antioch Law School. The institute was a part of the George Washington University Law School until February 1972. That school's dean, Robert Kramer, said he felt it was inappropriate for a law school or university to be "a plaintiff or moving party in any proceedings in any court or before any administrative body." While it was associated with the university, the institute brought several class-action suits against federal and local agencies.

Pre-Paid Legal Services. While the focus of recent efforts in the legal profession is on providing legal services for the poor, there is also concern that a vast segment of the middle class has been priced out of the nation's law offices. And this group of Americans, as many as 140-million by some estimates, are disqualified by their income levels from receiving free legal assistance. Speeking before the 1971 annual meeting of the Nebraska Bar Association, ABA President-elect Robert W. Meserve said: "We must concern ourselves with the vast middle economic group...having the ability to pay for legal services. This ability must be enhanced by arrangement that make payment less onerous and painful."

Since 1967 when the Supreme Court ruled that the United Mine Workers Union had "the right to hire attorneys on a salary basis to assist its members in the assertion of their legal rights," a number of organizations and unions have established pre-paid legal services. These programs are somewhat akin to the Blue Cross plan of health insurance. The three states which require disclosure of pre-paid legal plans—California, Florida and Missouri—report that more than 200 are in operation. Meserve estimated in September 1971 that as many as 4,000 might be in existence throughout the nation.[27]

The ABA itself is a sponsor of a project started in January 1971 at Shreveport, La., to provide pre-paid legal services to about 600 union members and their families. Each worker contributes about two cents an hour of his wages for a comprehensive package of legal benefits and a free choice of lawyers. The State Bar of California has contemplated starting a statewide "Legalcare" program modeled on the Kaiser Health Foundation plan. Members of participating organizations would pay $5 a month for basix legal services covering most foreseeable needs. For $10 a month, the member would get complete coverage as well as the right to iniate suits, and for a few dollars more, he could obtain coverage for his whole family.

Leon Jaworski has warned, however, that private plans for legal services may develop outside the framework of the legal profession and not be subject to its ethical standards. His warning comes at a time when complaints against both lawyers and judges over alleged misconduct are reported to be rising. For many years, national, state and local bar associations have been studying the ethical standards of the profession. There has been close to unanimous agreement that the organized bar is failing to police its own ranks. The study groups found that bar associations usually do not act until a formal complaint is made, that lawyers are reluctant to report their errant colleagues, that grievance committees are plagued with inadequate staffing and financial resources, that their procedures are invariably slow, complex and conducted in secrecy, that many lawyers found guilty are able to continue practicing law while appeals drag on for years, and that disbarred lawyers in one locality sometimes resume their practice elsewhere.

Complaints against judges are usually voiced privately—only rarely in a formal sense—by the lawyers who practice before them. The matter of misbehavior on the bench, whether it involves bribery or verbal abuse, prompted California in 1961 to set up a special commission to handle complaints against judges. Twenty-seven other states and the District of Columbia have adopted similar procedures although few judges have been censured. In California, only two of the state's 1,100 judges have been censured in the past 11 years.[28]

There are broader questions of ethics that have been asked since the beginning of the legal profession but have been brought back to heated discussion in recent years upon the insistent demand of law students and young activist lawyers. The questions deal essentially with defining the lawyer's proper role in society. Is it his duty always to see that justice is served, or only to see that his client is served if the client and justice do not happen to be on the same side? It is argued in the legal profession that the client has been too well served, especially if he happened to be rich. Much of the profession's current concern with its own well-being seems to focus on redressing the imbalance.

1 From the Latin *pro bono publico,* meaning for the common good. These firms provide legal services free or at low cost to the poor.

2 The 1971 *Lawyer Statistical Report,* based on data provided by the *Martindale and Hubbel* legal directory for the year 1970, listed the number of persons admitted to practice in the United States as 355,242. However, it was assumed that several thousand were not actually engaged in the practice of law.

3 For example, Robert H. Bork, a professor of law at Yale, has written: "In universities...presidents and deans are stripped of wide areas of discretion, rights and duties are spelled out, special tribunals for indictment, trial, and appeal are created. The analogy to formal legal systems is so powerful that these procedures begin to pick up elements of due process, right to counsel...and so forth."—*Fortune,* December 1971.

4 All except Washington, Madison, William H. Harrison, Taylor, Andrew Johnson, Grant, Garfield, T. R. Roosevelt, Harding, Hoover, Truman, Eisenhower, Kennedy and Johnson.

5 "The Gilt-Edged Profession," *Forbes,* Sept. 16, 1971, p. 38.

6 Peter Vanderwicken, "The Angry Young Lawyers." *Fortune,* September 1971, p. 77.

7 For details on Nader's organizations, see Congressional Quarterly *Weekly Report.* June 17, 1972, p. 1474.

8 Quoted by Lansing R. Shepard in *The Christian Science Monitor,* May 15, 1971.

9 Mark J. Green. "The Young Lawyers, 1972: Goodby to Pro Bono." *New York,* Feb. 21, 1972, p. 29.

10 Quoted by Roscoe Pound. *The Lawyer from Antiquity to Modern Times* (1953). p. 143.

11 Quoted by Erwin W. Griswold in *Law and Lawyers in the United States* (1965), p. 13.

12 Murray T. Bloom. *The Trouble with Lawyers* (1968), p. 333.

13 Two others, Lewis F. Powell Jr. of Richmond, Va., a former ABA president, and William H. Rehnquist, an assistant attorney general, were nominated and confirmed.

14 Albert P. Blausten and Charles O. Porter, *The American Lawyer* (1954), p. 166.

15 Quoted by Griswold, *op. cit.,* p. 41.

16 Some 9,103 women lawyers were counted in the United States in 1970.

17 James Willared Hurst. *The Growth of American Law* (1950). p. 305.

18 A. A. Berle Jr., *Encyclopedia of Social Sciences.* Vol. 9 (1933), p. 341

19 Goulden writes Washington Lawyer with a capital L. to distinguish him from the lawyer who happens to practice in the District of Columbia but involves himself in local litigation. He is a Washington lawyer without the capital L.

20 It is a firmly held belief in the legal profession that with access to a lawyer, the citizen is denied access to the law. A law professor has explained: "Non-lawyers can give advice on certain questions.... But with any case that has elements of novelty, the layman will not know how to relate the facts to legal issues."—Richard A. Posner. *The Law School Record* (University of Chicago), winter 1972, p. 19.

21 Quoted by Robert F. Buckhorn in *Nader: The People's Lawyer* (1972), p. 125.

22 *Consumer Newsletter,* Sept. 20, 1971.

23 Quintin Johnstone and Dan Hopson Jr., *Lawyers and Their Work* (1967), pp. 62-63.

24 Published in book form as *The Lawyer,* the Public, and Professional Responsibility (1972).

25 Ralph Nader, "Law Schools and Law Firms." *The New Republic,* Oct. 11, 1969, p. 21, 1969, p. 2.

26 *Antioch School of Law Nesletter,* Dec. 13, 1971.

27 *American Bar Association News,* Sept. 30, 1971.

28 According to figures reported by Lesley Oelsner in *The New York Times,* June 9, 1972.

JURY TRIAL UNDERGOING REEXAMINATION AND CHANGE

Deeply rooted in the American concept of freedom under law is the role of government as protector of the individual citizen—protector against abuse of power by officials of the government, and against harm from law-breaking individuals. At the heart of the concept is the system of justice, epitomized by the trial before a jury of one's peers. Today, the jury system is in a period of re-examination and change.

Congress acted in 1968 to require the inclusion of minority races, particularly Blacks, in the jury selection process. The Supreme Court ruled in 1970 that juries of fewer than 12 persons could hear state criminal cases, and on May 22, 1972, it upheld non-unanimous verdicts that had been obtained against defendants in state criminal courts. When the Supreme Court ruled, only 14 states[1] allowed juries of smaller size and only two, Louisiana and Oregon, allowed non-unanimous verdicts in felony cases. Now it is a question for the individual states to decide whether they will retain existing jury requirements or change them. *(Footnotes, p. 87)*

The non-unanimous rule has become subject to controversy in legal circles as a "law and order" decision obtained largely through President Nixon's appointees to the Supreme Court. It has been defended and denounced as a way of making convictions easier to obtain in criminal cases. And it has entered the political arena. The National Association for the Advancement of Colored People called on NAACP branches at its 1972 convention in July to lobby in the legislatures against state adoption of split verdicts.

There is little likelihood of a pell-mell rush by states to permit split verdicts in trials for serious offenses. The American Bar Association's handbook, "Trial by Jury," which recommends minimum standards for jury trials, points out that "the constitutions of the great majority of states" require unanimous verdicts. The process of constitutional change is slow and often deliberately cumbersome to give adequate time for public debate. In 21 states, however, the highest court in the state exercises complete rule-making authority in trials. In at least one state, Florida, the attorney general has asked for a rules change to permit non-unanimous verdicts.[2] If the Florida Supreme Court does not grant the change, he said he would take the issue to the legislature. Florida's trial procedures are controlled by both the high court and legislature.

It appears likely that before other states follow the Louisiana and Oregon example of allowing split verdicts in felony trials, they will take the lesser step of applying the rule in misdemeanor cases. Jury unanimity in such cases was not required in Montana, Oklahoma, Texas and Idaho, as well as in Louisiana and Oregon, at the time the Supreme Court rendered its decision.

Fairness, Delay and Disruption. Other events, too, set in motion the reexamination of the American jury system. Its ability to render a fair verdict for militant and minority defendants was roundly questioned, especially in the 1960s. Yale University President Kingman Brewster Jr., for one, declared he was "skeptical of the ability of black revolutionaries to achieve a fair trial anywhere in the United States." Some of his criticism has been dissipated by the refusal of juries to convict in such celebrated cases as Huey Newton's, Bobby Seale's and Angela Davis's. Brewster himself was later to modify his view.

In the meantime, new voices of concern were being raised over matters bearing on the jury system. President Nixon told the National Conference on the Judiciary in March 1971 that crime in the past decade rose 150 per cent. When criminals are caught there are "unconscionable delays," the President said, before they are brought to trial. Although statistical analyses show that only one felony charge out of seven results in a jury trial, the jury trial stands out as a lightning rod attracting criticism of a laggard system of justice. Four months were consumed in questioning 1,035 prospective jurors in the widely publicized 1971 trial of black militants in New Haven, Conn., the longest selection process in the nation's history.

On five occasions in 1970 and 1971, Chief Justice Warren E. Burger criticized defense lawyers who act as though "their zeal and effectiveness depend on how thoroughly they can disrupt the proceedings." The President, in his speech before the National Conference on the Judiciary, denounced "publicity seekers" who disrupt trials. Although the New York Bar later polled 1,600 judges, who reported only 99 cases of courtroom misconduct and only six contempt citations against lawyers, it is the exception that tends to shape public views on courtroom decorum.

Changing Nature of Criticism. Criticism of the jury system heard today differs from that voiced in earlier years in one significant way. Only rarely does a legal scholar suggest anymore that the jury system itself is out of date. In the 1940s and 1950s, it was fashionable to challenge the jury's ability to understand the complexity of "modern" law. Trial before a panel of judges would be a surer guarantee of justice, said critics such as Jerome Frank, a federal judge. "It is inconceivable that a body of 12 ordinary men...could, merely from listening to the instructions of the judge, gain the knowledge necessary to grasp the true import of the judge's words...."[3] Defense of the jury was couched in terms of faint praise. Judge Curtis Bok said trial by jury could never be excised from the Constitution because "the public wisely does not want the best of all possible systems in the best of all possible worlds. What the public has is a reasonably effective way of getting close to the truth but not too close."[4]

A monumental study published in 1966 largely squelched the theory of juror dunderheadedness. This study,[5] undertaken by Harry Kalven Jr. and Hans Zeisel at the University of Chicago Law School on a Ford Foundation grant, is frequently cited in Supreme Court opinions and in law journal treatises. From their research of the verdicts in 3,576 jury trials, the authors found ample evidence that jurors did indeed comprehend the testimony, and 78 per cent of the time reached verdicts with which the judge agreed. When there was disagreement, the jury was less lenient than the judge in 3 per cent of cases, and more lenient in 19 per cent. In their conclusion, the authors expressed admiration for the jury system.

A federal judge who had prior experience as a prosecutor and defense counsel wrote recently that his experiences convinced him that "juries generally perform their task with extraordinary conscientiousness and accuracy."[6] The American jury was not, however, to remain a stabilized institution, exempt from criticism or from fundamental change.

Approval of Small Juries. An attribute of jury trials once considered inviolable in criminal cases—a 12-member jury—was struck down by the Supreme Court June 22, 1970, in a 7-1 decision.[7] In the majority opinion, Justice Byron R. White conceded that English common law, from which much of the American judicial system was derived, did traditionally call for a 12-member jury. However, he said there was nothing in the "scanty history" of the evolvement of jury trial provisions during the Constitutional Convention of 1787 to show that every feature of common law was incorporated intact into the American system. Supreme Court rulings dating back to 1898 held that a criminal jury was by definition a body of 12 members.[8]

The 1970 decision, while holding that the Sixth Amendment guarantee of a fair and speedy trial does not require 12 jurors, did not specify how small a jury might be. "The number should probably be large enough to promote group deliberation, free from outside attempts at intimidation, and to provide a fair possibility for obtaining a fair cross section of the community," Justice White said. He anticipated the argument, made later by some critics of the decision, that the 12-member jury afforded protection to the defendant through safety in numbers. With 12 peers deciding his fate, the accused had a greater chance of finding one holdout for acquittal. White asserted that the argument is double-edged, since the prosecution needs only one holdout to prevent acquittal.

With the question in dispute as to whether a small jury favored the prosecution or the defense, the Supreme Court on the same day held that an accused person unable to pay for legal counsel was entitled to it free of charge at his initial hearing on a criminal charge and that he could insist on a jury trial if he faced a prison term longer than six months.

Some of the ensuing debate over jury size seemed to anticipate the 1972 ruling on non-unanimous verdicts. Hans Zeisel wrote in the *American Bar Association Journal* issue of April 1972, a month before the ruling was handed down, in defense of unanimous verdicts.

> The hung jury (he wrote) is an expression of respect for a strongly held dissenting view; it is one of the many noble features of our jury system.... In a 12-member jury, in which 10 are allowed to find a verdict, one or two minority dissenters can simply be disregarded.... A six-

member jury in which five jurors can find a verdict may still be a jury in name, but in fact it would be an institution very different from the 12-member unanimous jury.

A federal judge who was chairman of the American Bar Association's project to set minimum standards for criminal justice wrote earlier in favor of six-man juries hearing all criminal cases except those involving capital offenses. But he said that non-unanimous verdicts might erode public confidence in the system of justice. "Public support and respect for the jury system, which represents the *ad hoc* judgment of untrained laymen, may be due in large part to the fact that all the jurors agree."[9]

In Oregon, one of the states already permitting non-unanimous guilty verdicts, the editor of the state university's law journal said in 1968 the legislature should reconsider its "fallacious" reasoning behind the law. "It is well known in the human experience that minorities are often right, and an articulate minority on a jury may be able to persuade the majority.... The one or two dissenters may be the most intelligent and capable."[10]

Debate Over Split Verdicts. Then in 1972 came the Supreme Court ruling that jury verdicts against criminal defendants in state courts did not have to be unanimous.[11] The five-member majority in the case included the four Nixon appointees to the Court—Chief Justice Burger, Justices Harry A. Blackmun, Lewis F. Powell Jr. and William H. Rehnquist—and White, a Kennedy appointee who had frequently dissented in Warren Court decisions. Delivering the majority opinion, White said that state laws permitting less-than-unanimous verdicts did not violate the due process clause of the Constitution.[12]

He held, moreover, that the Court had never specifically required unanimity by jurors, and that dissent in the jury did not mean that the minority's arguments had not been heeded by other jurors. "That rational men disagree is not in itself equivalent to a failure of proof by the state, nor does it indicate infidelity to the reasonable doubt standard," White wrote. He suggested in a footnote that unanimity is an anachronism that may have developed "because early juries, unlike juries today, personally had knowledge of the facts of a case; the medieval mind assumed there could be only one correct view of the facts."

Justice Blackmun wrote that his vote with the majority did not mean he regarded the split verdict "a wise one" but merely that it was not "constitutionally offensive." If he were a state legislator deciding whether to adopt a split-verdict system, he would "disfavor" it. He added that any state rule that permitted conviction on a 7-5 vote "would afford me great difficulty." Furthermore, Powell balked at applying the split-verdict ruling to federal courts; his "no" was decisive on that issue.

Justice William O. Douglas, in the dissenting opinion, called the upholding of non-unanimous verdicts "a radical departure from American traditions" and "in the tradition of the inquisition." In all previous decisions on criminal law, he said, the Court had construed the "reasonable doubt" provision broadly, so as to err on the side of letting the guilty go free rather than sending the innocent to jail. "Up until today the price has never seemed too high. Now a 'law and order' judicial mood causes the barricades to be lowered." Douglas added that he believed the Court was overstepping its authority, saying: "The vast restructuring of American law which is entailed in today's decisions is for political, not for judicial action."

In the relatively brief time since the non-unanimity ruling has been handed down, legal scholars have studied it in conjunction with the earlier jury-size decision. Their opinion, on the whole, is disapproving. Alexander M. Bickel, the Yale law professor, said the split-verdict rule will have only slight effect in strengthening the prosecution of criminals. "The additional convictions will be very few, a drop in the bucket, statistically barely measurable. No more than 10 per cent or so of criminal cases go to trial. Most are disposed of on pleas of guilty. And most crimes never become cases because they are never solved. There's the real rub."[13]

Analyses of the decision were slow to appear in legal journals, probably because of the complexity of the Supreme Court's reasoning. In one of the first treatments of the decision, the Court was accused of raising "serious inconsistencies in federal-state criminal standards." John A. Burgess of Montpelier, Vt., wrote in the July-August 1972 issue of *Trial*, publication of the American Trial Lawyers Association, that the Court appeared to concede that common law and the Sixth Amendment require unanimous verdicts but held that the 14th Amendment does not impose the requirement on the states. Burgess called this "a convoluted reasoning pattern" and a "tortured rationale."

Evolvement of Jury System

Trial by jury and the other basic elements in the American system of justice were adapted by the Founding Fathers from English common law.[14] In turn, common law is a distillation of customs and usage derived from the native Britons, Picts and Scots; and from invaders of the British Isles, the Germanic Angles and Saxons, Norsemen, Romans, and Normans. Scholarly research turns up episodic use of some form of jury trials since the days of ancient Greece.

The Greeks maintained a list of 6,000 citizens, from which 200 to a thousand or so were drawn to hear evidence of wrongdoing and advise the government. The Romans borrowed the concept and used a judge-jury system of magistrates and advisers until Emperor Constantius II abolished it in 353 A.D., fearing that the courts had become too powerful. However, the idea had spread to some far reaches of the empire, surviving in Scandinavia, whence a raider named Rollo carried the jury concept into Normandy.

Frankish kings corrupted the concept of justice by jury trial, using it as an inquisitorial institution to preserve royal rights. The system had regained some of its original intent of preserving citizens' rights by the time William the Conqueror carried this feature of law into Britain with the Norman invasion of 1066. Although this date is given much significance in scholarly research, there is also some evidence of pre-Norman juries in England. King Alfred is said to have decreed the rough equivalent of jury trials around the beginning of the 10th century.

The Constitution states in Article III, Section 2, that "the trial of all crimes, except in cases of impeachment, shall be by jury." Three Bill of Rights amendments amplify jury protection. The Fifth states that trial for a "capital, or otherwise infamous crime" shall come only after indictment by a grand jury. The Sixth guarantees right to "a speedy and public trial, by an impartial jury of the State and district wherein the crime shall have been com-

---

Origins of 12-Member Juries

In a footnote to the Supreme Court's 1970 decision on jury size, an ancient Welsh king, Morgan of Gla-Morgan, is credited with adopting jury trials in 725 A.D. and basing his legal system upon "The Apostolic Law"; the judge and jury were likened to Christ and the 12 Apostles.

Religious origins are usually cited in research for applying the number 12 to jury size—the Apostles, or the 12 tribes of Israel, or Solomon's 12 officers. Julian Hartt of the *Los Angeles Times* wrote on June 28, 1970, his research indicated the first use of the figure in regard to trials came from Teutonic tribes, in apparent significance to the worship of the fire god Wotan.

At any rate, the Supreme Court said the origin of the traditional jury size rested on "little more than mystical or superstitious insights."

---

mitted...." The Seventh provides for jury trials in civil cases "where the value in controversy shall exceed twenty dollars."

Institution of Western Democracies. Trial by jury is almost exclusively a western, democratic political institution. It is becoming an increasingly American institution. It is estimated that at least 80 per cent of all criminal jury trials in the world today are held in the United States.[15] Few countries outside the orbit of the influence of Anglo-Saxon law have retained the jury system. Apparently the inclination of a nation's citizens to prefer the judgment of a group of laymen over that of learned judges reflects the same mode of thought that cherishes the imprecise workings of democratic government. An Englishman has said, "The jury system for deciding criminal trials is like democracy for deciding government; the worst system ever devised, except for all the others."[16]

Some countries which once had jury trials, including Portugal, Egypt, Czechoslovakia and Hungary, have abandoned them. Kalven and Zeisel observe that "historically, wherever the jury was adopted it became a symbol of democratic government, and any revival of absolutist forces became a threat to the existence of the jury."

Other countries have retained the form but little of the substance of the jury. Japan ended a brief experiment with jury trials in 1943; currently it sometimes invites a panel of citizens to participate in a trial by giving an opinion but not a verdict. In France, the judge sits in on the jury's deliberations and may turn the verdict aside if he feels it is in error. Austria's courts permit the three presiding judges, by unanimous vote, to overturn the jury's verdict. Common throughout northern, eastern and southern Europe are juries of judges and citizens in varied numerical combination. Russian law provides for a board of lay judges to sit with the professional judge and advise him. A 1967 English law permits non-unanimous jury verdicts, with one dissenter in some cases, two in others. In Scotland, a jury may bring in a verdict by bare majority.

Civil Rights Movement. The American jury system endured one of its severest crises during the height of the civil rights movement in the South during the 1960s.

When civil rights violations, including murder, were prosecuted, it became obvious that a double standard for meting out justice existed. The most obvious deficiency was the exclusion of Negroes from juries. Many offenses committed by whites against blacks were never brought to trial, and when they were, court leniency was the rule. There were notable exceptions, in which white defendants were severely punished, but even then the absence of black jurors was apparent.

A variation on the rule applied to whites charged with offenses against white civil rights workers. Mrs. Viola Gregg Liuzzo and Jonathan Daniels, both white, were murdered while engaged in civil rights activities around Selma, Ala. In separate trials in 1965, one of the white men accused of killing Mrs. Liuzzo was acquitted, as was the man charged with the Daniels slaying—both by all-white juries. Commenting later on the verdict in the Daniels case, Attorney General Nicholas deB. Katzenbach said, "This kind of outcome is expected from time to time.... It is difficult to get convictions in some areas. This is the price you have to pay for the jury system, but I don't think it is too high a price to pay."

Collie LeRoy Wilkins Jr., acquitted of murder in the Liuzzo case by a state jury, later was convicted by an all-white federal jury in Montgomery, Ala., Dec. 3, 1965, of violating an 1870 law outlawing conspiracy to deprive a citizen of his civil rights. The government used the same law to obtain convictions in the slaying of three civil rights workers near Philadelphia, Miss., in 1964.[17] Eighteen men went on trial before an all-white federal jury of five men and seven women. Eight were acquitted, the cases of three defendants resulted in hung juries, and seven were convicted in Meridian, Miss., on Oct. 20, 1967, on charges of conspiring to deny life or liberty without due process. Among those found guilty were the chief deputy sheriff of Neshoba County, Miss., Cecil R. Price, and the Imperial Wizard of the White Knights of the Ku Klux Klan, Sam H. Bowers Jr. However, the incidence of actual murder convictions in the South during the 1960s was spotty.

In his 1966 State of the Union message, President Johnson called for legislation "to establish unavoidable requirements for non-discriminatory jury selection in federal and state courts and to give the Attorney General the power necessary to enforce those requirements." A new law was regarded as necessary although the United States Criminal Code, provisions in earlier civil rights acts, and numerous Supreme Court decisions reaching back to 1880 seemed to ban racial discrimination in jury selection. *(Box this page)*

The Supreme Court, ruling in the famous Scottsboro case of the thirties,[18] spelled out the proof then required for a *prima facie* case of racial exclusion on juries. The accused had to prove that members of his race (1) constituted a substantial segment of the population within his community, (2) met the qualifications for jury service, and (3) had not been summoned to serve over an extended period. The loophole in this ruling was the scarcity of Negroes, particularly in the South, on tax lists and voter registration rolls from which jury lists were assembled. In other significant decisions, the Court ruled that deliberate inclusion of a minority race on juries was as unconstitutional as deliberate exclusion,[19] and that exclusion of a class of persons for reasons other than race also was in violation of the Constitution.[20] The net effect of

Racial Representation

Criminal Code. *Section 243*, based on a law passed in 1875, states: "No citizen possessing all other qualifications which are or may be prescribed by law shall be disqualified for service as grand or petit juror in any court of the United States, or of any state, on account of race, color or previous condition of servitude...."

Civil Rights Acts. The 1957 act stipulated that any citizen over 21 would be competent to serve as a grand or petit juror provided he had lived more than one year in a judicial district, was literate in English, was physically capable of jury duty, and was not a convicted felon. The 1964 act authorized the Attorney General to intervene in private suits brought by persons alleging denial of equal protection of the law under the 14th Amendment.

Supreme Court. In Strauder *v.* West Virginia, 100 U.S. 303 (1880), the Court struck down a West Virginia statute that excluded Negroes from jury service. The following year, in Neal *v.* Delaware, 103 U.S. 370 (1881), the Court overturned the indictment and conviction on a rape charge of a Delaware Negro on the ground that blacks had been excluded from duty on the grand and petit juries.

these rulings was token representation of blacks on jury lists and on juries.[21] The peremptory challenge was used widely to shunt aside black members of jury lists in selecting juries.

Moves to Ban Racial Exclusion. One provision of the Johnson administration's 1966 civil rights bill would have barred discrimination in the selection of state and federal juries. However, the jury-exclusion issue was not decisive in the controversy which led to the bill's defeat. This centered on Title IV, an open housing provision which caused a split in the coalition of Republicans and northern Democrats that had pushed through earlier civil rights bills. President Johnson resubmitted the rejected bill title by title in 1967 and the following year won approval for the federal voter selection provision.[22]

The Jury Selection and Service Act of 1968 contained these provisions:

• Federal juries must be selected at random from "a fair cross section of the community," without discrimination on account of race, color, religion, sex, national origin or economic status.

• Each U.S. district court must draw up a plan for selection of jurors which meets the act's standards, including random selection of names from voting lists with clearly defined rules for exclusion or exemption.

• A person's qualifications for jury service must be based solely on information contained on jury qualification forms and other "competent" evidence, with criteria based on age, residence, fluency and literacy in English, and lack of physical or mental infirmity or a criminal record.

• Procedures were established which must be followed for challenging compliance with jury selection requirements.

However, the act stopped short of affirmatively requiring the end of monoracial makeup on all juries. There was no provision covering state juries; a companion bill embodying what had been Title II of the 1966 civil rights bill, dealing with state court reform, was introduced in the Senate but received no action.

In the absence of congressional action, the Supreme Court has been requiring states to follow the same basic procedures used by federal courts in jury selection. In a far-reaching decision announced April 3, 1972, the Court placed upon the states the burden of proving that its jury-selection methods meet the test of constitutionality, even in the absence of any hard evidence that discriminatory practices were intended or used. It overturned the conviction of a Louisiana Negro on rape charges although finding no evidence to back the defendant's claim that the grand jury was consciously selected by race.

How, then, did Louisiana go wrong in its jury selection? The Court's answer was that the system "provided a clear and easy opportunity for racial discrimination." The critical flaw was that each potential juror—7,374 names drawn at random from the telephone directory, city directory and voter registration lists—was required to list his race on the form returned to the jury commission. Blacks "presumptively eligible" for jury service constituted 21 per cent of the population. On the "raw" jury selection list compiled by the commission, the percentage of blacks was down to 13.76. The final list of 400 persons contained 27 Negroes, 6.75 per cent. The Court, noting the statistical probability for such a reduction was one in 20,000, spoke of "a strong inference that racial discrimination and not chance produced this result...."

Problem of Jury Makeup

Legal scholars have looked on the Jury Selection and Service Act of 1968 as ineffective in bringing about substantial minority representation on juries. Proposals are being heard for still further reform, to redefine the concept of a jury of one's peers, emphasizing the importance of empaneling jurors whose personal experiences relate to an understanding of the circumstances of the case and affect the outcome.

A study of jury discrimination made at the time the 1968 law was beginning to take effect, the work of Roger S. Kuhn, associate professor of law at George Washington University, provides a reference point for further examination.[23] Kuhn concluded that *de facto* discrimination exists." He cited some of the "more subtle means of discrimination" which were replacing blatant exclusion of blacks from juries. Commissioners selecting grand jury membership place the names of Negroes at the bottom of the selection lists, decreasing the chances they would be selected to serve.

Another device in making up trial juries is to pack one panel with available black jurors and than bypass it in favor of another panel composed mostly or solely of whites. Some judges were said to cooperate in the use of peremptory challenges as a means of excluding blacks without running afoul of the law. Kuhn said some judges, "knowing what each side wants, simply excuse Negro jurors, in order to save the parties' peremptories for more serious business." There is little evidence that the 1968 law has made an effective direct assault on these practices. One study of the consequences of the 1968 act says it "ignores the *de facto* discrimination inherent" in the

voter rolls or other legally acceptable lists from which juries are drawn, and notes further that the lack of any control over state juries "is the (act's) most serious shortcoming."[24]

Another study finds that, despite reforms, "a prime feature of the American jury remains the absence of black citizens."[25] This study suggests that court districts be divided for jury selection purposes into something like the "vicinage"—the neighborhood—used in ancient common law. By drawing juries from the community where the crime occurred "we would ensure that the law for black people would be administered by substantially all-black juries."

Racial and Social Composition. Black defendants in criminal trials sometimes have contended that the racial makeup of the juries was of secondary importance to the sociological makeup. At the outset of the lengthy prosecution of Black Panther co-founder Huey P. Newton in California, his attorneys argued that a jury of his peers meant "not an exclusively black jury, but one consisting of people from and involved in his community, West Oakland, a lower-class predominantly black ghetto...(people) able to empathize with him where middle- and upper-class whites would not."[26]

A law professor who surveyed the jury system for the Center for the Study of Democratic Institutions said: "It has never been asserted that persons from one district or from one part of town are any better at sifting evidence and arriving at facts" than persons from elsewhere. But jurors drawn from the defendant's community "are more likely to be sensitive to the significance of the crime and the appropriateness of applying the law to the defendant's act."[27] The professor's thesis is that the more intimately knowledgeable a jury is of the pocket of society which produced the crime and the accused, the more responsible will be the jury's actions in exercising its inherent power of nullification. This is the power of the jury to refuse to apply the specific law, as presented to them by the trial judge, to the given set of evidence.

In the journal of the American Trial Lawyers Association, an attorney active in defending militants— Howard Moore Jr., then director of the Southern Legal Assistance Project in Atlanta, Ga.—denounced all prior jury reforms as "simplistic." He said that since whites and blacks do not enjoy the same legal status, "it must be concluded that a trial before an all-white or biracial jury of an accused black is not a trial before his peers."[28]

Moore conceded that any requirement for all-black juries would be viewed as "reverse racism" and was unlikely to win official approval. But reforms which appeared possible, he said, include wide latitude in the questioning of prospective jurors to cull the prejudiced, and an absolute standard of proportional representation of the races in each community. Moore, who later served as chief counsel for Angela Davis at her California trial, said in an interview in July 1972 that neither Miss Davis' acquittal nor any other verdicts setting black militants free during the previous two years had changed his opinions as to the unfairness of American justice.

There were, however, enough instances in which black militants were freed after jury trials to defuse the controversy. Critics of the American judicial system's ability to provide fair trials for militants and minorities reached a peak in the late 1960s, a period of highly publicized indictments, and receded in the early 1970s, a period marked by acquittals and hung juries. Panther leader Huey Newton spent 33 months in jail awaiting and undergoing trial, but in the end he went free. So did Bobby Seale, whose approaching trial for murder in New Haven, Conn., prompted Kingman Brewster Jr. to express doubt that any black revolutionary could get a fair trial.[29] When Brewster next commented publicly on the issue, he said: "The ability of a Connecticut judge to dismiss a murder complaint because he doubted whether a new trial could be fair encouraged many in their belief that law could still serve justice as well as order."[30]

Controversy Over Panther Trials. Another critic, William M. Kunstler, acknowledged that trial justice for radical defendants was not beyond achievement. Kunstler, a member of the Center for Constitutional Rights and defense attorney for a number of militants, including H. Rap Brown, said: "For many the inability of prosecutors (in recent trials of radicals) to convince any—or even most—of their respective panels that the defendants were guilty of the crimes with which they were charged has been regarded as a stunning vindication of our legal system. For others, including myself, these results only indicate that just verdicts are, under certain conditions, attainable...."[31] The current dichotomy over the state of American justice is perhaps typified by the remark of Angela Davis after her acquittal June 4, 1972, that it was the happiest day of her life. She added, "A fair trial would have been no trial at all."

Howard Moore Jr., Miss Davis's chief counsel, said the all-white jury which acquitted her was selected through a unique investigative effort. The defense organized a pool of investigators, including law school faculty members and psychologists. They were aided by 150 "contacts," residents who already knew or could learn the attitudes of each member of the venire list. The entire effort was designed to identify persons emphathetic to the defendant.

Application of Modern Techniques. For many persons called to jury service the experience is more tedious than festive because of "overcall." The Administrative Office of the United States Courts reported recently that on a daily average, 46 per cent of all persons present in federal courts for jury duty do nothing but sit and wait. If the overcall were cut to 25 per cent, the estimated annual saving to the federal court system would be $2.5-million. Acting on this report, one of the least efficient of the 93 federal districts in juror utilization, the Second District of New York, began calling—and paying—fewer jurors, and cut its operating costs $600,000 a year. Now, the Administrative Office for federal courts has a team of management experts available to advise district courts.

Computers have been used to help courts identify and correct the causes of wasted time. A judge in the U.S. District Court for Eastern Pennsylvania noted that workmen's compensation cases involving dockworkers rose from 6 per cent of all cases before the court in 1961 to 23 per cent in 1966 but the number of such cases tried remained static. A computer printout pointed to the reason. Two law firms were representing 95 per cent of all dockworker plaintiffs. One lawyer was responsible for 52 cases. Two other firms were handling the lawsuits

for 95 per cent of the shipowner defendants. By persuading the firms to spread out the work load among attorneys who were less busy, a two-year backlog of cases was cleared up in two months.[32]

---

1 Florida, Louisiana, South Carolina, Texas and Utah for cases in which the criminal penalty exceeded one year in prison; Alaska, Georgia, Iowa, Kentucky, Mississippi, New York, Oklahoma, Oregon and Virginia for cases in which the criminal penalty was no more than a year in prison.

2 Attorney General Robert L. Shevin asked the Florida Supreme Court on July 12, 1972, to adopt administrative rules allowing jury verdicts of 10 to 2 and 5 to 1.

3 Jerome Frank, *Courts On Trial* (1949), p. 116.

4 Curtis Bok (Judge of Philadelphia Court of Common Pleas), "The Jury System in America," *Annals of the American Academy of Political and Social Science,* May 1953.

5 Harry Kalven Jr. and Hans Zeisel, *The American Jury* (1966).

6 Irving R. Kaufman, "Harbingers of Jury Reform," *American Bar Association Journal,* July 1972.

7 *Williams v. Florida,* 399 U.S. 78.100 (1970). The defendant in the case, accused of robbery, was convicted by a six-member jury.

8 The "leading" case is *Thompson v. Utah,* 170 U.S. 343 (1898). Justice White said that this decision assumed the inviolability of the 12-man jury "long after scholars had exposed this ancient error." He called the number 12 a "historical accident, unrelated to the great issues which gave rise to the jury in the first place."

9 Edward Lumbard, (Judge of the U.S. Court of Appeals, Second Circuit, New York), "Let the Jury Be—But Modified," *Trial,* November-December, 1971.

10 Laird C. Kirkpatrick, "Unanimous Jury Verdicts?" *Oregon Law Review,* June 1968.

11 At issue were the cases of Johnson v. Louisiana, a 9-3 conviction, and Apodaca et al. v. Oregon, testing Oregon's "10 of 12" verdict rule.

12 Section 1 of the 14th Amendment states, in part: "No State shall make or enforce any law which shall abridge the privileges or immunities of citizens of the United States; nor shall any State deprive any person of life, liberty, or property, without due process of law."

13 Alexander M. Bickel, "Law and Order Cases: Powell's Day," *The New Republic,* June 10, 1972.

14 See "Fair Trial by Jury," *E.R.R.,* 1966 Vol. I, pp. 103-120.

15 Kalven and Zeisel, *op. cit,* p. 13.

16 Bernard Levin in *The Times* (of London), July 22, 1971.

17 The victims were James E. Chaney, a 21-year-old black plasterer from Meridian; Michael H. Schwerner, 24, of New York, a white field worker for the Congress of Racial Equality; and Andrew Goodman, 20, a white college student from New York.

18 *Norris v. Alabama,* 294 U.S. 587 (1935). Nine Negro boys accused of raping two white girls were indicted and tried originally in Scottsboro, Ala. The case became a *cause celebre.* After seven years of litigation, including appeals to the Supreme Court, five of the defendants were sent to prison and the other four freed.

19 *Akins v. Texas,* 325 U.S. 398 (1945), and others.

20 *Hernandez v. Texas,* 347 U.S. 475 (1954).

21 In *Brown v. Allen,* 344 U.S. 443 (1953), the Supreme Court in effect approved a 7 per cent Negro representation on juries although Negroes accounted for 38 per cent of the names on tax lists from which juries were selected.

22 See *Congressional Quarterly, Congress and the Nation,* Vol. II (1969), p. 385.

23 Roger S. Kuhn, "Jury Discrimination, Next Phase," *Southern California Law Review,* winter, 1968.

24 Jennie Rhine, "The Jury: Reflection of the Prejudices in a Community," *The Hastings Law Journal,* May 1969, p. 1441.

25 "The Case for Black Juries," *Yale Law Journal,* January 1970, p. 533.

26 Jennie Rhine, *op. cit.,* p. 1417.

27 Jon M. Van Dyke, "The Jury as a Political Institution," *The Center Magazine,* March-April 1970.

28 Howard Moore Jr., "The Jury Challenge," *Trial,* June-July 1970.

29 As quoted by *The New York Times,* April 25, 1970, Brewster said the basis for his doubt "has been created by police actions and prosecutions against the Panthers in many parts of the country. It is also one more inheritance from the centuries of racial discrimination and oppression."

30 Kingman Brewster Jr., "Reflections on Our National Purpose," *Foreign Affairs,* April 1972, p. 401.

31 *The New York Times,* June 24, 1972.

32 *The Christian Science Monitor,* Aug. 9, 1968.

ANCIENT INSTITUTION GAINING IN PROMINENCE IN 1970's

The grand jury has been condemned as an arbitrary and capricious Star Chamber and lauded as a people's panel which seeks out truth while protecting ordinary citizens from overzealous prosecutors. Ignored and unnoticed for much of American history—"a hidden corner of American law"[1] —the system has come increasingly under scrutiny in recent years. In the early 1970s, grand juries were used extensively to investigate Black Panthers, Catholic leftists and anti-war militants. In 1973, they heard evidence against such prominent former members of the Nixon administration as Spiro T. Agnew, John N. Mitchell, Maurice Stans, H.R. Haldeman and John D. Ehrlichman. Mitchell, Stans and Ehrlichman were indicted and face trial while Agnew pleaded no contest to income tax evasion and resigned as Vice President before indictments were returned. *(Footnotes, p. 93)*

The controversy over possession of tape recordings made in President Nixon's Oval Office pitted him against a federal grand jury and brought on a constitutional crisis. It was on behalf of the grand jury in Washington, D.C., that Special Prosecutor Archibald Cox sought nine of the presidential tapes for the Watergate investigation, and it was on the grand jury's behalf that U.S. District Court Judge John J. Sirica ruled that they must be released to him for review. The President's appeal of Sirica's order and temporary defiance of it—before capitulation—set in motion a yet-unresolved crisis in government and a threat of presidential impeachment of Nixon in Congress.

Watergate-related investigations had meanwhile been conducted by a second grand jury in Washington, and by grand juries in New York City, Los Angeles, Houston, and Orlando, Fla. Vice President Agnew, the administration's chief law-and-order spokesman, became the unhappy subject of a federal grand jury investigation in Baltimore that led to his resignation from office, although the investigation did not concern Watergate developments. It dealt with possible violations of bribery, conspiracy, extortion and tax laws by Agnew when he was Baltimore County executive, governor of Maryland and Vice President.

Attorney General Elliot L. Richardson, in announcing the Agnew investigation on Sept. 25, said that Justice Department attorneys would present evidence to the grand jury and that it would be used, "in accordance with well-established practice, as an investigative body. This is the traditional function of a federal grand jury, whose role, as representative of the community, is to ensure the fairness of the investigative process." Three days later, Agnew asked U.S. District Judge Walter E. Hoffman in Baltimore to bar the grand jury from "conducting any investigation looking to possible indictment" and from "issuing any indictment, presentment or other charge or statement." The request was based on two arguments: first, that the Constitution forbids indictment of an incum-

bent Vice President, and, second, that Justice Department officials had engaged in a "steady campaign of statement to the press" which had so prejudiced the grand jury that Agnew could not get a fair judgment on the charges against him. On Oct. 10, two days before a scheduled hearing on these questions, the Vice President resigned and pleaded *nolo contendere* (no contest) to charges of evading income taxes in 1967.

Criticism. Federal and state grand juries have two main functions. The first is to require the prosecution to show, behind closed doors, that it has sufficient evidence to bring formal charges against individuals. If the grand jury decides, by majority vote, that the prosecutor has demonstrated that there is probable cause to believe the suspect has committed a crime, it issues a "true bill," an indictment or formal accusation, recommending that the person be brought to trial. If the majority decides that the prosecution's case does not have sufficient merit, it issues a "no bill." The second function of a grand jury is to investigate wrongdoing, seeking to pry out facts that eventually may lead to criminal indictments. In 1919, the Supreme Court upheld the grand jury's broad investigatory powers.[2] On the basis of an investigation, a grand jury can issue reports or indictments.

As the authors of the Bill of Rights envisioned it, the grand jury was a key defense against unfair criminal prosecution. Thus, the Fifth Amendment to the Constitution gurarantees that "No person shall be held to answer for a capital, or otherwise infamous crime, unless on a presentment or indictment of a Grand Jury, except in cases arising in the land or naval forces or in the Militia, when in actual service in time of War or public danger..." By no means are all criminal cases referred to a grand jury, however. Panels are required in federal criminal cases in which a conviction would result in a prison term of more than one year. Less than half of the states use that standard. Others use grand juries irregularly and some have abandoned the system entirely.

Critics contend that contemporary grand juries are not fulfilling the function intended by the founding fathers. Theoretically, grand jurors have the right to extend or broaden investigations, call and question witnesses, and request that evidence be brought in. Detractors argue that grand juries serve merely as rubber stamps for the prosecution, indicting when the government asks them to indict and giving the prosecution absolute control over what questions are asked and what investigations are undertaken.

Justice William O. Douglas, dissenting in a Supreme Court case in January 1973, said: "It is indeed common knowledge that the grand jury, having been conceived as a bulwark between the citizen and the government, is now a tool of the executive (branch)."[3] William J. Campbell, a former prosecutor who is now a federal judge, shares that view. "Today," he wrote, "the grand jury is the total captive of the prosecutor who, if he is candid, will concede that he can indict anybody, at any time, for almost anything, before a grand jury."[4]

Prosecutors typically deny that grand juries serve as rubber stamps and frequently cite cases of "runaway" bodies that refuse to comply with the prosecutor's wishes. Nevertheless, available evidence suggests that independent grand juries are rare. A study conducted in 1930 by Wayne L. Morse, then dean of the University of Oregon Law School, surveyed 162 prosecutors from 21 states and found that of 6,543 cases, grand juries disagreed with the prosecutor in only 348 cases—about 5 per cent. The National Advisory Commission on Criminal Justice Standards and Goals reported early in 1973 that in Baltimore "the grand jury returned indictments in 98.18 per cent of the cases presented to it in 1969, but 42 per cent of those indictments were dismissed before trial."

Through the grand jury, the prosecutor is able to subpoena witnesses, ask them questions on almost any subject and grant them immunity. According to Rule Six of the Federal Rules of Criminal Procedure, district court clerks are authorized to issue blank grand jury subpoenas to U.S. attorneys. The prosecutor fills in the names of witnesses he wishes to call. Commenting on this procedure, two lawyers have said that "federal prosecuting officials—who themselves have no power of subpoena— are using the coercive powers of the grand jury for police and intelligence work."[5]

A grand jury witness who chooses not to answer questions may plead the Fifth Amendment privilege against self-incrimination. However, if the prosecution decides that his testimony is necessary, it can grant him immunity from prosecution and thereby compel him to answer questions, at the risk of a contempt citation and possibly imprisonment. There are two types of immunity: *transactional* and *use*. The first protects a witness from prosecution for any offense mentioned in or related to his testimony, regardless of independent evidence against him. The second gives protection only from the use of a witness's own testimony against himself.[6]

Critics are unhappy about the manner of selecting most grand juries. In the federal judiciary and in most state judicial systems, grand jurors are chosen at random from voter-registration rolls. In California, however, jurors are drawn by lot from a panel of about 30 persons who are usually selected by a judge. Federal grand juries must have from 16 to 23 members; state bodies are generally smaller. It is argued that most grand juries, even if chosen from voter lists, tend to exclude radicals, blacks, low-income persons or those who are likely to question the government's case.[7]

Individual Rights, News Leaks. Grand jury investigations in the last few years have led to charges that the system is perverting rather than protecting individual rights, including: the First Amendment protection of political beliefs, and freedom of speech and press; Fourth Amendment guarantees against unlawful searches and seizures; Fifth Amendment protection against self-incrimination; Sixth Amendment provisions that in all criminal cases the accused must be told of the charges against him, confronted by witnesses against him, allowed witnesses in his favor and given the right to counsel; and Ninth Amendment assurances of the right to privacy.

Secrecy in grand jury proceedings provides another area for argument between defenders and detractors of the grand jury system. Grand jurors, on assuming their duties, are sworn to secrecy. There are four reasons generally cited for doing so: (1) to prevent the accused from escaping before he is indicted or arrested, or to prevent him from tampering with witnesses; (2) to prevent disclosure of derogatory information presented to the grand jury against an accused person who has not been indicted; (3) to encourage complainants and witnesses to come before the grand jury and speak freely; and (4) to encourage grand jurors to engage in uninhibited investigation and deliberation.[8]

On the other hand, it is said that secrecy may mask prosecution abuses or that it may be ineffective. Witnesses are not sworn to secrecy and grand juries are able to issue reports about their investigations which may damage personal reputations. In addition, prosecutors sometimes leak information to the news media. This issue was raised recently by Vice President Agnew.

In a televised statement on Aug. 21, Agnew demanded an inquiry into news leaks about the investigation of his activities. "This is a clear and outrageous effort to influence the outcome of possible grand jury deliberations," he said. On Sept. 28, Agnew's lawyers filed a motion in U.S. district court in Baltimore to stop the grand jury investigation on the two grounds that a Vice President could not be indicted and that news leaks could "prejudice" the case. Finally on Oct. 5, Agnew's lawyers had subpoenas served on eight reporters and two national news magazines to require them to reveal their sources of information about the case.[9]

Confidentiality, Presidential Immunity. Agnew resigned from office and submitted his plea of no contest on the day before the newsmen were scheduled to appear

---

Definition of Terms

Contempt. Refusal to comply with a court order. In *civil contempt,* the person who refuses to testify before a grand jury is punished, usually with a jail sentence, until he changes his mind or until the grand jury term ends. In *criminal contempt,* he is sentenced to a specified jail term; if for more than six months on each count, a jury trial may be requested to determine guilt or innocence.

Immunity. The witness is offered protection from prosecution in exchange for his testimony. For distinction between *transactional* and *use* immunity, see this page, second column.

Information. Direct accusation by the prosecutor.

Indictment. A formal written statement from the grand jury, decided by majority vote, charging one or more persons with specified offenses.

Petit or Trial Jury. Decides guilt or innocence in open trial.

Presentment. Written grand jury report to the court which does not charge persons with specific law violations. Used in some states but rare in federal practice.

Subpoena. Order to present one's self for questioning before a grand jury court trial or legislative hearing.

in court for questioning. Even though the case was abruptly terminated, it revived an old conflict between the government and the press over the mandatory appearance of newsmen before grand juries seeking to learn their sources of confidential information. The question reached the Supreme Court in 1972 cases involving three newsmen—Earl Caldwell of *The New York Times,* Paul M. Branzburg of the Louisville *Courier-Journal,* and Paul Pappas of television station WTEV in New Bedford, Mass. They had refused to disclose confidential information to separate grand juries and were cited for contempt of court.

The Caldwell, Pappas and Branzburg appeals were considered together by the Supreme Court and became known as the *Caldwell* case. In a 5-4 decision on June 29, 1972, the Court held that "the great weight of authority is that newsmen are not exempt (by the First Amendment's freedom-of-press provision) from the normal duty of appearing before a grand jury and answering questions relevant to a criminal investigation."[10] None of the three defendants was jailed in the wake of the decision, but several other newsmen were.[11]

Justice Byron R. White, in writing the majority decision, spoke of the "long standing principle that 'the public has a right to every man's evidence,' except for those persons protected by the Constitution, common law or statutory privilege." The question has since arisen as to whether this protection applies to the President or Vice President while in office.[12]

The Justice Department, in a 23-page brief filed in federal district court in Baltimore on Oct. 5, challenged Agnew's argument that he was constitutionally immune as Vice President from criminal prosecution. As for the President, Justice argued that he is constititionally immune from prosecution while he holds office. That issue presumably will not be settled, however, without a Supreme Court ruling. Judge Sirica and the U.S. Court of Appeals for the District of Columbia have rejected claims of presidential immunity in regard to making tape recordings available to a grand jury.[13]

Grand Jury History

The grand jury system, as it is known today, is usually traced to the Assize of Clarendon in 1166. It was then that King Henry II provided that 12 "good and lawful" men among every 104 lawful men in each village reveal under oath the names of those thought guilty of criminal offenses. Reports by the body were made to the royal sheriff and royal justices. Those accused of specific crimes could defend themselves before the King's representatives by denying the charges under oath and submitting to the ordeal by water. If, after being lowered into the water, the suspect sank, he was delared innocent; if he floated, he was deemed guilty.

The grand jury was conceived as an instrument to enlarge and centralize royal power, not to protect individual rights. Richard H. Kuh pointed out in the December 1955 issue of the *Columbia Law Review*: "This new instrument for charging crime only increased the number of persons standing trial...." But "the logic of using persons drawn from the locale of the crime...was gradually recognized, and hence the petit (trial) jury slowly developed from the Grand Assize."

The first known case of grand jury independence came in 1681 when a panel refused to indict the Earl of Shaftesbury on charges of treason, despite the insistence of Charles II. "In that case, the King's counsel insisted that the grand jury hear, in open court, testimonial evidence.... The jurors demanded and were refused the right to interview witnesses in private chambers. Nevertheless, they were allowed to hear witnesses one by one.... The indictment was ultimately returned by the jury with the word 'Ignoramus' (we know nothing of it) written across it. The jurors would give no reason for refusing to indict. By establishing the concept of grand jury secrecy, the case thereafter was celebrated as a bulwark against the oppression and despotism of the Crown."[14] A year later, Lord Chancellor John Somers wrote in a tract called *The Security of Englishmen's Lives:* "Grand juries are our only security in as much as our lives cannot be drawn into jeopardy by all the malicious crafts of the devil, unless such a number of our honest countrymen shall be satisfied in the truth of the accusations."[15]

Early American Practice. American colonists transplanted and grand jury concept to the New World during the 17th and 18th centuries. In 19635, the Massachusetts Bay Volony impanelled the first regular grand jury in America. Before 1700, panels concerned themselves with violations of the law, including such offenses as "having been instigated of the devil," murder, robbery and wife beating. Some chastised officials for laxity and private citizens for not taking proper care of their property.

"The Fifth Amendment introduces us to the oldest institution known to the Constitution, the grand jury,"

—Edward S. Corwin, *Understanding the Constitution*

Richard D. Younger notes in *The People's Panel* (1963) that after 1700 the American colonists gradually came to realize the value of the grand juries as a means of obtaining redress of grievances from the proprietors and of opposing the power of royal officials. "By the end of the Colonial period the grand jury had become an indispensable part of government in each of the American colonies," he wrote. "Grand juries served as more than panels of public accusers. They acted as local representative assemblies ready to make known the wishes of the people. They proposed new laws, protested against abuses in government, and peformed many administrative tasks. They wielded tremendous authority in their power to determine who should and who should not face trial."[16]

A Boston grand jury refused to indict leaders of the Stamp Act riots in 1765. Three years later, another grand jury rejected demands that charges be brought against the editors of the *Boston Gazette* for libeling the royal governor, Francis Bernard. In 1770, a Philadelphia panel, in addition to refusing to indict those charged by the Crown, proposed a union with other colonies to oppose British taxes. During the Revolutionary War, grand juries in virtually all the colonies were unabashedly sympathetic to the cause of independence. Thus, in the early years of the new republic, the people's panel enjoyed wide public support.

Charles E. Goodell writes: "The Constitution, when it went into effect in 1789, made no mention of grand juries.

Several state ratifying conventions expressed uneasiness that the new Constitution left citizens to rely on the unfettered discretion of federal authorities to protect them against repressive prosecutions; the Fifth Amendment was ratified in 1791 to eliminate that danger.... The hopes of those who drafted the Fifth Amendment with activist pre-Revolutionary grand juries in mind have been largely disappointed. Thomas Jefferson charged that by 1791 the Federalists had already transformed grand juries 'from a legal to a political engine' by inviting them 'to become inquisitors on the freedom of speech.' "[17]

Charges of grand jury partisanship in the last decade of the 18th century were followed in the early 1800s by accusations that the people's panel was inefficient and costly and should be replaced by professionally trained prosecutors. Responding to these arguments, a number of states abolished the grand jury and many others limited its powers. The Fourteenth Amendment, ratified in 1868, forbade states to "deprive any person of life, liberty or property without due process of law." Some states construed the amendment to mean that they were not required to prosecute crimes by indictment nor prohibited from prosecuting on the basis of an information—a direct accusation by the prosecutor.

The Supreme Court, sustaining a murder conviction, in 1884 upheld the right of states to proceed by information rather than indictment.[18] Justice John M. Harlan, in a much quoted dissent in that case, argued: "Anglo-Saxon liberty would, perhaps, have perished long before the adoption of our Constitution, had it been in the power of government to put the subject on trial for his life whenever a justice of the peace, holding his office at the will of the Crown, should certify that he had committed a capital crime.... One of the peculiar benefits of the grand jury system, as it exists in this country and England, is that it is composed, as a general rule, of a body of private persons, *who do not hold office at the will of the government, or at the will of the voters* (Harlan's emphasis)...."

20th Century Use. Younger pointed out that by the time the United States entered World War I in 1917, reformers had succeeded "in making long strides toward abolishing the grand inquest.... Legal circles were generally anti-jury on the grounds of inefficiency, expense and lay interference in professional matters. Further, vast areas in the United States had done away with it. In the East the reformers had succeeded only partially, in the South hardly at all, and in the West overwhelmingly. Only four western states, Texas, California, Oregon and New Mexico, summoned grand jurors regularly."

Little credit was being given to the grand jury's effectiveness in combating municipal corruption and big-business abuses. A New York panel played an important role in exposing the thievery and corruption of the Tweed Ring in the early 1870s. Between 1890, when the Sherman Anti-Trust Act was enacted, and 1916, federal grand juries had indicted 84 corporations for violations of that law to prohibit restraint of trade. Around 1930, grand jury investigations of crime and corruption were given wide publicity. One of the most important was that of a special New York panel established to investigate racketeering and organized crime in the city. Led by Special Prosecutor Thomas E. Dewey, a grand jury in 1935-36 exposed and indicted underworld figures and prominent racketeers. Other cities followed suit.

Grand jury success in exposing crime and corruption led the Better Government Association, in a 1931 study, to conclude: "The grand jury...is the greatest engine that can be created for the destruction of crime and graft in public office. It can get information where the most acute investigators would fail."[19] The same year, however, the Report on Prosecution by the National Commission on Law Observance and Enforcement recommended that the grand jury system be abolished.

McCarthy Era, Ellsberg and Berrigan. During the 1950s, grand juries summoned by the Justice Department's Internal Security Division, were used to investigate persons suspected of being or aiding Communists. John K. Fairbank, director of the East Asian Research Center at Harvard, recalled the effect of these investigations during the McCarthy era. "In the absence of any evidence of criminal conduct...a subpoena has the effect of intimidation both on the person subpoenaed and on those who might have contact with him."[20]

The common picture of grand jury proceedings "is one of a lone witness, thrust into the legal darkness of the grand jury room, barricaded from his lawyer, threatened by all sorts of unseen dangers...."

—Herald P. Fahringer, *Trial* magazine

Charles E. Goodell contends that the Nixon administration's use of the grand jury in the early 1970s was "rooted in this aberration of the Fifties, not in the colonial grand juries and the tradition underlying the Fifth Amendment." In the last few years, federal grand juries have concentrated on three highly political groups: young radicals, anti-war intellectuals and the Catholic left. Special prosecutors from the Internal Security Division have been aided in their investigations by Title I and Title II of the Organized Crime Control Act of 1970. Title I authorized special grand juries to sit in heavily populated areas, or where designated by the Attorney General, for periods of up to 36 months. Title II allowed prosecutors to grant use immunity, rather than the broader transactional immunity.[21]

There have been a number of organizations formed to aid persons called before so-called political grand juries. Two of the most active groups are the Grand Jury Defense Office[22] of the National Lawyers Guild, in San Francisco, and the Coalition to End Grand Jury Abuse, in New York. Both offer legal advice to those compelled to testify. In addition, the New England Free Press has published a booklet, "Are You Now or Have You Ever? ...." (1971), which suggests about 10 ways of challenging a grand jury subpoena.

Grand jury indictments of the Catholic left proved to be embarrassing to the government. A grand jury investigation grew out of a statement by FBI Director J. Edgar Hoover to a Senate Appropriations subcommittee on Nov. 27, 1970. Hoover testified that two activist priests, the brothers Philip and Daniel Berrigan, and a group known as the East Coast Conspiracy to Save Lives were plotting to kidnap presidential assistant Henry A Kissinger, now the secretary of state, and blow up heating systems for federal buildings in the capital.

One of the most publicized grand jury investigations in recent years involved Dr. Daniel Ellsberg, who was accused by the government of making the secret Pentagon Papers[23] available to the press in 1971. Among those subpoenaed to appear before panels in Boston and Los Angeles were professors, friends and neighbors of Ellsberg, government consultants, congressional aides, and Ellsberg's 15-year-old son, mother-in-law, and co-defendant Anthony Russo. Ellsberg and Russo were indicted by Los Angeles grand juries, but all charges against them—of espionage, theft and conspiracy—were dismissed at their trial by Judge W. Matthew Byrne of the U.S. District Court in Los Angeles on May 11, 1973. In declaring a mistrial, Byrne said government misconduct in the case had precluded "a fair and dispassionate consideration of issues by the jury."

A grand jury in Harrisburg, Pa., heard the government's evidence and indicted six persons and named seven others as co-conspirators.[24] In an apparent attempt to bolster its case, the government called the grand jury back into session to hear 34 additional witnesses, including priests and nuns. A superseding indictment was returned with new counts inserted. The case went to trial before a federal district court jury in Harrisburg and on April 5, 1972, the jury announced it was unable to reach a verdict on the main charges. Only two of the six defendants were convicted—Philip Berrigan and Elizabeth McAlister for the offense of smuggling letters in and out of the federal prison where he was serving a sentence for anti-war activity.

Grand Jury Reform

With the exception of one issue—wiretapping—prosecution methods have not been challenged very successfully by those who would reform the grand jury system. The 1968 Omnibus Crime Control and Safe Streets Act and the 1970 Organized Crime Control Act both prohibit prosecutors from questioning grand jury witnesses on matters derived from unauthorized wiretaps. In 1972 the Supreme Court, with all four Nixon appointees dissenting, reversed a witness's contempt citation for refusing to answer questions because the Justice Department would not reveal whether the witness had been wiretapped.[25] However, unless the witness specifically demands to know if the government used illegal wiretapping, there is no way of finding out how the information was obtained.

Jack Nelson and Ronald J. Ostrow pointed out in *The FBI and the Berrigans* (1972) that the Supreme Court's ruling "established the precedent that grand jury witnesses threatened with contempt for refusing to testify could require the government either to disclose whether they had been picked up on wiretaps or drop the contempt proceedings, a choice prosecutors were loath to make." In October 1973, the Justice Department agreed to drop a grand jury indictment of 15 Weathermen accused of planning a campaign of terrorism and bombing in Flint, Mich., after U.S. District Court Judge Damon J. Keith ordered the government to disclose whether it had used burglaries, wiretapping, sabotage or other "espionage techniques" against the radicals. The prosecutors argued that they would have had to disclose "foreign intelligence

information deemed essential to the security of the United States."

Among the changes that have been suggested in the grand jury system are more rigorous standards for investigation, court supervision of subpoena and questioning powers, giving witnesses the right to have an attorney with them during the proceedings, and routinely providing them transcripts of their testimony. According to one school of thought, prosecutors should be required to file reports with the courts on the reasons for investigations and for calling certain witnesses. Others urge that similar restraints be placed on the questions that prosecutors ask.

Probably the most frequently mentioned proposal for reform is that of allowing defense counsel to be present to object to questions, and to cross-examine the prosecutor. Some argue that the attorney's function should be limited to advising his client on the questions he should answer, lest the grand jury proceeding become like a regular court trial. In an interview after his release from prison for not answering questions before a grand jury in the Pentagon Papers investigation, Harvard professor Samuel L. Popkin confessed to having had mixed feelings on the subject.

> For me (Popkin said), I see an advantage for the lawyer to be in the hall because I can get the question down perfectly and then we have a slight amount of privacy where I can relax and talk out loud about how I should answer the question.... On the other hand, I think a lawyer in the grand jury room may be necessary for the average witness, who does not have a Ph.D. and has not been working with a lawyer for six months to help make the distinctions that only a lawyer is used to making.[26]

Rights of Witnesses. There are at least three reasons offered as to why witnesses should be given a transcript of their testimony after the grand jury has announced its findings. First, a transcript could help a witness prove he had been granted immunity by one grand jury if he were called before a second grand jury or threatened with prosecution. Second, it might deter a prosecutor from intimidating witnesses. Third, it could protect newsmen and other recipients of confidential material by permitting them to show their sources that they had not violated any confidences. Finally, it is argued that grand jurors should be instructed about their rights to ask questions, challenge the prosecution's case and undertake independent investigations on their own.[27]

However, Hugo L. Black, the late civil libertarian and Supreme Court justice, insisted that many proposed changes in grand-jury operations were neither necessary nor desirable. The grand jury, Black said for the Court's majority in a 1956 case, is an "institution in which laymen conduct their inquiry unfettered by technical rules. Neither justice nor the concept of a fair trial requires... a change. In a trial on the merits, defendants are entitled to a strict observance of all the rules designed to bring about a fair verdict. Defendants are not entitled, however, to a rule which would result in interminable delay but add nothing to the assurance of a fair trial."

Abolishing the Grand Jury. Detractors of the grand jury system who do not argue for reform want to have the system abolished. They point out that Britain did away with grand juries in 1933 without jeopardizing that country's system of criminal justice. The National Advisory Commission on Criminal Justice Standards and Goals was critical of the grand jury system but was unwilling to recommend abolishment. It said that grand jury indictments should not be required in any criminal prosecution. If an indictment is issued, the commission added, the prosecutor should disclose to the defense all testimony before the grand jury directly relating to the charges contained in the indictment against the defendant. However, "the grand jury can perform an important role in the investigation and accusation that leads to the prosecution of crime, a role not satisfactorily filled by the prosecutor-information system in some serious, doubtful, or politically sensitive cases...."

The Supreme Court has upheld the right of states, through legislation or referendum, to abolish grand juries. But federal grand juries could be outlawed only by repeal of the Fifth Amendment. The only constitutional amendment ever to have been repealed was the 18th, which forbade the manufacture, sale or transporation of intoxicating liquors. Grand juries are not yet as unpopular as prohibition.

It is possible to argue that the grand jury system, in theory and often in practice, is a sound institution. In this view, criticism of the people's panel should be directed not at what it is but at how it is being used. However, the uses for which it is praised or condemned often depend on the political views of critics and defenders. Thus, liberals can applaud grand juries for investigating Watergate and denounce them for intimidating militants. Conservatives might just as easily reprove them for the former and commend them for the latter. The important question about grand juries is whether they are an effective instrument for protecting the innocent and bringing the guilty to trial. Could the American system of justice work more efficiently and fairly without the grand inquest? Or would the panel's investigatory functions be better conducted by other agencies, like legislative committees? On these questions, the jury is still out.

---

1 So characterized by Harvard Professor Samuel L. Popkin, who was jailed briefly for refusal to answer certain questions before a grand jury investigating the Pentagon Papers case.

2 Blair *v.* United States, 250 U.S. 273.

3 Dionisio *v.* United States, 410 U.S. 1.

4 "Eliminate the Grand Jury," *The Journal of Criminal Law and Criminology* (Northwestern University Law School publication), 1973 Vol. 64, No. 2, p. 174.

5 Frank J. Donner and Eugene Cerruti, "The Grand Jury Network," *Nation,* Jan. 3, 1972, p. 5.

6 Title II of the Organized Crime Control Act of 1970 provided for use immunity. On May 22, 1973, the Supreme Court in Kastigar *v.* United States held that a grant of use immunity was sufficient to allow the government to compel the testimony of a witness who invoked the Fifth Amendment. The same day, in Zicarelli *v.* New Jersey, the Court upheld a state statute that provided only for use immunity—not transactional immunity.

7 Size and composition of trial juries is also an issue. See "American Jury System: Re-examination and Change," *Editorial Research Reports* 1972 Vol. II, pp. 687-704.

8 Livingston Hall, Yale Kamisar, Wayne LaFave and Jerold H. Israel, *Modern Criminal Procedure* (1969), p. 829.

9 *The Wall Street Journal* broke the story on Aug. 7 that Agnew was under investigation. In the ensuing weeks, a number of other papers, especially *The Washington Post,* published stories about the investigation that were attributed to unidentified sources.

10 The majority decision was written by Justice Byron R. White and supported by the four Nixon appointees to the Court—Chief Justice Warren E. Burger and Justices Harry A Blackmun, Lewis F. Powell Jr., and William H. Rehnquist.

11 The first to be jailed after the Caldwell ruling was Peter J. Bridge, a reporter for the now-defunct Newark, N.J., *News,* on Oct. 4, 1972. Among the latest to be ordered to jail for contempt was Lucy Ware Morgan of the *St. Petersburg Times,* who refused to tell the source of a story disclosing portions of a Pasco County (Fla.) grand jury presentment. She was sentenced Nov. 1, 1973, to five months in jail but remained free on bond pending appeal.

12 White cited an opinion by Chief Justice Marshall, given as presiding judge in the 1807 treason trial of Aaron Burr, suggesting that the President could be subpoenaed to appear in court. Marshall, in fact, issued a subpoena on President Thomas Jefferson but it was never served.

13 For background on arguments over executive-privilege and separation-of-powers doctrines invoked by the White House, see "Separation of Powers," *Editorial Research Reports,* 1973 Vol. II, pp. 691-708.

14 William P. Cannon, "The Propriety of a Breach of Grand Jury Secrecy When No Indictment Is Returned," *Houston Law Review,* 1970 Vol. 7, No. 34, pp. 343-344.

15 George J. Edwards Jr. offers a different view in his book *The Grand Jury* (1973), pp. 29-30. While the grand jurors' stand was bold, he wrote, "the Earl of Shaftesbury was a very powerful nobleman.... The sheriff...was an open adherent of Shaftesbury, and it is reasonable to assume that the panel was composed of those whose sympathies were inclined toward the Earl."

16 *The People's Panel (1963), pp. 19, 26.*

17 Charles E. Goodell, *Political Prisoners in America* (1973). Goodell is a former Republican senator from New York.

18 Hurtado *v.* United States, 110 U.S. 516.

19 The *Grand Jury: Its Powers and Duties in Relation to the Officials' Oath of Office,* p. 1.

20 Quoted by Frank K. Donner and Eugene Cerruti in *Nation,* Jan. 3, 1972, p. 19.

21 Between 1970 and January 1973, a small group of Justice Department lawyers presented evidence to more than 100 grand juries in 36 states and 84 cities. The grand juries returned about 410 indictments.—Paul Cowan, "The New Grand Jury," *The New York Times Magazine,* April 29, 1973.

22 Barry Winograd and Martin Fassier of the Grand Jury Defense Office wrote on "The Political Question" concerning grand juries in the January-February 1973 issue of *Trial* magazine published by the Association of Trial Lawyers of America.

23 *The New York Times* and later several other newspapers published excerpts from a 7,000-page *History of the United States Decision-Making Process on Vietnam Policy,* popularly known as the Pentagon Papers. For background, see "Secrecy in Government," *Editorial Research Reports,* 1971 Vol. II, pp. 629-637.

24 Those indicted were Eqbal Ahmed, Philip Berrigan, Elizabeth McAlister, Neil McLaughlin, Anthony Scoblick and Joseph Wenderoth. Named as co-conspirators were Daniel Berrigan, Thomas Davidson, Margorie Shuman, Beverly Bell, Paul Mayer, Bill Davidon and Jogues Egan.

25 Two cases were combined for the court's decision on June 26, 1972, in Gelbard *v.* United States, 408 U.S. 41.

26 Interview with Eda M. Gordon, *Trial,* January-February 1973, p. 22.

27 On the matter of obtaining transcripts, the Federal Rules of Criminal Procedure state that a defendant may obtain a transcript of his own testimony.

Appendix

WATERGATE: A CASE STUDY IN THE POWER OF THE COURTS

Without the federal judiciary, Watergate would have been a different story. Now, among its legacies, remains a powerful and provocative case study of judicial power, its exercise, its impact, and its limits.

It was federal grand juries, an arm of the federal courts, which investigated various aspects of the mushrooming scandal across the country. It was federal courtrooms in which the original Watergate defendants were tried—and where the determined probing by Federal District Judge John J. Sirica produced revelations which raised the burglary to the level of a national scandal. The federal courts were the forum to which the Senate Watergate Committee and the White House came to battle out the matter of the committee's subpoena of White House tapes, and it was there too that constitutional experts argued whether one part of the Executive Branch, the White House, had to give up subpoenaed tapes to another part, the Special Prosecutor acting for the grand jury. After the dramatic announcement that the President would allow Sirica to examine the tapes, it was in Sirica's courtroom that the saga of the tapes unfolded.

Caution was the signal characteristic of judicial moves in the Watergate matter. Cognizant both of the historic nature of the confrontation mounted over the presidential tapes—and of the judiciary's inability to enforce its orders—the courts sought a middle road, a compromise instead of collision.

Stating clearly that he was attempting to "walk the middle ground," Sirica in his Aug. 29 decision on the tapes battle ordered Nixon to turn over to him, for private inspection and a decision on the claim of executive privilege, the tapes subpoenaed by the grand jury Charles Alan Wright, the president's attorney, had claimed that the President had the right to keep the tapes secret, under executive privilege. Archibald Cox, the special prosecutor, had argued that they must be delivered to the grand jury.

Wright, in arguing against enforcement of the subpoena had emphasized the far-reaching impact of such a precedential decision; Cox, to the contrary, had emphasized the uniqueness of the particular situation, and therefore, the limited use to which Sirica's ruling could be put as precedent.

Sirica's Order

"There can be executive privileges that will bar the production of evidence," said Sirica. "The court is willing here to recognize and give effect to an evidentiary privilege based on the need to protect presidential privacy."

But it was not up to the President alone to decide when executive privilege was properly asserted, continued Sirica. When that decision affected the avail-

ability of evidence, it fell also within the province of the courts. "Executive fiat is not the mode" for resolving such problems, he said.

"In all candor, the court fails to perceive any reason for suspending the power of the courts to get evidence and rule on questions of privilege in criminal matters simply because it is the President of the United States who holds the evidence," declared Sirica.

The court had the right to avail itself of a private examination of the documents or

Judge John J. Sirica

tapes, held Sirica. "To call for the tapes *in camera* is thus tantamount to fully enforcing the subpoena as to any unprivileged matter." He had concluded, he said, that the court had the authority to order a President to obey the command of a grand jury subpoena as it related to unprivileged evidence in his possession.

It was up to the President, he continued, "to define exactly what it is about his office that court process commanding the production of evidence (a subpoena) cannot reach there.... What distinctive quality of the Presidency permits its incumbent to withhold evidence?"

Separation of Powers. Sirica found unpersuasive the arguments that the need for presidential privacy and respect for the separation of powers justified withholding of evidence: "the special prosecutor has correctly noted that the framers' intention to lodge the powers of government in separate bodies also included a plan for interaction between departments."

"A 'watertight' division of different functions was never their design. The legislative branch may organize the judiciary and dictate the procedures by which it transacts business. The judiciary may pass upon the constitutionality of legislative enactments and in some instances define the bounds of congressional investigations. The executive may veto legislative enactments, and the legislature may override the veto. The executive appoints judges and justices and may bind judicial decisions by lawful executive orders. The judiciary may pass on the constitutionality of executive acts."

It is immaterial whether the court has the physical power to enforce an order against the President, continued Sirica. "Regardless of its physical power...the court has a duty to issue appropriate orders." Agreeing with the special prosecutor's argument concerning grand jury powers, Sirica stated: "The grand jury derives its authority directly from the people, and when that group, independent in its sphere, acts according to its mandate, the court cannot justifiably withhold its assistance, nor can anyone, regardless of his station, withhold from it evidence not privileged."

The Claim of Privilege. The eventual decision on the width of the protection of executive privilege as applied to the tapes would be heavily influenced, Sirica indicated, by the well documented and imposing need for the tapes as evidence.

"This is a criminal investigation....

"The special prosecutor cites a substantial possibility, based on the sworn testimony of participants, that the privilege is improperly invoked as a cloak for serious criminal wrong-doing." Should that be the case, said Sirica—"if the interest served by a privilege is abused or subverted—the claim of privilege is invalid.

But Sirica found himself unable, under the circumstances of Aug. 29, to rule that the present claim of privilege by Nixon was invalid. "The court...is extremely reluctant to finally stand against a declaration of the President of the United States on any but the strongest possible evidence. Need for the evidence requires that a claim not be rejected lightly. The court is simply unable to decide...without inspecting the tapes."

He admitted that if the tapes were indeed protected by executive privilege, even his private inspection of them would compromise that privilege. But "it would be an extremely limited infraction and in this case an unavoidable one.... The court is unable to design a more cautious approach.... The court has attempted to walk the middle ground between a failure to decide the question of privilege...and a wholesale delivery of tapes to the grand jury at the other. The one would be a breach of duty; the other an inexcusable course of conduct."

"If it be apparent that the tapes are irrelevant to the investigation, or that for state reasons they cannot be introduced into the case, the subpoena *duces tecum* would be useless. But if this be not apparent, if they *may* be important in the investigation, if they *may* be safely heard by the grand jury, if only in part, would it not be a blot on the page which records the judicial proceedings of this country, if, in a case of such serious import as this, the court did not at least call for an inspection of the evidence in chambers?"

The Appeal

Both sides chose to appeal Sirica's ruling—and thus, by an odd circumstance, Sirica himself had to find attorneys to argue on behalf of his order before the full court of appeals in the District of Columbia circuit. The arguments took place Sept. 11 and on Sept. 13 the appeals court, in an unusual move in an unusual case, sent a memorandum to Nixon, Sirica and Cox, asking them to try to settle their dispute without further court action:

"The doctrine under which courts seek resolution of a controversy without a constitutional ruling is particularly applicable here....

"Whereas Judge Sirica contemplated an *in camera* examination of the subpoenaed tapes, which would have necessitated the presence of the judiciary, we contemplate an examination of the tapes by the Chief Executive or his delegate, assisted by both his own counsel, Professor Wright, and the special prosecutor, Professor Cox.

"We say this without intimating a decision on any question of jurisdiction or privilege advanced by any party. Apart from noting that the likelihood of successful settlement along the lines indicated contemplates a voluntary submission of such portions of the tapes to the two counsels as satisfies them, we do not presume to prescribe the details....

"This procedure may permit the different approaches of the parties to converge. The President has maintained that he alone should decide what is necessarily privileged and should not be furnished the grand jury. The special prosecutor has maintained that he should have the opportunity of examining the material and asserting its relevance and importance to the grand jury investigation. If the President and the special prosecutor agree as to the material needed for the grand jury's functioning, the national interest will be served. At the same time, neither the President nor the special prosecutor would in any way have surrendered or subverted the principles for which they have contended...."

A week later, Wright and Cox informed the court that they had failed to reach any agreement. It was then up to the appeals court to decide the issue it had hoped to avoid.

Appeals Court Decision

"Sovereignty remains at all times with the people, and they do not forfeit through elections the right to have the law construed against and applied to every citizen," stated the court of appeals Oct. 12. That afternoon, by a 5-2 vote, the court upheld the order of Judge Sirica directing President Nixon to turn over to Sirica the nine tapes of presidential conversations sought by the original grand jury investigating the Watergate break-in and cover-up.

A view of their decision as limited in its impact—and of executive privilege as a qualified privilege to be weighed by courts against competing public interests—emerged from the unsigned *(per curiam)* 44-page majority opinion. Joining in that opinion were Chief Judge David L. Bazelon and Judges J. Skelly Wright, Carl McGowan, Harold Leventhal and Spottswood W. Robinson III. All five were appointed by Democratic presidents: Bazelon by Truman, Wright and McGowan by Kennedy, Leventhal and Robinson by Johnson.

On the other hand, the far-reaching impact of their decision—and a view of executive privilege as absolute and exercised at the sole discretion of the President—marked the two lengthy dissenting opinions written by Judges George E. MacKinnon and Malcolm R. Wilkey, both Nixon appointees. Not participating in the consideration or decision of the matter were two other members of the appeals court—Edward Allen Tamm, appointed by Johnson, and Roger Robb, another Nixon appointee.

Before addressing the questions raised on appeal, the majority emphasized the limited nature of the case:

"We deem it essential to emphasize the narrow contours of the problem that compels the court to address the issues raised by this case. The central question before us is, in essence, whether the President may, in his sole discretion, withhold from a grand jury evidence in his possession that is relevant to the grand jury's investigations. It is our duty to respond to this question, but we limit our decision strictly to that required by the precise and entirely unique circumstances of the case."

The grand jury's need for the tapes was clearly shown. "The strength and particularity of this showing were made possible by a unique intermeshing of events unlikely soon, if ever, to recur."

Because Nixon had allowed his present and former aides to testify before the Senate committee on the Watergate affair, because their testimony had revealed a strong possibility that a high-level conspiracy had existed, important evidence of which was contained in statements made during conversations of those aides with Nixon, there was a clear need for the taped records to clear up questions about exactly what was said during those conversations, the court stated.

"Most importantly...significant inconsistencies in the sworn testimony of these advisers relating to the content of the conversations raised a distinct possibility that perjury had been committed," the opinion said. And so the special prosecutor could make his case that the tapes contained "evidence critical to the grand jury's decisions as to whether and whom to indict."

Courts have frequently ordered officials of the executive branch to produce evidence, the opinion noted. It then pointed out the signal instance of the steel seizure case in which the Supreme Court directed the secretary of commerce not to follow President Truman's order to assume control of the nation's steel mills.

It made no difference that in the case at hand Nixon personally assumed possession of the tapes and therefore was personally the object of the court order: "The practice of judicial review would be rendered capricious—and very likely impotent—if jurisdiction vanished whenever the President personally denoted an executive action or omission as his own."

Thus the court ruled that the President then is not immune from such orders: "The Constitution makes no mention of special presidential immunities." Yet the President's counsel asked the court to "infer immunity from the President's political mandate, or from his vulnerability to impeachment, or from his broad discretionary powers. These are invitations to refashion the Constitution and we reject them."

"Though the President is elected by nationwide ballot and is often said to represent all the people, he does not embody the nation's sovereignty. He is not above the law's commands."

No Absolute Privilege. "Whenever a privilege is asserted...it is the courts that determine the validity of the assertion and the scope of the privilege," stated the Court.

But, Wright argued for the President, separation of powers dictated that this executive privilege be absolute, asserted without question by the President alone. Such a claim, the majority held, misconstrued the purpose and the operation of separated powers: "To leave the proper scope and application of executive privilege to the President's sole discretion would represent a mixing, rather than a separation, of executive and judicial functions."

Such an absolute privilege is unnecessary for workable government, the court held. "If the claim of absolute privilege was recognized, its mere invocation by the President or his surrogates could deny access to all documents in all the executive departments to all citizens and their representatives, including Congress, the courts as well as grand juries, state governments, state officials and all state subdivisions. The Freedom of Information Act could become nothing more than a legislative statement of unenforceable rights. Support for this kind of mischief simply cannot be spun from incantation of the doctrine of separation of powers."

In a footnote, the majority added that the reason separation of powers was adopted by the founding fathers as the basic form of American government was not to promote efficiency but "to preclude the exercise of arbitrary power. The purpose was not to avoid friction, but, by means of the inevitable friction incident to the distribution of governmental power among three departments, to save the people from autocracy."

If the privilege is not absolute, the instances of its proper application depend upon a balancing, in each case, of "the public interest protected by the privilege against the public interests that would be served by disclosure." In this case the interest in confidentiality of White House conversations fails to outweigh the grand jury's—and the public's need for this evidence, the court held.

In Dissent. "The ultimate issue is the effect that our decision will have upon the constitutional independence of the presidency for all time," MacKinnon wrote in his 65-page dissenting opinion. "The preservation of the confidentiality of the presidential decision-making process is of overwhelming importance to the effective functioning of our three branches of government. Therefore, I would recognize an absolute privilege for confidential presidential communications."

"To allow the courts to breach presidential confidentiality whenever one of 400 federal trial judges considers that the circumstances...demonstrate a compelling need...would frustrate the privilege's underlying policy.... The lessons of legal history teach that it will be impossible to contain this breach of presidential confidentiality if numerous federal judges may rummage through presidential papers."

In MacKinnon's view, only a minimal role existed for the courts. Once executive privilege is invoked, "the only inquiry is whether the...invocation...promotes the policy which the privilege was designed to protect."

It is for the executive, not the courts, to decide when and to what extent executive privilege may be properly asserted, Wilkey said in his 79-page dissent. Any weighing of competing public interests should be done by the president, not the courts, he held.

"It was and is the President's right to make that decision initially, and it is the American people who will be the judge as to whether the President has made the right decision.... If the decision is not visibly on sound grounds of national public interest, in political terms the decision may be ruinous for the President, but it is his to make.

The grand design has worked; the separate independent branch remains in charge of and responsible for its own papers, processes and decisions, not to a second or third branch, but it remains responsible to the American people."

Inherent in the system of separated powers, conceded Wilkey, is the possibility of irreconcilable conflict. "Leaving the three branches in an equilibrium of tension was just one of their devices to guard against oppression," Wilkey stated.

A Dramatic Turn-Around

White House spokesmen had earlier said that President Nixon would only comply with a "definitive" Supreme Court ruling to hand over the tapes. Yet, although given a grace period by the appeals court, within which to appeal its decision to the Supreme Court, the President chose not to do so—thus agreeing to the finality of the appeals court ruling. A week after the appeals court decision, further efforts to settle the tug-of-war over the tapes exploded in the "Saturday night massacre"—the firing of Cox, the resignations of William D. Ruckelshaus and Elliot L. Richardson. As a storm of public reactions gained strength across the nation, Wright came again to Sirica's courtroom on the following Tuesday—to announce quietly that the President would comply with Sirica's order as modified by the appeals court.

The system, it appeared, had triumphed. The ultimate confrontation had been avoided. Law had prevailed. But such conclusions proved premature.

Wright's announcement of the President's decision did not end the tapes controversy. Instead, it only set the stage for another set of disquieting discoveries of coincidental absences of certain material. First it was disclosed, in Sirica's courtroom, that two of the subpoenaed tapes did not exist at all. Hearings were begun on the tapes, before Sirica, in an effort to trace their production, safekeeping, and the record of persons who had had access to them. During these sessions, still more revelations emerged—chief among them the fact that significant "gaps" existed in the remaining seven subpoenaed tapes.

The Committee's Suit

Sirica's action in the suit brought by the Watergate Committee, seeking enforcement of its subpoena of certain presidential tapes, made clear the limits of federal court power.

Federal courts are courts of limited jurisdiction, and in this particular situation, Sirica found that Congress had never acted to give his court—or any other federal court—jurisdiction over such a case. Thus, on Oct. 17, he dismissed the committee's case.

In an 18-page opinion, Sirica discussed each of the four reasons that the committee attorneys had argued as the basis for federal court jurisdiction over their civil suit for enforcement of the subpoenas. Each was dismissed by the judge as insufficient. Because he dismissed the case on the threshold question of whether the case should be in his court at all, Sirica did not consider the other basic questions raised by the case.

In civil suits, he explained, "jurisdiction is a threshold issue.... For the federal courts, jurisdiction is not automatic and cannot be presumed. Thus, the presumption in each instance is that a federal court lacks jurisdiction until it can be shown that a specific grant of jurisdiction applies. Federal courts may exercise only that judicial power provided by the Constitution in Article III and conferred by Congress. All other judicial power or jurisdiction is reserved to the states.... When it comes to jurisdiction of the federal courts, truly, to paraphrase the scripture, the Congress giveth, and the Congress taketh away...(and) jurisdictional requirements cannot be waived."

Sirica then considered the four bases which the committee claimed gave the court jurisdiction:

- Federal law providing that federal courts have jurisdiction over "all civil actions, suits or proceedings commenced by the United States." But, Sirica said, other provisions of the law make clear that the attorney general and the Justice Department are the only ones who can qualify to litigate as the United States under that law.

- Federal law granting the federal courts jurisdiction over any effort to get an order to compel an official of the United States to perform a duty owed to a citizen. Sirica found that the President had no official duty to comply with the committee's subpoenas "regardless of whatever duty...(he) may owe the select committee as a citizen."

- The Administrative Procedure Act, which Sirica held did not confer jurisdiction when a suit would not otherwise be properly before the federal courts.

- Federal law providing that federal courts have jurisdiction over all civil cases involving "a matter in controversy" of more than $10,000. In this case, Sirica found no "matter in controversy...capable of valuation in dollars and cents." The tapes and documents were not worth that much; access to that information could not be considered as worth that amount; the rights and responsibilities of legislators were not measurable in dollars and cents; nor was Nixon's interest in keeping the tapes secret.

"No jurisdictional statute known to the court," Sirica concluded, "warrants an assumption of jurisdiction, and the court is therefore left with no alternative here but to dismiss the action....

"The court has here been requested to invoke a jurisdiction which only Congress can grant but which Congress has heretofore withheld. Whether such jurisdiction ought to be conferred is the prerogative of the Congress. Plaintiffs...are free to pursue whatever remedy they now deem appropriate, but the court cannot, consistent with law and the constitutional principles that reserve to Congress the conferral of jurisdiction, validate the present course."

TEXT OF JUDGE SIRICA'S OPINION ON PRESIDENTIAL TAPES

Following are excerpts from District Court Chief Judge John J. Sirica's Aug. 29, 1973 opinion on the presidential tapes:

The Court has found it necessary to adjudicate but two questions for the present: (1) whether the Court has jurisdiction to decide the issue of privilege, and (2) whether the Court has authority to enforce the subpoena *duces tecum* by way of an order requiring production for inspection *in camera*. A third question, whether the materials are in fact privileged as against the grand jury, either in whole or in part, is left for subsequent adjudication. For the reasons outlined below, the Court concludes that both of the questions considered must be answered in the affirmative.

A search of the Constitution and the history of its creation reveals a general disfavor of government privileges, or at least uncontrolled privileges. Early in the Convention of 1787, the delegates cautioned each other concerning the dangers of lodging immoderate power in the executive department. This attitude persisted throughout the Convention, and executive powers became a major topic in the subsequent ratification debates. The Framers regarded the legislative department superior in power and importance to the other two and felt the necessity of investing it with some privileges and immunities, but even here an attitude of restraint, as expressed by James Madison, prevailed.... The upshot...regarding a definition of executive privileges was that none were deemed necessary, or at least that the Constitution need not record any.

...Are there, then, any rights or privileges consistent with, though not mentioned in, the Constitution which are necessary to the Executive? One answer may be found in the Supreme Court decision, *United States v. Reynolds,* 346 U.S. 1 (1953). The Court recognized an executive privilege, evidentiary in nature, for military secrets. *Reynolds* held that when a court finds the privilege is properly invoked under the appropriate circumstances, it will, in a civil case at least, suppress the evidence. Thus, it must be recognized that there can be executive privileges that will bar the production of evidence. The Court is willing here to recognize and give effect to an evidentiary privilege based on the need to protect Presidential privacy.

The Court, however, cannot agree with Respondent that it is the Executive that finally determines whether its privilege is properly invoked. The availability of evidence including the validity and scope of privileges, is a judicial decision.... In all the numerous litigations where claims of executive privilege have been interposed, the courts have not hesitated to pass judgment. Executive fiat is not the mode of resolution....

The measures a court should adopt in ruling on claims of executive privilege are discussed under Part III herein.

If after judicial examination *in camera,* any portion of the tapes is ruled not subject to privilege, that portion will be forwarded to the grand jury at the appropriate time. To call for the tapes *in camera* is thus tantamount to fully enforcing the subpoena as to any unprivileged matter. Therefore, before the Court can call for production *in camera*, it must have concluded that it has authority to order a President to obey the command of a grand jury subpoena as it relates to unprivileged evidence in his possession. The Court has concluded that it possesses such authority.

Analysis of the question must begin on the well established premises that the grand jury has a right to every man's evidence and that for purposes of gathering evidence, process may issue to anyone.... The important factors are the relevance and materiality of the evidence.... The burden here then, is on the President to define exactly what it is about his office that court process commanding the production of evidence cannot reach there. To be accurate, court process in the form of a subpoena *duces tecum* has already issued to the President, and he acknowledges that...courts possess authority to direct such subpoenas to him. A distinction is drawn, however, between authority to issue a subpoena and authority to command obedience to it. It is this second compulsory process that the President contends may not reach him. The burden yet remains with the President, however, to explain why this must be so. What distinctive quality of the Presidency permits its incumbent to withhold evidence? To argue that the need for Presidential privacy justifies it, is not persuasive. On the occasions when such need justifies suppression, the courts will sustain a privilege. The fact that this is a judicial decision has already been discussed at length, but the opinion of Chief Justice Marshall *(United States v. Burr,* 25 Fed. Cas. 30, 1807) on the topic deserves notice here. When deciding that a subpoena should issue to the President, the Chief Justice made it clear that if certain portions should be excised, it being appropriate to sustain a privilege, the Court would make such a decision upon return of the subpoena....

To argue that it is the constitutional separation of powers that bars compulsory court process from the White House, is also unpersuasive. Such a contention overlooks history. Although courts generally, and this Court in particular, have avoided any interference with the discretionary acts of coordinate branches, they have not hesitated to rule on non-discretionary acts when necessary. Respondent points out that these and other precedents refer to officials other than the President, and that this distinction renders the precedents inapplicable. Such an argument tends to set the White House apart as a fourth branch of government....

The Special Prosecutor has correctly noted that the Framer's intention to lodge the powers of government in separate bodies also included a plan for interaction between departments. A "watertight" division of different functions was never their design. The legislative branch may organize the judiciary and dictate the procedures by which it transacts business. The judiciary may pass upon the constitutionality of legislative enactments—and in some instances define the bounds of Congressional investigations. The executive may veto legislative enactments, and the legislature may override the veto. The executive appoints judges and justices and may bind judicial decisions by lawful executive orders. The judiciary may pass on the constitutionality of executive acts....

That the Court has not the physical power to enforce its order to the President is immaterial to a resolution of the issues. Regardless of its physical power to enforce them, the Court has a duty to issue appropriate orders. The Court cannot say that the Executive's persistence in withholding the tape recordings would "tarnish its reputation," but must admit that it would tarnish the Court's reputation to fail to do what it could in pursuit of justice. In any case, the courts have always enjoyed the good faith of the Executive Branch, even in such dire circumstances as those presented by *Youngstown Sheet & Tube Co. v. Sawyer,* 343 U.S. 579 (1952), and there is no reason to suppose that the courts in this instance cannot again rely on that same good faith. Indeed, the President himself has publicly so stated.

It is important also to note here the role of the grand jury. Chief Justice Marshall, in considering whether a subpoena might issue to the President of the United States observed:

> In the provisions of the constitution, and of the statute, which give to the accused a right to the compulsory process of the court, there is no exception whatever. *(United States. v. Burr,* 25 Fed. Cas. 20, 1807)*

Aaron Burr, it will be remembered, stood before the court accused though not yet indicted. The Chief Justice's statement regarding the accused is equally true with regard to a grand jury: "there is no exception whatever" in its right to the compulsory process of the courts. The Court, while in a position to lend its process in assistance to the grand jury, is thereby in a position to assist justice....

In all candor, the Court fails to perceive any reason for suspending the power of courts to get evidence and rule on questions of privilege in criminal matters simply because it is the President of the United States who holds the evidence. The Burr decision left for another occasion a ruling on whether compulsory process might issue to the President in situations such as this. In the words of counsel, this is a new question," with little in the way of precedent to guide the Court. But Chief Justice Marshall clearly distinguished the amenability of the King to appear and give testimony under court process and that of this nation's chief magistrate. The conclusion reached here cannot be inconsistent with the view of that great Chief Justice nor with the spirit of the Constitution.

In deciding whether these tape recordings or portions thereof are properly the objects of a privilege, the Court must accommodate two competing policies. On the one hand, as has been noted earlier, is the need to disfavor privileges and narrow their application as far as possible. On the other hand, lies a need to favor the privacy of Presidential deliberations; to indulge a presumption in favor of the President. To the Court, respect for the President, the Presidency, and the duties of the office, gives the advantage to this second policy. This respect, however, does not decide the controversy....

The teaching of *Reynolds* is that a Court should attempt to satisfy itself whether or not a privilege is properly invoked without unnecessarily probing into the material claimed to be privileged. A decision on how far to go will be dictated in part by need for the evidence....

The grand jury's showing of need here is well documented and imposing. The Special Prosecutor has specifically identified by date, time and place each of the eight meetings and the one telephone call involved. Due to the unusual circumstances of having access to sworn public testimony of participants to these conversations, the Special Prosecutor has been able to provide the Court with the conflicting accounts of what transpired. He thus identifies the topics discussed in each instance, the areas of critical conflict in the testimony, and the resolution it is anticipated the tape recordings may render possible. The relative importance of the issues in doubt is revealed....

The point is raised that, as in *Reynolds,* the sworn statements of witnesses should suffice and remove the need for access to documents deemed privileged. Though this might often be the case, here, unfortunately, the witnesses differ, sometimes completely, on the precise matters likely to be of greatest moment to the grand jury. Ironically, need for the taped

evidence derives in part from the fact that witnesses *have* testified regarding the subject matter, creating important issues of fact for the grand jury to resolve. It will be noted as well in contradistinction to *Reynolds,* that this is a criminal investigation. Rather than money damages at stake, we deal here in matters of reputation and liberty. Based on this indisputably forceful showing of necessity by the grand jury, the claim of privilege cannot be accepted lightly

In his Brief in Support, the Special Prosecutor outlines the grand jury's view regarding the validity of the Respondent's claim of privilege. Its opinion is that the right of confidentiality is improperly asserted here. Principally, the Special Prosecutor cites a substantial possibility, based on the sworn testimony of participants, that the privilege is improperly invoked as a cloak for serious criminal wrongdoing....

If the interest served by a privilege is abused or subverted, the claim of privilege fails. Such a case is well described in *Clark* v. *United States,* 289 U.S. 1 (1933), a decision involving the privilege of secrecy enjoyed by jurors....

These principles are, of course, fully applicable throughout government. A court would expect that if the privacy of its deliberations, for example, were ever used to foster criminal conduct or to develop evidence of criminal wrongdoings, any privilege might be barred and privacy breached. So it is that evidentiary privileges asserted against the grand jury may be ruled inapplicable if the interest served by the privilege is subverted.

Nevertheless, without discrediting the strength of the grand jury's position, the Court cannot, as matters now stand, rule that the present claim of privilege is invalid. The President contends that the recorded conversations occurred pursuant to an exercise of his duty to "take care that the laws be faithfully executed." Although the Court is not bound by that conclusion, it is extremely reluctant to finally stand against a declaration of the President of the United States on any but the strongest possible evidence. Need for the evidence requires that a claim not be rejected lightly. The Court is simply unable to decide the question of privilege without inspecting the tapes....

It is true that if material produced is properly the subject of privilege, even an inspection *in camera* may constitute a compromise of privilege. Nevertheless, it would be an extremely limited infraction and in this case an unavoidable one. If privileged and unprivileged evidence are intermingled, privileged portions may be excised so that only unprivileged matter goes before the grand jury (which also meets in secret proceedings). If privileged and unprivileged evidence are so inextricably connected that separation becomes impossible, the whole must be privileged and no disclosure made to the grand jury....

EXCERPTS FROM APPEALS COURT DECISION ON TAPES

Following are excerpts from the District of Columbia Circuit Court of Appeals decision Oct. 12 affirming Judge Sirica's Aug. 29 order and from the dissenting opinions of Judges George E. MacKinnon and Malcolm R. Wilkey:

PER CURIAM. This controversy concerns an order of the District Court for the District of Columbia entered on August 29, 1973, by Chief Judge John J. Sirica as a means of enforcing a grand jury subpoena *duces tecum* issued to and served on President Richard M. Nixon. The order commands the President, or any subordinate official, to produce certain items identified in the subpoena so that the Court can determine, by *in camera* inspection, whether the items are exempted from disclosure by evidentiary privilege.

Both the President and Special Prosecutor Archibald Cox, acting on behalf of the grand jury empanelled by the District Court in June, 1972, challenge the legality of this order. All members of this Court agree that the District Court had, and this Court has, jurisdiction to consider the President's claim of privilege. The majority of the Court approves the District Court's order, as clarified and modified in part, and otherwise denies the relief requested....

We turn...to the merits of the President's petition. Counsel for the President contend on two grounds that Judge Sirica lacked jurisdiction to order submission of the tapes for inspection. Counsel argue, first, that, so long as he remains in office, the President is absolutely immune from the compulsory process of a court; and, second, that Executive privilege is absolute with respect to presidential communications, so that disclosure is at the sole discretion of the President. This immunity and this absolute privilege are said to arise from the doctrine of separation of powers and by implication from the Constitution itself. It is conceded that neither the immunity nor the privilege is express in the Constitution....

We must...determine whether the President is *legally* bound to comply with an order enforcing a subpoena.

We note first that courts have assumed that they have the power to enter mandatory orders to Executive officials to compel production of evidence.

The courts' assumption of legal power to compel production of evidence within the possession of the Executive surely stands on firm footing. *Youngstown Sheet & Tube v. Sawyer,* in which an injunction running against the Secretary of Commerce was affirmed, is only the most celebrated instance of the issuance of compulsory process against Executive officials.... If *Youngstown* still stands, it must stand for the case where the President has himself taken possession and control of the property unconstitutionally seized, and the injunction would be framed accordingly. The practice of judicial review would be rendered capricious—and very likely impotent—if jurisdiction vanished whenever the President personally denoted an Executive action or omission as his own. This is not to say that the President should lightly be named as a party defendant.... Here, unfortunately, the court's order must run directly to the President, because he has taken the unusual step of assuming personal custody of the Government property sought by the subpoena.

The President also attempts to distinguish *United States v. Burr,* in which Chief Justice Marshall squarely ruled that a subpoena may be directed to the President. It is true that *Burr* recognized a distinction between the issuance of a subpoena and the ordering of compliance with that subpoena, but the distinction did not concern judicial power or jurisdiction. A subpoena *duces tecum* is an order to produce documents or to show cause why they need not be produced. An order to comply does not make the subpoena more compulsory; it simply maintains its original force....

The clear implication is that the President's special interests may warrant a careful judicial screening of subpoenas after the President interposes an objection, but that some subpoenas will nevertheless be properly sustained by judicial orders of compliance.....

The Constitution makes no mention of special presidential immunities. Indeed, the Executive Branch generally is afforded none. This silence cannot be ascribed to oversight. James Madison raised the question of Executive privileges during the Constitutional Convention, and Senators and Representatives enjoy an express, if limited, immunity from arrest, and an express privilege from inquiry concerning "Speech and Debate" on the floors of Congress. Lacking textual support, counsel for the President nonetheless would have us infer immunity from the President's political mandate, or from his vulnerability to impeachment, or from his broad discretionary powers. These are invitations to refashion the Constitution, and we reject them.

Though the President is elected by nationwide ballot, and is often said to represent all the people, he does not embody the nation's sovereignty. He is not above the law's commands: "With all its defects, delays and inconveniences men have discovered no technique for long preserving free government except that the Executive be under the law...." Sovereignty remains at all times with the people, and they do not forfeit through elections the right to have the law construed against and applied to every citizen.

Nor does the Impeachment Clause imply immunity from routine court process. While the President argues that the Clause means that impeachability precludes criminal prosecution of an incumbent, we see no need to explore this question except to note its irrelevance to the case before us.... By contemplating the possibility of post-impeachment trials for violations of law committed in office, the Impeachment Clause itself reveals that incumbency does not relieve the President of the routine legal obligations that confine all citizens....

We of course acknowledge, the longstanding judicial recognition of Executive privilege.... The Judiciary has been sensitive to the considerations upon which the President seems to rest his claim of absolute privilege: the candor of Executive aides and functionaries would be impaired if they were persistently worried that their advice and deliberations were later to be made public. However, counsel for the President can point to no case in which a court has accepted the Executive's mere assertion of privilege as sufficient to overcome the need of the party subpoenaing the documents. To the contrary, the courts have repeatedly asserted that the applicability of the privilege is in the end for them and not the Executive to decide....

To do otherwise would be effectively to ignore the clear words of *Marbury v. Madison,* that "(i)t is emphatically the province and duty of the judicial department to say what the law is."... Whenever a privilege is asserted, even one expressed in the Constitution, such as the Speech and Debate privilege, it is the courts that determine the validity of the assertion and the scope of the privilege. To leave the proper scope and application of Executive privilege to the President's sole discretion would represent a mixing, rather than a separation, of Executive and Judicial functions.... The Constitution mentions no Executive privileges, much less any absolute Executive privileges....

If the claim of absolute privilege was recognized, its mere invocation by the President or his surrogates could deny access to all documents in all the Executive departments to all citizens and their representatives, including Congress, the courts as well as grand juries, state governments, state officials and all state subdivisions. The Freedom of Information Act could become nothing more than a legislative statement of unenforceable rights. Support for this kind of mischief simply cannot be spun from incantation of the doctrine of separation of powers....

The President's privilege cannot, therefore, be deemed absolute. We think the *Burr* case makes clear that application of Executive privilege depends on a weighing of the public interest protected by the privilege against the public interests that would be served by disclosure in a particular case. We direct our attention, however, solely to the circumstances here. With the possible exception of material on one tape, the President does not assert that the subpoenaed items involve military or state secrets; nor is the asserted privilege directed to the particular kinds of information that the tapes contain. Instead, the President asserts that the tapes should be deemed privileged because of the great public interest in maintaining the confidentiality of conversations that take place in the President's performance of his official duties....

Our conclusion that the general confidentiality privilege must recede before the grand jury's showing of need, is established by the unique circumstances that made this showing possible. In his public statement of May 22, 1973, the President said: "Executive privilege will not be invoked as to any testimony concerning possible criminal conduct or discussions of possible criminal conduct, in the matters presently under investigation, including the Watergate affair and the alleged cover-up." We think that this statement and its consequences may properly be considered as at least one factor in striking the balance in this case. Indeed, it affects the weight we give to factors on both sides of the scale. On the one hand, the President's action presumably reflects a judgment by him that the interest in the confidentiality of White House discussions in general is outweighed by such matters as the public interest, stressed by the Special Prosecutor, in the integrity of the level of the Executive Branch closest to the President, and the public interest in the integrity of the electoral process... it supports our estimation of the great public interest that attaches to the effective functioning of the present grand jury....

At the same time, the public testimony given consequent to the President's decision substantially disminishes the interest in maintaining the confidentiality of conversations pertinent to Watergate.

The simple fact is that the conversations are no longer confidential...(w)e see no justification, on confidentiality grounds, for depriving the grand jury of the best evidence of the conversations available....

Nonetheless, we hold that the District Court may order disclosure of all portions of the tapes relevant to matters within the proper scope of the grand jury's investigations, unless the Court judges that the public interest served by nondisclosure of *particular* statements or information outweighs the need for that information demonstrated by the grand jury.

The question remains whether, in the circumstances of this case, the District Court was correct in ordering the tapes produced for *in camera* inspection, so that it could determine whether and to what extent the privilege was properly claimed.... It is our hope that our action in providing what has become an unavoidable constitutional ruling, and in approving, as modified, the order of the District Court, will be followed by maximum cooperation among the parties. Perhaps the President will find it possible to reach some agreement with the Special Prosecutor as to what portions of the subpoenaed evidence are necessary to the grand jury's task.

Should our hope prove unavailing, we think that *in camera* inspection is a necessary and appropriate method of protecting the grand jury's interest in securing relevant evidence. The exception that we have delineated to the President's confidentiality privilege depends entirely on the grand jury's showing that the evidence is directly relevant to its decisions. The residual problem of this case derives from the possibility that there are elements of the subpoenaed recordings that do not lie within the range of the exception that we have defined....

With the rejection of this all-embracing claim of prerogative, the President will have an opportunity to present more particular claims of privilege, if accompanied by an analysis in manageable segments....

1. In so far as the President makes a claim that certain material may not be disclosed because the subject matter relates to national defense or foreign relations, he may decline to transmit that portion of the material and ask the District Court to reconsider whether *in camera* inspection of the material is necessary. The Special Prosecutor is entitled to inspect the claim and showing and may be heard thereon, in chambers. If the judge sustains the privilege, the text of the government's statement will be preserved in the Court's record under seal.

2. The President will present to the District Court all other items covered by the order, with specification of which segments he believes may be disclosed and which not. This can be accomplished by itemizing and indexing the material, and correlating indexed items with particular claims of privilege. On request of either counsel, the District Court shall hold a hearing in chambers on the claims. Thereafter the Court shall itself inspect the disputed items.

Given the nature of the inquiry that this inspection involves, the District Court may gave the Special Prosecutor access to the material for the limited purpose of aiding the Court in determining the relevance of the material to the grand jury's investigations.... And, here, any concern over confidentiality is minimized by the Attorney General's designation of a distinguished and reflective counsel as Special Prosecutor. If, however, the Court decides to allow access to the Special Prosecutor, it should, upon request, stay its action in order to allow sufficient time for application for a stay to this Court.

Following the *in camera* hearing and inspection, the District Court may determine as to any items (a) to allow the particular claim of privilege in full; (b) to order disclosure to the grand jury of all or a segment of the item or items; or, when segmentation is impossible; (c) to fashion a complete statement for the grand jury of those portions of an item that bear on possible criminality. The District Court shall provide a reasonable stay to allow the President an opportunity to appeal. In case of an appeal to this Court of an order either allowing or refusing disclosure, this Court will provide for sealed records and confidentiality in presentation.

We end, as we began, by emphasizing the extraordinary nature of this case. We have attempted to decide no more than the problem before us—a problem that takes its unique shape from the grand jury's compelling showing of need. The procedures we have provided require thorough deliberation by the District Court before even this need may be satisfied. Opportunity for appeals, on a sealed record, is assured.

We cannot, therefore, agree with the assertion of the President that the District Court's order threatens "the continued existence of the Presidency as a functioning institution." As we view the case, the order represents an unusual and limited requirement that the President produce material evidence. We think this required by law, and by the rule that even the Chief Executive is subject to the mandate of the law when he has no valid claim of privilege.

Dissenting Opinions

MacKINNON, *Circuit Judge....*

By recognizing an absolute privilege, my opinion places the presidential communications privilege on an equal footing with that recognized for military or state secrets.... Military or state secrets are never subject to disclosure regardless of the weight of countervailing interests.

The rationale underlying the absolute privilege for military or state secrets is the policy judgment that the nation's interest in keeping this information secret always outweighs any particularized need for disclosure. A similar policy judgment supports an absolute privilege for communications between a President and his advisers on matters of official concern.

The interest supporting an absolute privilege for presidential communications is the confidentiality essential to insure thorough and unfettered discussion between a President and his advisers....

To allow the courts to breach presidential confidentiality whenever one of 400 federal trial judges considers that the circumstances of the moment demonstrate a compelling need for disclosure would frustrate the privilege's underlying policy of encouraging frank and candid presidential deliberations....

The lessons of legal history teach that it will be impossible to contain this breach of presidential confidentiality if numerous federal judges may rummage through presidential papers to determine whether a President's or a litigant's contentions should prevail in a particular case. Furthermore, the decision in this case inevitably will be precedent for assaults on the presently asserted absolute privileges of Congress and the Judiciary.....

...The greatest vice of the decision sought by the Special Prosecutor is that it would establish a precedent that would subject every presidential conference to the hazard of eventually being publicly exposed at the behest of some trial judge trying a civil or criminal case. It is this precedential effect which transforms this case from one solely related to the recordings sought here, to one which decides whether this President, and all future Presidents, shall continue to enjoy the independency of executive action contemplated by the Constitution and fully exercised by all their predecessors.

After the President has claimed the privilege, the court must satisfy itself that "the circumstances are appropriate for the claim of privilege." In determining whether the privilege is appropriate in a particular case, the only inquiry is whether there is a "reasonable danger" that disclosure of the evidence would expose matters which the privilege is designed to protect. Since the presidential communications privilege is an absolute rather than a qualified privilege, there is no occasion to balance the particularized need for the evidence against the governmental interest in confidentiality. The balance between these competing interests was examined and resolved when the absolute presidential communications privilege was formulated. Having concluded that the privilege is available, the only inquiry is whether the President's invocation of the privilege promotes the policy which the privilege was designed to protect....

Yet the court must make this determination without forcing disclosure of the very communication which the privilege protects. Thus an *in camera* inspection is proper only if the court cannot otherwise satisfy itself that the privilege should be sustained. In the present case, we are satisfied that appropriate circumstances do exist and, therefore, would hold that even *in camera* inspection is improper.

WILKEY, *Circuit Judge....*

I respectfully submit that the errors in the *Per Curiam's* analysis stem from a frequent source of confusion, the failure to recognize and separate the two origins of the Executive Branch privilege: on one hand, the common sense-common law privilege of confidentiality necessary in government administration, which has been partly codified in statutes such as the Freedom of Information Act; on the other hand, the origin of the privilege in the Constitutional principle of separation of powers....

In theory, if only the ancient customary Governmental confidentiality privilege is involved, whether the Chief Executive should disclose the information should be decided no differently from the case of any other Government official.... It would be permissible for the courts to talk in terms of balancing the public interest of those seeking disclosure versus the public interest of the President in retaining confidentiality....

As a practical matter, as history shows, the theory breaks down. Not only is the grist of the Presidential mill of a higher quality than that processed by the average bureaucrat, but the institutions or individuals daring to confront the Chief Executive directly have been of a character and power to invoke immediately the other source of the Chief Executive's privilege, the Constitutional doctrine of separation of powers.... If the Chief Executive can be "coerced" by the Judicial Branch into furnishing records hitherto throughout our history resting within the exclusive control of the Executive, then the Chief Executive is no longer "master in his own house."

This is not a matter of "coercing" the Executive to "obey the law"; there has never before in 184 years been any such law that the Executive could be compelled by the Judiciary to surrender Executive records to the Judiciary. This is an assertion of privilege by the Executive, not a refusal to obey a court's interpretation of the law. This the Executive has *always* done, even when the Executive's interpretation of the law was different.... But also, the Executive has *always* been the one who decided whether the Executive Branch privilege of confidentiality of its records should be asserted, and to what extent, when confronted with demand of another Branch for such records....

...(W)here the privilege of the Chief Executive is derived from the *Constitutional principle* of separation of powers, it is no more subject to weighing and balancing than any other Constitutional privilege can be weighed and balanced by extraneous third parties....

We all know that when a Constitutional privilege under the Fifth Amendment is asserted by the humblest individual, the court does not weigh and balance the public interest in having the individual's testimony. All the court can do is make a preliminary inquiry as to a prima facie justification for the assertion of the privilege.... If the Constitutional privilege has been asserted, then no court has the right to determine what the President will or will not produce....

Throughout this nation's 184-year Constitutional history, Congress and the Executive have succeeded in avoiding any near-fatal confrontation over attempts by Congress to procure documents in the Executive's possession. In recognition of the delicate balance created by the doctrine of separation of powers, the two Branches have generally succeeded in fashioning a *modus vivendi* through mutual deference and cooperation....

Congressional demands for Executive papers are as numerous as autumn leaves, and frequently fall due to a frost between the two ends of Pennsylvania Avenue. In contrast, Judicial demands for Executive documents can be summarized in the drama and legal intricacies of one *cause celebre,* the two trials of Aaron Burr in 1807, the major historical example of the issuance by a federal court of a subpoena *duces tecum* directing the President to produce documents. Although the United States Circuit Court for Virginia, per Chief Justice Marshall,

issued the subpoena *duces tecum* to President Jefferson, the court never directly decided the question of the scope of the President's asserted privilege to withhold documents or portions thereof, nor did it determine who should decide the scope of the privilege....

If we go on *what was actually done,* the Burr Trials prove that the final "weighing of the public interest" is done by the Chief Executive. If we go on what was *said* by Marshall, the *Burr* trials leave the ultimate issue of Who finally decides the public interest completely undecided, for Marshall never faced up, even verbally, to a confrontation with the President himself with the issue drawn on the question of separation of powers.

These two great Constitutional and political antagonists— Marshall and Jefferson, Chief Justice and President—had circled each other warily, each maintaining his position, each, out of respect for the other and for the delicate fabric of the Constitution, not forcing the ultimate issue. Who *should* decide the scope and applicability of the Chief Executive's privilege? The portions of the letter determined by the President to be confidential remained confidential; the full letter was never produced to the court....

...(T)he real issue...is whether it is appropriate for the court to determine the legal validity of a claim of privilege by the President, or whether the Constitutional principle of separation of powers requires the court to yield to the President's judgment as to where the public interest lies. My answer would be the latter....

It was and is the President's right to make that decision initially, and it is the American people who will be the judge as to whether the President has made the right decision, *i.e.,* whether it is or is not in the public interest that the papers (tapes) in question be furnished or retained. If his decision is made on visibly sound grounds, the people will approve the action of the Executive as being in the public interest. If the decision is not visibly on sound grounds of national public interest, in political terms the decision may be ruinous for the President, but it is his to make. The grand design has worked; the separate, independent Branch remains in charge of and responsible for its own papers, processes and decisions, not to a second or third Branch, but it remains *responsible* to the American people....

The Founding Fathers were not looking for the *most efficient* government design. After all, they had been subject to and rebelled against one of the most efficient governments then existing. What the Founding Fathers designed was *not efficiency, but protection against oppression.* Leaving the three Branches in an equilibrium of tension was just one of their devices to guard against oppression.

This healthy equilibrium of tension will be destroyed if the result reached by the *Per Curiam* is allowed to stand. My colleagues cannot confine the effect of their decision to Richard M. Nixon.

The precedent set will inevitably have far-reaching implications on the vulnerability of any Chief Executive to judicial process, not merely at the behest of the Special Prosecutor in the extraordinary circumstances of Watergate, but at the behest of Congress. Congress may have equally plausible needs for similar information. The fact that Congress is usually or frequently locked in political battle with the Chief Executive cannot mean that Congress' need or right to information in the hands of the Chief Executive is any less than it otherwise would be....

To put the theoretical situation and possibilities in terms of "absolute" privilege sounds somewhat terrifying—*until one realizes that this is exactly the way matters have been for 184 years of our history,* and the Republic still stands. The practical capacity of the three independent Branches to adjust to each other, their sensitivity to the approval or disapproval of the American people, have been sufficient guides to responsible action, without imposing the authority of one co-equal Branch over another....

GLOSSARY OF COMMON LEGAL TERMS

Accessory. In criminal law, a person not present at the commission of an offense who commands, advises, instigates or conceals the offense.

Acquittal. Discharge of a person from a charge of guilt. A person is acquitted when a jury returns a verdict of not guilty. However, a person may also be acquitted when a judge determines that there is insufficient evidence to convict or that a violation of due process precludes a fair trial. *(See Due Process)*

Adjudicate. To determine finally by the exercise of judicial authority; as to decide a case.

Affidavit. A voluntarily made written statement of facts or charges affirmed under oath.

Amicus Curiae. "A friend of the court." A person, not a party to the litigation, who volunteers or is invited by the court to give advice on a matter pending before it.

Appeal. To take a case to a higher court for review. Generally, a party losing in a trial court may appeal once to an appellate court as a matter of right. If he loses in the appellate court, appeal to a higher court is within the discretion of the higher court. Most appeals to the U.S. Supreme Court are within the court's discretion *(See Writ of Certiorari)*. However, when the highest court in a state rules that a U.S. statute is unconstitutional or upholds a state statute against the claim that it is unconstitutional, appeal to the Supreme Court is a matter of right.

Appellant. The party that appeals a lower court decision to a higher court. *(See Appellee, Appeal)*

Appellee. One who has an interest in upholding the decision of a lower court and is compelled to respond when the case is appealed to a higher court by the appellant. *(See Appellant, Appeal)*

Arraignment. Process of calling an indicted person before the court, reading him the indictment, asking whether he pleads guilty or not guilty, and entering his plea. *(See Indictment, Pleas)*

Bail. The security, usually money, given as assurance of a prisoner's due appearance at a designated time and place (as in court) in order to procure in the interim his release from jail.

Bailiff. A minor officer of a court usually serving as an usher or a messenger.

Brief. A document prepared by counsel to serve as the basis for an argument in an appellate court.

Case Law. As distinguished from statutes and other sources of law, case law is the law as defined by previously decided cases. *(See Code, Statutes, Common Law)*

Civil Law. Body of law dealing with the private rights of individuals, as distinguished from criminal law.

Class Action. A lawsuit brought by one person or group on behalf of all persons similarly situated.

Code. A collection of laws, arranged systematically.

Common Law. Collection of principles and rules of action, particularly from unwritten English law, which derive their authority from longstanding usage and custom or from courts recognizing and enforcing these customs. Sometimes used synonomously with case law. *(See Civil Law, Criminal Law, Statute, Case Law)*

Consent Decree. A court sanctioned agreement entered into by the consent of the parties.

Contempt (Civil and Criminal). Civil contempt consists in the failure to do something which the party is ordered by the court to do for the benefit of another party. Criminal contempt occurs when a person willfully exhibits disrespect for the court or obstructs the administration of justice.

Conviction. Final judgment or sentence that the defendant is guilty as charged.

Criminal Law. That branch of law which deals with the enforcement of laws and the punishment of persons who, by breaking laws, commit crimes. *(See Civil Law)*

Declaratory Judgment. A court pronouncement declaring a legal right or interpretation but not ordering a specific action.

Defendant. In a civil action, the party denying or defending itself against charges brought by a plaintiff. In a criminal action, the person indicted for commission of an offense. *(See Plaintiff)*

Deposition. Oral testimony from a witness taken out of court in response to written or oral questions, committed to writing, and intended to be used in the preparation of a case.

Dicta. Opinions of a judge which are not part of the resolution or determination of the court; non-binding statements included in a court decision.

Dismissal. Order disposing of a case without a trial.

Docket. See Trial Docket.

Due Process. Constitutional guarantee of the Fifth and Fourteenth Amendments providing that a person may not be "deprived of life, liberty or property" without opportunity to prepare a defense and present it.

Ex Parte. "On one side only." Application to a court on behalf of only one party.

Grand Jury. Group of 12 to 23 persons impanelled to hear in private evidence presented by the state against persons accused of crime and to issue indictments when a majority of the jurors find that probable cause exists to believe that the accused has committed a crime. Called a "grand" jury because it comprises a greater number of persons than a "petit jury." *(See Petit Jury)*

Grand Jury Report. A public report released by a grand jury after an investigation into activities of public officials that fall short of criminal actions. Grand jury reports are often called "presentments."

Guilty. A word used by a defendant in entering a plea or by a jury in returning a verdict, indicating that the defendant is legally responsible as charged for a crime or other wrongdoing.

Habeas Corpus. A writ to inquire whether a person is lawfully imprisoned or detained. *(See Writ)*

Sources for Definitions

Black's Law Dictionary. West Publishing Company, St. Paul, Minn. 1968.

Random House Dictionary. Random House, New York, N.Y., 1966.

Webster's Third International Dictionary. G. & C. Merriam Company, Springfield, Mass., 1961.

Immunity. A grant of exemption from prosecution in return for evidence or testimony. *(See Transactional Immunity and Use Immunity)*

In Camera. "In chambers." Refers to court hearings in private without spectators.

In Re. In the affair; concerning. Frequent title of judicial proceedings where there are no adversaries, but rather where a matter itself requires judicial actions, as a bankrupt's estate.

Indictment. A formal written statement based on evidence presented by the prosecutor from a grand jury decided by a majority vote, charging one or more persons with specified offenses. *(See Grand Jury)*

Information. A written set of accusations, similar to an indictment, but filed directly by a prosecutor without intervention by a grand jury.

Injunction. A court order prohibiting the person to whom it is directed from performing a particular act.

Interlocutory Decree. A provisional decision of the court before completion of a legal action which temporarily settles an intervening matter.

Judgment. Official decision of a court based on the rights and claims of the parties to a case which was submitted for determination.

Jurisdiction. Exists when a court has the right and power to hear a case in question, when the proper parties are present, and when the point to be decided is within the issues authorized to be handled by the particular court.

Juries. See Grand Jury and Petit Jury.

Magistrate. A judicial officer having jurisdiction to try minor criminal cases and conduct preliminary examinations of persons charged with serious crimes.

Mandamus. "We command." An order issued from a superior court directing a lower court or other authority to perform a particular act.

Moot. Unsettled; undecided. A moot question is also one which is no longer material.

Motion. Written or oral application to a court or a judge to obtain a rule or an order.

Nolo Contendere. "I will not contest it." A plea entered by a defendant at the discretion of the judge with the same legal effect as a plea of guilty, but it may not be cited in other proceedings as an admission of guilt.

Parole. A conditional release from imprisonment under conditions that if the prisoner abides by the law and other restrictions that may be placed upon him, he will not have to serve the remainder of his sentence. But if he does not abide by specified rules, he will be returned to prison to finish his time.

Per Curiam. "By the court." An unsigned opinion of the court, or an opinion written by the whole court.

Petit Jury. Originally, a panel of 12 persons who tried to reach a unanimous verdict on questions of fact in criminal and civil proceedings. Since 1970, the Supreme Court has upheld the legality of state juries with fewer than 12 persons and of non-unanimous verdicts. Because it comprises fewer persons than a "grand jury," it is called a "petit" jury. *(See Grand Jury)*

Petitioner. One who files a petition with a court seeking action or relief, including a plaintiff or an appellant. But a petitioner is also a person who files for other court action where charges are not necessarily made; for example, a party may petition the court for an order requiring another person or party to produce documents. The opposite party is called the respondent. When a writ

of certiorari is granted by the Supreme Court, the parties to the case are called petitioner and respondent in contrast to the appellant and appellee terms used in an appeal. *(See Appeal, Respondent, Writ of Certiorari)*

Plaintiff. A party who brings a civil action or sues to obtain a remedy for injury to his rights. The party against whom action is brought is termed the defendant.

Plea Bargaining. Negotiations between prosecutors and the defendant aimed at eliciting a plea of guilty from the defendant in exchange for concessions by the prosecutors, such as reduction of charges or a request for leniency. Sixty-four per cent of all criminal cases settled in the federal courts in 1972 were settled by plea bargains.

Pleas. See Guilty and Nolo Contendere.

Presentment. See Grand Jury Report.

Prima Facie. "At first sight." Referring to a fact or other evidence presumably sufficient to establish a defense or a claim unless otherwise contradicted.

Probation. Process under which a person convicted of an offense, usually a first offense, receives a suspended sentence and is given his freedom, usually under the guardianship of a probation officer.

Quash. To overthrow, annul or vacate; as to quash a subpoena. *(See Vacate)*

Recognizance. A obligation entered into before a court or magistrate requiring the performance of a specified act—usually to appear in court at a later date. It is an alternative to bail for pre-trial release.

Remand. To send back. In the event of a decision being remanded, it is sent back by a higher court to the court from which it came for further action.

Respondent. One who is compelled to answer the claims or questions posed in court by a petitioner. A defendant and an appellee may be called respondents, but the term also includes those parties who answer in court during actions where charges are not necessarily brought or where the Supreme Court has granted a writ of certiorari. *(See Petitioner, Appeal, Writ of Certiorari)*

Stare Decisis. The doctrine of law that principles of law established by judicial decision be accepted as authoritative in cases similar to those from which such principles were established.

Statute. A written law enacted by a legislature. A collection of statutes for a particular governmental division is called a code. *(See Code)*

Stay. To halt or suspend further judicial proceedings.

Subpoena. An order to present one's self before a grand jury, court or legislative hearing.

Subpoena Duces Tecum. An order to produce specified documents or papers.

Transactional Immunity. Protects a witness from prosecution for any offense mentioned in or related to his testimony, regardless of independent evidence against him.

Trial Docket. A calendar prepared by the clerks of the court listing the cases set to be tried.

Use Immunity. Protects a witness against the use of his own testimony against him in prosecution.

Vacate. To make void, annul or rescind.

Writ. A written court order commanding the designated recipient to perform or not perform acts specified in the order.

Writ of Certiorari. Discretionary writ issued from the U.S. Supreme Court or a state supreme court to an inferior court ordering the lower court to prepare the records of a case and to send them up for review.

NIXON'S APPOINTEES TO FEDERAL JUDICIARY 1969-73

1969

Party affiliations of appointees for the years 1969 and 1970 were made available by the Justice Department, and for the years 1971, 1972 and 1973 from entries in *Who's Who in American Politics* and from the senators of the states involved. Information is listed in the following order: jurisdiction, salary, appointee, voting residence, occupation at time of appointment, date and place of birth, party affiliation and date of confirmation.

U.S. SUPREME COURT

Chief Justice of the United States, $62,500—**Warren E. Burger;** Arlington, Va.; associate judge, U.S. Court of Appeals for the District of Columbia; Sept. 17, 1907 in St. Paul, Minn.; Rep.; June 9.

U.S. CIRCUIT COURTS OF APPEALS

Judge for the Third Circuit, $42,500—**Arlin M. Adams;** Philadelphia, Pa.; lawyer; April 16, 1921, in Philadelphia, Pa.; Rep.; Oct. 1.

Judge for the Third Circuit, $42,500—**John J. Gibbons;** Newark, N.J.; lawyer; Dec. 8, 1924, in Newark; Rep.; Dec. 17.

Judge for the Fifth Circuit, $42,500—**George H. Carswell;** Tallahassee, Fla.; U.S. District Judge; Dec. 22, 1919 in Irwinton, Ga.; Rep.; June 19.

Judge for the Fifth Circuit, $42,500—**Harles Clark;** Jackson, Miss.; lawyer; Sept. 12, 1925, in Memphis, Tenn.; Dem.; Oct. 15.

Judge for the Fifth Circuit, $42,500—**Joe McDonald Ingraham;** Houston, Texas; U.S. District Judge for the Southern District of Texas; July 5, 1903, in Pawnee Co., Okla.; Rep.; Dec. 17.

Judge for the Sixth Circuit, $42,500—**Henry L. Brooks;** Louisville, Ky.; U.S. District Judge for the District of Ky.; Aug. 29, 1908 in Jackson, Tenn.; Rep.; Dec. 10.

Judge for the Ninth Circuit, $42,500—**John F. Kilkenny;** Portland, Ore.; U.S. District Judge; Oct. 26, 1901, in Hepner, Ore.; Rep.; Sept. 12.

Judge for the Ninth Circuit, $42,500—**Ozell M. Trask;** Phoenix, Ariz.; lawyer; July 4, 1909, in Wakita, Okla.; Rep.; Sept. 12.

Judge for the Ninth Circuit, $42,500—**Eugene A. Wright;** Seattle, Wash.; vice president, Pacific National Bank of Seattle; Rep.; Sept. 12.

Judge for the District of Columbia Circuit, $42,500 **George E. MacKinnon;** Long Lake, Minn.; general counsel and vice president, Investors Mutual Corp.; April 22, 1906, in St. Paul, Minn.; Rep.; May 5.

Judge for the District of Columbia Circuit, $42,500—**Roger Robb;** Washington, D.C.; lawyer; July 7, 1907, in Bellows Falls, Vt.; Rep.; May 5.

U.S. COURT OF CUSTOMS AND PATENT APPEALS

Associate Judge, $42,500—**Donald E. Lane;** Washington, D.C.; commissioner, U.S. Court of Claims; June 10, 1909 in Chevy Chase, Md.; June 19.

U.S. DISTRICT COURTS

Judge for the Northern District of Alabama, $40,000—**Frank H. McFadden;** Birmingham, Ala.; lawyer; Nov. 20, 1925, in Oxford, Miss.; Rep.; Aug. 8.

Judge for the Northern District of California, $40,000—**Gerald S. Levin;** San Francisco, Calif.; judge, Superior Court of California; Jan. 9, 1906, in Danville, Ill.; Rep.; July 11.

Judge for the Eastern District of California, $40,000—**Philip C. Wilkins;** Sacramento, Calif.; lawyer; Jan. 27, 1913, in Sacramento; Rep.; Dec. 17.

Judge for the Central District of California, $40,000—**David W. Williams;** Los Angeles, Calif.; California state judge; March 20, 1910, in Atlanta, Ga.; Rep.; June 19.

Judge for the Northern District of Florida, $40,000—**David L. Middlebrooks Jr.;** Pensacola, Fla.; lawyer; June 27, 1926, in Pensacola; Rep.; Dec. 10.

Judge for the District of Montana, $40,000—**James F. Battin;** Billings, Mont.; Member, U.S. House of Representatives; Feb. 13, 1922, in Wichita, Kan.; Rep.; Feb. 25.

Judge for the District of New Jersey, $40,000—**George H. Barlow;** Trenton, N.J.; New Jersey State Judge; Jan. 4, 1921, in Trenton; Rep.; Dec. 17.

Judge for the District of New Jersey, $40,000—**Leonard I. Garth;** Paterson, N.J.; lawyer; April 7, 1921, in Brooklyn, N.Y.; Rep.; Dec. 17.

Judge for the District of Oregon, $40,000—**Alfred T. Goodwin;** Salem, Ore.; Associate Justice, Oregon Supreme Court; Aug. 29, 1923, in Bellingham, Wash.; Rep.; Dec. 17.

Judge for the Eastern District of Pennsylvania, $40,000—**John B. Hannum;** Unionville, Pa.; lawyer; March 9, 1915, in Chester, Pa.; Rep.; May 5.

Judge for the Middle District of Pennsylvania, $40,000—**R. Dixon Herman;** Harrisburg, Pa.; judge, Dauphin Co. Court of Common Pleas; Sept. 24, 1911, in Northumberland, Pa.; Rep.; Dec. 10.

Judge for the Western District of Virginia, $40,000—**H. Emory Widener Jr.;** Bristol, Va.; lawyer; April 20, 1923, in Abingdon, Va.; Rep.; July 11.

Judge for the District of Columbia, $40,000—**Barrington D. Parker;** Washington, D.C.; lawyer; Nov. 17, 1915, in Rosslyn, Va.; Rep.; Dec. 18.

Judge for the District of the Virgin Islands, $40,000—**Almeric L. Christian;** St. Thomas, V.I.; U.S. Attorney for the Virgin Islands; Nov. 23, 1919, in St. Croix, V.I.; Dem.; Aug. 8.

Judge for the District of Guam, $40,000—**Cristobal C. Duenas;** Agana, Guam; Judge, Guam Island Court; Sept. 12, 1920 in Agana; Rep.; Dec. 10.

1970

U.S. SUPREME COURT

Associate Justice, $60,000—**Harry Andrew Blackmun;** Rochester, Minn.; U.S. Circuit Court judge; Nov. 12, 1908, in Nashville, Ill.; Rep.; May 12.

U.S. CIRCUIT COURTS OF APPEALS

Judge for the Third Circuit, $42,500—**Max Rosenn;** Kingston, Pa.; lawyer; Feb. 4, 1910, in Plaine, Pa.; Rep.; Oct. 6.

Judge for the Fifth Circuit, $42,500—**Paul H. Roney;** St. Petersburg, Fla.; partner in the law firm of Roney, Ulmer, Woodworth and Jacobs; Sept. 5, 1921, in Olney, Ill.; Rep.; Oct.13.

Judge for the Sixth Circuit, $42,500—**W. Wallace Kent;** Kalamazoo, Mich.; Judge for the Western District of Michigan; May 1, 1916, in Galesburg, Mich.; Rep.; Dec. 16.

Judge for the Sixth Circuit, $42,500—**William E. Miller;** Nashville, Tenn.; Judge for the Middle District of Tenn.; Feb. 3, 1908, in Johnson City, Tenn.; Rep.; July 26.

Judge for the Seventh Circuit, $42,500—**Wilbur F. Pell Jr.;** Shelbyville, Ind.; senior partner in the law firm of Pell and Matchett; Dec. 6, 1915, in Shelbyville, Ind.; Rep.; April 23.

Judge for the Seventh Circuit, $42,500—**John Paul Stevens;** Chicago, Ill.; partner in the law firm of Rothschild,

Stevens, Barry and Myers; April 20, 1920, in Chicago, Ill.; Rep.; Oct. 8.

Judge for the Eighth Circuit, $42,500—**Donald R. Ross;** Omaha, Neb.; partner in the law firm of Swarr, May, Royce, Smith, Andersen and Ross; June 8, 1922, in Orleans, Neb.; Rep.; Dec. 11.

Judge for the Tenth Circuit, $42,500—**Robert Hugh McWilliams Jr.;** Denver, Colo.; Chief Justice, Colorado Supreme Court; April 27, 1916, in Salina, Kan.; Rep.; Oct. 8.

Judge for the District of Columbia Circuit, $42,500—**Malcom R. Wilkey;** New York, N.Y.; general counsel, Kennecott Copper Corp.; Dec. 6, 1918, in Murfreesboro, Tenn.; Rep.; Feb. 24.

U.S. DISTRICT COURTS

Judge for Northern District of Alabama, $40,000—**Sam C. Pointer Jr.;** partner in the law firm of Brown, Pointer and Pointer; Nov 15, 1934, in Birmingham, Ala.; Rep.; Oct. 8.

Judge for the District of Arizona, $40,000—**William C. Frey;** Tucson, Ariz.; Judge, County of Pima Superior Court, Ariz.; July 24, 1919, in Tucson, Ariz.; Rep.; Nov. 25.

Judge for the Eastern District of Arkansas $40,000 **G. Thomas Eisele;** Little Rock, Ark.; lawyer; Nov. 3, 1923, in Hot Springs, Ark.; Rep.; Aug. 5.

Judge for the Central District of California, $40,000—**Robert J. Kelleher;** Beverly Hills, Calif.; lawyer; March 5, 1913, in New York, N.Y.; Dec. 17.

Judge for the Northern District of California, $40,000—**Samuel Conti;** Concord, Calif.; Judge, County of Contra Costa Superior Court, Calif.; July 16, 1922, in Los Angeles, Calif.; Rep.; Oct. 13.

Judge for the Northern District of California, $40,000—**Robert H. Schnacke;** San Francisco, Calif.; Judge, County of San Francisco Superior Court. Calif.; Oct. 8, 1913, in San Francisco, Calif.; Rep. Oct. 13.

Judge for the Southern District of California, $40,000—**J. Clifford Wallace;** La Mesa, Calif.; partner in the law firm of Gray, Cary, Ames & Frye; Dec. 11, 1928, in San Diego, Calif.; Rep.; Oct. 13.

Judge for the Southern District of California, $40,000—**Gordon Thompson Jr.;** San Diego, Calif.; partner in the law firm of Thompson and Thompson; Dec. 28, 1929, in San Diego, Calif.; Rep.; Oct. 13.

Judge for the District of Colorado, $40,000—**Fred M. Winner;** Denver, Colo.; partner in the law firm of Winner, Berge, Martin & Clark; April 8, 1912, in Denver, Colo.; Rep.; Dec. 16.

Judge for the District of Delaware, $40,000—**Walter K. Stapleton;** Wilmington, Del.; lawyer, former Deputy Attorney General of Delaware; June 2, 1934, in Cuthbert, Ga.; Rep.; Oct. 8.

Judge for the Middle District of Florida, $40,000—**Gerald B. Tjoflat;** Jacksonville, Fla.; Judge, Fourth Judicial Circuit of Florida, Jacksonville; Dec. 6, 1929, in Pittsburgh, Pa.; Rep.; Oct. 13.

Judge for the Southern District of Florida, $40,000—**James L. King;** Miami, Fla.; Circuit Judge (elected), Eleventh Judicial Circuit, Florida; Dec. 20, 1927, in Miami, Fla.; Dem.; Oct. 13.

Judge for the Southern District of Florida, $40,000—**Peter T. Fay;** Miami, Fla.; partner in the law firm of Frates, Fay, Floyd & Pearson; Jan. 18, 1929, in Rochester, N.Y.; Rep. Oct. 13.

Judge for the Northern District of Georgia, $40,000—**Charles A. Moye Jr.;** Atlanta, Ga.; partner in the law firm of Gambrell, Russell, Moye & Killorin; July 13, 1918, in Atlanta, Ga.; Rep.; Oct. 13.

Judge for the Northern District of Georgia, $40,000—**William C. O'Kelley;** Norcross, Ga.; partner in the law firm of O'Kelley, Hopkins & Van Gerpen; Jan. 2, 1930, in Atlanta, Ga.; Rep.; Oct. 13.

Judge for the Northern District of Illinois, $40,000—Frank **J. McGarr;** Melrose Park, Ill., Assistant Attorney General, Illinois; Feb. 25, 1921, in Chicago, Ill.; Rep.; Oct. 8.

Judge for the Western District of Kentucky, $40,000—**C. Rhodes Bratcher;** Owensboro, Ky.; senior partner in the law firm of Bratcher, Cooper & Flaherty; Dec. 23, 1917, in Morgantown, Ky.; Rep.; Oct. 13.

Judge for the Western District of Louisiana, $40,000—**Nauman S. Scott;** Alexandria, La.; partner in the law firm of Provosty, Sadler & Scott; June 15, 1916, in New Roads, La.; Rep.; Oct. 13.

Judge for the District of Maryland, $40,000—**James R. Miller Jr.;** Rockville, Md.; partner in the law firm of Miller, Miller & Canby; June 15, 1931, in Sandy Spring, Md.; Rep.; Oct. 13.

Judge for the Western District of Michigan, $40,000—**Albert J. Engel;** Muskegon, Mich.; Judge, State of Michigan Circuit Court (14th Circuit); March 21, 1924, in Lake City, Mich.; Rep.; Dec. 17.

Judge for the Eastern District of Michigan, $40,000—**John Feikens;** Grosse Pointe Park, Mich.; partner in the law firm of Feikens, Dice, Sweeney & Sullivan; Dec. 3, 1917, in Clifton, N.J.; Rep.; Nov. 25.

Judge for the Eastern District of Michigan, $40,000—**Cornelia G. Kennedy;** Grosse Pointe Woods, Mich.; Judge, Wayne County Circuit Court, Detroit, Mich.; Aug. 4, 1923, in Detroit, Mich.; Rep.; Oct. 6.

Judge for the Eastern District of Michigan, $40,000—**Philip Pratt;** Pontiac, Mich.; Circuit Judge, Sixth Circuit in Oakland, Mich.; July 14, 1924, in Pontiac, Mich.; Rep.; Nov. 25.

Judge for the Eastern District of Missouri, $40,000—**William H. Webster;** St. Louis, Mo.; U.S. Attorney, Eastern District of Missouri; March 8, 1924, in St. Louis, Mo.; Rep.; Dec. 17.

Judge for the Eastern and Western Districts of Missouri, $40,000—**H. Kenneth Wangelin;** Poplar Bluff, Mo.; partner in the law firm of Wangelin and Friedewald; May 10, 1913, in Des Moines, Iowa; Rep.; Dec. 17.

Judge for the District of Nebraska, $40,000—**Warren K. Urbom;** Lincoln, Neb.; lawyer, Dec. 17, 1925, in Atlanta, Neb.; Apr. 23.

Judge for the District of New Jersey, $40,000—**Clarkson S. Fisher;** West Long Branch, N.J.; Judge, State of New Jersey Superior Court; July 8, 1921, in Long Branch, N.J.; Rep.; Oct. 13.

Judge for the District of New Jersey, $40,000—**John J. Kitchen;** Bridgeport, N.J.; Judge, Gloucester County Superior Court; Dec. 29, 1911, in Camden, N.J.; Rep.; Oct. 13.

Judge for the District of New Jersey, $40,000—**Frederick B. Lacey;** Glen Ridge, N.J.; U.S. Attorney, District of New Jersey; Sept. 9, 1920, in Newark, N.J.; Rep.; Oct. 13.

Judge for the District of New Mexico, $40,000—**Edwin L. Mechem;** Mesilla Park, N.M.; partner in the law firm of Barden, Mechem & Sage; member, U.S. Senate, 1962-65; Governor of New Mexico, 1951-52, 57-59, 61-62; July 2, 1912, in Alamogordo, N.M.; Rep.; Oct. 8.

Judge for the Eastern District of North Carolina, $40,000—**Franklin T. Dupree Jr.;** Raleigh, N.C.; senior partner in the law firm of Dupree, Weaver, Horton, Cockman & Alvis; Oct. 8, 1913, in Angier, N.C.; Rep.; Dec. 11.

Judge for the Northern District of Ohio, $40,000—**Robert B. Krupansky;** Independence, Ohio; U.S. Attorney, Ohio; Aug. 15, 1921, in Cleveland, Ohio; Rep.; Oct. 13.

Judge for the Northern District of Ohio, $40,000—**Nicholas J. Walinski Jr.;** Toledo, Ohio; Judge, Lucas County Common Pleas Court; Nov. 29, 1920, in Toledo, Ohio; Rep.; Oct. 13.

Judge for the Middle District of Pennsylvania, $40,000—**Malcolm Muir;** Muncy, Pa.; lawyer; Oct. 20, 1914, in Englewood, N.J.; Rep.; Oct. 8.

Judge for the Middle District of Pennsylvania, $40,000—**Edward R. Becker;** Philadelphia, Pa.; partner in the law firm of Becker, Becker & Fryman; May 4, 1933, in Philadelphia, Pa.; Rep.; Oct. 8.

Judge for the Eastern, District of Pennsylvania, $40,000—**J. William Ditter Jr.**; Ambler, Pa., Judge, Montgomery County Court of Common Pleas; Oct. 19, 1921, in Philadelphia, Pa.; Rep.; Oct. 8.

Judge for the Eastern District of Pennsylvania, $40,000— **James H. Gorbey**; Chester, Pa.; Judge, 32nd Judicial District, Delaware County Court of Common Pleas, Pa.; July 30, 1920, in Chester, Pa.; Rep.; Dec. 17.

Judge for the Eastern District of Pennsylvania, $40,000— **Daniel H. Huyett 3rd**; Reading, Pa.; Public Utilities Commissioner, Pennsylvania; May 2, 1921, in Reading Pa.; Rep.; Oct. 8.

Judge for the Eastern District of Pennsylvania, $40,000 **Donald W. Van Artsdalen**; Doylestown, Pa.; partner in the law firm of Barnes, Van Artsdalen, Pratt, Gathright & Price; Oct. 21, 1919, in Doylestown, Pa.; Rep.; Oct. 8.

Judge for the Western District of Pennsylvania, $40,000— **William W. Knox**; Erie, Pa.; partner in the law firm of Knox, Graham, Pearson and McLaughlin; June 18, 1911, in Erie, Pa.; Rep.; Oct. 8.

Judge for the Western District of Pennsylvania, $40,000— **Barron P. McCune**; Washington, Pa.; Judge, Court of Common Pleas of the 27th Judicial Circuit; Feb. 19, 1915, in West Newton, Pa.; Rep.; Dec. 16.

Judge for the Western District of Pennsylvania, $40,000— **Hubert I. Teitelbaum**; Pittsburgh, Pa.; partner in the law firm of Morris, Safier & Teitelbaum; July 2, 1915, in Pittsburgh, Pa.; Rep.; Dec. 11.

Judge for the Western District of Pennsylvania, $40,000— **Joseph F. Weis Jr.,**; Pittsburgh, Pa.; judge; March 12, 1923, in Ross Township, Pa.; April 23.

Judge for the District of Puerto Rico, $40,000—**Jose V. Toledo**; San Juan, Puerto Rico; partner in the law firm of Toledo & Cordova; Aug. 14, 1931, in Arecibo, Puerto Rico; New Progressive Party of Puerto Rico; Nov. 25.

Judge for the District of South Dakota, $40,000—**Andrew W. Bogue**; Canton S.D.; judge; May 23, 1919, in Yankton, S.D.; April 23.

Judge for the Western District of Tennessee, $40,000— **Harry W. Wellford**; Memphis, Tenn.; partner in the law firm of McCloy, Wellford & Clark; Aug. 6, 1924, in Memphis, Tenn.; Rep.; Dec. 11.

Judge for the Middle District of Tennessee, $40,000—**L. Clure Morton**; Knoxville, Tenn.; partner in the law firm of Morton, Lewis & King; Feb. 20, 1916, in Knox County, Tenn.; Rep.; Oct. 8.

Judge for the Northern District of Texas, $40,000—**Robert M. Hill**; Dallas, Texas; partner in the law firm of Woodruff Hill, Kendall & Smith; Jan. 13, 1928, in Dallas, Texas; Rep.; Nov. 25.

Judge for the Eastern District of Texas, $40,000—**William M. Steger**; Tyler, Texas; partner in the law firm of Wilson, Siller, Spivey & Steger; Aug. 22, 1920, in Dallas, Texas; Rep.; Nov. 25.

Judge for the Western District of Texas, $40,000—**John H. Wood Jr.**; San Antonio, Texas; partner in the law firm of Backmann, Standard, Wood & Keene; March 31, 1916, in Rockport, Texas; Rep.; Nov. 25.

Judge for the Southern District of Texas, $40,000—**Carl O. Blue Jr.**; Houston, Texas; partner in the law firm of Royston & Rayzor; March 27, 1922, in Chicago, Ill.; Rep.; Oct. 13.

Judge for the Southern District of Texas, $40,000—**Owen D. Cox**; Corpus Christi, Texas, partner in the law firm of Boone, Davis, Cox & Hales; March 20, 1910, in Joplin, Mo.; Rep.; Nov. 25.

Judge for the District of Vermont, $40,000—**James L. Oakes**; Brattleboro, Vt.; lawyer; Feb. 21, 1924, in Springfield, Ill.; April 23.

Judge for the Southern District of West Virginia—$40,000— **Dennis R. Knapp**; Nitro, W. Va.; Judge Kanawha County Court of Common Pleas; May 13, 1912, in Bee, W.Va.; Rep.; Dec. 16.

1971

U.S. SUPREME COURT

Associate Justice, $60,000—**Lewis F. Powell Jr.**; Richmond, Va.; partner in the law firm of Hunton, Gay, Powell and Gibson; Sept. 19, 1907, in Suffolk, Va.; Dem.; Dec. 6.

Associate Justice, $60,000—**William H. Rehnquist**; Phoenix, Ariz.; Assistant Attorney General (office of legal counsel); Oct. 1, 1924, in Milwaukee, Wis.; Rep.; Dec. 10.

U.S. CIRCUIT COURTS OF APPEALS

Judge for the Second Circuit, $42,500—**Walter R. Mansfield**; New York City; U.S. district judge, Southern District of New York; July 1, 1911, in Boston, Mass.; Rep.; May 20.

Judge for the Second Circuit, $42,500—**William Hughes Mulligan**; Bronxville, N.Y.; dean and professor, Fordham University Law School; March 5, 1918, in Bronx, N.Y.; Rep.; May 20.

Judge for the Second Circuit, $42,500—**James L. Oakes**, Brattleboro, Vt.; U.S. district judge, District of Vermont; Feb. 21, 1924, in Springfield, Ill.; Rep.; May 20.

Judge for the Second Circuit, $42,500—**William H. Timbers**; Darien, Conn.; U.S. District Judge, District of Connecticut; Sept. 5, 1915, in Yonkers, N.Y.; Rep.; July 29.

Judge for the Third Circuit, $42,500—**James Hunter III**; Haddonfield, N.J.; partner in the law firm of Archer, Breiner, Hunter & Read; Dec. 26, 1916, in Westville, N.J.; Rep.; Sept. 21.

Judge for the Third Circuit, $42,500—**James Rosen**; West New York, N.J.; judge of the Superior Court of New Jersey; Oct. 23, 1909, in Brooklyn, N.Y.; Rep.; Sept. 21.

Judge for the Fourth Circuit, $42,500—**John A. Field Jr.**; Charleston, W.Va.; U.S. District Judge, Southern District of West Virginia; Rep.; Sept. 21.

Judge for the Fourth Circuit, $42,500—**Donald Stuart Russell**; Spartanburg, S.C.; U.S. district judge, District of South Carolina; Feb. 22, 1906, in Lafayette Springs, Miss.; Dem.; April 21.

Judge for the Seventh Circuit, $42,500—**Robert A. Sprecher**; Evanston, Ill.; partner in the law firm of Crowley, Sprecher, Barrett & Karaba; May 30, 1917, in Chicago, Ill.; Rep.; April 21.

Judge for the Eighth Circuit, $42,500—**Roy L. Stephenson**; Des Moines, Iowa; U.S. district judge, Southern District of Iowa; March 14, 1917, in Spirit Lake, Iowa; Rep.; June 18.

Judge for the Ninth Circuit, $42,500—**Herbert Y. C. Choy**; Honolulu, Hawaii; partner in the law firm of Fong, Miho, Choy & Robinson; Jan. 6, 1916, in Makaweli, Kauai, Hawaii; Rep.; April 21.

Judge for the Ninth Circuit, $42,500—**Alfred T. Goodwin**; Portland, Ore.; U.S. district judge, district of Oregon; June 29, 1923, in Bellingham, Wash.; Rep.; Nov. 23.

Judge for the Tenth Circuit, $42,500—**James E. Barrett**; Cheyenne, Wyo.; attorney general, State of Wyoming; April 8, 1922, in Lusk, Wyo.; Rep.; April 21.

Judge for the Tenth Circuit, $42,500—**William E. Doyle**; Denver, Colo.; U.S. district judge, District of Colorado; Feb. 5, 1911, in Denver, Colo.; Dem.; April 21.

U.S. COURT OF CUSTOMS

Judge, $40,000—**Nils A. Boe**; Sioux Falls, S.D.; director, Office of Intergovernmental Affairs (also former Governor of South Dakota from 1965-69); Sept. 10, 1913, in Baltic, S.D.; Rep.; Aug. 6.

Judge for the Southern District of Iowa, $40,000—**William C. Stuart**; Chariton, Iowa; judge on the Iowa supreme court; April 28, 1920, in Knoxville, Iowa; Rep.; Oct. 28.

U.S. TAX COURT

Judge for the term expiring Nov. 4, 1986, $40,000—**William A. Goffe**; Sulphur, Okla.; lawyer; Aug. 30, 1929, in Sulphur, Okla.; Rep.; Oct. 28.

U.S. COURT OF MILITARY APPEALS

Judge for the term expiring May 1, 1986, $42,500—**Robert M. Duncan**; Columbus, Ohio; judge on the Ohio supreme court, Aug. 24, 1927, in Urbana, Ohio; Rep.; Oct. 6.

U.S. DISTRICT COURTS

Judge for the Southern District of Alabama, $40,000— **William Brevard Hand**; Mobile, Ala.; partner in the law firm of Hand, Arendall, Bedsole, Creaves & Johnson; Jan. 18, 1924, in Mobile, Ala.; Rep.; Sept. 21.

Judge for the Middle District of Alabama, $40,000—**Robert E. Varner**; Montgomery, Ala.; partner in the law firm of Jones, Murray, Stewart & Varner; June 11, 1921, in Montgomery, Ala.; Rep.; April 21.

Judge for the Central District of California, $40,000— **William M. Byrne Jr.**; Los Angeles, Calif.; executive director, Presidential Commission on Campus Unrest; Sept. 3, 1930, in Los Angeles, Calif.; Dem.; May 20.

Judge for the Central District of California, $40,000—**Malcolm M. Lucas**; Los Alamitos, Calif.; judge of Superior Court, County of Los Angeles; April 19, 1927, in Berkeley, Calif.; Rep.; July 29.

Judge for the Central District of California, $40,000— **Lawrence T. Lydick**; California; partner in the law firm of Adams, Duque and Hazeltine; June 22, 1916, in San Diego, Calif.; Rep.; July 29.

Judge for the Southern District of California, $40,000— **Leland C. Nielsen**; La Jolla, Calif.; judge, Superior Court in San Diego, Calif.; June 14, 1919, in Vasper, Kan.; Rep.; May 20.

Judge for the Northern District of California, $40,000— **Charles B. Renfrew**; San Francisco, Calif.; partner in the law firm of Pillsbury, Madison and Sutro; Oct. 31, 1928, in Detroit, Mich.; Dem.; Dec. 2.

Judge for the Northern District of California, $40,000— **Spencer M. Williams**; Sacramento, Calif.; of counsel for firms of Evans, Jackson & Kennedy, and Rankin, Oneal, Center, Luckhardt, Bonney, Marlain & Lund; Feb. 24, 1922, in Reading, Mass.; Rep.; July 29.

Judge for the District of Colorado, $40,000—**Sherman G. Finesilver**; Denver, Colo.; judge, Denver District Court; Oct. 1, 1927, in Denver, Colo.; Rep.; Sept. 21.

Judge for the District of Columbia District, $40,000—**Thomas A. Flannery**; Springfield, Md.; U.S. Attorney for the District of Columbia (Justice Department); May 10, 1918, in Washington, D.C.; Rep.; Dec. 1.

Judge for the District of Columbia District, $40,000— **Charles R. Richey**; Potomac, Md.; general counsel, Maryland Public Service Commission; Oct. 16, 1923, in Middleburg, Ohio; Rep.; April 29.

Judge for the Southern District of Georgia, $40,000— **Anthony A. Alaimo**; Sea Island, Ga.; partner in the law firm of Alaimo, Taylor & Bishop; March 29, 1920, in Termini, Sicily, Italy; Rep.; Dec. 2.

Judge for the Northern District of Georgia, $40,000— **Richard C. Freeman**, Atlanta, Ga.; partner in the law firm of Haas, Holland, Freeman, Levison & Gilbert; Dec. 14, 1926, in Atlanta, Ga.; Rep.; April 21.

Judge for the Northern District of Illinois, $40,000—**Richard W. McLaren**; Winnetka, Ill.; Assistant Attorney General (antitrust); April 21, 1918, in Chicago, Ill.; Rep.; Dec. 2.

Judge for the Northern District of Illinois, $40,000—**Thomas R. McMillen**; Winnetka, Ill.; judge, Circuit Court of Cook County; June 8, 1916, in Decatur, Ill.; Rep.; April 21.

Judge for the Northern District of Illinois, $40,000—**Philip W. Tone**; Park Ridge, Ill.; lawyer with the law firm of Jenner and Block; April 9, 1923, in Chicago, Ill.; Rep.; Dec. 2.

Judge for the Southern District of Iowa, $40,000—**William C. Stuart**; Chariton, Iowa; judge on the Iowa supreme court; April 28, 1920, in Knoxville, Iowa; Rep.; Oct. 28.

Judge for the District of Kansas, $40,000—**Earl E. O'Connor**; Topeka, Kansas; judge on the Kansas supreme court; Oct. 6, 1922, in Paola, Kan.; Rep.; Oct. 28.

Judge for the Western District of Kentucky, $40,000— **Charles M. Allen**; Louisville, Ky.; judge on the Jefferson County Circuit Court (Fourth Division); Nov. 22, 1916, in Louisville, Ky.; Rep.; Nov. 23.

Judge for the Eastern District of Louisiana, $40,000—**Jack M. Gordon**; Metairie, La.; partner in the law firm of Phelps, Dunbar, Marks, Clavarie & Sims; Feb. 13, 1931, in Lake Charles, La.; Rep.; June 18.

Judge for the Eastern District of Louisiana, $40,000—**R. Blake West**; New Orleans, La.; partner in the law firm of Phelps, Dunbar, Marks, Claverie & Sims; May 10, 1928, in New Orleans, La.; Rep.; June 18.

Judge for the District of Maryland, $40,000—**C. Stanley Blair**; Darlington, Md.; private law practice (also candidate for Governor of Maryland in 1970); Dec. 20, 1927, in Kinsville, Md.; Rep.; July 29.

Judge for the District of Maryland, $40,000—**Herbert F. Murray**; Baltimore, Md.; partner in the law firm of Smith, Somerville & Case; Dec. 29, 1923, in Waltham, Mass.; Rep.; July 29.

Judge for the District of Maryland, $40,000—**Joseph H. Young**; Baltimore, Md.; partner in the law firm of Piper & Marbury; July 18, 1922, in Hagerstown, Md.; Rep.; July 29.

Judge for the District of Massachusetts, $40,000—**Levin H. Campbell**; Cambridge, Mass.; associate justice, Superior Court for the Commonwealth of Massachusetts; Jan. 2, 1927, in Summit, N.J.; Rep.; Nov. 23.

Judge for the Eastern District of Michigan, $40,000—**Robert E. DeMascio**; Detroit, Mich.; judge in the Recorder's Court in Detroit, Mich.; Jan. 11, 1923, in Coraopolis, Pa.; Rep.; July 22.

Judge for the District of Nebraska, $40,000—**Robert V. Denney**; Fairbury, Neb.; member, U.S. House of Representatives (R Neb. 1967-1971); April 11, 1916, in Council Bluffs, Iowa; Rep.; March 4.

Judge for the District of Nebraska, $40,000—**Richard A. Dier**; Omaha, Neb.; U.S. Attorney (Justice Department) in Omaha; Feb. 27, 1914, in Exeter, Neb.; Rep.; Dec. 6.

Judge for the Southern District of New York, $40,000— **Charles L. Brieant Jr.**; Ossining, N.Y.; assistant counsel for the New York State Joint Legislative Committee on Fire Insurance Rates; March 13, 1923, in Ossining, N.Y.; Rep.; July 29.

Judge for the Eastern District of New York, $40,000—**Mark A. Costantino**; Staten Island, N.Y.; acting justice of the Supreme Court of the Second Judicial District, Richmond and King Counties, N.Y.; April 9, 1920, in Staten Island, N.Y.; Rep.; May 20.

Judge for the Southern District of New York, $40,000— **Murray I. Gurfein**; New York City; partner in the law firm of Goldstein, Gurfein, Shames and Hyde; Nov. 17, 1907, in New York City; Rep.; May 20.

Judge for the Eastern District of New York, $40,000—**Edward R. Neaher**; Garden City, N.Y.; U.S. Attorney for the Eastern District of New York; May 2, 1912, in Brooklyn, N.Y.; Rep.; July 22.

Judge for the Southern District of New York, $40,000— **Lawrence W. Pierce**; East Chatham, N.Y.; professor of criminal justice in Graduate School of Criminal Justice, State University of New York; Dec. 31, 1924, in Philadelphia, Pa.; Rep.; May 20.

Judge for the District of North Dakota, $40,000—**Paul Benson**; Grand Forks, N.D.; partner in the law firm of Shaft, Benson, Shaft & McConn; June 1, 1918, in Verona, N.D.; Rep.; July 29.

Judge for the Northern District of Ohio, $40,000—**Leroy J. Contie Jr.**; Canton, Ohio; judge, Common Pleas Court in Stark County, Ohio; April 2, 1920, in Canton, Ohio; Rep.; Dec. 1.

Judge for the Southern District of Ohio, $40,000—**Carl B. Rubin**; Cincinnati, Ohio; partner in the law firm of Tyler, Kane and Rubin; March 27, 1920, in Cincinnati, Ohio; Rep.; May 20.

Judge for the Eastern District of Pennsylvania, $40,000— **Raymond J. Broderick**; Philadelphia, Pa.; lieutenant governor of Pennsylvania; May 29, 1914, in Philadelphia, Pa.; Rep.; April 21.

Judge for the Eastern District of Pennsylvania, $40,000—**Clarence C. Newcomer**; Lancaster, Pa.; partner in the law firm of Newcomer, Roda and Morgan; Jan. 18, 1923, in Mount Joy, Pa.; Rep.; Nov. 23.

Judge for the Western District of Pennsylvania, $40,000—**Ralph F. Scalera**; Beaver, Pa.; partner in the law firm of Wallover, Scalera, Reed and Steff; June 28, 1930, in Midland, Pa.; Rep.; Nov. 23.

Judge for the District of South Carolina, $40,000—**Solomon Blatt Jr.**; Barnwell, S.C.; partner in the law firm of Blatt, Fales, Peeples, Bedingfield & Loadholt; Sept. 20, 1921, in Sumter, S.C.; Dem.; May 26.

Judge for the District of South Carolina, $40,000—**Robert F. Chapman**; Spartanburg, S.C.; associate and senior member of the law firm of Butler, Chapman, Parler & Morgan; April 24, 1926, in Inman, S.C.; Rep.; May 26.

Judge for the District of Utah, $40,000—**Aldon J. Anderson**; Salt Lake City, Utah; instructor parttime at Latter Day Saints Business College and the University of Utah; Jan. 3, 1917, in Salt Lake City, Utah; Rep.; July 22.

Judge for the District of Vermont, $40,000—**James S. Holden**; North Bennington, Vt.; chief justice of Supreme Court of Vermont; Jan. 29, 1914, in Bennington, Vt.; Rep.; Nov. 23.

Judge for the Eastern District of Virginia, $40,000—**Albert V. Bryan Jr.**; Alexandria, Va.; judge in the 16th Judicial Circuit of Virginia; Nov. 8, 1926, in Alexandria, Va.; Rep.; July 29.

Judge for the Western District of Washington, $40,000—**Walter T. McGovern**; Seattle, Wash.; associate justice, Supreme Court of State of Washington; May 24, 1922, in Seattle, Wash.; Rep.; April 21.

Judge for the Western District of Washington, $40,000—**Morell E. Sharp**; Bellevue, Wash.; associate justice, Supreme Court of Washington; Sept. 12, 1920, in Portland, Ore.; Rep.; Dec. 2.

Judge for the Southern District of West Virginia, $40,000—**Kenneth K. Hall**; Charleston, W.Va.; administrative hearing examiner, Bureau of Hearing and Appeals in the Social Security Administration; Feb. 24, 1918, in Greenview, W.Va.; Dem.; Dec. 1.

1972

U.S. CIRCUIT COURTS OF APPEALS

Judge for the First Circuit, $42,500—**Levin H. Campbell**; Cambridge, Mass.; U.S. District Judge, District of Massachusetts; Jan. 2, 1927, in Summit, N.J.; Rep.; June 28.

Judge for the Fourth Circuit, $42,500—**H. Emory Widener Jr.**; Bristol, Va.; U.S. District Judge, Western District of Virginia; April 30, 1923, in Abingdon, Va.; Rep.; Oct. 12.

Judge for the Sixth Circuit, $42,500—**Frederick Pierce Lively**; Danville, Ky.; partner in the law firm of Lively & Rodes; Aug. 17, 1921, in Louisville, Ky.; Rep.; Oct. 3.

Judge for the Ninth Circuit, $42,500—**J. Clifford Wallace**; La Mesa, Calif.; U.S. District Judge, Southern District of California; Dec. 11, 1928, in San Diego, Calif.; Rep.; June 28.

U.S. COURT OF CUSTOMS AND PATENT APPEALS

Chief Judge, $42,500—**Howard T. Markey**; Chicago, Ill.; attorney; Nov. 10, 1920, in Chicago, Ill.; June 21.

U.S. DISTRICT COURTS

Judge for the Southern District of California, $40,000—**William B. Enright**; La Mesa, Calif.; partner in the law firm of Enright, Knutson, Tobin & Meyer; July 12, 1925, in Long Island, N.Y.; Dem.; June 28.

Judge for the Southern District of Florida, $40,000—**Norman C. Roettger Jr.**; Ft. Lauderdale, Fla.; partner in the

law firm of Fleming, O'Bryan & Fleming; Nov. 3, 1930, in Lucasville, Ohio; Rep.; May 31.

Judge for the Middle District of Georgia, $40,000—**Wilbur D. Owens Jr.**; Macon, Ga.; partner in the law firm of Block, Hall, Hawkins & Owens; Feb. 1, 1930, in Albany, Ga.; Rep.; Feb. 17.

Judge for the District of Hawaii, $40,000—**Samuel P. King**; Honolulu, Hawaii; attorney; April 13, 1916, in Hankow, China; Rep.; June 28.

Judge for the District of Massachusetts, $40,000—**Frank H. Freedman**; Springfield, Mass.; mayor of Springfield, Mass.; Dec. 15, 1924, in Springfield, Mass.; Rep.; Oct. 12.

Judge for the District of Massachusetts, $40,000—**Joseph L. Tauro**; Marblehead, Mass.; partner in the law firm of Jaffee & Tauro; Sept. 26, 931, in Winchester, Mass.; Rep.; Oct. 12.

Judge for the Eastern District of Michigan, $40,000—**Charles W. Joiner**; Ann Arbor, Mich.; dean and professor of law, Wayne State University Law School; Jan. 14, 1916, in Maquoketa, Iowa; Rep.; June 8.

Judge for the Southern District of New York, $40,000—**Robert L. Carter**; New York City; partner in the law firm of Poletti, Freidin, Parshker, Feldman & Gartner; March 11, 1917, in Caryville, Fla.; Dem.; July 21.

Judge for the Southern District of New York, $40,000—**Kevin Thomas Duffy**; Bronxville, N.Y.; regional administrator, Securities and Exchange Commission; Jan. 10, 1933, in New York City; Rep.; Oct. 12.

Judge for the Southern District of New York, $40,000—**Thomas P. Griesa**; New York City; partner in the law firm of Davis, Polk & Wardwell; Oct. 11, 1930, in Kansas City, Mo.; Rep.; June 28.

Judge for the Southern District of New York, $40,000—**Whitman Knapp**; New York City; partner in the law firm of Barrett, Knapp, Smith, Schapiro & Simon; Feb. 24, 1909, in New York City; Rep.; June 28.

Judge for the Southern District of New York, $40,000—**Charles E. Stewart Jr.**; Ardsley-On-Hudson, N.Y.; member of the law firm of Dewey, Ballantine, Bushby, Palmer & Wood; Sept. 1, 1916, in Glen Ridge, N.J.; Rep.; June 28.

Judge for the Southern District of New York, $40,000—**Robert J. Ward**; New York City; partner in the law firm of Aranow, Brodsky, Bohlinger, Benetar, Einhorn & Dann; Jan. 31, 1926, in New York City; Rep.; Oct. 12.

Judge for the Middle District of North Carolina, $40,000—**Hiram H. Ward**; Denton, N.C.; partner in the law firm of DeLapp & Ward; April 29, 1923, in Thomasville, N.C.; Rep.; June 28.

Judge for the District of Oregon, $40,000 **Otto R. Skopil Jr.**; Salem, Ore.; senior partner in the law firm of Williams & Skopil; June 3, 1919, in Portland, Ore.; Rep.; May 25.

Judge for the District of Oregon, $40,000—**James M. Burns**; Portland, Ore.; Judge, circuit court of Oregon; Nov. 24, 1924, in Portland, Ore.; Rep.; May 25.

Judge for the District of Puerto Rico, $40,000—**Hernan G. Pesquera**; Santurce, Puerto Rico; partner in the law firm of Geigel, Silva & Pesquera; May 25, 1924, in Santurce, Puerto Rico; Oct. 12.

Judge for the Northern District of Texas, $40,000—**Eldon B. Mahon**; Fort Worth, Texas; U.S. Attorney, northern district of Texas; April 9, 1918, in Loraine, Texas; Dem.; June 28.

Judge for the District of Vermont, $40,000—**Albert W. Coffrin**; Burlington, Vt.; partner in the law firm of Coffrin, Pierson & Affolter; Dec. 21, 1919, in Burlington, Vt.; Rep.; June 8.

Judge for the Western District of Virginia, $40,000—**James C. Turk**; Radford, Va.; senior partner in the law firm of Dalton, Turk & Stone; May 3, 1923, in Roanoke County, Va.; Rep.; Oct. 12.

Judge for the Eastern District of Washington, $40,000—**Marshall A. Neill**; Olympia, Wash.; associate justice, Washington Supreme Court; Aug. 23, 1914, in Pullman, Wash.; Rep.; Aug. 2.

1973

The following persons were confirmed to federal judgeships between Jan. 1, 1973 and Oct. 23, 1973.

U.S. CIRCUIT COURTS OF APPEALS

Judge for the third circuit, $42,500—**Leonard I. Garth;** Paterson, N.J.; judge for the district of New Jersey; April 7, 1921, in Brooklyn, N.Y.; Rep.; Aug. 3.

Judge for the third circuit, $42,500—**Joseph F. Weis Jr.;** Pittsburgh, Pa.; judge for the western district of Pennsylvania; March 12, 1923, in Ross Township, Pa.; Rep.; March 14.

Judge for the fifth circuit, $42,500—**Thomas G. Gee;** Austin, Texas; partner in the law firm of Graves, Dougherty, Gee, Hearon, Moody & Garwood; Dec. 9, 1925, in Jacksonvill, Fla.; Rep.; July 13.

Judge for the eighth circuit, $42,500—**William H. Webster;** St. Louis, Mo.; judge for the eastern district of Missouri; March 8, 1924, in St. Louis, Mo.; Rep.; July 13.

Judge for the ninth circuit, $42,500—**Joseph T. Sneed;** Durham, N.C.; deputy attorney general, Justice Department; July 21, 1920, in Calvert, Texas; Rep.; Aug. 3.

U.S. COURT OF CUSTOMS AND PATENT APPEALS

Associate Judge, $42,500—**Jack R. Miller;** Sioux City, Iowa; U.S. senator (R Iowa 1961-73); June 6, 1916, in Chicago, Ill.; Rep.; June 28.

U.S. DISTRICT COURTS

Judge for the northern district of Alabama, $40,000—**J. Foy Guin Jr.;** Russellville, Ala.; senior partner in the law firm of Guin, Guin, Bouldin & Porch; Feb. 2, 1924, in Russellville, Ala.; Rep.; April 10.

Judge for the northern district of Alabama, $40,000—**James H. Hancock;** Brimingham, Ala.; partner in the law firm of Balch, Bingham, Baker, Hawthorne & Williams; April 30, 1931, in Montgomery, Ala.; Rep.; April 10.

Judge for the middle district of Florida, $40,000—**John A. Reed Jr.;** West Palm Beach, Fla.; chief judge, Florida Fourth District Court of Appeals; June 29, 1931, in Washington, D.C.; Rep.; Aug. 3.

Judge for the northern district of Illinois, $40,000—**Prentice H. Marshall;** Urbana, Ill.; hearing officer, Illinois Fair Employment Practices Commission and professor of law, University of Illinois College of Law; Aug. 7, 1926, in Oak Park, Ill.; Ind.; July 13.

Judge for the sourthern district of Illinois, $40,000—**Harlington Wood Jr.;** Springfield, Ill.; assistant attorney general (civil), Justice Department; April 17, 1920, in Springfield, Ill.; Rep.; July 13.

Judge for the northern district of Indiana, $40,000—**Allen Sharp;** Williamsport, Ind.; judge, Appellate Court of Indiana; Feb. 11, 1932, in Washington, D.C.; Rep.; Oct. 4.

Judge for the eastern district of Missouri, $40,000—**John F. Nangle;** Brentwood, Mo.; attorney in private practice; June 8, 1922, in St. Louis, Mo.; Rep.; July 13.

Judge for the district of Nebraska, $40,000—**Albert G. Schatz;** Omaha, Neb.; partner in the law firm of Gross, Welch, Vinardi, Kauffman, Schatz & Day; Aug. 4, 1921, in Omaha, Neb.; Rep.; May 10.

Judge for the district of New Jersey, $40,000—**Vincent P. Biunno,** Glen Ridge, N.J.; partner in the law firm of Lum, Biunno & Tompkins; Feb. 2, 1916, in Newark, N.J.; Rep.; April 10.

Judge for the eastern district of Pennsylvania, $40,000—**Herbert A. Fogel;** Philadelphia, Pa.; partner in the law firm of Obermayer, Rebmann, Maxwell & Hippel; April 20, 1929, in Philadelphia, Pa.; Rep.; March 14.

Judge for the western district of Pennsylvania, $40,000—**Daniel J. Snyder;** Greensburg, Pa.; senior partner in the law firm of Costello, Snyder, Berk & Horner; May 2, 1916, in Greensburg, Pa; Rep.; April 10.

ACTS OF CONGRESS HELD UNCONSTITUTIONAL 1789—1973

**SOURCE: U.S. Library of Congress,
Congressional Research Service**

1. Act of September 24, 1789 (1 Stat. 81, sec. 13, in part).

Provision that "...(the Supreme Court) shall have power to issue... writs of mandamus, in cases warranted by the principles and usages of law, to any...persons holding office, under authority of the United States" as applied to the issue of mandamus to the Secretary of State requiring him to deliver to plaintiff a commission (duly signed by the President) as justice of the peace in the District of Columbia, *held* an attempt to enlarge the original jurisdiction of the Supreme Court, fixed by Article III, section 2.

Marbury v. Madison, 1 Cr. 137 (February 24, 1803).

2. Act of February 20, 1812 (2 Stat. 677).

Provisions establishing board of revision to annul titles conferred many years previously by governors of the Northwest Territory were *held* violative of the due process clause of the Fifth Amendment.

Reichart v. Felps, 6 Wall. 160 (March 16, 1868).

3. Act of March 6, 1820 (3 Stat. 548, sec. 8, proviso).

The Missouri Compromise, prohibiting slavery within the Louisiana Territory north of 36 30', except Missouri, *held* not warranted as a regulation of Territory belonging to the United States under Article IV, section 3, clause 2 (and *see* Fifth Amendment).

Dred Scott v. Sandford, 19 How. 393 (March 6, 1857).

4. Act of February 25, 1862 (12 Stat. 345, sec. 1); July 11, 1862 (12 Stat. 532, sec. 1); March 3, 1863 (12 Stat. 711, sec. 3), each in part only.

"Legal tender clauses," making noninterest-bearing United States notes legal tender in payment of "all debts, public and private," so far as applied to debts contracted before passage of the act, *held* not within express or implied powers of Congress under Article I, section 8, and inconsistent with Article I, section 10, and Fifth Amendment.

Hepburn v. Griswold, 8 Wall. 603 (February 7, 1870; overruled in *Knox v. Lee* (Legal Tender Cases), 12 Wall. 457 (May 1, 1871).

5. Act of March 3, 1863 (12 Stat. 756, sec. 5).

"So much of the fifth section...as provides for the removal of a judgment in a State court, and in which the cause was tried by a jury to the circuit court of the United States for a retrial on the facts and law, is not in pursuance of the Constitution, and is void" under the Seventh Amendment.

The Justices v. Murray, 9 Wall. 274 (March 14, 1870).

6. Act of March 3, 1863 (12 Stat. 766, sec. 5)

Provision for an appeal from the Court of Claims to the Supreme Court—there being, at the time, a further provision (sec. 14) requiring an estimate by the Secretary of the Treasury before payment of final judgments, *held* to contravene the judicial finality intended by the Constitution, Article III.

Gordon v. United States, 2 Wall. 561 (March 10, 1865). (Case was dismissed without opinion; the grounds upon which this decision was made were stated in a posthumous opinion by Chief Justice Taney printed in the appendix to volume 117 of the U.S. Reports at p. 697.)

7. Act of June 30, 1864 (13 Stat. 311, sec. 13).

Provision that "any prize cause now pending in any circuit court shall, on the application of all parties in interest...be transferred by that court to the Supreme Court...," as applied in a case where no action had been taken in the Circuit Court on the appeal from the district court, *held* to propose an appeal procedure not within Article III, section 2.

The Alicia, 7 Wall. 571 (January 25, 1869).

8. Act of January 24, 1865 (13 Stat. 424).

Requirement of a test oath (disavowing actions in hostility to the United States) before admission to appear as attorney in a federal court by virtue of any previous admission, *held* invalid as applied to an attorney who had been pardoned by the President for all offenses during the Rebellion—as *ex post facto* (Article I, section 9, clause 3) and an interference with the pardoning power (Article II, section 2, clause 1).

Ex parte Garland, 4 Wall. 333 (January 14, 1867).

9. Act of March 2, 1867 (14 Stat. 484, sec. 29).

General prohibition on sale of naphtha, etc., for illuminating purposes, if inflammable at less temperature than 110 F., *held* invalid "except so far as the section named operates within the United States, but without the limits of any State," as being a mere police regulation.

United States v. Dewitt, 9 Wall. 41 (February 21, 1870).

10. Act of May 31, 1870 (16 Stat. 140, secs. 3, 4).

Provisions penalizing (1) refusal of local election officials to permit voting by persons offering to qualify under State laws, applicable to any citizens; and (2) hindering of any person from qualifying or voting, *held* invalid under Fifteenth Amendment.

United States v. Reese et al., 92 U.S. 214 (March 27, 1876).

11. Act of July 12, 1870 (16 Stat. 235).

Provisions making Presidential pardons inadmissible in evidence in Court of Claims, prohibiting their use by that court in deciding claims or appeals, and requiring dismissal of appeals by the Supreme Court in cases where proof of loyalty had been made otherwise than as prescribed by law, *held* an interference with judicial power under Article III, section 1, and with the pardoning power under Article II, section 2, clause 1.

United States v. Klein, 13 Wall. 128 (January 29, 1872).

12. Act of June 22, 1874 (18 Stat. 1878, sec. 4).

Provision authorizing federal courts, in suits for forfeitures under revenue and custom laws, to require production of documents, with allegations expected to be proved therein to be taken as proved on failure to produce such documents, was *held* violative of the search and seizure provision of the Fourth Amendment and the self-incrimination clause of the Fifth Amendment.

Boyd v. United States, 116 U.S. 616 (February 1, 1886).

13. Revised **Statutes** 1977 (Act of May 31, 1870, 16 Stat. 144).

Provision that "all persons within the jurisdiction of the United States shall have the same right in every State and Territory to make and enforce contracts...as is enjoyed by white citizens...," *held* invalid under the Thirteenth Amendment.

Hodges v. United States, 203 U.S. 1 (May 28, 1906).

14. Revised Statutes 4937-4947 (Act of July 8, 1870, 16 Stat. 210), and Act of August 14, 1876 (19 Stat. 141).

Original trademark law, applying to marks "for exclusive use within the United States," and a penal act designed solely for the protection of rights defined in the earlier measure, *held* not supportable by Article I, section 8, clause 8 (copyright clause), nor Article I, section 8, clause 3, by reason of its application to intrastate as well as interstate commerce.

Trade-Mark Cases, 100 U.S. 82 (November 17, 1879).

15. Revised Statutes 5132, subdivision 9 (Act of March 2, 1867, 14 Stat. 539).

Provision penalizing "any person respecting whom bankruptcy proceedings are commenced...who, within 3 months before the commencement of proceedings in bankruptcy, under the false color and pretense of carrying on business and dealing in the ordinary course of trade, obtains on credit from any person any goods or chattels with intent to defraud...," *held* a police regulation not within the bankruptcy power (Article I, section 4, clause 4).

United States v. Fox, 95 U.S. 670 (January 7, 1878).

16. Revised Statutes 5507 (Act of May 31, 1870, 16 Stat. 141, sec. 4).

Provision penalizing "every person who prevents, hinders, controls, or intimidates another from exercising...the right of suffrage, to whom that right is guaranteed by the Fifteenth Amendment to the Constitution of the United States, by means of bribery...," *held* not authorized by the said Fifteenth Amendment.

James v. Bowman, 190 U.S. 127 (May 4, 1903).

17. Revised Statutes 5519 (Act of April 20, 1871, 17 Stat. 13, sec. 2).

Section providing punishment in case "two or more persons in any State...conspire...for the purpose of depriving...any person...of the equal protection of the laws...or for the purpose of preventing or hindering the constituted authorities of any State...from giving or securing to all persons within each State...the equal protection of the laws...," *held* invalid as not being directed at State action proscribed by the Fourteenth Amendment.

United States v. Harris, 106 U.S. 629 (January 22, 1883).

In *Baldwin v. Franks*, 120 U.S. 678 (March 17, 1887), an attempt was made to distinguish the Harris case and to apply the statute to a conspiracy directed at aliens within a State, but the provision was held not enforceable in such limited manner.

18. Revised Statutes of the District of Columbia, section 1064 (Act of June 17, 1870, 16 Stat. 154, sec. 3).

Provision that "prosecutions in the police court (of the District of Columbia) shall be by information under oath, without indictment by grand jury or trial by petit jury," as applied to punishment for conspiracy, *held* to contravene Article III, section 2, clause 3, requiring jury trial of all crimes.

Callan v. Wilson, 127 U.S. 540 (May 14, 1888).

19. Act of March 1, 1875 (18 Stat. 336, secs. 1,2).

Provision "That all persons within the jurisdiction of the United States shall be entitled to the full and equal enjoyment of the accommodations...of inns, public conveyances on land or water, theaters, and other places of public amusement; subject only to the conditions and limitations established by law, and applicable alike to citizens of every race and color, regardless of any previous condition of servitude"—subject to penalty, *held* not to be supported by the Thirteenth or Fourteenth Amendments.

Civil Rights Cases, 109 U.S. 3 (October 15, 1883), as to operation within States.

20. Act of March 3, 1875 (18 Stat. 479, sec. 2).

Provision that "if the party (i.e., a person stealing property from the United States) has been convicted, then the judgment against him shall be conclusive evidence in the prosecution against (the) receiver that the property of the United States therein described has been embezzled, stolen, or purloined," *held* to contravene the Sixth Amendment.

Kirby v. United States, 174 U.S. 47 (April 11, 1899).

21. Act of July 12, 1876 (19 Stat. 80, sec. 6, in part).

Provision that "postmasters of the first, second, and third classes... may be removed by the President by and with the advice and consent of the Senate," *held* to infringe the executive power under Article II, section 1, clause 1.

Myers v. United States, 272 U.S. 52 (October 25, 1926).

22. Act of August 14, 1876 (19 Stat. 141, trademark act), *see* Revised Statutes 4937, above, No. 14.

23. Act of August 11, 1888 (25 Stat. 411).

Clause, in a provision for the purchase or condemnation of a certain lock and dam in the Monongahela River, that "...in estimating the sum to be paid by the United States, the franchise of said corporation to collect tolls shall not be considered or estimated...," *held* to contravene the Fifth Amendment.

Monongahela Navigation Co. v. United States, 148 U.S. 312 (March 27, 1893).

24. Act of May 5, 1892 (27 Stat. 25, sec. 4).

Provision of a Chinese exclusion act, that Chinese persons "convicted and adjudged to be not lawfully entitled to be or remain in the United States shall be imprisoned at hard labor for a period not exceeding 1 year and thereafter removed from the United States..." (such conviction and judgment being had before a justice, judge, or commissioner upon a summary hearing), *held* to contravene the Fifth and Sixth Amendments.

Wong Wing v. United States, 163 U.S. 228 (May 18, 1896).

25. Joint Resolution of August 4, 1894 (28 Stat. 1018, No. 41).

Provision authorizing the Secretary of the Interior to approve a second lease of certain land by an Indian chief in Minnesota (granted to lessor's ancestor by art. 9 of a treaty with the Chippewa Indians), *held* an interference with judicial interpretation of treaties under Article III, section 2, clause 1 (and repugnant to the Fifth Amendment).

Jones v. Meehan, **175 U.S. 1 (October 30, 1899).**

26. Act of August 27, 1894 (28 Stat. 553-560, secs. 27-37).

Income tax provisions of the tariff act of 1894. "The tax imposed by sections 27 and 37, inclusive...so far as it falls on the income of real estate and of personal property, being a direct tax within the meaning of the Constitution, and, therefore, unconstitutional and void because not apportioned according to representation (Article I, section 2, clause 3), all those sections, constituting one entire scheme of taxation, are necessarily invalid" (158 U.S. 601, 637).

Pollock v. Farmers' Loan & Trust Co., 157 U.S. 429 (April 8, 1895) and rehearing, 158 U.S. 601 (May 20, 1895).

27. Act of January 30, 1897 (29 Stat. 506).

Prohibition on sale of liquor "...to any Indian to whom allotment of land has been made while the title to the same shall be held in trust by the Government...," *held* a police regulation infringing State powers, and not warranted by the commerce clause, Article I, section 8, clause 3.

Matter of Heff, **197 U.S. 488 (April 10, 1905)**, *overruled* in *United States v. Nice*, **241 U.S. 591 (1916).**

28. Act of June 1, 1898 (30 Stat. 428).

Section 10, penalizing "any employer subject to the provisions of this act" who should "threaten any employee with loss of employment... because of his membership in...a labor corporation, association or organization" (the act being applicable "to any common carrier...engaged in the transportation of passengers or property...from one State...to another State...," etc.), *held* an infringement of the Fifth Amendment, and not supported by the commerce clause.

Adair v. United States, 208 U.S. 161 (January 27, 1908).

29. Act of June 13, 1898 (30 Stat. 451, 459).

Stamp tax on foreign bills of lading, *held* a tax on exports in violation of Article I, section 9.

Fairbank v. United States, 181 U.S. 283 (April 15, 1901).

30. Same (30 Stat. 451, 460).

Tax on charter parties, as applied to shipments exclusively from ports in United States to foreign ports, *held* a tax on exports in violation of Article I, section 9.

United States v. Hvoslef, 237 U.S. 1 (March 22, 1915).

31. Act of June 6, 1900 (31 Stat. 359, sec. 171).

Section of the Alaska Code providing for a six-person jury in trials for misdemeanors, *held* repugnant to the Sixth Amendment, requiring "jury" trial of crimes.

Rassmussen v. United States, 197 U.S. 516 (April 10, 1905).

32. Act of March 3, 1901 (31 Stat. 1341, sec. 935).

Section of the District of Columbia Code granting the same right of appeal, in criminal cases, to the United States or the District of Columbia as to the defendant, but providing that a verdict was not to be set aside for error found in rulings during trial, *held* an attempt to take an advisory opinion, contrary to Article III, section 2.

United States v. Evans, 213 U.S. 297 (April 19, 1909).

33. Act of June 11, 1906 (34 Stat. 232).

Act providing that "every common carrier engaged in trade or commerce in the District of Columbia...or between the several States...shall be liable to any of its employees...for all damages which may result from the negligence of any of its officers...or by reason of any defect...due to its negligence in its cars, engines...roadbed," etc., *held* not supportable under Article I, section 8, clause 3 because it extended to intrastate as well as interstate commercial activities.

The Employers' Liability Cases, 207 U.S. 463 (January 6, 1908). (The act was upheld as to the District of Columbia in *Hyde v. Southern R. Co.*, 31 App. D.C. 466 (1908); and as to the Territories, in *El Paso & N.E. Ry. v. Gutierrez*, 215 U.S. 87 (1909).

34. Act of June 16, 1906 (34 Stat. 269, sec. 2).

Provision of Oklahoma Enabling Act restricting relocation of the State capital prior to 1913, *held* not supportable by Article IV, section 3, authorizing admission of new States.

Coyle v. Oklahoma, 221 U.S. 559 (May 29, 1911).

35. Act of February 20, 1907 (34 Stat. 889, sec. 3).

Provision in the Immigration Act of 1907 penalizing "whoever...shall keep, maintain, control, support, or harbor in any house or other place, for the purpose of prostitution...any alien woman or girl, within 3 years after she shall have entered the United States," *held* an exercise of police power not within the control of Congress over immigration (whether drawn from the commerce clause or based on inherent sovereignty).

Keller v. United States, 213 U.S. 138 (April 5, 1909).

36. Act of March 1, 1907 (34 Stat. 1028).

Provisions authorizing certain Indians "to institute their suits in the Court of Claims to determine the validity of any acts of Congress passed since...1902, insofar as said acts...attempt to increase or extend the restrictions upon alienation...of allotments of lands of Cherokee citizens...," and giving a right of appeal to the Supreme Court, *held* an attempt to enlarge the judicial power restricted by Article III, section 2, to cases and controversies.

Muskrat v. United States, 219 U.S. 346 (January 23, 1911).

37. Act of May 27, 1908 (35 Stat. 313, sec. 4).

Provision making locally taxable "all land (of Indians of the Five Civilized Tribes) from which restrictions have been or shall be removed," *held* a violation of the Fifth Amendment, in view of the Atoka Agreement, embodied in the Curtis Act of June 28, 1898, providing tax-exemption for allotted lands while title in original allottee, not exceeding 21 years.

Choate v. Trapp, 224 U.S. 665 (May 13, 1912).

38. Act of August 19, 1911 (37 Stat. 28).

A proviso in section 8 of the Federal Corrupt Practices Act fixing a maximum authorized expenditure by a candidate for Senator "in any campaign for his nomination and election," as applied to a primary election, *held* not supported by Article I, section 4, giving Congress power to regulate the manner of holding elections for Senators and Representatives. *Newberry v. United States*, **256 U.S. 232 (May 2, 1921). Overruled in *United States v. Classic*, 313 U.S. 299 (1941).**

39. Act of June 18, 1912 (37 Stat. 136, sec. 8).

Part of section 8 giving the Juvenile Court of the District of Columbia (proceeding upon information) concurrent jurisdiction of desertion cases (which were, by law, punishable by fine or imprisonment in the workhouse at hard labor for 1 year), *held* invalid under the Fifth Amendment, which gives right to presentment by a grand jury in case of infamous crimes.

United States v. Moreland, 258 U.S. 433 (April 17, 1922).

40. Act of March 4, 1913 (37 Stat. 988, part of par. 64).

Provision of the District of Columbia Public Utility Commission Act authorizing appeal to the United States Supreme Court from decrees of the District of Columbia Court of Appeals modifying valuation decisions of the Utilities Commission, *held* an attempt to extend the appellate jurisdiction of the Supreme Court to cases not strictly judicial within the meaning of Article III, section 2.

Keller v. Potomac Elec. Co., 261 U.S. 428 (April 9, 1923).

41. Act of September 1, 1916 (39 Stat. 675).

The original Child Labor Law, providing "that no producer...shall ship...in interstate commerce...any article or commodity the product of any mill...in which within 30 days prior to the removal of such product therefrom children under the age of 14 years have been employed or permitted to work more than 8 hours in any day or more than 6 days in any week...," *held* not within the commerce power of Congress.

Hammer v. Dagenhart, 247 U.S. 251 (June 3, 1918).

42. Act of September 8, 1916 (39 Stat. 757, sec. 2(a), in part).

Provision of the income tax law of 1916, that a "stock dividend shall be considered income, to the amount of its cash value," *held* invalid (in spite of the Sixteenth Amendment) as an attempt to tax something not actually income, without regard to apportionment under Article I, section 2, clause 3.

Eisner v. Macomber, 252 U.S. 189 (March 8, 1920).

43. Act of October 6, 1917 (40 Stat. 395).

The amendment of sections 24 and 256 of the Judicial Code (which prescribe the jurisdiction of district courts) "saving...to claimants the rights and remedies under the workmen's compensation law of any State," *held* an attempt to transfer federal legislative power to the States—the Constitution, by Article III, section 2, and Article I, section 8, having adopted rules of general maritime law.

Knickerbocker Ice Co. v. Stewart, 253 U.S. 149 (May 17, 1920).

44. Act of September 19, 1918 (40 Stat. 960).

Specifically, that part of the Minimum Wage Law of the District of Columbia which authorized the Wage Board "to ascertain and declare... (a) Standards of minimum wages for women in any occupation within the District of Columbia, and what wages are inadequate to supply the necessary cost of living to any such women workers to maintain them in good health and to protect their morals...," *held* to interfere with freedom of contract under the Fifth Amendment.

Adkins et al. v. Children's Hospital and Adkins et al. v. Lyons, 261 U.S. 525 (April 9, 1923), *overruled* in *West Coast Hotel Co. v. Parrish*, 300 U.S. 379 (March 29, 1937).

45. Act of February 24, 1919 (40 Stat. 1065, sec. 213, in part).

That part of section 213 of the Revenue Act of 1918 which provided that "...for the purposes of this title...the term 'gross income'...includes gains, profits, and income derived from salaries, wages, or compensation for personal service (including in the case of...judges of the Supreme and inferior courts of the United States...the compensation received as such)..." as applied to a judge in office when the act was passed, *held* a violation of the guaranty of judges' salaries, in Article III, section 1.

Evans v. Gore, 253 U.S. 245 (June 1, 1920).

Miles v. Graham, 268 U.S. 501 (June 1, 1925), held it invalid as applied to a judge taking office subsequent to the date of the act.

46. Act of February 24, 1919 (40 Stat. 1097, sec. 402(c)).

That part of the estate tax law providing that "gross estate" of a decedent should include value of all property "to the extent of any interest therein of which the decedent has at any time made a transfer or with respect to which he had at any time created a trust, in contemplation of or intended to take effect in possession or enjoyment at or after his death (whether such transfer or trust is made or created before or after the passage of this act), except in case of a *bona fide* sale..." as applied to a transfer of property made prior to the act and intended to take effect "in possession or enjoyment" at death of grantor, but not in fact testamentary or designed to evade taxation, *held* confiscatory, contrary to Fifth Amendment.

Nicholas v. Coolidge, 274 U.S. 531 (May 31, 1927).

47. Act of February 24, 1919, title XII (40 Stat. 1138, entire title).

The Child Labor Tax Act, providing that "every person...operating... any...factory (etc.)...in which children under the age of 14 years have been employed or permitted to work...shall pay...in addition to all other taxes imposed by law, an excise tax equivalent to 10 percent of the entire net profits received...for such year from the sale...of the product of such... factory...," *held* beyond the taxing power under Article I, section 8, clause 1, and an infringement of State authority.

Bailey v. Drexel Furniture Co. (Child Labor Tax Case), 259 U.S. 20 (May 15, 1922).

48. Act of October 22, 1919 (41 Stat. 298, sec. 2), amending Act of August 10, 1917 (40 Stat. 277, sec. 4).

(a) Section 4 of the Lever Act, providing in part "that it is hereby made unlawful for any person willfully...to make any unjust or unreasonable rate or charge in handling or dealing in or with any necessaries..." and fixing a penalty, *held* invalid to support an indictment for charging an unreasonable price on sale—as not setting up an ascertainable standard of guilt within the requirement of the Sixth Amendment.

United States v. Cohen Grocery Co., 255 U.S. 81 (February 28, 1921).

(b) That provision of section 4 making it unlawful "to conspire, combine, agree, or arrange with any other person to...exact excessive prices for any necessaries" and fixing a penalty, *held* invalid to support an indictment, on the reasoning of the Cohen Grocery case.

Weeds, Inc. v. United States, 255 U.S. 109 (February 28, 1921).

49. Act of August 24, 1921 (42 Stat. 187, Future Trading Act).

(a) Section 4 (and interwoven regulations) providing a "tax of 20 cents a bushel on every bushel involved therein, upon each contract of sale of grain for future delivery, except...where such contracts are made by or through a member of a board of trade which has been designated by the Secretary of Agriculture as a 'contract market'...," *held* not within the taxing power under Article I, section 8.

Hill v. Wallace, 259 U.S. 44 (May 15, 1922).

(b) Section 3, providing "That in addition to the taxes now imposed by law there is hereby levied a tax amounting to 20 cents per bushel on each bushel involved therein, whether the actual commodity is intended to be delivered or only nominally referred to, upon each...option for a contract either of purchase or sale of grain...," *held* invalid on the same reasoning.

Trusler v. Crooks, 269 U.S. 475 (January 11, 1926).

50. Act of November 23, 1921 (42 Stat. 261, sec. 245, in part).

Provision of Revenue Act of 1921 abating the deduction (4 percent of mean reserves) allowed from taxable income of life insurance companies in general by the amount of interest on their tax-exempts, and so according no relative advantage to the owners of the tax-exempt securities, *held* to destroy a guaranteed exemption. (*See* Fifth Amendment.)

National Life Ins. v. United States, 277 U.S. 508 (June 4, 1928).

51. Act of June 10, 1922 (42 Stat. 634).

A second attempt to amend sections 24 and 256 of the Judicial Code, relating to jurisdiction of district courts, by saving "to claimants for compensation for injuries to or death of persons other than the master or members of the crew of a vessel, their rights and remedies under the workmen's compensation law of any State...," *held* invalid on authority of *Knickerbocker Ice Co. v. Stewart*.

Washington v. Dawson & Co., 264 U.S. 219 (February 25, 1924).

52. Act of June 2, 1924 (43 Stat. 313).

The gift tax provisions of the Revenue Act of 1924, applicable to gifts made during the calendar year, were *held* invalid under the Fifth Amendment insofar as they applied to gifts made before passage of the act.

Untermeyer v. Anderson, 276 U.S. 440 (April 9, 1928).

53. Act of February 26, 1926 (44 Stat. 70, sec. 302, in part).

Stipulation creating a conclusive presumption that gifts made within two years prior to the death of the donor were made in contemplation of death of donor and requiring the value thereof to be included in computing the death transfer tax on decedent's estate was *held* to effect an invalid deprivation of property without due process.

Heiner v. Donnan, 285 U.S. 312 (March 21, 1932).

54. Act of February 26, 1926 (44 Stat. 95, sec. 701).

Provision imposing a special excise tax of $1,000 on liquor dealers operating in States where such business is illegal, was *held* a penalty, without constitutional support following repeal of the Eighteenth Amendment.

United States v. Constantine, 296 U.S. 287 (December 9, 1935).

55. Act of March 20, 1933 (48 Stat. 11, sec. 17, in part).

Clause in the Economy Act of 1933 providing "...all laws granting or pertaining to yearly renewable term war risk insurance are hereby repealed," *held* invalid to abrogate an outstanding contract of insurance, which is a vested right protected by the Fifth Amendment.

Lynch v. United States, 292 U.S. 571 (June 4, 1934).

56. Act of May 12, 1933 (48 Stat. 31).

Agricultural Adjustment Act providing for processing taxes on agricultural commodities and benefit payments therefrom to farmers, *held* not within the taxing power under Article I, section 8, clause 1.

United States v. Butler, 297 U.S. 1 (January 6, 1936).

57. Joint Resolution of June 5, 1933 (48 Stat. 113, sec. 1).

Abrogation of gold clause in Government obligations, *held* a repudiation of the pledge implicit in the power to borrow money (Article I, section 8, clause 2), and within the prohibition of the Fourteenth Amendment, against questioning the validity of the public debt. (The majority of the Court, however, held plaintiff not entitled to recover under the circumstances.)

Perry v. U.S., 294 **U.S. 330 (February 18, 1935).**

58. Act of June 16, 1933 (48 Stat. 195, the National Industrial Recovery Act).

(a) Title I, except section 9.

Provisions relating to codes of fair competition, authorized to be approved by the President in his discretion "to effectuate the policy" of the act, *held* invalid as a delegation of legislative power (Article I, section 1) and not within the commerce power (Article I, section 8, clause 3).

Schechter Corp. v. United States, 295 U.S. 495 (May 27, 1935).

(b) Section 9(c).

Clause of the oil regulation section authorizing the President "to prohibit the transportation in interstate...commerce of petroleum...produced or withdrawn from storage in excess of the amount permitted...by any State law..." and prescribing a penalty for violation of orders issued thereunder, *held* invalid as a delegation of legislative power.

Panama Refining Co. v. Ryan, 293 U.S. 388 (January 7, 1935).

59. Act of June 16, 1933 (48 Stat. 307, sec. 13).

Temporary reduction of 15 percent in retired pay of judges, retired from service but subject to performance of judicial duties under the Act of March 1, 1929 (45 Stat. 1422), was *held* a violation of the guaranty of judges' salaries in Article III, section 1.

Booth v. United States, 291 U.S. 339 **(February 5, 1934).**

60. Act of April 27, 1934 (48 Stat. 646, sec. 6), amending section 5(i) of Home Owners' Loan Act of 1933.

Provision for conversion of State building and loan associations into federal associations, upon vote of 51 percent of the votes cast at a meeting of stockholders called to consider such action, *held* an encroachment on reserved powers of State (Amendment 10).

Hopkins Savings Assn. v. Cleary, 296 U.S. 315 (December 9, 1935).

61. Act of May 24, 1934 (48 Stat. 798).

Provision for readjustment of municipal indebtedness, though "adequately related" to the bankruptcy power, was *held* invalid as an interference with State sovereignty (Amendment 10).

Ashton v. Cameron County Dist., 298 U.S. 513 (May 25, 1936).

62. Act of June 27, 1934 (48 Stat. 1283).

The Railroad Retirement Act, establishing a detailed compulsory retirement system for employees of carriers subject to the Interstate Commerce Act, *held*, not a regulation of commerce within the meaning of Article I, section 8, clause 3, and violative of the due process clause (Amendment 5).

Retirement Board v. Alton R. Co., 295 U.S. 330 (May 6, 1935).

63. Act of June 28, 1934 (48 Stat. 1289, ch. 869).

The Frazier-Lemke Act, adding subsection(s) to section 75 of the Bankruptcy Act, designed to preserve to mortgagors the ownership and enjoyment of their farm property and providing specifically, in paragraph 7, that a bankrupt left in possession has the option at any time within 5 years of buying at the appraised value—subject meanwhile to no monetary obligation other than payment of reasonable rental, *held* a violation of property rights, under the Fifth Amendment.

Louisville Bank v. Radford, 295 U.S. 555 (May 27, 1935).

64. Act of August 24, 1935 (49 Stat. 750).

Amendments of Agricultural Adjustment Act *held* not within the taxing power.

Rickert Rice Mills v. Fontenot, 297 U.S. 110 (January 13, 1936).

65. Act of August 30, 1935 (49 Stat. 991).

Bituminous Coal Conservation Act of 1935, *held* to impose, not a tax within Article I, section 8, but a penalty not sustained by the commerce clause (Article I, section 8, clause 3).

Carter v. Carter Coal Co., 298 U.S. 238 (May 18, 1936).

66. Act of June 25, 1938 (52 Stat. 1040).

Federal Food, Drug, and Cosmetic Act of 1938, section 301 (f), prohibiting the refusal to permit entry or inspection of premises by federal officers *held* void for vagueness and as violative of the due process clause of the Fifth Amendment.

United States v. Cardiff, 344 U.S. 174 (December 8, 1952).

67. Act of June 30, 1938 (52 Stat. 1251).

Federal Firearms Act, section 2(f), establishing a presumption of guilt based on a prior conviction and present possession of a firearm, *held* to violate the test of due process under the Fifth Amendment.

Tot v. United States, 319 U.S. 463 (June 7, 1943).

68. Act of October 14, 1940 (54 Stat. 1169, sec. 401(g)); as amended by Act of January 20, 1944 (58 Stat. 4, sec. 1).

Provision of Aliens and Nationality Code (8 U.S.C. 1481(a) (8)), derived from the Nationality Act of 1940, as amended, that citizenship shall be lost upon conviction by court martial and dishonorable discharge for deserting the armed services in time of war, *held* invalid as imposing a cruel and unusual punishment barred by the Eighth Amendment and not authorized by the war powers conferred by Article I, section 8, clauses 11 to 14.

Trop v. Dulles, 356 U.S. 86 (March 31, 1958).

69. Act of November 15, 1943 (57 Stat. 450).

Urgent Deficiency Appropriation Act of 1943, section 304, providing that no salary should be paid to certain named federal employees out of moneys appropriated, *held* to violate Article I, section 9, clause 3, forbidding enactment of bill of attainder or *ex post facto* law.

United States v. Lovett, 328 U.S. 303 (June 3, 1946).

70. Act of May 5, 1950 (64 Stat. 107).

Article 3(a) of the Uniform Code of Military Justice subjecting civilian ex-serviceman to court martial for crime committed while in military service *held* to violate Article III, section 2 and the Fifth and Sixth Amendments.

Toth v. Quarles, 350 U.S. 11 (November 7, 1955).

71. Act of May 5, 1950 (64 Stat. 107).

Insofar as Article 2(11) of the Uniform Code of Military Justice subjects civilian dependents accompanying members of the armed forces overseas in time of peace to trial, in capital cases, by court martial, it is violative of Article III, section 2, and the Fifth and Sixth Amendments.

Reid v. Covert, 354 U.S. 1 (June 10, 1957).

Insofar as the aforementioned provision is invoked in time of peace for the trial of noncapital offenses committed on land bases overseas by employees of the armed forces who have not been inducted or who have not voluntarily enlisted therein, it is violative of the Sixth Amendment.

McElroy v. United States, 361 U.S. 281 (January 18, 1960).

Insofar as the aforementioned provision is invoked in time of peace for the trial of noncapital offenses committed by civilian dependents accompanying members of the armed forces overseas, it is violative of Article III, section 2, and the Fifth and Sixth Amendments.

Kinsella v. United States, 361 U.S. 234 (January 18, 1960).

Insofar as the aforementioned provision is invoked in time of peace for the trial of a capital offense committed by a civilian employee of the armed forces overseas, it is violative of Article III, section 2, and the Fifth and Sixth Amendments.

Grisham v. Hagan, 361 U.S. 278 (January 18, 1960).

72. Act of September 27, 1944 (58 Stat. 746, sec. 401 (J)); and Act of June 27, 1952 (66 Stat. 163, 267-268, sec. 349(a) (10)).

Section 401(J) of Immigration and Nationality Act of 1940, added in 1944, and section 349(a) (10) of the Immigration and Nationality Act of 1952 depriving one of citizenship, without the procedural safeguards guaranteed by the Fifth and Sixth Amendments, for the offense of leaving or remaining outside the country, in time of war or national emergency, to evade military service are invalid.

Kennedy v. Mendoza-Martinez, 372 U.S. 144 (February 18, 1963).

73. Act of June 27, 1952 (66 Stat. 163, 269, sec. 352(a) (1)).

Section 352(a) (1) of the Immigration and Nationality Act of 1952 depriving a naturalized person of citizenship for "having a continuous residence for three years" in state of his birth or prior nationality is violative of the due process clause of the Fifth Amendment.

Schneider v. Rusk, 377 U.S. 163 (May 18, 1964).

74. Act of September 23, 1950 (64 Stat. 993, sec. 6).

Subversive Activities Control Act of 1950, section 6, providing that any member of a Communist organization, which has registered or has been ordered to register, commits a crime if he attempts to obtain or use a passport, *held* violative of due process under the Fifth Amendment.

***Aptheker v. Secretary of State,* 378 U.S. 500 (June 22, 1964).**

75. Act of October 11, 1962 (76 Stat. 832, 840, sec. 305(a)).

Postal Service and Federal Employees Salary Act of 1962, section 305 (a), providing for detention by Postmaster General upon arrival of certain foreign mail matter containing Communist political propaganda and delivery thereof only after notification of addressee and receipt of his request therefor, *held* invalid as abridging freedom of speech and press contrary to Amendment I.

Lamont v. Postmaster General, 381 U.S. 301 (May 24, 1965).

76. Act of September 14, 1959 (73 Stat. 519, 536, sec. 504).

Labor-Management Reporting and Disclosure Act of 1959, sec. 504, which makes it a crime for a member of the Communist Party to serve as an officer or employee (other than in clerical or custodial post) of a labor union, *held* invalid as a bill of attainder proscribed by Article I, section 9, clause 3.

United States v. Brown, 381 U.S. 437 (June 7, 1965).

77. Act of September 23, 1950 (64 Stat. 987, 995, sec. 8 (a, c)).

Enforcement of Subversive Activities Control Act of 1950, sec. 8 (a, c) requiring members of a Communist-action organization, upon default of the latter to register pursuant to a final order of the Subversive Activities Control Board, to register with the Board as a member of such organization, *held* to subject said members to a denial of their Fifth Amendment privilege against self-incrimination.

Albertson v. Subversive Board, 382 U.S. 70 (November 15, 1965).

78. Act of September 2, 1958 (72 Stat. 1275, 1399, sec. 201).

Excise Technical Changes Act of 1958, sec. 201 (26 U.S.C. 5601 (b) (1) providing that presence of a defendant at the site of an illegal distilling apparatus shall be evidence of unlawful possession, custody or control thereof, *held* violative of due process under the Fifth Amendment for the reason that there is no rational connection between the fact proved and the fact presumed.

United States v. Romano, 382 U.S. 136 (November 22, 1965).

79. Act of June 27, 1952 (66 Stat. 267).

Section 349(a)(5) of the Immigration and Nationality Act of 1952 (8 U.S.C. 1481(a)(5)) providing that a United States citizen shall lose his citizenship by voting in a political election in a foreign state, held violative of the Citizenship Clause of Amendment 14 which protects "every citizen...against a congressional forcible destruction of his citizenship."

Afroyim v. Rusk, 387 U.S. 253 (May 29, 1967).

80. Act of September 23, 1950 (64 Stat. 987, 992, Sec. 5(a)(1)(D).

Section 5(a)(1)(D) of the Subversive Activities Control Act of 1950 (50 U.S.C. 784(a)(1)(D) which provided that when a Communist-action organization, such as the Communist Party, has been required to register under that Act, it shall be unlawful for any member of the organization to be employed in any defense facility designated as such by the Secretary of Defense effected an unconstitutional abridgment of the right of association protected by Amendment I; for it indiscriminately encompassed all types of associations with Communist-action groups without regard to the quality and degree of membership.

U.S. v. Robel, 389 U.S. 258 (December 11, 1967).

81. Act of August 16, 1954 (68A Stat. 725, 728, Secs. 5841, 5851). Sec. 3841 of the Internal Revenue Code of 1954 (26 U.S.C. 5841) providing that every one possessing a firearm (shotguns with barrels less than 18 inches long; rifles with barrels less than 16 inches long; weapons made from a rifle or shotgun with an overall length of less than 26 inches; machine guns' automatic firearms; mufflers and silencers; and other firearms other than pistols and revolvers, capable of being concealed on one's person) shall register the same with the Secretary of the Treasury; and Sec. 5851 of said Code (26 U.S.C. 5851) providing that it shall be unlawful for any person to possess any firearm which has not been registered as required by Sec. 5841, cannot constitutionally be enforced against one who, having acquired such firearm by impermissible means, invokes the privilege against self-incrimination of Amendment 5 as a defense to a prosecution founded upon either of said provisions.

Haynes v. U.S., 390 U.S. 85 (January 29, 1968). Note: Although Chief Justice Warren, who dissented, disagrees, the Court held that these provisons were not unconstitutional "on their face."

82. Act of August 16, 1954 (68A Stat. 525, 527, Secs. 4401, 4411, 4412).

Sec. 4401 of the Internal Revenue Code of 1954 (26 U.S.C. 4401) imposing an excise of 10 percent of the amount of the wager upon every person engaged in the business of accepting wagers; sec. 4411 of said Code (26 U.S.C. 4411) imposing an annual occupational fee upon said persons; and sec. 4412 (26 U.S.C. 4412) which requires every person paying the latter tax to register his name and place of residence with the director of the internal revenue district in which such person conducts his business cannot constitutionally be enforced against noncompliants who invoke the privilege against self-incrimination guaranteed by Amendment 5 on the ground that federal disclosure of their compliance with these provisions would expose them to prosecutions for violating federal and state anti-gambling laws.

Marchetti v. U.S., 390 U.S. 39, and *Grosso v. U.S.,* 390 U.S. 62, both January 29, 1968.

Note: Although Chief Justice Warren, who dissented, disagreed, the Court maintained that the aforesaid provisions were not constitutionally impermissible on their face nor unenforceable against taxpayers ineligible to invoke the privilege.

83. Act of June 25, 1948 (62 Stat. 683, 760. Sec. 1201(a)). That part of the Federal Kidnaping Act. 18 U.S.C. 1201(a) which provides that in an interstate kidnaping case, where the victim has not been liberated unharmed, the defendant, if found guilty, shall be punished by death, if the verdict of the jury so recommends, is unconstitutional for the reason that "it makes 'the risk of death' the price for asserting the right to a jury trial, and thereby impairs...free exercise" of that constitutional right (Amendment 6).

U.S. v. Jackson, 390 U.S. 570 (April 8, 1968)

84. Act of October 15, 1962 (76 Stat. 914).

Provision of District of Columbia laws requiring that a person to be eligible to receive welfare assistance must have resided in the District for at least one year impermissibly classified persons on the basis of an assertion of the right to interstate travel and therefore *held* to violate the due process clause of the Fifth Amendment.

Shapiro v. Thompson, 394 U.S. 618 (April 21, 1969).

85. Marijuana Tax Act (26 U.S.C. 4744(a)(2) and Narcotic Drugs Import and Export Act (70 Stat. 570; 21 U.S.C. 176a). The Marijuana Tax Act provides that those who deal in marijuana must register with the Internal Revenue Service and pay a transfer tax upon all transfers of marijuana. The Narcotic Drugs Import and Export Act makes it a crime to transport marijuana with knowledge of its illegal importation and creates a presumption of such knowledge from the mere possession of marijuana. *Held,* the Marijuana Tax Act violates the Fifth Amendment in that it requires self-incrimination, and the Drug Import and Export Act in Sec. 176a violates the Due Process Clause of the Fifth Amendment because the presumption of knowledge is irrational and arbitrary when it arises from mere possession.

Leary v. U.S. 395 U.S. 6 (May 19, 1969).

86. Act of August 10, 1956 (70A Stat. 65. Uniform Code of Military Justice, Articles 80, 130, 134).

Servicemen may not be charged under the Act and tried in military courts because of the commission of non-service connected crimes committed off-post and off-duty which are subject to civilian court jurisdiction where the guarantees of the Bill of Rights are applicable.

O'Callahan v. Parker, 395 U.S. 258 (June 2, 1969).

87. Act of August 10, 1956 (70A Stat. 35; 10 U.S.C. 772 f).

Section of the law permitting the wearing of a military uniform by a civilian "in a theatrical or motion-picture production...if the portrayal does not tend to discredit that armed force" *held* to violate First Amendment right of free speech of one who protests military policies while garbed in military uniform during performance of skit against war. The Court struck out from the statue as unconstitutional the phrase "if the portrayal does not tend to discredit that armed force."

Schact v. United States, 398 U.S. 58 (May 25, 1970).

88. Act of February 9, 1909 (2.35 Stat. 614, as amended).

Provision of Narcotic Drugs Import and Export Act creating a presumption that possessor of cocaine knew of its illegal importation into the United States *held,* in light of the fact that more cocaine is produced domestically than is brought into the country and in absence of any showing that defendant could have known his cocaine was imported, if it was, inapplicable to support conviction from mere possession of cocaine.

Turner v. United States, 396 U.S. 398 (June 8, 1970)

89. Act of June 22, 1970 (ch. III. 84 Stat. 318).

Provision of Voting Rights Act Amendments of 1970 which set a minimum voting age qualification of 18 in state and local elections *held* to be unconstitutional because beyond the powers of Congress to legislate.

Oregon v. Mitchell 400 U.S. 112 (December 21, 1970).

90. Act of August 16, 1950 (64 Stat. 451, as amended).

Statutory scheme authorizing the Postmaster General to close the mails to distributors of obscene materials *held* unconstitutional in the absence of procedural provisions which would assure prompt judicial determination that protected materials were not being restrained.

Blount v. Rizzi, 400 U.S. 410 (January 14, 1971).

91. Act of August 16, 1954 (68A Stat. 867. Int. Rev. Code of 1954. Sec. 7302).

Provision of tax laws providing for forfeiture of property used in violating internal revenue laws may not be constitutionally used in face of invocation of privilege against self-incrimination to condemn money in possession of gambler who had failed to comply with the registration and reporting scheme held void in *Marchetti v. United States,* 390 U.S. 39 (1968).

United States v. United States Coin & Currency, 401 U.S. 715 (April 5, 1971).

92. Act of December 16, 1973 (77 Stat. 378. 20 U.S.C. Sec. 754).

Provision of Higher Education Facilities Act of 1963 which in effect removed restriction against religious use of facilities constructed with federal funds after 20 years *held* to violate the establishment clause of the First Amendment inasmuch as the property will still be of considerable value at the end of the period and removal of the restriction would constitute a substantial governmental contribution to religion.

Tilton v. Richardson, 403 U.S. 672 (June 28, 1971).

93. Act of July 31, 1946 (60 Stat. 719, sec. 7).

District Court decision voiding enjoining enforcement of statute forbidding parades and assemblages on grounds of United States Capitol as an infringement of the free speech clause of the First Amendment and the due process clause of the Fifth Amendment is summarily affirmed.

Chief of the Capitol Police v. Jeanette Rankin Brigade, 409 U.S. 972 (November 6, 1972).

94. Act of July 30, 1965 (79 Stat. 363, sec. 308(d) (6), 339 (a), amending Social Security Act).

Insofar as these provisions discriminate against illegitimate children in payment of benefits on death of wage earning parent by reducing benefits to them to the extent the amount available is not adequate to meet maximum payments to wife and legitimate children of father, district court decisions holding the provisions unconstitutional and enjoining the discrimination are affirmed.

Richardson v. Davis, 409 U.S. 1069 (December 18, 1972).

Richardson v. Griffin, 409 U.S. 1069 (December 18, 1972)

95. Act of September 2, 1958 (72 Stat. 14446, 10 U.S.C. sec. 1072), and Act of September 7, 1962 (76 Stat. 469, 37 U.S.C. sec. 401).

Insofar as these statutes discriminate between male and female members of the armed forces in the provision of quarters allowances and medical and dental benefits to dependents, they are invalid as a denial of due process under the Fifth Amendment.

Frontiero v. Richardson, 411 U.S. 676 (May 14, 1973).

96. Act of January 11, 1971, (sec. 3(e), 84 Stat. 2048, amending Food Stamp Act of 1964).

Provision excluding from participation in food stamp program any household containing an individual who is unrelated to any other household member creates an irrational classification clearly irrelevant to the stated purposes of the Act and is void under the due process clause of the Fifth Amendment.

U.S. Department of Agriculture v. Moreno, 413 U.S.—(June 25, 1973).

97. Act of January 11, 1971 (sec. 5(b), 84 Stat. 2048, amending Food Stamp Act of 1964).

Provision making ineligible for participation in food stamp program any household which includes a member who has reached his 18th birthday and who is claimed as a dependent child for federal income tax purposes by a taxpayer who is not a member of the household creates an invalid presumption and denies any such household the opportunity to rebut the presumption, thereby violating the due process clause of the Fifth Amendment.

U.S. Department of Agriculture v. Murry, 413 U.S.—(June 25, 1973).

The following six statutes were not held unconstitutional in their entirety and were not therefore inoperative. Their application to specific factual situations was held to be prohibited by the Constitution, but the provisions otherwise continued to be enforceable.

(a) Act of July 13, 1866 (14 Stat. 138), amending Act of June 30, 1864 (13 Stat. 284, sec. 122).

Tax on dividends and interest payable on indebtedness of railroads and other corporations, deducted from payments made by such corporations and surrendered to the Government, was *held* to be inapplicable to a municipal corporation owning such certificates of indebtedness or bonds by reason of the Tenth Amendment.

United States v. Railroad Company, 17 Wall. 322 (April 8, 1873).

(b) Act of March 2, 1867 (14 Stat. 477, sec. 13), amending Act of June 30, 1864 (13 Stat. 281, sec. 116).

Tax on income of "...every person residing in the United States... whether derived from...salaries...or from any source whatever...," as applied to the income of state judges, was *held* to interfere with the reserved powers of the States (Amendment 10).

The Collector v. Day, 11 Wall. 113 (April 3, 1871).

(c) Act of June 13, 1898 (30 Stat. 451, 461).

Tax on policies of marine insurance against perils of the sea was *held* inapplicable to insurance on a voyage to foreign ports; for, thus applied, the tax would be one on exports in violation of Article I, section 9.

Thames & Mersey Ins. Co. v. United States, 237 U.S. 19 (April 5, 1915).

(d) Act of October 3, 1917 (40 Stat. 302, secs. 4, 201, 1206) amending 39 Stat. 765, sec. 10; and Act of February 24, 1919 (40 Stat. 1075, secs. 230, 301).

Income and excess profits taxes on income of "every corporation," applied to income of an oil corporation from leases of land granted by the United States to a State, for the support of common schools, etc., was *held* to interfere with a State governmental function (Amendment 10).

Burnet v. Coronado Oil & Gas Co., 285 U.S. 393 (April 11, 1932).

(e) Act of October 3, 1917 (40 Stat. 316, sec. 600(f).

The tax "upon all tennis balls, rackets, golf clubs, baseball bats... balls of all kinds, including baseballs,...sold by the manufacturer, producer or importer...," when imposed on articles sold by a manufacturer to a commission merchant for exportation, was *held* to amount to a tax on exports prohibited by Article I, section 9.

Spalding & Bros. v. Edwards, 262 U.S. 66 (April 23, 1923).

(f) Revenue Act of June 2, 1924 (43 Stat. 322, sec. 600).

Excise tax on certain articles "sold or leased by the manufacturer" and measured by the sales price (specifically, "(z)...Motorcycles...5 per centum"), when sought to be collected on sales of motorcycles to a municipality for police uses, was *held* to infringe State immunity under the principle of *Collector v. Day*.

Indian Motorcycle Co. v. U.S., 283 U.S. 570 (May 25, 1931).

CONSTITUTION OF THE UNITED STATES

We the People of the United States, in Order to form a more perfect Union, establish Justice, insure domestic Tranquility, provide for the common defence, promote the general Welfare, and secure the Blessings of Liberty to ourselves and our Posterity, do ordain and establish this Constitution for the United States of America.

Article I

Section 1. All legislative Powers herein granted shall be vested in a Congress of the United States, which shall consist of a Senate and House of Representatives.

Section 2. The House of Representatives shall be composed of Members chosen every second Year by the People of the several States, and the Electors in each State shall have the Qualifications requisite for Electors of the most numerous Branch of the State Legislature.

No Person shall be a Representative who shall not have attained to the age of twenty five Years, and been seven Years a Citizen of the United States, and who shall not, when elected, be an Inhabitant of that State in which he shall be chosen.

Representatives and direct Taxes shall be apportioned among the several States which may be included within this Union, according to their respective Numbers, which shall be determined by adding to the whole Number of free Persons, including those bound to Service for a Term of Years, and excluding Indians not taxed, three fifths of all other Persons. The actual Enumeration shall be made within three Years after the first Meeting of the Congress of the United States, and within every subsequent Term of ten Years, in such Manner as they shall by Law direct. The Number of Representatives shall not exceed one for every thirty Thousand, but each State shall have at Least one Representative; and until such enumeration shall be made, the State of New Hampshire shall be entitled to chuse three, Massachusetts eight, Rhode-Island and Providence Plantations one, Connecticut five, New-York six, New Jersey four, Pennsylvania eight, Delaware one, Maryland six, Virginia ten, North Carolina five, South Carolina five, and Georgia three.

When vacancies happen in the Representation from any State, the Executive Authority thereof shall issue Writs of Election to fill such Vacancies.

The House of Representatives shall chuse their Speaker and other Officers; and shall have the sole Power of Impeachment.

Section. 3. The Senate of the United States shall be composed of two Senators from each State, chosen by the Legislature thereof, for six Years; and each Senator shall have one Vote.

Immediately after they shall be assembled in Consequence of the first Election, they shall be divided as equally as may be into three Classes. The Seats of the Senators of the first Class shall be vacated at the Expiration of the second Year, of the second Class at the Expiration of the fourth Year, and of the third Class at the Expiration of the sixth Year, so that one third may be chosen every second Year; and if Vacancies happen by Resignation, or otherwise, during the Recess of the Legislature of any State, the Executive thereof may make temporary Appointments until the next Meeting of the Legislature, which shall then fill such Vacancies.

No Person shall be a Senator who shall not have attained to the Age of thirty Years, and been nine Years a Citizen of the United States, and who shall not, when elected, be an Inhabitant of that State for which he shall be chosen.

The Vice President of the United States shall be President of the Senate, but shall have no Vote, unless they be equally divided.

The Senate shall chuse their other Officers, and also a President pro tempore, in the Absence of the Vice President, or when he shall exercise the Office of President of the United States.

The Senate shall have the sole Power to try all Impeachments. When sitting for that Purpose, they shall be on Oath or Affirmation. When the President of the United States is tried the Chief Justice shall preside: And no Person shall be convicted without the Concurrence of two thirds of the Members present.

Judgment in Cases of Impeachment shall not extend further than to removal from Office, and disqualification to hold and enjoy any Office of honor, Trust or Profit under the United States: but the Party convicted shall nevertheless be liable and subject to Indictment, Trial, Judgment and Punishment, according to Law.

Section. 4. The Times, Places and Manner of holding Elections for Senators and Representatives, shall be prescribed in each State by the Legislature thereof; but the Congress may at any time by Law make or alter such Regulations, except as to the Places of chusing Senators.

The Congress shall assemble at least once in every Year, and such Meeting shall be on the first Monday in December, unless they shall by Law appoint a different Day.

Section. 5. Each House shall be the Judge of the Elections, Returns and Qualifications of its own Members, and a Majority of each shall constitute a Quorum to do Business; but a smaller Number may adjourn from day to day, and may be authorized to compel the Attendance of absent Members in such Manner, and under such Penalties as each House may provide.

Each House may determine the Rules of its Proceedings, punish its Members for disorderly Behaviour, and, with the Concurrence of two thirds, expel a Member.

Each House shall keep a Journal of its Proceedings, and from time to time publish the same, excepting such Parts as may in their Judgment require Secrecy; and the Yeas and Nays of the Members of either House on any question shall, at the Desire of one fifth of those Present, be entered on the Journal.

Neither House, during the Session of Congress, shall, without the Consent of the other, adjourn for more than three days, nor to any other Place than that in which the two Houses shall be sitting.

Section. 6. The Senators and Representatives shall receive a Compensation for their Services, to be ascertained by Law, and paid out of the Treasury of the United States. They shall in all Cases, except Treason, Felony and Breach of the Peace, be privileged from Arrest during their Attendance at the Session of their respective Houses, and in going to and returning from the same; and for any Speech or Debate in either House, they shall not be questioned in any other Place.

No Senator or Representative shall, during the Time for which he was elected, be appointed to any civil Office under the Authority of the United States, which shall have been created, or the Emoluments whereof shall have been encreased during such time; and no Person holding any Office under the United States, shall be a Member of either House during his Continuance in Office.

Section. 7. All Bills for raising Revenue shall originate in the House of Representatives; but the Senate may propose or concur with amendments as on other Bills.

Every Bill which shall have passed the House of Representatives and the Senate, shall, before it become a Law, be presented to the President of the United States; If he approve he shall sign it, but if not he shall return it, with his Objections to that House in which it shall have originated, who shall enter the Objections at large on their Journal, and proceed to reconsider it. If after such Reconsideration two thirds of that House shall agree to pass the Bill, it shall be sent, together with the Objections, to the other House, by which it shall likewise be reconsidered, and if approved by two thirds of that House, it shall become a Law. But in all such Cases the Votes of both

Houses shall be determined by yeas and Nays, and the Names of the Persons voting for and against the Bill shall be entered on the Journal of each House respectively. If any Bill shall not be returned by the President within ten Days (Sunday excepted) after it shall have been presented to him, the Same shall be a Law, in like Manner as if he had signed it, unless the Congress by their Adjournment prevent its Return, in which Case it shall not be a Law.

Every Order, Resolution, or Vote to which the Concurrence of the Senate and House of Representatives may be necessary (except on a question of Adjournment) shall be presented to the President of the United States; and before the Same shall take Effect, shall be approved by him, or being disapproved by him, shall be repassed by two thirds of the Senate and House of Representatives, according to the Rules and Limitations prescribed in the Case of a Bill.

Section. 8. The Congress shall have Power To lay and collect Taxes, Duties, Imposts and Excises, to pay the Debts and provide for the common Defence and general Welfare of the United States; but all Duties, Imposts and Excises shall be uniform throughout the United States;

To borrow Money on the credit of the United States;

To regulate Commerce with foreign Nations, and among the several States, and with the Indian Tribes;

To establish an uniform Rule of Naturalization, and uniform Laws on the subject of Bankruptcies throughout the United States;

To coin Money, regulate the Value thereof, and of foreign Coin, and fix the Standard of Weights and Measures;

To provide for the Punishment of counterfeiting the Securities and current Coin of the United States;

To establish Post Offices and post Roads;

To promote the Progress of Science and useful Arts, by securing for limited Times to Authors and Inventors the exclusive Right to their respective Writings and Discoveries;

To constitute Tribunals inferior to the supreme Court;

To define and punish Piracies and Felonies committed on the high Seas, and Offences against the Law of Nations;

To declare War, grant Letters of Marque and Reprisal, and make Rules concerning Captures on Land and Water;

To raise and support Armies, but no Appropriation of Money to that Use shall be for a longer Term than two Years;

To provide and maintain a Navy;

To make Rules for the Government and Regulation of the land and naval Forces;

To provide for calling forth the Militia to execute the Laws of the Union, suppress Insurrections and repel Invasions;

To provide for organizing, arming, and disciplining, the Militia, and for governing such Part of them as may be employed in the Service of the United States, reserving to the states respectively, the Appointment of the Officers and the Authority of training the Militia according to the discipline prescribed by Congress;

To exercise exclusive Legislation in all Cases whatsoever, over such District (not exceeding ten Miles square) as may, by Cession of Particular States, and the Acceptance of Congress, become the Seat of the Government of the United States, and to exercise like Authority over all Places purchased by the Consent of the Legislature of the State in which the Same shall be, for the Erection of Forts, Magazines, Arsenals, dock-Yards, and other needful Buildings;—And

To make all Laws which shall be necessary and proper for carrying into Execution the foregoing Powers, and all other Powers vested by this Constitution in the Government of the United States, or in any Department or Officer thereof.

Section. 9. The Migration or Importation of such Persons as any of the States now existing shall think proper to admit, shall not be prohibited by the Congress prior to the Year one thousand eight hundred and eight, but a Tax or duty may be imposed on such Importation, not exceeding ten dollars for each Person.

The Privilege of the Writ of Habeas Corpus shall not be suspended, unless when in Cases of Rebellion or Invasion the public Safety may require it.

No Bill of Attainder or ex post facto Law shall be passed.

No Capitation, or other direct, Tax shall be laid, unless in Proportion to the Census of Enumeration herein before directed to be taken.

No Tax or Duty shall be laid on Articles exported from any State.

No Preference shall be given by any Regulation of Commerce or Revenue to the Ports of one State over those of another; nor shall Vessels bound to, or from, one State, be obliged to enter, clear or pay Duties in another.

No Money shall be drawn from the Treasury, but in Consequence of Appropriations made by Law; and a regular Statement and Account of the Receipts and Expenditures of all public Money shall be published from time to time.

No Title of Nobility shall be granted by the United States: And no Person holding any Office of Profit or Trust under them, shall, without the Consent of the Congress, accept of any present, Emolument, Office, or Title, of any kind whatever, from any King, Prince or foreign State.

Section. 10. No State shall enter into any Treaty, Alliance, or Confederation; grant Letters of Marque and Reprisal; coin Money; emit Bills of Credit; make any Thing but gold and silver Coin a Tender in Payment of Debts; pass any Bill of Attainder, ex post facto Law, or Law impairing the Obligation of Contracts, or grant any Title of Nobility.

No State shall, without the Consent of the Congress, lay any Imposts or Duties on Imports or Exports, except what may be absolutely necessary for executing it's inspection Laws: and the net Produce of all Duties and Imposts, laid by any State on Imports or Exports, shall be for the Use of the Treasury of the United States; and all such Laws shall be subject to the Revision and Controul of the Congress.

No State shall, without the Consent of Congress, lay any Duty of Tonnage, keep Troops, or Ships of War in time of Peace, enter into any Agreement or Compact with another State, or with a foreign Power, or engage in War, unless actually invaded, or in such imminent Danger as will not admit of delay.

Article II

Section. 1. The executive Power shall be vested in a President of the United States of America. He shall hold his Office during the Term of four Years, and, together with the Vice President, chosen for the same Term, be elected, as follows

Each State shall appoint, in such Manner as the Legislature thereof may direct, a Number of Electors, equal to the whole Number of Senators and Representatives to which the State may be entitled in the Congress: but no Senator or Representative, or Person holding an Office of Trust or Profit under the United States, shall be appointed an Elector.

The Electors shall meet in their respective States, and vote by Ballot for two Persons, of whom one at least shall not be an Inhabitant of the same State with themselves. And they shall make a List of all the Persons voted for, and of the Number of Votes for each; which List they shall sign and certify, and transmit sealed to the Seat of the Government of the United States, directed to the President of the Senate. The President of the Senate shall, in the Presence of the Senate and House of Representatives, open all the Certificates, and the Votes shall then be counted. The Person having the greatest Number of Votes shall be the President, if such Number be a Majority of the whole Number of Electors appointed; and if there be more than one who have such Majority, and have an equal Number of Votes, then the House of Representatives shall immediately chuse by Ballot one of them for President; and if no Person have a Majority, then from the five highest on the List the said House shall in like Manner chuse the President. But in chusing the President, the Votes shall be taken by States, the Representation from each State having one Vote; a quorum for this Purpose shall consist of a Member or Members from two thirds of the States, and a Majority of all the States shall be necessary to a Choice. In every Case, after the Choice of the President, the Person having the greatest Number of Votes of the Electors shall be the Vice President. But if there should remain two or more who have equal Votes, the Senate shall chuse from them by Ballot the Vice President.

The Congress may determine the Time of chusing the Electors, and the Day on which they shall give their Votes; which Day shall be the same throughout the United States.

No Person except a natural born Citizen, or a Citizen of the United States, at the time of the Adoption of this Constitution, shall be eligible to the Office of President; neither shall any person be eligible to that Office who shall not have attained to the Age of thirty five Years, and been fourteen Years a Resident within the United States.

In Case of the Removal of the President from Office, or of his Death, Resignation, or Inability to discharge the Powers and Duties of the said Office, the Same shall devolve on the Vice President, and the Congress may by Law provide for the Case of Removal, Death, Resignation or Inability, both of the President and Vice President, declaring what Officer shall then act as President, and such Officer shall act accordingly, until the Disability be removed, or a President shall be elected.

The President shall, at stated Times, receive for his Services, a Compensation, which shall neither be encreased nor diminished during the Period for which he shall have been elected, and he shall not receive within that Period any other Emolument from the United States, or any of them.

Before he enter on the Execution of his Office, he shall take the following Oath or Affirmation:—"I do solemnly swear (or affirm) that I will faithfully execute the Office of President of the United States, and will to the best of my Ability, preserve protect and defend the Constitution of the United States."

Section. 2. The President shall be Commander in Chief of the Army and Navy of the United States, and of the Militia of the several States, when called into the actual Service of the United States; he may require the Opinion, in writing, of the principal Officer in each of the executive Departments, upon any Subject relating to the Duties of their respective Offices, and he shall have Power to grant Reprieves and Pardons for Offenses against the United States, except in Cases of Impeachment.

He shall have Power, by and with the Advice and Consent of the Senate, to make Treaties, provided two thirds of the Senators present concur; and he shall nominate, and by and with the Advice and Consent of the Senate, shall appoint Ambassadors, other public Ministers and Consuls, Judges of the supreme Court, and all other Officers of the United States, whose Appointments are not herein otherwise provided for, and which shall be established by Law: but the Congress may by Law vest the Appointment of such inferior Officers, as they think proper, in the President alone, in the Courts of Law, or in the Heads of Departments.

The President shall have Power to fill up all Vacancies that may happen during the Recess of the Senate, by granting Commissions which shall expire at the End of their next Session.

Section. 3. He shall from time to time give to the Congress Information of the State of the Union, and recommend to their Consideration such Measures as he shall judge necessary and expedient; he may, on extraordinary Occasions, convene both Houses, or either of them, and in Case of Disagreement between them, with Respect to the Time of Adjournment, he may adjourn them to such Time as he shall think proper; he shall receive Ambassadors and other public Ministers; he shall take Care that the Laws be faithfully executed, and shall Commission all the Officers of the United States.

Section. 4. The President, Vice President and all Civil Officers of the United States, shall be removed from Office on Impeachment for, and Conviction of, Treason, Bribery, or other high Crimes and Misdemeanors.

Article III

Section. 1. The judicial Power of the United States, shall be vested in one supreme Court, and in such inferior Courts as the Congress may from time to time ordain and establish. The Judges, both of the supreme and inferior Courts, shall hold their Offices during good Behaviour, and shall, at stated Times, receive for their Services, a Compensation, which shall not be diminished during their Continuance in Office.

Section. 2. The judicial Power shall extend to all Cases, in Law and Equity, arising under this Constitution, the Laws of the United States, and Treaties made, or which shall be made, under their Authority;—to all Cases affecting Ambassadors, other public Ministers and Consuls;—to all Cases of admiralty and maritime Jurisdiction;—to Controversies to which the United States shall be a Party;—to Controversies between two or more States;—between a State and Citizens of another State;—between Citizens of different States;—between Citizens of the same State claiming Lands under Grants of different States, and between a State, or the Citizens thereof, and foreign States, Citizens or Subjects.

In all Cases affecting Ambassadors, other public Ministers and Consuls, and those in which a State shall be Party, the supreme Court shall have original jurisdiction. In all the other Cases before mentioned, the supreme Court shall have appellate Jurisdiction, both as to Law and Fact, with such Exceptions, and under such Regulations as the Congress shall make.

The Trial of all Crimes, except in cases of Impeachment, shall be by Jury; and such Trial shall be held in the State where the said Crimes shall have been committed; but when not committed within any State, the Trial shall be at such Place or Places as the Congress may by Law have directed.

Section. 3. Treason against the United States, shall consist only in levying War against them, or in adhering to their Enemies, giving them Aid and Comfort. No Person shall be convicted of Treason unless on the Testimony of two Witnesses to the same overt Act, or on Confession in open Court.

The Congress shall have Power to declare the Punishment of Treason, but no Attainder of Treason shall work Corruption of Blood, or Forfeiture except during the Life of the Person attainted.

Article IV

Section. 1. Full Faith and Credit shall be given in each State to the public Acts, Records, and judicial Proceedings of every other State. And the Congress may by general Laws prescribe the Manner in which such Acts, Records and Proceedings shall be proved, and the Effect thereof.

Section. 2. The Citizens of each State shall be entitled to all Privileges and Immunities of Citizens in the several States.

A Person charged in any State with Treason, Felony, or other Crime, who shall flee from Justice, and be found in another State, shall on Demand of the executive Authority of the State from which he fled, be delivered up, to be removed to the State having Jurisdiction of the Crime.

No Person held to Service or Labour in one State, under the Laws thereof, escaping into another, shall, in Consequence of any Law or Regulation therein, be discharged from such Service or Labour, but shall be delivered up on Claim of the Party to whom such Service or Labour may be due.

Section. 3. New States may be admitted by the Congress into this Union; but no new State shall be formed or erected within the Jurisdiction of any other State; nor any State be formed by the Junction of two or more States, or Parts of States, without the Consent of the Legislatures of the States concerned as well as of the Congress.

The Congress shall have Power to dispose of and make all needful Rules and Regulations respecting the Territory or other Property belonging to the United States; and nothing in this

Constitution shall be so construed as to Prejudice any Claims of the United States, or of any particular State.

Section. 4. The United States shall guarantee to every State in this Union a Republican Form of Government, and shall protect each of them against Invasion; and on Application of the Legislature, or of the Executive (when the Legislature cannot be convened) against domestic Violence.

Article V

The Congress, whenever two thirds of both Houses shall deem it necessary, shall propose Amendments to this Constitution, or, on the Application of the Legislatures of two thirds of the several States, shall call a Convention for proposing Amendments, which, in either Case, shall be valid to all Intents and Purposes, as Part of this Constitution, when ratified by the Legislatures of three fourths of the several States, or by Conventions in three fourths thereof, as the one or the other Mode of Ratification may be proposed by the Congress; Provided that no Amendment which may be made prior to the Year One thousand eight hundred and eight shall in any Manner affect the first and fourth Clauses in the Ninth Section of the First Article; and that no State, without its Consent, shall be deprived of its equal Suffrage in the Senate.

Article VI

All Debts contracted and Engagements entered into, before the Adoption of this Constitution, shall be as valid against the United States under this Constitution, as under the Confederation.

This Constitution, and the Laws of the United States which shall be made in Pursuance thereof; and all Treaties made or which shall be made, under the Authority of the United States, shall be the supreme Law of the Land; and the Judges in every State shall be bound thereby, any Thing in the Constitution or Laws of any State to the Contrary notwithstanding.

The Senators and Representatives before mentioned, and the Members of the several State Legislatures, and all executive and judicial Officers, both of the United States and of the several States, shall be bound by Oath or Affirmation, to support this Constitution; but no religious Test shall ever be required as a Qualification to any Office or public Trust under the United States.

Article VII

The Ratification of the Conventions of nine States, shall be sufficient for the Establishment of this Constitution between the States so ratifying the Same. Done in Convention by the Unanimous Consent of the States present the Seventeenth Day of September in the Year of our Lord one thousand seven hundred and Eighty seven and of the Independence of the United States of America the Twelfth In witness whereof We have hereunto subscribed our Names.

AMENDMENTS

Amendment I
(First ten amendments ratified Dec. 15, 1791.)

Congress shall make no law respecting an establishment of religion, or prohibiting the free exercise thereof; or abridging the freedom of speech, or of the press; or the right of the people peaceably to assemble, and to petition the Government for a redress of grievances.

Amendment II

A well regulated Militia, being necessary to the security of a free State, the right of the people to keep and bear Arms, shall not be infringed.

Amendment III

No Soldier shall, in time of peace be quartered in any house, without the consent of the Owner, nor in time of war, but in a manner to be prescribed by law.

Amendment IV

The right of the people to be secure in their persons, houses, papers, and effects, against unreasonable searches and seizures, shall not be violated, and no Warrants shall issue, but upon probable cause, supported by Oath or affirmation, and particularly describing the place to be searched, and the persons or things to be seized.

Amendment V

No person shall be held to answer for a capital, or otherwise infamous crime, unless on a presentment or indictment of a Grand Jury, except in cases arising in the land or naval forces, or in the Militia, when in actual service in time of War or public danger; nor shall any person be subject for the same offence to be twice put in jeopardy of life or limb; nor shall be compelled in any criminal case to be a witness against himself, nor be deprived of life, liberty, or property, without due process of law; nor shall private property be taken for public use, without just compensation.

Amendment VI

In all criminal prosecutions, the accused shall enjoy the right to a speedy and public trial, by an impartial jury of the State and district wherein the crime shall have been committed, which district shall have been previously ascertained by law, and to be informed of the nature and cause of the accusation; to be confronted with the witnesses against him; to have compulsory process for obtaining witnesses in his favor, and to have the Assistance of Counsel for his defence.

Amendment VII

In Suits at common law, where the value in controversy shall exceed twenty dollars, the right of trial by jury shall be preserved, and no fact tried by a jury, shall be otherwise reexamined in any Court of the United States, than according to the rules of the common law.

Amendment VIII

Excessive bail should not be required, nor excessive fines imposed, nor cruel and unusual punishments inflicted.

Amendment IX

The enumeration in the Constitution, of certain rights, shall not be construed to deny or disparage others retained by the people.

Amendment X

The powers not delegated to the United States by the Constitution, nor prohibited by it to the States, are reserved to the States respectively, or to the people.

Amendment XI *(Ratified Jan. 8, 1798)*

The Judicial power of the United States shall not be construed to extend to any suit in law or equity, commenced or prosecuted against one of the United States by Citizens of another State, or by Citizens or Subjects of any Foreign State.

Amendment XII *(Ratified Sept. 25, 1804)*

The Electors shall meet in their respective states and vote by ballot for President and Vice-President, one of whom, at least, shall not be an inhabitant of the same state with themselves; they shall name in their ballots the person voted for as President, and in distinct ballots the person voted for as Vice-President, and they shall make distinct lists of all persons voted for as President, and of all persons voted for as Vice-President, and of the number of votes for each, which lists they shall sign and certify, and transmit sealed to the seat of the government of the United States, directed to the President of the Senate;—The President of the Senate shall, in the presence of the Senate and House of Representatives open all the certificates and the votes shall then be counted;—The person having the greatest number of votes for President, shall be the President, if such number be a majority of the whole number of Electors appointed; and if no person have such majority, then from the persons having the highest numbers not exceeding three on the list of those voted for as President, the House of Representatives shall choose immediately, by ballot, the President. But in choosing the President, the votes shall be taken by states, the representation from each state having one vote; a quorum for this purpose shall consist of a member or members from two-thirds of the states, and a majority of all the states shall be necessary to a choice. And if the House of Representatives shall not choose a President whenever the right of choice shall devolve upon them, before the fourth day of March next following, then the Vice-President shall act as President, as in the case of the death or other constitutional disability of the President—The person having the greatest number of votes as Vice-President, shall be the Vice-President, if such number be a majority of the whole number of electors appointed, and if no person have a majority, then from the two highest numbers on the list, the Senate shall choose the Vice-President; a quorum for the purpose shall consist of two-thirds of the whole number of Senators, and a majority of the whole number shall be necessary to a choice. But no person constitutionally ineligible to the office of President shall be eligible to that of Vice-President of the United States.

Amendment XIII *(Ratified Dec. 18, 1865)*

Section 1. Neither slavery nor involuntary servitude, except as a punishment for crime whereof the party shall have been duly convicted, shall exist within the United States, or any place subject to their jurisdiction.

Section 2. Congress shall have power to enforce this article by appropriate legislation.

Amendment XIV *(Ratified July 28, 1868)*

Section 1. All persons born or naturalized in the United States and subject to the jurisdiction thereof, are citizens of the United States and of the States wherein they reside. No State shall make or enforce any law which shall abridge the privileges or immunities of citizens of the United States; nor shall any State deprive any person of life, liberty, or property, without due process of law; nor deny to any person within its jurisdiction the equal protection of the laws.

Section 2. Representatives shall be apportioned among the several States according to their respective numbers, counting the whole number of persons in each State, excluding Indians not taxed. But when the right to vote at any election for the choice of electors for President and Vice President of the United States, Representatives in Congress, the Executive and Judicial officers of a State, or the members of the Legislature thereof, is denied to any of the male inhabitants of such State, being twenty-one years of age, and citizens of the United States, or in any way abridged, except for participation in rebellion, or other crime, the basis of representation therein shall be reduced in the proportion which the number of such male citizens shall bear to the whole number of male citizens twenty-one years of age in such State.

Section 3. No person shall be a Senator or Representative in Congress, or elector of President and Vice President, or hold any office, civil or military, under the United States, or under any State, who, having previously taken an oath, as a member of Congress, or as an officer of the United States, or as a member of any State legislature, or as an executive or judicial officer of any

State, to support the Constitution of the United States, shall have engaged in insurrection or rebellion against the same, or given aid or comfort to the enemies thereof. But Congress may by a vote of two-thirds of each House, remove such disability.

Section 4. The validity of the public debt of the United States, authorized by law, including debts incurred for payment of pensions and bounties for services in suppressing insurrection or rebellion, shall not be questioned. But neither the United States nor any State shall assume or pay any debt or obligation incurred in aid of insurrection or rebellion against the United States, or any claim for the loss or emancipation of any slave; but all such debts, obligations and claims shall be held illegal and void.

Section 5. The Congress shall have power to enforce, by appropriate legislation, the provisions of this article.

Amendment XV *(Ratified March 30, 1870)*

Section 1. The right of citizens of the United States to vote shall not be denied or abridged by the United States or by any State on account of race, color, or previous condition of servitude.

Section 2. The Congress shall have power to enforce this article by appropriate legislation.

Amendment XVI   *(Ratified Feb. 25, 1913)*

The Congress shall have power to lay and collect taxes on incomes, from whatever source derived, without apportionment among the several States, and without regard to any census or enumeration.

Amendment XVII   *(Ratified May 31, 1913)*

The Senate of the United States shall be composed of two Senators from each State, elected by the people thereof, for six years; and each Senator shall have one vote. The electors in each State shall have the qualifications requisite for electors of the most numerous branch of the State legislatures.

When vacancies happen in the representation of any State in the Senate, the executive authority of such State shall issue writs of election to fill such vacancies: *Provided,* That the legislature of any State may empower the executive thereof to make temporary appointments until the people fill the vacancies by election as the legislature may direct.

This amendment shall not be so construed as to affect the election or term of any Senator chosen before it becomes valid as part of the Constitution.

Amendment XVIII   *(Ratified Jan. 29, 1919)*

Section 1. After one year from the ratification of this article the manufacture, sale, or transportation of intoxicating liquors within, the importation thereof into, or the exportation thereof from the United States and all territory subject to the jurisdiction thereof for beverage purposes is hereby prohibited.

Sec. 2. The Congress and the several States shall have concurrent power to enforce this article by appropriate legislation.

Sec. 3. This article shall be inoperative unless it shall have been ratified as an amendment to the Constitution by the legislatures of the several States, as provided in the Constitution, within seven years from the date of the submission hereof to the States by the Congress.

Amendment XIX   *(Ratified Aug. 26, 1920)*

The right of citizens of the United States to vote shall not be denied or abridged by the United States or by any State on account of sex.

Congress shall have power to enforce this article by appropriate legislation.

Amendment XX   *(Ratified Feb. 6, 1933)*

Section 1. The terms of the President and Vice President shall end at noon on the 20th day of January, and the terms of

Senators and Representatives at noon on the 3d day of January, of the years in which such terms would have ended if this article had not been ratified; and the terms of their successors shall then begin.

Sec. 2. The Congress shall assemble at least once in every year, and such meeting shall begin at noon on the 3rd day of January, unless they shall by law appoint a different day.

Sec. 3. If, at the time fixed for the beginning of the term of the President, the President elect shall have died, the Vice President elect shall become President. If a President shall not have been chosen before the time fixed for the beginning of his term, or if the President elect shall have failed to qualify, then the Vice President elect shall act as President until a President shall have qualified; and the Congress may by law provide for the case wherein neither a President elect nor a Vice President elect shall have qualified, declaring who shall then act as President, or the manner in which one who is to act shall be selected, and such person shall act accordingly until a President or Vice President shall have qualified.

Sec. 4. The Congress may by law provide for the case of the death of any of the persons from whom the House of Representatives may choose a President whenever the right of choice shall have devolved upon them, and for the case of the death of any of the persons from whom the Senate may choose a Vice President whenever the right of choice shall have devolved upon them.

Sec. 5. Sections 1 and 2 shall take effect on the 15th day of October following the ratification of this article.

Sec. 6. This article shall be inoperative unless it shall have been ratified as an amendment to the Constitution by the legislatures of three-fourths of the several States within seven years from the date of its submission.

Amendment XXI *(Ratified Dec. 5, 1933)*

Section 1. The eighteenth article of amendment to the Constitution of the United States is hereby repealed.

Sec. 2. The transportation or importation into any State, Territory or possession of the United States for delivery or use therein of intoxicating liquors, in violation of the laws thereof, is hereby prohibited.

Sec. 3. This article shall be inoperative unless it shall have been ratified as an amendment to the Constitution by conventions in the several States, as provided in the Constitution, within seven years from the date of the submission hereof to the States by the Congress.

Amendment XXII *(Ratified Feb. 26, 1951)*

Section 1. No person shall be elected to the office of the President more than twice, and no person who has held the office of President, or acted as President, for more than two years of a term to which some other person was elected President shall be elected to the office of the President more than once. But this Article shall not apply to any person holding the office of President when this Article was proposed by the Congress, and shall not prevent any person who may be holding the office of President, or acting as President, during the term within which this Article becomes operative from holding the office of President or acting as President during the remainder of such term.

Sec. 2. This Article shall be inoperative unless it shall have been ratified as an amendment to the Constitution by the legislatures of three-fourths of the several States within seven years from the date of its submission to the States by the Congress.

Amendment XXIII *(Ratified March 29, 1961)*

Section 1. The District constituting the seat of Government of the United States shall appoint in such manner as the Congress may direct:

A number of electors of President and Vice President equal to the whole number of Senators and Representatives in Congress to which the District would be entitled if it were a State, but in no event more than the least populous State; they shall be in addition to those appointed by the States, but they shall be considered, for the purposes of the election of President and Vice President, to be electors appointed by a State; and they shall meet in the District and perform such duties as provided by the twelfth article of amendment.

Sec. 2. The Congress shall have power to enforce this article by appropriate legislation.

Amendment XXIV *(Ratified Jan. 23, 1964)*

Section 1. The right of citizens of the United States to vote in any primary or other election for President or Vice President, for electors for President or Vice President, or for Senator or Representative in Congress, shall not be denied or abridged by the United States or any State by reason of failure to pay any poll tax or other tax.

Section 2. The Congress shall have power to enforce this article by appropriate legislation.

Amendment XXV *(Ratified Feb. 10, 1967)*

Section 1. In case of the removal of the President from office or of his death or resignation, the Vice President shall become President.

Sec. 2. Whenever there is a vacancy in the office of the Vice President, the President shall nominate a Vice President who shall take office upon confirmation by a majority vote of both Houses of Congress.

Sec. 3. Whenever the President transmits to the President pro tempore of the Senate and the Speaker of the House of Representatives his written declaration that he is unable to discharge the powers and duties of his office, and until he transmits to them a written declaration to the contrary, such powers and duties shall be discharged by the Vice President as Acting President.

Sec. 4. Whenever the Vice President and a majority of either the principal officers of the Executive departments or of such other body as Congress may by law provide transmit to the President pro tempore of the Senate and the Speaker of the House of Representatives their written declaration that the President is unable to discharge the powers and duties of his office, the Vice President shall immediately assume the powers and duties of the office as Acting President.

Thereafter, when the President transmits to the President pro tempore of the Senate and the Speaker of the House of Representatives his written declaration that no inability exists, he shall resume the powers and duties of his office unless the Vice President and a majority of either the principal officers of the executive departments or of such other body as Congress may by law provide transmit within four days to the President pro tempore of the Senate and the Speaker of the House of Representatives their written declaration that the President is unable to discharge the powers and duties of his office. Thereupon Congress shall decide the issue, assembling within forty-eight hours for that purpose if not in session. If the Congress, within twenty-one days after receipt of the latter written declaration, or, if Congress is not in session, within twenty-one days after Congress is required to assemble, determines by two-thirds vote of both houses that the President is unable to discharge the powers and duties of his office, the Vice President shall continue to discharge the same as Acting President; otherwise, the President shall resume the powers and duties of his office.

Amendment XXVI *(Ratified June 30, 1971)*

Section 1. The right of citizens of the United States, who are eighteen years of age or older, to vote shall not be denied or abridged by the United States or by any State on account of age.

Sec. 2. The Congress shall have power to enforce this article by appropriate legislation.